Economic Sociology

Economic sociology re-emerged in the 1980s as a vibrant subfield confronting economic theory and important economic issues. However, work in this field is scattered and inaccessible to the novice. This insightful new book addresses this problem and presents the clearest, most comprehensive and wide-ranging account of economic sociology to date. In so doing, Hass makes the insights, claims, and logic of economic sociology accessible to students while exposing the realities of today's complex economic world and the challenges of studying economies and societies.

This introductory text:

- Provides a sophisticated yet approachable analysis of economic behavior and phenomena.
- Explores economic structures and change from a global perspective – by using comparisons and data from the United States, Europe, East Asia, Latin America, and post-socialist countries to show how domestic and international economic forces work over time to shape modern economies.
- Takes a critical perspective of both economic sociology and economics to establish useful insights.
- Presents historical narratives showing the development of today's economic structures and institutions.
- Addresses important economic issues directly impacting on students' lives – from the more visible (economic inequality and organizations) to the less visible (international economic trends, public policy, post-socialism).

Incorporating illustrations, case studies, a glossary of key terms and concepts, chapter notes, and a comprehensive bibliography of key readings, this student-friendly text also puts forward suggestions for further project work by showing the reader areas that require further investigation.

Broad in scope, interactive and accessible, this book is a key resource for students of economics, sociology and political economy.

Jeffrey K. Hass is an Associate Professor in sociology at the University of Richmond, Virginia, USA. His main areas of interest include social change, political sociology, economic sociology, organizational sociology, power, and culture. He has spent time at Harvard, Princeton and the University of Reading, UK and has taught extensively on a range of introductory sociology courses, including economic sociology, in the UK and US.

Economic Sociology

An Introduction

Jeffrey K. Hass

R Routledge
Taylor & Francis Group

LONDON AND NEW YORK

First published 2007 by
Routledge
2 Park Square, Milton Park, Abingdon, Oxon OX14 4RN

Simultaneously published in the USA and Canada by
Routledge
711 Third Ave, New York, NY 10017

Routledge is an imprint of the Taylor & Francis Group, an informa business

© 2007 Jeffrey K. Hass

Typeset in Univers and Rotis by
Florence Production Ltd, Stoodleigh, Devon

British Library Cataloguing in Publication Data
A catalogue record for this book is available from the British Library

Library of Congress Cataloging in Publication Data
Hass, Jeffrey Kenneth, 1967–
 Economic sociology: an introduction/Jeffrey K. Hass.
  p. cm.
  Includes bibliographical references and index.
 1. Economics–Sociological aspects. I. Title.
 HM548.H375 2007
 306.3–dc.22   2006017346

ISBN10: 0–415–39222–5 (pbk)
ISBN10: 0–415–39221–7 (hbk)
ISBN10: 0–203–08731–3 (ebk)

ISBN13: 978–0415–39222–8 (pbk)
ISBN13: 978–0415–39221–1 (hbk)
ISBN13: 978–0203–08731–2 (ebk)

To Daniel and Peter, and in memory of Mitchell
(August 15, 2000 to February 11, 2002)

Contents

Illustrations

Figures

Tables

Boxes

Preface

To most students economics can seem dry, dull, and daunting. The reality is that it is not only extremely important – it can also be very fascinating. The history of economies is not just about inflation, currencies, trade, and gross domestic product. It is also about power and resistance, different cultural concepts of a "normal" economy, games of legitimacy, and lots of confusion and conflict. This is the side of economics that economic sociology uncovers. In this vein I have several goals in this book. The first goal is to acquaint students as to how economies operate: how structure, culture, power, and practice operate across space and time. The second goal is to show intellectual assumptions at work. There is theory here, because theory really does drive what people say about and do to the economy. The policies that the American government and World Bank implement are not just functions of elite interests and power; they also reflect ideologies and intellectual fashions. Further, no existing paradigm is perfect; we are far away from a "grand unifying theory" of all economics. While the reader will probably figure out my own position, I try to show insights and warts for all positions. The third goal is to give the reader an intellectual journey through economic issues, events, and histories. This is not only a weapon against the dullness that sometimes comes with economics; it is also a way to make sense of economic sociology itself.

The book begins with an overview of economic sociology and a basic economic theory: this is so that the reader can better understand the debates of the day, and why economic sociologists have done what they have done. Much economic sociology is a reaction to the over-simplifications and claims of neoclassical economic theory. The two are not intractable enemies: there is overlap, and there is much sociologists can learn (and have learned) from economists, especially those who address institutions (new institutional economics) and meaningful interaction (game theory). From there we will explore economic development – the coming and spread of capitalism, and forces behind economic growth. This remains an extremely important issue, one that has not been definitively solved. There is no magic theory of growth, but we have made breakthroughs, especially in analyses that include power, structure, and the state. The state is so important that it has its own chapter (Chapter 4), where we will see how states operate in the economy, how different states have different policy styles and cultures, and how these persist and lead to different national economic structures and practices. For example, one cannot understand why American and Asian economies are different by reference to "culture" alone. Culture must be linked to institutions that reproduce it, including the state. With these broad structures and processes in place we can turn our attention to the organization of the economy, from organizations such as corporations to class, race/ethnic, and gender inequality. The book ends with two chapters that try to bring together the lessons of economic sociology: an overview of post-socialist experiments to build capitalism where it did not exist, and the challenge of "globalization" (the hot topic as of this writing) and of organizing better the insights and intellectual agenda of economic sociology – not only for research and teaching, but also to expand public discourse and activism. One word of warning: the reader will see more about Russia than he or she likely expected. This is for two reasons: first, Russia is my area of research; second, Russia's post-socialist experiment in market-building is a social laboratory whose data remain to be studied adequately.

While I want the reader to gain as much relevant data as possible, I do not want to bludgeon that reader with table after table and citations in every sentence. Thus, rather than cite every possible journal article or book, I have followed one of my teacher's tactics of focusing on "signposts": key readings not only give data but also make non-trivial contributions to the discourse of the field. The bibliography is only the beginning of economics and economic sociology, but from those references one can build up a library. I am also developing a website to go along with this book. This will provide additional citations and data sources, as well as questions for discussion or rumination. I hope that these can convey the wonder and excitement that studying economics really can bring – that attracted me to the subject, and kept me with it for so many years. Happy reading!

Acknowledgements

Ironically, I did not enter graduate school intending to study economic sociology. (In fact, I started a Ph.D. in sociology quite by accident – but that's another story.) I wanted to study political sociology – democracy and dictatorship, revolutions, and social change attracted my interest. I began economic sociology from scratch with my Ph.D. dissertation on Russia's post-Soviet experiment with a market economy. I was then drawn into the field, not only by the many interesting studies and debates, but also because of the potential for contributions. In my own journey through the world of economic sociology, I have benefited from many conversations with many intelligent scholars (not all of whom study economic sociology as directly as I do), and here I would like to offer them my thanks. My teachers at Princeton instilled the basics of economic sociology and comparative-historical work as well as a love for the subfield: Miguel Centeno, Paul DiMaggio, Frank Dobbin, and Viviana Zelizer. After my Ph.D., I have had (and continue to have) many discussions of economic issues with Richard Colignon, Robert Donnorummo, the late Valerii Golofast, Nikita Lomagin, John Markoff, Jorge Rodriguez, and Maxim Storchevoi, and I hope they will not mind my using the fruition of our talks here. Andy Buck and I have discussed Russia's economy, and economic sociology generally, more times than I can remember, and I thank him as well for taking the time to look over the manuscript as a fellow teacher of economic sociology. My deepest thanks to Gerhard Boomgaarden and Constance Sutherland at Routledge, for proposing and supporting this project from start to finish – in the process reawakening my faith in academic publishers. I also thank the many students I have taught in three different countries. Their attention, and their questions, kept me on my toes. Hopefully this work reflects their input as well.

My final, and greatest, thanks are to my family for support over these years, including the mad rush to finish this manuscript. My father and mother have supported me through this long trip from Ph.D. to Professor. My wife Irina has been patient with writing and rewriting, not only during "job" hours but also on weekends and evenings until 1 a.m. My greatest thanks, and love, go to my children, who convince me every day that research and writing have some pay-off, that discovery is truly a gift, and that the world out there is worth fighting for. I only wish my eldest son could see the result of this labor. This is for them.

1 Economic sociology unbound

Our pensions and futures depend on the performance of large corporations with offices or factories flung across dozens of countries – and so future livelihood is dependent on decisions of many managers, the structure of their corporations, the labor available to them, and the policies of the countries where they work. Our buying power depends on the value of our currencies (American dollars, euros) – but that value is shaped by how brokers and investors on international currency markets evaluate American and European policies, and whether their economies conform to investors' ideals of a "normal" economy. In America, the dot-com bubble and Enron scandal still echo on Wall Street, the "war on terror" increases the budget deficit and insecurities about the global economy, rocketing oil prices hinder growth (but not quite as many feared), and inequality persists – yet the American economy fuels the world and the dollar is closest to a world currency. In the United States and Great Britain, politicians and people discuss welfare programs while ignoring why they were adopted and how reducing them might have done more harm than good – yet "corporate welfare" and CEOs' enormous salaries merit less discussion. In Russia, former KGB officials battle financial elites (who made their wealth by politics as much as entrepreneurship), and China stands tall but looks over its shoulder as the Indian and Brazilian economies begin to pick up steam.

As communism collapsed, capitalism stood triumphant in the 1990s – but then East Asian economies suffered currency problems, America's high-tech bubble economy burst, myriad problems persisted in former Soviet economies, oil prices surged, and al-Qaeda plugged into global capitalism for its terrorist benefit. It appeared that the gatekeepers of economic reform – the International Monetary Fund, the World Bank, government technocrats in Washington, Tokyo, and Frankfurt – knew less than believed about how economies work. Perhaps it is time to turn from the pundits of glossy magazines and television programs, from politicians and radio talk-show hosts, to contributions from one area that so far has its contributions in academic seminars but not yet in the public domain: economic sociology. This subfield of sociology returned with dynamism in the 1980s, just in time to confront conundrums and failures of economic theory and the uncertain future of the new millennium.

Economic sociology is not stereotypical sociology. Most laypeople and probably many sociologists think sociology is basically about inequality (class, race, gender), culture (mass and youth culture, religion), social work, and criminology. Economic sociology's areas of interest are labor markets, economic development, organizations, even policy – themes most people do not associate with sociology. This is partly due to youth – an irony, as classical sociology is economic sociology. Further, economic departments and business schools have greater legitimacy in the study of economics. The economy is their turf. If one wants to study economics, why do sociology, when graduates with an economics BA or MBA have socially recognized "wisdom" in giving economic advice? In contrast, sociologists have yet to elevate their own authority among the public, politicians, and bureaucrats.[1] This is unfortunate, for economic sociology has already made powerful discoveries about the realities of economies: the importance of power and structure, for example, or mechanisms of organizational change and function. Yet there are also limitations that must be overcome – the worst being that sometimes it restates the obvious, such as persistently noting the importance of personal networks to economic life (something most undergraduates intuitively already know). This book aims to expand the insights while suggesting ways around the limitations.

When intellectually unbound, economic sociology has much to offer. Consider some important issues we face today:

- **Poverty and underdevelopment:** forms and sources of inequality, the impact of changes in the global economy on general well-being, and political ramifications – e.g. whether markets or states alleviate inequality and poverty, and whether we are likely to see more equality or more poverty and political instability as a result;
- **Organizational changes:** whether corporations or small networked firms are the wave of the future in the context of the "new economy" of the internet – e.g. whether WalMart or dot-coms are the face of the future;
- **The state's role in the economy:** whether state policies can make positive contributions to growth *and* social justice and well-being, or whether unfettered markets and business freedom deliver these promises better – e.g. whether we are at the mercy of impersonal market forces, or whether states can improve the human condition;
- **Economic structures:** to what extent national economies are remaining distinctly different or integrating into a global economy, and the impact this has on people – e.g. whether there are "best" public policies, and whether a truly global economy will emerge;
- **Market capitalism:** how it emerged in its different forms, how economies change, and how market capitalism can be constructed – e.g. the lessons of economic reform in post-socialist Russia and China, and their lessons for economic theory;
- **Work:** how labor was organized in the past, how it is changing, and what this means for employee autonomy and well-being – e.g. whether temp work is the wave of the future, with its uncertainties and low benefits.

These issues dominated headlines over the past decade, and other issues are as important but lack media coverage. Unfortunately, public discussions on economic issues are too simplistic. Economists explain these issues with convoluted language and mathematics, creating the impression of sophistication and depth that hides profound misunderstandings about how human beings think and act (McCloskey 2003). Politicians and pundits do not have the background, time, or interest for a comprehensive public discussion of these issues. Some elected officials might be far too busy helping constituents to study theory and data; others fear detailed discussions will hurt their interests (power) or those of their allies. Politicians and the media seem wedded to sound bites. Business publications provide woefully inadequate analyses of economic reality. Average citizens are too busy or feel too distant to engage issues with rigor.

My goal here is to give the reader a picture of the complexity underlying these important issues, to relate the accumulated knowledge from economic sociology, and to loosen its intellectual constraints by expanding on its insights and suggesting fruitful advances. I hope the reader will better understand how economies operate and how to ride the waves of economic change in the twenty-first century. I hope this book – and questions it leaves *unanswered* – inspire the reader to look further into this subfield. I assume that the reader has some familiarity with basic socio-logical concepts. I do not assume that the reader has formally studied economics, although I assume some acquaintance with very basic ideas. In Chapter 2 I present the rudimentary logic of economic theory, although without the math and technical detail of introductory microeconomics.

For the remainder of this chapter I will take the reader on a journey involving the intellectual history and foundations of economic sociology. That is, I want to "decon-struct" economic sociology and point out its assumptions, logic, and limitations. This will prepare the reader for sociological analyses of global economies and develop-ment, economic change, economic organization (especially the rise and current state of the corporation), and inequality (that aspect of economic sociology which every student will face).

Intellectual history and foundations: legacies of classical sociology

Much classical sociology could be called "economic sociology" (although nineteenth-century "sociology" did not have proper subfields). Sociology's founding fathers were concerned with the modern world emerging around them. Capitalism and industrialization, urbanization, rapid technological development (including application to warfare), collective action and revolutions (beginning with 1789 France) – these aspects of the new modern world deeply worried Karl Marx and Friedrich Engels, Max Weber, and Emile Durkheim. (I provide only a cursory overview of classical theory here.) While these great thinkers analyzed such stereotypical sociological topics as culture, social power, ideology, religion, and class, economic structure and practice were central to their investigations. For Marx and Engels and Weber, the economy was an important, if not *the* important, engine of social change and reproduction. For Durkheim, non-economic factors underpin economies, and so he provided an interesting alternative to analyzing economic organization. Because these founding fathers were concerned with the *genesis* of modernity (including capitalism), I address their explanations for the rise of modern economies in Chapter 3. For now. I give a basic overview of key logics, variables, and causal relations they thought central to social and economic interaction. Marx and Engels thought that *structure*, especially class structure, held the key to social relations. For Weber, *institutions and organizations* are crucial to understanding economies; for Durkheim, *rituals and meanings (culture)* create social structures and identities. Let us look at each briefly.

The best-known classical sociology is that of Karl Marx and Friedrich Engels. While best known for communism, their studies of capitalism still provide insights. In the Marxist vision, economic resources and power are central to all social life; and social life is ultimately *class structure* and history is *class struggle*. Society is organized around the economy (the "base"), especially the *mode and relations of production*: the physical basis of production, and the nature of ownership.[2] In antiquity, economies were grounded in slave labor, creating two primary classes: slaves (labor power) and slave-owners (who controlled that labor power). In feudal societies, economic production was agriculture, and land was the primary economic commodity. The landowning nobility owed its social power to status granted by the monarch. Part of that status was the right to own land and control serfs – peasants tied to working the land, turning over produce to their aristocratic masters. Under capitalism, the primary mode of production is in the factory, where raw materials are turned into physical products. The remaining social institutions are "superstructure," which emerges from the base and class relations. States defend private property. Schools propagate and legitimate individualism, profit, and property rights as normal and natural, and reproduce the working class by alienating working-class youth from white-collar logic (Bowles and Gintis 1976).

The capitalist economy in the Marxist vision is a web of class relations that impact upon the remaining social structure. Economic organizations, from small firms to large corporations, are imbued with class logics, from exploitation and power to group interests and ideology. Marxists understand relations between managers and employees and enterprise structure through this class lens. But their inquiry does not stop there. Marxist class analysis has interesting things to say about why markets take the form they do, why the welfare state was born and then diminished, why Latin American countries have had historical difficulties with development, and so on. While in the end I may reject a Marxist explanation, I need to consider its insights seriously, as I will in the chapters that follow.

The common story is that Max Weber stood in opposition to Marx and Engels on the rise and operation of capitalism, but this is wrong. While Weber did treat "class" and "structure" differently and had a somewhat different logic, he did agree with Marx that conflict and power were important in the economy. It is also not entirely inaccurate to say that Weber added two dimensions to Marx: that *culture* is as important as material resources and classes; and that *organizations* are not simple outgrowths of the base but have a life of their own. The popular belief is that Weber opposed Marx's stress on material forces, believing instead that capitalism emerged from *culture*, in particular the "Protestant ethic" and religious values (Weber 1930). Yet Weber was wise enough to see that ideas and material resources were *equally* important, articulated in his famous "switchman" metaphor. Material resources and interests are the rails on which a train runs. No rails, no train. Culture directs the organization and use of resources – like a switchman, diverting the train between rails and directions of travel. Further, Weber claimed that *bureaucracy* was central to capitalism – part of his definition of capitalism is the production of material goods by bureaucratically organized private enterprise. Weber added organizations to our analysis of economies.

Because he notes the importance of organizations such as states and firms, and sees culture as equally important to material resources, Weber's model is ultimately *institutional* (Weber 1987 [1923]; see also Collins 1980). For Weber, as for Marx and Engels, private property is a crucial institution, but it is not alone: Weber also sees bureaucracy as crucial to capitalism. Bureaucracies mobilize a large number of people towards a common goal, whether producing goods (factories and corporations) or producing violence (the state). Bureaucracies manage this by creating *dependence*: bureaucratic employees are dependent on the organization for wages (and thus for survival) and for social status. Bureaucracies create specified tasks for each position and lines of authority – producing relatively effective coordination of a large number of people. For Weber, capitalism required not only private property but also bureaucracy. Further, Weber saw the importance of practices and culture, especially *rationalization*. Rationalization made capitalism different from and superior to earlier economies. Capitalist firms and owners calculated profit and gain by sophisticated *measuring* of the economic world. For example, a crucial capitalist practice was *double-entry bookkeeping* – we take this for granted today, but it was a major step to the coming of capitalism. This allowed entrepreneurs to calculate costs and returns, fostering efficiency, innovation, and investment.

The third "founding father" of sociology, Emile Durkheim, did not focus as squarely on the economy as did Marx and Weber, but it did not elude him, either. His insights from other studies, for example, of religion, provide important insights into social organization that we can apply to the study of economies. In particular, in his later work (on suicide, the professions, and religion), Durkheim demonstrated the importance of social structures over human volition. "Structure" for Durkheim is broader and more nebulous than for Marx, and in it he includes micro-level structures such as family and networks. Durkheim's mature work, *The Elementary Forms of Religious Life* (1965), shows how our identities and beliefs are created and reproduced as we participate in rituals that make up the social world around us. Later scholars took these non-economic insights and applied them to economic issues. For example, Randall Collins (1981) hypothesized that class is "interactive ritual chains," rituals of authority and deference between individuals that add up to "classes." As we will see in Chapter 5, economic sociologists have examined organizations (especially firms) as ritualized myths and ceremonies (Meyer and Rowan 1977). These scholars suggest that firms are in *fields* (communities of firms, usually in the same sector), and that managers play ritual games of watching each other's structures and strategies (DiMaggio and Powell 1983). The upshot of this theory is that economic strategy and structure are less maximizing profits and minimizing expenditures, as economists assume, than playing by stable rules and *satisficing*, or making enough profit to satisfy personal and organizational needs.

These classical analyses of economy and society are important not only for an historical excursion alone; their insights are the foundations for much economic sociology today. Contemporary political economy and state-centered economic sociology combine Marx's structural approach with Weber's appreciation of organizations, especially the state. Sociological neoinstitutionalism, the reigning theory of why firms take on forms and strategies, draws insights from Durkheim's sociology of religion. This does not exhaust the "classical" canon, although other thinkers of the nineteenth century so far have not had the same impact. Georg Simmel has traditionally had a mixed reception, although scholars lately have taken greater interest in his analysis of money and society (e.g. Zelizer 1997; Woodruff 1999). Alexis de Tocqueville is better known for his studies of democracy and politics, but his analysis of civic association has inspired work on "civil society" and how more advanced civil society creates better conditions for growth (Putnam 1993).

As classical sociology was emerging, economics was undergoing its own development. Towards the end of the nineteenth century European economists engaged in a "war of the methods" between two major camps, basically debating the proper way to study economics, including the role of mathematics and fundamental assumptions. The first camp – which ultimately lost (but for whom sociologists have sympathy) – thought economic study should include mathematical, quantitative analysis, but that it should also encompass the study of history and institutions. This camp was intellectually closer to the "political economy" of Marx's time, for which one had to understand politics to fully grasp economics. The second group, which emerged victorious and shaped economics to this day, threw out institutions and history. The "marginalists," as they were called, viewed economics as a mathematical, deductive science whose theories hold for all places at all times – something the first camp could not swallow. (Joseph Schumpeter understood that economics was embedded in history – a view that marginalized him by the end of his career.) With the marginalists' victory, economic theory became deductive, quantitative, mathematical, parsimonious, and constrained by rigorous (but simplistic) assumptions about human nature. By the early twentieth century, economics as we know it had taken shape. Further scholarship would mostly advance the existing paradigm. Dissent would lead to subgroups – for example, new institutional economics, an important branch of economic theory we will explore in Chapters 2 and 3. Sociology (let alone economic sociology) was still gestating. As economic sociology came into being, economists were long engaged in their studies.

While economists were forming and consolidating their discipline, sociology after Marx, Weber, and Durkheim retreated from directly studying economies. Partly this was due to institutional politics (cf. Hart 1990). Economics departments in the United States had established themselves earlier than sociology. Any sociological study of the economy would be seen as an intrusion on to another's turf. To gain acceptance for his discipline, Talcott Parsons accepted the division of labor in which economists studied economics and sociologists studied everything else. Partially for political reasons – to keep economists from feeling threatened and blocking the expansion of fledgling sociology departments in American universities – and perhaps for intellectual reasons as well, Parsons accepted economists' theories and methods as legitimate and did not question them, legitimating economic theory and discouraging vigorous sociological inquiry into economics, at least in the United States.

This said, there was still some research that would provide important material for economic sociology's rebirth.[3] Industrial sociology provided interesting insights into how employees and managers really worked, focusing in particular on how employees appreciated autonomy and self-realization on the job, as well as the central role of informal networks in bureaucratic firms (Dalton 1959; Straus 1992 [1955]). In *The Great Transformation*, Karl Polanyi (1944) reinterpreted the rise of market capitalism in England, demolishing economists' claims that markets arise naturally – they are created by states. Polanyi (1957) also claimed that economic action was embedded in social structure and culture, a theme which Mark Granovetter (1985) expanded to pave the way for new economic sociology. Sociologists were also studying stratification, although they seldom questioned how social groups such as the professions could shape the economy to their advantage. Sociologists studied aspects of economic life that seemed more natural to sociology. But a direct examination of stereotypical "economic" issues, such as exchanging goods and money, corporations and firms, and even consumer behavior, remained off the radar for the time being.

Rebirth: political economy and new economic sociology

Economic sociology's rebirth stemmed from two sources: the return of political economy and the emergence of economic imperialism. In the 1960s and 1970s, graduate students working in archives or in the field noticed that economic organization and change did not follow the simple notions of modernization theory (based on Parsons' sociological theory) or neoclassical economics. Scholars in Latin American showed how underdevelopment was due to global structures and inequality (Cardoso and Faletto 1979), and Western neo-Marxists followed them and questioned reigning paradigms of economic development, sociology's modernization theory and economic theory (Frank 1967). Young scholars expanded Marxism, focusing as much on the *state* as on class relations, explaining international development through reference to relations between states, local elites, and multinational corporations (Evans 1979). This was economic sociology's first real challenge to economic theory.

While some scholars were studying development in the Third World, other sociologists were taking a new look at Western economies and returning to Marx and Weber for inspiration. Economists assumed that employment followed a normal market pattern, with wages (a form of reward) reflecting objective market value. Structural functionalism, the dominant paradigm of 1950s and 1960s sociology (an outgrowth of Talcott Parsons' work), claimed that labor relations reflected a society's functional needs: for example, certain jobs attracted higher wages, status, or authority because those jobs were more important to social survival (Davis and Moore 1945). A new generation of sociologists drew on the ideas of Marx and Weber to challenge these notions, demonstrating the importance of power and history to the formation of labor markets and hierarchies of wages and status (a theme I return to in Chapter 6). Marxist-inspired studies discussed exploitation and deskilling (cf. Braverman 1974), "games" of power between managers and employees (Burawoy 1979), and contradictions between welfare and capitalist development and the threats this held for Western societies (Offe 1984). Weber-inspired scholars looked at managerial authority, showing how relations between managers and employees differed between countries (such as Great Britain, the United States, and Russia) and emerged from unique political histories rather than some universal logic, as economists would expect (Bendix 1974).

It may have been natural for sociologists to return eventually to studying markets and economies, but this trend was helped by a powerful catalyst: economic imperialism. Emboldened by confidence in their framework (which I explore below), economists expanded beyond purely economic phenomena to analyze social phenomena, such as racism, discrimination, collective action, and families (cf. Becker 1976, 1981). This expansion into traditional sociological fields led to a turf war and backlash. If economists could tread on sociological ground, why couldn't sociologists take the battle to economists' own court? Economic behavior and organization, after all, are social, so why not use sociological tools to analyze economies? Sociologists had been formulating responses, such as John Meyer and Brian Rowan's (1977) cultural approach to firms, DiMaggio and Powell's (1983) seminal article introducing Bourdieu's concept of "fields" to the study of firms, and Harrison White's work on networks and his demonstration (White 1981) that markets cannot work according to the principles of economic theory. But the real challenge to economics, and the rallying point for economic sociology, was Mark Granovetter's (1985) manifesto that made "embeddedness" the central concept for economic sociology and its counterattack on economic theory and imperialism. Granovetter focused mainly on "social embeddedness" – how economic action was not simply driven by profit and cost alone but was really embedded in dense networks of personal relations. However, he allowed room for other forms of embeddedness as well: class, power and politics, institutions, and culture. Economies are embedded in all these factors, and they shape how businesspeople, managers, entrepreneurs, employees, and the like behave in the marketplace. To ignore them or reduce them to individual rational calculation seemed erroneous, and sociologists turned their attention to reformulating economic issues in sociological terms – taking the battle to economists' turf.

Since the 1980s sociologists and their brethren elsewhere (e.g. political science, anthropology) have explored such topics as the structure of labor markets (Sabel 1982), the various forms of networks and their different impacts on economic behavior (Powell and Smith-Doerr 1994), the importance of political culture to economic policies (Dobbin 1994), the social roots of organizational structure (Fligstein 1990), the changing social and economic value of children (Zelizer 1985), and the formation of new economic elites and institutions in former socialist economies (Eyal *et al.* 2001). Some economists have begun to question economic theory on prices (Blinder *et al.* 1998) and economic performance (North 1990).

New economic sociology: fundamental concepts

Economic sociology is grounded in central concepts – a vocabulary of analysis – that make discussion of economic issues possible: structure, culture, institutions, and power. These concepts are familiar to students of sociology, and I give them only a cursory treatment here. *Structure* is patterned relations between two or more social entities (individuals, groups, classes, organizations). We should not think of "structure" as a *thing* but rather as a process of who interacts with whom and how: between two people who know each other (networks) or between two groups in different positions *vis-à-vis* power (managers versus employees – those who control labor versus those who work). Structure shapes action by providing resources – people who provide information or other help, rights to use money and property, and so on. That is, *structure is the distribution of resources and the power to act.*

Culture is a problematic term, for it has different meanings for different people, and even a rigorous classification might note different "levels" of culture, from values (superficial level) to scripts and preconscious habits (DiMaggio 1990). Following Robert Wuthnow (1987: 4), I define culture as the "symbolic-expressive aspect of social behavior." That is, "culture" includes symbols, meanings, our understandings about normal or natural social life and behavior, and categories (e.g. "minutes," "property"). Culture is important because it is literally what we know and how to do it. "Private property" does not exist as you or I do – "real," physical entities – but rather is a category and meaning about control of some entity. At one point in history, people could be "property" (slaves), but this aspect of the meaning of "property" is now considered abnormal. That land can be considered "property" is not universal: historically, peasants have often thought of land as belonging to no one and to everyone (cf. Pipes (1990) on Russian peasants' views of landownership). Even "economy" is an artificial idea that has become prominent only with modernity. That such activities as buying and selling should be considered different from politics, home life, and religion is a rather new concept in human history. Hence, culture is crucial in the economy, for it is the meanings and understandings we hold about what a "normal" economy is and how it operates.

Power is a crucial sociological concept, yet it is notoriously difficult to define and to operationalize and measure. Robert Dahl (1957), echoing Weber's logic, defined power as follows: person A has power over person B to the extent that A can get B to do what B otherwise would not do. William Roy defines power as "the extent to which the behavior of one person is explained in terms of the behavior of another" (Roy 1997: 13). Both definitions get across the central aspect of power: shaping the behavior of others by defining their choices and being able to punish or reward them in some way. One crucial point should be kept in mind: people can wield power without intending to do so. "Power" need not be motivated or conscious. It may not be directly observable, either. When businesses hire economics undergraduates and avoid sociology majors, they are wielding power over students' choice of degree: those who choose sociology will be punished by "the market," and power is in operation, even though business managers are not consciously trying to influence students' choice of studies (e.g. Roy 1997: ch. 1). Economists say little about power except in certain specific cases, such as how monopolies wield (illegitimate) power over consumers. Power becomes an *anomaly* in economic analysis. In economic sociology, power cannot be avoided. Firms, states, classes, unions, and other organized actors create and wield power to advance or defend their interests or to defend "normality." Power also need not be negative: Michel Foucault noted that power can serve positive purposes, such as organizing people to alter nature and society to produce useful goods (Foucault 1980).

Finally, *institutions* are probably the central variable for economic sociology, for institutions reproduce structure, culture, and power (even as these then reproduce institutions). One might think of institutions as collective rules of interaction. Institutions shape action by prescribing roles, identities, and normal interaction between roles. A "bank" and a "corporation" are institutions, because they are collections of roles and categories and the rules governing them: money, bankers, accountants, managers, employees, and the like. "Property" and "contract" are not only categories: they are institutions, because they are categories that involve roles and interaction. For example, contract is a promise between two parties that defines how they will interact. Property is control of one entity by another, and denial of that right to any others. What is crucial to remember is that institutions are *collective* and that they are repeated because people take these rules for granted – this is the world "as it is." (As we shall see in Chapter 2, economists have a different understanding of what "institutions" are – a more simplistic and superficial understanding than that of sociologists.)

The importance of these concepts will become clearer in the chapters that follow: for example, the rise of the corporation is a story about the rise of *cultural categories* and how these are enforced through *power* to become *institutions* – which in turn create *social structure* and classes with vested interests in defending existing institutions, relations of power, and culture. Some economic sociologists follow power, culture, structure, and institutions over time – an historical approach – and how their interaction in the past sets the stage for present and future activity, a condition known as *path dependence* (when future paths are dependent on past practices and relations).[4] This allows economic sociologists to understand the *processes* that give birth to the present state of the economy, and from there to try to guess what the future will look like. This powerful set of tools has been used to examine the rise of markets and capitalism (Chapter 3), different forms of public policy and their effects on the economy (Chapter 4), the rise of the corporation and different structures of firms in different countries and different times (Chapter 5), economies and social inequality, including racial, ethnic, and gender inequality (Chapter 6), the great social experiment of the past twenty years and test of social and economic theories, the attempt to create market capitalism in formerly communist countries of East Europe and the former Soviet Union (Chapter 7), and consideration of changes in the international dimension, including just what "globalization" is (Chapter 8). I conclude with a brief discussion of the lessons and future needs of economic sociology.

For better or worse, these stories, like reality, are never tidy. If markets and corporations had straightforward histories, we would have fewer troubles creating prosperity in Latin America, East Europe, and Africa. Those people who think economies are easy and straightforward give advice that ends up creating even more problems, as Russia since 1991 has demonstrated. However, I do guarantee that the issues and stories in the following chapters will be fascinating and involve different ideas and explanations from what most people are told by their parents, many teachers, politicians, pundits, and journalists. But this is the strength and joy of sociology, especially economic sociology.

The basics of economic sociology

From the classical tradition, insights from other sociological subfields, and the competition with neoclassical economics, new economic sociology has developed as a vibrant tradition. Like any scholarly endeavor, it is not a uniform subfield – there are debates, disagreements, and differing approaches, which in the end help propel theoretical and empirical research. (One wonders whether the uniformity of the economics discipline – where graduate students must tow the line of formal neoclassical theory and the single quantitative methodology – has actually restricted its intellectual growth.) Some economic sociologists focus on networks; others privilege class or organizational structures. What all have in common – the central idea holding contemporary economic sociology together – is "embeddedness," the centerpiece to Granovetter's criticism of economic theory and its insistence that humans be treated as atomized individuals.[5] Networks were Granovetter's first candidate for embeddedness, but embeddedness can take many forms. Zukin and DiMaggio (1990) have suggested different forms of embeddedness: structural, cognitive, cultural, institutional, and political.

Structural embeddedness

The most common embeddedness is individuals in a social structure that constrains and enables. "Structure" is patterned relations and so can take different forms. "Micro" structure is networks. People we know and how we know them influence information we have and actions we can undertake. For example, Granovetter (1973) suggested that "weak ties" – people with whom we do not interact often – are sometimes more useful than "strong ties" – people with whom we constantly interact – because they provide non-redundant information (information we do not have). This makes sense, because weak ties live in different social circles (or else we would always interact with them and they would be strong ties).[6] Networks can create trust when people learn about each other and can reasonably predict each other's behavior. Networks also have different characteristics, related to the degree of trust in a society. Networks and "social capital" (the way people generally interact) might be characterized as "horizontal," where all are equal and cooperate and there is trust, or as "vertical," where people are linked through relations of authority in clans, and where different clans do not trust each other. Robert Putnam (1993) suggests that this is the case in northern and southern Italy – the north has horizontal social capital and trust, the south is organized in clans and distrust between them. Economic cooperation is easier in the north, risks and innovations are shared, and the north's economy has prospered. Distrust and lack of cooperation have created economic stagnation in southern Italy. The advantage of networks is that if they create trust, they can facilitate sharing information and resources so that groups can take risks and spread both benefits and potential losses. This can make it easier for entrepreneurs to undertake risky ventures that may have a large pay-off for them and for society – which contributed to the development of the computer industry in Silicon Valley and Route 128 in Massachusetts, and of industries in Italy's Po Valley (Piore and Sabel 1984). However, if groups are too closely networked, they may feel obligated to stick together even if incompetence or inability to produce or innovate effectively leads to economic losses (Uzzi 1997).

Networks can also create opportunity and advantage. Consider the following example, where you are person A, and there are two other people in businesses B and C. Consider two different ways you all interact (see Figure 1.1). In Figure 1.1(a), A and B can interact independently of C, B and C independent of A, and A and C independently of B. In Figure 1.1(b), A knows B and C, but B and C *do not know each other*. If B and C need to interact, A is a go-between, and B and C are *dependent* on him/her to relay information and coordinate action. The gap between B and C is a "structural hole" (Burt 1992), and you (A) gain a strategic advantage by bridging that hole. In this way networks can provide advantage and opportunity (for you) or constraint (e.g. B and C are constrained because they must go through you to deal with each other).

Another form of structural embeddedness comes from the Marxist tradition – class structure. In democracies, political elites require resources to run for office, and these come often from corporations and economic elites. Politicians must be careful about the policies they enact for fear of breaking alliances with capitalist elites, who would not support them in further elections. In addition, in the global economy, a state must be careful about demands which it makes (regulations, high taxes) on

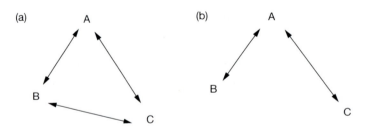

Figure 1.1   Networks and structural holes

corporations and economic elites. If taxes are too high or laws too strict, elites and corporations may take their business to other countries – depriving the home country of employment for its citizens and tax income for its own coffers and operation. The relative power of states, on the one hand, and economic elites and corporations, on the other, and the latter's capacity to go elsewhere, have shaped the general way different economies operate. An interesting combination of these two ways of thinking about social embeddedness is in work on "interlocking directorates" (cf. Mizruchi 1996). Capitalist elites, by right of property ownership, sit on several boards of directors. This brings them into contact with other elites who they otherwise may not have met. Institutions of private property and boards of directors – the plaything of the upper class – create networks within the upper class that help elites share strategies and realize their common interests, especially *vis-à-vis* the state, labor unions, and other external groups (Domhoff 1998). Class creates networks that reinforce class – social structure at work!

Cognitive embeddedness

"Cognitive embeddedness" is how the way we think influences economic action: we cannot escape how our brains work. While we examine economic theory and its assumptions in Chapter 2, let me skip ahead for a moment. Economists assume we have perfect (or near-perfect) information about what we want, that our tastes and preferences are stable over time, and that we calculate objectively and rationally. Experimental psychologists challenge these assumptions. First, we suffer "bounded rationality." We cannot have perfect information but rather have incomplete information, sometimes because we just cannot get all the information about a partner or good that we need or want. As a result, we create short cuts to live without perfect information. For example, we create rituals in firms and bureaucracies, or else we would have to gather and evaluate reams of information for *every* decision we make. Sometimes it is easier to follow a simple rule.

Let us consider universities and the case of Professors A and B. In universities we measure how good a professor is by looking at his/her curriculum vitae (academic résumé). The more publications a professor has and the higher his/her teaching evaluations, the better he/she must be. If you think about it, this is problematic. Students may give good evaluations because a professor gives easy grades for little work. He/she may publish superficial papers that contribute little real knowledge, rather than focusing on one good, path-breaking article. But: quantity is apparent, and quality is not. Professor A has written ten articles, while Professor B has written one. B's article is intelligent, but some colleagues disagree with B's conclusions or methods (or may feel threatened by B's innovations and intelligence). Professor A has clearly written more, and it is easier to rank A over B on one easy, visible measure: *quantity*. To rank B ahead of A would require thinking, discussing, and arguing over the non-measurable merits of B's one article. Hence, we use a simple rubric (quantity) that allows us to deal with the problem of information that is lacking (B's real productivity) or difficult to interpret (is B's article really that good?).

Second, our thinking is not "objective," and the information we hold is not objective either: we do not see the world perfectly, but rather we filter information from the surrounding social world through *categories* that help us make sense of all the raw data our senses provide us every day. For example, we meet many people in our lives, and the information we could have about them is too immense for us. As a shortcut, we tend to categorize people according to race, gender, nationality, and the like, so that it becomes possible to predict others' behavior (Berger and Luckmann 1967). Otherwise we would be very uncertain (and likely fearful) of all the interactions we have around us. This means that we do not examine the world objectively, as economists think, but rather we filter the world through our categories. This is important for public policies: politicians can legislate only what they know to legislate, only according to categories they have. Finally, the way we process information when making decisions is not as objective or rational as economists would like us to believe. Amos Tversky and Daniel Kahneman (1974, 1981) conducted interesting experiments to demonstrate this. I discuss this in Chapter 2.

Cultural embeddedness

We are constrained by categories through which we interpret the world, assumptions about how the social world normally operates, and knowledge of social action. This is "cultural embeddedness": categories, assumptions, and rituals from contexts of our social lives shape our decisions and actions. This may seem commonsensical, but economic theory ignores culture. Economists tend to believe that the rest of the world thinks as they do and that only hard economic rationality is important. But culture is a powerful force in economic behavior and organization.[7] As Viviana Zelizer (2002) suggests, our categories and assumptions of the social world shape the tactics we use and the policies which state elites enact. "Gender" is a category with historical meanings of hierarchy: men as leaders, women as led. This legitimated and reproduced patriarchy in the home and workplace that survives as wage inequality, "ghettoization" of women in low-wage jobs, and the glass ceiling. Different societies, and groups within societies, have different ideas about "natural" or "normal" economic organization. Europeans think it natural that states should be active in the economy, shielding society from its harmful effects. This reflects a different history and assumptions about the normal form of state–society relations. Americans, on the other hand, see government as run by society, but also see government as a potential intruder into the economy. Governments may be elected and answerable to the people, but to let the government run the economy is an invitation to tyranny – the state would free itself from popular control and trample citizens' rights.

Institutional embeddedness

Economies are not just immediate exchanges between buyer and seller – they are also rules that structure exchange and production of goods and services, working conditions and employment, and the like. Those rules structure economies in two ways. First, institutions are rules of action that have enforcement behind them, whether through sanctions such as shaming or social marginalization (ignoring the offender) to use of coercion and violence to uphold institutional procedures (North 1990). In this way, institutions shape costs of action: if an action is against the law or rules and those laws and rules are enforced, I run the risk of punishment if I am caught, and so I am more likely to follow rules and procedures. This is how economists think of institutions – known as an *instrumental* approach to institutions – and there is some truth here. However, sociologists see institutions as more complex. Institutions also *constitute* social action. They are not only rules – they also set categories and logics of how people think, interpret their social worlds, and act on them. Because institutions involve us in social rituals with other people, they inject meanings, identities, and strategies into us – reproducing institutions and the social order. This is a *constitutive* approach to institutions.

Consider two centerpieces to market capitalism: private property and contract. These are not just rules about control (property) and promises (contract): they are also categories of roles (buyer and seller, owner and owned). "Property" becomes more than a law of ownership: it becomes a *sacred* aspect of the economy, something no economy can live without. Property becomes to "normal" capitalism what the crucifix is to Catholicism. Consider another institution vital to capitalism: money. Money is a piece of paper or metal that is imbued with some meaning and value: the state supports it, and businesses regularly accept that this paper or metal is valid in return for a good or service. But the logic of money – a number representing value – can then be transferred to other aspects of life, such as time or the environment. (Economists think of ecological problems in terms of the costs – monetary costs – of health risks or cleaning up after ecological disasters.)

Political embeddedness

Economies are not immune to politics. Market capitalism – the economy we know so well and that dominates the globe – partly came about because state leaders wanted to increase political power. Kings and presidents fought wars with each other, but to do so they needed weapons. The production of weapons – what we call an arms race – provided profit to entrepreneurs, who then invested even more money in industrial production. State leaders have courted political support by supporting corporate profits through tax benefits or legal changes; at other times, presidents and prime ministers have tried to calm radicalized workers by legislating welfare and legalizing unions and the right to strike, which altered the way labor was organized and controlled in the economy. The modern corporation was born partly because New Jersey politicians wanted the support of industrialists. State leaders want power but to have power they must have economies that are stable and growing – providing both weapons or other goods and a tax base – and a workforce that is calm and willing to work. Politicians have their own designs on economies. Corporate managers and owners will fight or compromise with state leaders to get their own concessions.

One warning is necessary: embeddedness does not mean we are programmed to particular action. Culture, cognition, politics, institutions, and structure "constrain and enable": they make certain actions more difficult but may make others easier. Consider cultural embeddedness. Knowledge is one aspect of culture, and we cannot do those things that we do not know. Here culture constrains. However, we can also call on different symbols and knowledge to engage in action. For example, labor unions are possible because workers imported the idea of democracy – an idea and symbol from politics – into the workplace. Union representation is democracy within the factory. So culture also enables. The trick is to understand the nature of that social context in which we are embedded (Table 1.1).

Traditions within economic sociology

Economic sociology is not a unified field with one way of thinking about the economy. Views and explanations are diverse and rich. However, to make sense of the field, I will group most work into three camps. The differences between them are research questions, and what they identify as the crucial variables and processes. The first camp is state-centered political economy, which harkens back to Marx and Weber and makes class organization and state power and policies the centerpiece for analysis. This camp examines economies by looking at the interaction between states and organizes classes, for example, different industrialists or agricultural interests. Class leaders try to influence policies, but states may sometimes resist or compromise. State policies shape economies, in turn shaping class organization – and so the process continues. Key issues for study have traditionally been: the rise of the welfare state and the different forms it takes across the globe (Skocpol 1992;

Table 1.1   Forms of embeddedness

Type of embeddedness	How it constrains and enables
Structural	Linkages to resources or people: provide resources (money, property, knowledge, allies)
Cognitive	How we process information from our surroundings; natural inclinations (e.g. avoiding risk rather than maximising profit, engaging in routines)
Cultural	How we conceive, define, and rationalize decisions: how we understand legitimate, normal practices; categories we use to make sense of the world and routines and practices we use to act
Institutional	Collective rules and roles that shape costs of action or suggest available categories and paths of action; produced by and reproduce structures and culture
Political	Relations and motives of power that impinge on distribution of (material, economic) resources

Weir and Skocpol 1985); different types of national economies and the reasons for economic growth or stagnation (Evans 1995); and the rise of the corporation (Roy 1997).

A second emerging tradition focuses on the role of networks in the economy. Institutions by themselves are less meaningful than how people actually use them, and people's ability to act depends on their access to resources – which is a function of people's personal networks. At the elite level, networks between elites become the foundation for political and business alliances that shape what kinds of policies are accepted and rejected by national and local governments (Domhoff 1998). Beyond elite politics and business, networks can provide necessary knowledge about others to help build trust for business deals or to find a job. What is crucial is that networks shape the information which people have available to them and provide the possibility to mobilize other people and their resources – something difficult to ascertain from a study of "classes," "institutions," and structures generally.

A third tradition, sociological neoinstitutionalism, looks at culture and institutions and the social construction of economies. Social myths, assumptions, and ideologies, rather than pure competition or efficiency, shape public policy, organizations, and labor markets. A strength of neoinstitutionalism is that it takes seriously the ritualistic nature of economic life, showing that what we take for granted as "economic laws" and reality are cultural understandings. In Durkheim's view of society, collective rituals (church services, parades, football games) reinforce shared meanings and make us believe that these meanings are real. When we gather together, we repeat the same chants and interactions and come to believe that we are actually a "community" when in reality we are isolated individuals. The "United States" and "Pittsburgh Steelers" do not exist in the same way as you and I, but by constantly engaging in rituals we share the importance of these symbols and act as if they are real. The same is true for economies. As Meyer and Rowan (1977) point out, organizations are really "myths and ceremonies" – firms exist because they are rituals – we act together as if they exist.

Recently, Neil Fligstein (1996, 2001a) has brought together insights from these paradigms into a "political-cultural" approach, in which economies are really about power and culture. To neoinstitutionalism's insights about culture he adds organized power. Firms may be myths and ceremonies, but they remain powerful myths and ceremonies because the state accepts that they are "real" and designs laws accordingly. Groups with power enforce their ideas of what is "real." The political-cultural approach has affinity with aspects of classical sociology, especially Weber's claim that social action is grounded in *verstehen* – actors' own understandings of the social world – and Durkheim's later work, in which social life is reproduced through rituals which make our own subjective meaning appear to be a true reflection of reality. While I review economic sociology's overall contributions, I favor the political-cultural approach, as it attempts to unify economic sociology into a coherent paradigm. I also attempt to expand the political-cultural approach's understandings of power and culture.

Limitations of new economic sociology

New economic sociology is not a perfect paradigm, and we will have to confront its limitations if we are to learn from it and improve on it. Perhaps the greatest limitation stems from the constant engagement with economic theory. As we will see in Chapter 2, economic theory is based on several assumptions that appear elegant but are unrealistic at best. Human behavior, for example, is often far from rational and calculated. Emotions and rituals are just as important, and humans are motivated as much by status, meaning, and other factors that are difficult to quantify, measure, and calculate.[8] Unfortunately, some economic sociology has tried to show the ridiculousness of economists' assumptions – and in the process these sociologists point out what most average people figured out long ago from their own experiences. Consider networks. There is much to learn about how networks matter in the economy – for example, "structural holes." However, much network-based economic sociology appears to spend time and energy showing us the general result that networks are important in the economy. Most people understand that who you know is important in much of life. To advance economic sociology we must avoid spending our time making trivial claims. Unfortunately, because economic sociology has spent so much time engaging the unrealism of economic theory, pointing out everyday truth becomes a minor academic triumph. While I will point out economists' assumptions and claims, I will try to move us away from the simple job of refuting economists, to the better job of suggesting alternatives to their theories.

Another limitation is the conceptualization of *power*. Power is a crucial variable in most sociology, especially political sociology and inequality. In economic sociology, power is not always invoked, and when it is it requires unpacking of concepts and operation. Much economic sociology uses networks to explain variation and operation of economic processes. Yet networks are an arrangement of individuals and social distance between them. There is little sense of authority here (e.g. charisma or dependence). We all have seen charismatic authority – the leader of a group of friends, the co-worker who inspires and leads the others. Sometimes network power operates because of dependence – we need someone for favors or because they control something we need, for example, money. (We have all experienced this form of dependence at one point in our lives.) In addition, culture involves power: power enforces culture, and culture supports the authority of certain classes and professions (e.g. owners and managers). The link between power, culture, and economies requires more study. We will not ignore this important side to economic life.

Economic sociology was at the heart of classical sociology, but soon disappeared from view. It has reappeared only relatively recently. It has developed many rich insights, but there is still much more to do. I will spend the rest of this book showing its triumphs and discoveries, as well as suggesting what work remains to be done.

2 Sociology and economics
Economic theory and its sociological critique

Economic sociology is not only a continuation of classical sociology – it is also a response to neoclassical economic theory and new institutional economics. To understand economic sociology one has to understand economic theory. Economic sociology is not only a response to the turf war between the two disciplines and economic imperialism. It is also an intellectual response to a particular paradigm that has had incredible power over public policy and has impacted – often negatively – on the lives and livelihoods of millions of people.

Contemporary economic theory is founded on assumptions that most economists take as given, either because they believe this is human nature or because such simplifications are justified for building theory.[1] The assumptions simplify economic life, often to the point that what is examined seems surreal. This is best captured in a joke. A physicist, chemist, and economist are stranded on an island with only a can of corn. The physicist says that if they find a coconut tree, the impact of a falling coconut will split open the can. The chemist figures out the composition of the can and devises an acid to open it. The economist has the easiest solution: "Assume we have a can opener." This may sound light, and the reader might think that the following discussion cannot be serious – it has too many simplistic assumptions of human behavior (despite increasingly sophisticated mathematics of models). This has not stopped economic theory dominating policy and discourse. One variant of economic theory, neoliberalism, has dominated policy discussion and reforms in recent decades, despite theoretical problems and over-simplifications that create as much harm as good (e.g. increasing elite wealth, stagnation or decline in real income for the working and middle classes,[2] disruption of many families, and the weakening of welfare safety nets) (Gray 1998).

A brief discussion of the logic of basic economic theory is in order for two reasons. First, this social science paradigm dominates organizations that control resources: the International Monetary Fund (IMF), World Bank, and state funding agencies. Second, economic sociology since the 1980s has been engaged in a confrontation with economic theory, in particular with neoliberalism. Many of the issues and research dominating economic sociology make less sense unless they are seen in this context. That sociologists spend much time talking about networks would appear odd – the importance of networks in social life and business should seem obvious – until we see that economic theory has little room for networks. When economists admit the importance of networks, they do so in spite of their own theory.

The significant other: neoclassical economics and institutional economics

Much of the following discussion may seem dry, but it is important to slog through it because this is the foundation for economic theory – and the basis for problematic policies that have often created social problems in the developed and developing worlds. Contemporary economic theory is complex, mathematically sophisticated, and sometimes subtle. Yet it all boils down to a few assumptions that sociologists find problematic. Economists claim that these assumptions provide an accurate understanding of human behavior when *all other things are equal* (known as *ceteris parabis*). When actors consider goods or actions, they judge according to prices (or value) and resources available (time, money). (Sociologists usually counter that all things are not equal. Goods have a price but also a status, and consuming goods is linked to people's desire for status recognition.)

Rational actors and rational choice

The first assumption is that individuals are *rational actors*. This assumption goes back to Adam Smith, although one can find philosophical discussions of rationality versus emotion in human behavior, and how to bring about peace by elevating the former and reducing the latter (Hirschman 1977). For Smith, people do not follow their hearts when they buy or sell or work – they follow their wallets (Smith 1981 [1776]) – although Smith (1982 [1759]) also understood that rational exchange was embedded in social mores that constrained the destructive potential of pure market behavior. In modern economics, "rational actor" is pretty rigorous: it is more than simply buying the cheaper of two goods. First, individuals have a *utility function* based on their *preferences* for goods or other objects. These preferences are stable, change slowly, and are transitive.[3] Possessing or consuming these goods brings utility (use). Let me use a crude example to illustrate: reading sociology and eating ice-cream. Both bring me utility – they give me something of worth. They are my preferences, and for me reading sociology has more utility than eating ice-cream. If my choice is reading sociology or eating ice-cream – let us assume that I cannot do both at the same time – I will spend time and money on a sociology book rather than on a quart of Ben and Jerry's. However, consumption has marginal returns: at some point consuming more does not bring more value. If I keep reading sociology in one evening I will get tired, and the words will just blow by me. (Every student has experienced this, especially before exams!) Continuing to read sociology brings no more utility. At this point I have free time to eat ice-cream, adding to my utility.

This example is crude – to be fair, economists posit complex utility functions and preferences. The point is to illustrate utility maximization with a simple example. But there is more. Rational choice assumes we *can* calculate costs and benefits of objects we desire: somehow we *count* costs and benefits, even if roughly, and *numerically*. Back to reading sociology versus eating ice-cream. I may *really* want to read sociology, but the books I need are in the library. It takes thirty minutes to walk to the library, and it is raining. I have ice-cream at home in my freezer. I may decide the *cost* of reading sociology – walking thirty minutes in the rain to the library, looking for the books, checking them out (if they are available), and walking home through the rain – is large. The difference between benefit and cost for reading sociology is less than the difference between the benefit of eating ice-cream (lower than reading sociology) and the cost of eating ice-cream – as I have ice-cream at home, I spend no time getting it. By eating ice-cream rather than reading sociology, I gain less utility – the benefit is less – but the cost of reading sociology is much greater than the cost of eating ice-cream. In the end, the benefit from reading sociology is reduced by its higher cost.

Let us take another example. I want to make dinner but have no food at home. I can leave my apartment and walk five minutes to the local store or walk thirty minutes to a supermarket where the same food is cheaper. (Assume brands and quality are the same, that service is the same, and that I do not care about local store owners versus corporate chains – this is "all else being equal.") The costs and benefits are time and money. If money is no problem, the cost–benefit balance suggests I go to the corner store. If money is tight and I am in no hurry (and can walk thirty minutes with two armfuls of food), the supermarket is the logical solution. If money is tight but I am in a hurry I have a real problem – the cost–benefit balance between store and supermarket is close.

Rational choice makes it easier to model and study human behavior by simplifying it. If we think of human decision-making in terms of costs, we can measure those costs (time, monetary value) and analyze them via quantitative techniques (e.g. advanced statistics) for large data sets. Rational choice sometimes does provide insights on what people do. In banal circumstances we choose a good or action because of benefit. Real insights of rational choice come in game theory, which we briefly examine later. Much as physicists begin their studies of motion by assuming a frictionless surface (but later adding friction into their calculations), economists assume rational choice so as to begin modeling complex phenomena.

Criticism of rational choice

Rational choice is seductive because it is simple and, perhaps, because it is cynical: everyone has his or her price. It has gained popularity in political science and has made inroads into sociology as well, where some scholars see it as a useful way of analyzing various forms of social behavior: creating social organization, norms and compliance, revolution, and so on (Coleman 1998; Heckathorn 1990). Sociology's rational choice is "softer" than its economics cousin and has its own problems, but I will leave it aside here.

A powerful criticism of rational choice is that it is *tautological*: true by definition, not by support of empirical evidence – a sign a theory is "cheating" and making itself seem true by sleight-of-hand. The problem of tautology lies in *preferences*. How do we know people's preferences? Paul Samuelson claimed we can know "revealed preferences," that people show their preferences – what they want, the value they attach to goods, the order of their likes and preferences – through their choices and actions. However, this begs the question: perhaps people make many decisions on a whim, or they feel pressured from outside influences. Let me put this in graphic terms. Rational choice claims that preferences lead directly to choices. Our preferences lead to our choices, since we maximize utility of our preferences. To test this, we would need to know people's preferences *first*, and then examine what they really did. We may find that half the time they calculate to maximize utility, but half the time they do not – they are irrational from an economist's perspective. However, economists usually measure *choices* and then *assume* that these reflect preferences. They then claim that this supports the theory. However, this is where the tautology enters. It is no good to start by assuming that preferences lead to choices, looking at choices, saying this reveals preferences, and saying this proves the theory – when all the time *no one* is measuring people's preferences! We have an assumption that says very little about what people decide, and even less about what their preferences really are or where they come from. This is useful for economists because it makes human behavior very simple and easy to model – but the model becomes weak when we ask where people's tastes (e.g. in goods or services) come from. (Sociologists claim that tastes are grounded in such contexts as class (Bourdieu 1984).)

Some criticize rational choice for being too simple or cynical: people calculate for personal gain sometimes, but not always. Much of human behavior is ritualistic: we do things in a proper context because we have always acted this way. We sit in the same place in lectures (if we go to lectures) because this is ritualistic: we don't have to think about it, so we don't. We go to the same bar, the same store, the same friends, not because we think of gain but because this is habit. At other times people act on impulse or emotion or from a sense of morality. People often do what they do because it gives them *meaning*, not because it brings tangible gain. Sometimes decisions involve a combination of all these factors, which makes action more complex than rational choice can handle. Consider work. It is not always about money alone. It can also be about identity and meaning: what we do is who we are, especially for people with skills. Rational choice cannot address this. For example, at the start of the Industrial Revolution, weavers came into competition with textile factories, where cloth was woven more cheaply than by hand. Weavers responded to competition by lowering the price of their cloth – because weavers worked for themselves, they were lowering their own wages, to the point that their wages were lower than alternative jobs they could have taken. Rather than give up weaving for a better wage, weavers continued to weave – as if their job were more than a cost–benefit calculus or a simple source of income (Reddy 1984).

Another criticism concerns measurement. Rational choice assumes everything has a cost that can be measured – time, money, and even "psychic costs" (Becker 1976) that account for the pain of changing jobs. This may work for abstract mathematics, but actually measuring the value which people put on different activities or tastes is extraordinarily difficult, if even possible. Even money has multiple meanings: wages, charity donations or receipts, "blood money" (money received because of tragedy, i.e. an insurance payment for a family member's death), and the like may seem to be the same – it's all money, isn't it? – yet people do not always code or treat money from different sources in the same way (Zelizer 1997). If average people do not measure money in the same way as economists, how can we be sure that people can measure everything else about their lives through some numerical means? Probably the most classic example is gifts, especially gifts of blood (Titmus 1971) or organs (e.g. livers or kidneys) donated for use by those desperately in need. Most people code gifts as having a value above money or some numeric value coldly calculated: in fact, to do so would be profane and insulting to courtesy and values of proper behavior and thought.

In short, rational choice over-simplifies how people think. The model assumes people know *how* to calculate and *what* they are supposed to calculate. This is not always the case. Managers calculate different things at different times: they worry about profit, but this is one of many worries. At a psychological level, rational choice is wrong about *cognitive* aspects of decision-making. For example, rational choice assumes that we use only relevant information when making a decision, and that we can filter and organize information to make the proper choice. Psychologists Amos Tversky and Daniel Kahneman tested decision-making by giving subjects (often students) a series of tests (Tversky and Kahneman 1974, 1981; Frank 1990). They discovered that for the same situation, people will make different decisions if the situation is framed differently. For example, subjects of such studies were presented with the same choice – using a new drug on suffering patients – but also framed in terms of risk (a certain number of people will die) versus hope (the same number of people may live but are more likely to die). Subjects chose overwhelmingly to use the drug in the "hope" case but not in the "risk" case, even though the choices offered were exactly the same.

Let us take another example, that of the "halo effect." According to rational choice, we ignore information that is irrelevant to the decision at hand. However, irrelevant information may skew decision-making by making one choice appear better – it gains a "halo" because irrelevant information makes that (irrelevant) choice seem a good deal. Let me demonstrate with another example, illustrated in Figure 2.1 (taken from Frank 1990). Students are given a choice for an apartment: a more expensive apartment near campus (A), or a cheaper apartment further away (B). Psychologists

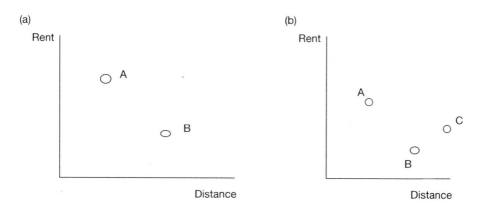

Figure 2.1   Framing of choice and halo effects

can do surveys until they find a price and distance, such that half of the students choose A and half choose B. Psychologists then add a third choice (C), further away but more expensive than B. C should be irrelevant data for the choice: B is closer and cheaper. (Assume apartments B and C are in the same condition.) However . . . the split between A and B is no longer 50:50, as rational choice predicts. Instead it is 30:70, because C gives choice B a halo effect. Suddenly, B seems attractive not because it is better than A – students don't suddenly become cheapskates – but because B seems to be a really good bargain when compared to C. Some students who would choose A now think B is *really* a good buy. Irrelevant information skews the outcome of decisions.

The gist of these criticisms is that human beings suffer from *bounded rationality* (Simon 1945): we do not have all the information we need, and obtaining information is costly. This criticism has been taken into account by champions of new institutional economics, who include information costs into their models and explain many important economic arrangements that neoclassical economic theory cannot explain, such as the existence of corporations. More important for sociology is that bounded rationality is not only information costs: it is how people *process* "information." Just what is a "cost," and what social entities are assigned a numeric "cost"? How do we go about analyzing cost and benefit and judging correct action? These questions are not as straightforward as they appear at first glance, and much economic sociology examines just how people assign value, what they assign value to, and how they go about formulating strategies. Economic sociology takes seriously the *sociology of knowledge*: that knowledge is not objective but instead is socially created and shaped by forces such as structure, culture, institutions, class, and the like.

Competition and assuming markets: efficiency, equilibrium, and evolution

Except for certain strands of economics (new institutional economics), economic theory assumes that the market is the state of nature and exists everywhere – not only in the buying and selling of goods (books, cars, ice-cream), but even families (cf. Becker 1981). This is an "atomized" view: essentially, society is nothing but individuals with no real ties to other individuals. We are all rather egotistic, following our own interests rather than collective beliefs, emotional bonds, or public pressures. In this atomized social world, it is literally every person for himself or herself; competition is the normal state of nature. Compromises, negotiations, and alliances are just temporary pacts that bring each member of the group individual gain – there is no collective identity or solidarity. Further, "consumers" are king: a good or service produced has no value unless it is purchased, and so producers constantly compete with each other for consumers' dollars or pounds or attention. The theory also assumes that consumers have near-perfect information about the real value of a good, about the quality of the good, about where to buy the good and where competitors may be found, and so on. Some critics find this assumption ludicrous: obtaining information is not easy and can cost time and money. In fact new institutional economics – an improvement on neoclassical theory but far less wide-spread, except in legal studies – emerged to address "information costs."

This assumption about the real state of human beings has certain important theoretical consequences. First, in an individualized, atomized state of nature, where rationally acting consumers will try to get the most utility for the least cost, competition will lead to innovation and improvement and efficient use of resources. Those producers who cannot produce goods well or cheaply will suffer in competition with others. Why would rational utility maximizers buy a worse or more expensive good when a better or cheaper alternative is available? For example, take the production of cars. Firm A produces high-quality, expensive cars. Firm B produces cheaper, lower quality cars. Firm C produces cars of the same quality as B but at a higher price. In the pure market world of economic theory, Firm C should not last long because it loses in quality and price to A and B.

Underlying this is an *efficiency imperative* central to economic theory. Only efficient firms, entrepreneurs, and institutions survive a competitive, rational environment. Note how each assumption is key. Rational actors want maximum gain for minimal cost, and they take goods from the most efficient producer (producing the best at the lowest price). Competition forces firms, states, entrepreneurs, workers, or others to produce efficiently, or else rational consumers will choose the better producer. Finally, in an atomized society, social pressures from networks, collective identities, and the like can overcome rational utility maximization and undercut the efficiency results of competition. (For example, consider the patriot who buys only products made in America. Just because a good is made in my motherland does not mean it is automatically the best or cheapest. If I buy that good out of patriotism alone, I am not contributing to competition, nor am I acting rationally.)[4] Further, producers must by atomized: if they create cartels (alliances to control prices and output), competition is undercut and efficiency is hurt. If efficiency is hurt, an economy is not producing as well as it could, because resources (e.g. income, investment) are not being used wisely. If goods are produced efficiently, more profit can be made (fewer expenses for producers, and more money for consumers to spend), and this money can find its way into wages and investments – further driving economic health, wealth, and growth.[5] Further, in the competitive state of nature, anything that exists – any organizational form, any state policy, any form of production – exists because it is competitive and efficient. (Alternatively, there may be market interference – for example, states providing subsidies or tariffs. But this is an aberration outside the realm of neoclassical economic theory – and in fact such aberrations should eventually disappear as rational actors exert pressure for efficient production.) Or so the neoclassical story goes.

Let me give two brief examples to get this point across. Private property exists because it was an efficient solution to the problem of equating individual and social returns. Building a factory would benefit society – goods and employment. But why should I build a factory, which is costly, unless I could reap rewards? Private property emerged as an efficient way to get investment with both individual and social returns (see North and Thomas (1973) for a basic discussion of this view). Take another example: the rise of the modern multi-divisional corporation. Economists claim these bureaucratic monsters exist because they are the most efficient means of coordinating production and distribution of a large number of goods across a large territory (Chandler 1977). Further, investment in corporations is through limited liability: one can lose only that money one has invested. This lowers risk, and in doing so attracts investment – another efficient solution to the problem of risk and investment. (We will see in later chapters that these approaches are erroneous.)

By assuming a competitive state of nature and the market, economists assume that *efficiency* ultimately decides what firms, strategies, goods, and the like survive, and which do not. This also implies a process called *regression to the norm* (or, sometimes, regression to the *mean*). If a type of firm, or product, or strategy is not as efficient as a competitor, its price or cost will be too high, and it will lose out in competition and disappear – an evolutionary process. Take an example of two automobile factories producing for the same market. If Firm X produces efficiently, its cars cost $10,000. Firm Y produces less efficiently: perhaps Firm Y has low labor productivity and discipline, or pays less attention to the quality of its goods, or is not as competent at discovering what consumers want. It may produce the same car as Firm X, but because it is inefficient, its car costs $12,000. Consumers will buy the X-car, not the Y-car (unless the consumer is irrational). Perhaps Firm Y produces its car for $10,000, but its marketing and advertising are inefficient. Or Firm Y does not know what consumers want, so while its car costs $10,000 (just like the X-car), the Y-car does not meet consumers' tastes. Consumers buy the X-car, and Firm Y will have to improve the efficiency of its production and sales – improve labor productivity (to lower labor costs), improve marketing research and quality control. Otherwise, Firm Y will not make any money and will go bankrupt. Firm Y will be weeded out. In the marketplace, only the fittest survive.

Now, consumers are not always irrational – economic sociology does not suggest this. *All other things being equal*, consumers will choose the X-car over the Y-car. But this is where all else is not equal. Do consumers really have all the information they need to make a choice about the quality of the two cars? How much do they really shop around? Are their tastes set in stone, or can dealers for the Y-car wheel and deal successfully and convince buyers that the Y-car is really what they need? I love Hondas and cannot understand why anyone would buy a similarly priced Ford, Renault, or GM (except for minivans, where Chrysler puts out a good product). Yet GM, Ford, and Renault are still in business. People buy their cars. Why? Tastes are different. In the United States some people prefer to "buy American." The upshot is that "efficiency" is a notoriously slippery term. *What* is supposed to be efficient for a firm's success? Who ultimately decides whether a firm is "efficient"? Microsoft is a giant in the software field – is this because its products are almost always superior, or because Microsoft has market power and leverage over consumers?

One result of this is that we often meet the following argument: if products, organizational structures, or laws exist, it *must be* because they are the most efficient – otherwise, more efficient competitors would have driven them out of the marketplace. This is regression to the norm: strategies and structures move towards the most efficient form for fear of competition. This argument is applied not just to products or production processes and technology: it is also applied to state policies, institutions, labor markets and work, national economies – just about anything under the economic sun. This often seems to an outsider like hand-waving, and in fact is tautological: anything that happens must be efficient because the theory says so.[6] To be fair, not all economists buy into this, and some informally admit this problem to neoclassical theory. However, efficiency dominates formal models and discourse.

Critique of efficiency and evolution

Economic sociologists and some economists have been rather wary of assumptions about the market state of nature and efficiency. Some have noted historical anomalies that do not fit the efficiency logic of economics. Probably the most popular is QWERTY (Arthur 1989): the current design of computer/typewriter keyboards. It is *not* the most efficient arrangement of letters on your keyboard. Originally, typewriters would jam if one typed too fast, and typewriter-making firms used a less efficient keyboard to slow people down. As typewriters improved, jamming was less of a problem. (Computers do not jam from typing too fast.) Why do we retain QWERTY? Economists and sociologists argue that there is a short-term *lock-in* cost. Millions of secretaries and other professionals already know the QWERTY design and are used to typing on it. To change to a new keyboard would take up time, and probably money. Even if, over the long run, switching to a different, more efficient keyboard layout makes sense, in the immediate future the cost is just too great – and so we keep using an inefficient keyboard layout.

This is not the only example. Take systems of weight and measurement. Europe uses the metric system. The United States uses not meters and kilometers but yards and miles; not liters but quarts (except for two-liter bottles of soda); not centigrade but Fahrenheit. The metric system, based on tens, is easier to use in calculations, which is why scientists work in metrics (even in the United States). Average Americans stick to the non-metric system: the cost of adjusting to a new system is not worth it. Under President Jimmy Carter (1977–1980) American federal and state governments experimented with "going metric" (e.g. highway speed limits and distance signs were in miles and kilometers, and elementary and junior high school students were introduced to conversions from non-metric to metric). The experiment was abandoned by 1981. An efficient system did not take root because it was resisted for a plethora of reasons – including confusion and "sunk costs" (people would have to learn a new system of measurement) and national pride.[7] To take root a clearly efficient measurement system would to be *enforced*. This hardly sounds like competition.

Yet economic theory and economists miss this crucial fact: "efficiency" is embedded in social institutions and contexts, especially power and culture. Efficiency can be a strong stimulus, but only where economic structure allows market entry to competitors and where states and other institutions enforce competition. Yet efficiency may be less central than economists think. Managers and owners have various motives for strategies: maintaining stability in the firm and the field; improving power or status; improving personal profits. These can drive owners and managers to various strategies, of which addressing efficiency is but one tactic. Owners and managers may lobby states to enact beneficial tax laws or to allow firms to minimize legal or financial liability while reaping profits (cf. Chapter 5). Business elites may obtain property or survive competition because of networks to state elites, as happened in 1990s post-socialist Russia. If we follow this argument further, we note that "efficiency" is not only embedded in relations of power and politics; it is also embedded in cultural understandings. Just what is "efficiency" anyway, and who decides what is efficient and how to measure and evaluate whether a practice or organization is efficient? Is an "efficient" firm one that produces quality for minimal cost? Or is it a firm that establishes and supports rules which bring it maximum benefit – which might include cultivating favorable informal relations with elites and the state? Perhaps the most efficient firms are not those that produce the best for minimal cost, but those whose owners and managers are able to use networks to capture markets. Is Microsoft an effective and efficient producer because its products are superior, or because Microsoft has market power? Is Bill Gates a genius software visionary, or a genius at conquering markets – a latter-day Alexander the Great? In the real world, this becomes much murkier than straightforward, internally consistent, mathematical economic theory. But these questions about "efficiency" do not fit into the assumptions and hard-nosed mathematics of contemporary neoclassical theory.

Overall evaluation: economics and its sociological critique

This discussion of economic theory does not address all its richness, especially for advanced models (e.g. those that model information costs, interests of different groups such as employees versus managers, complex models of investment returns and equilibrium points). That said, these assumptions are crucial to most economic theory and especially to economics as realized in its general claims and policy recommendations. The sociological critiques do not pull any punches, and they demonstrate that economic sociologists have serious problems with how economists analyze and understand economies. Sociologists have been satisfied for the present with critiquing economics' general foundations and its claims in fields where sociologists do work: firms, development, public policy, and inequality, to name a few. Sociologists have not really ventured into fields such as finance and investment, although some general stabs have been made (e.g. Mintz and Schwartz 1990). Until economic sociology further develops its own paradigm it cannot take on economics in every possible area – but that time will come. For now, economics and sociology challenge each other in limited areas, and the most important of these are the topics of the chapters that follow.

There are other differences we do not address because they involve advanced, complicated, or "stratospheric" aspects of theory and epistemology. Economics is deductive and theory-driven: theoretical claims emerge from logical deductions out of first principles. (Economic theory resembles mathematics and geometry: start with givens and then logically conclude further claims.) Economic data and data collection methods are far more tailored to rational choice and deduction than in sociology. Sociology is far more data-driven and inductive: theory grows out of the empirical accounts, and methods of data collection are much more varied (for example, widespread use of participant observation and open-ended surveys in addition to closed-ended surveys and statistical techniques). There are important differences in what constitutes acceptable data; economists are far more restrictive, preferring "hard" data – data that can be easily counted ("quantified"), such as income, costs, and the like.

Hirsch and colleagues (1990) suggested crucial differences between the logics of economics and economic sociology. While this is an idealized difference between the two, there is some truth to it. Economists see people as (usually) highly rational and society as an aggregate of individuals; sociologists see rationality as variable and society as more than the sum of its individuals. Economists prize deduction and parsimony in their theories; sociologists tend to prefer inductive theorizing and complex patterns of variables. Economists' theory is materialist in nature, while sociological theories usually give equal weight to symbols and meaning. Differences between sociology and economics can run deep, even into the nature of theory and "correct" methods. One issue deserves some attention: the importance of parsimony. Some economists – especially those who apply the model to non-economic issues – often trumpet parsimony as a sign of economists' superiority. In short, parsimony is the claim to explaining the most variation (the most events) with the fewest variables. Darwin's theory of evolution is sometimes cited as an example of parsimony at work. The assumption is that the best theory uses the fewest variables to explain the most: it is that "best" theory because it is the simplest, and therefore must be true (a misapplication of Occam's Razor). Further, economists claim that their theories predict events (despite their legendary inability to predict economic events). Even if a theory seems unsound but can predict, it is good theory (Friedman 1953) – something sociologists would never claim. Sociologists focus less on prediction and more on *explaining* past events and variation – the defense being that one should be able to explain accurately *why* events and variation occur before being able to claim one has an accurate, "true" theory. Sociologists do see the importance of parsimony – one should limit the number of variables one uses or else theory becomes so complex as to be unwieldy – but they are less fixated on parsimony. (The exceptions are sociologists wedded to rational choice or strict positivism.)

Quite possibly the fundamental difference between economics and sociology is that economists assume markets and that people are natural-born market actors. Sociologists, on the contrary, see all social action as embedded in historical and social contexts. Markets are not "natural," but then again, nothing social is. Markets are political and social as well. Markets are sets of institutions of control (e.g. property), exchange (e.g. contract and boundaries), value (e.g. forms of money), and organization (historical forms, such as firms and fields). Classes and states are key actors, and the forms of economic organization are not without influence: the American corporation gave birth to new forms of property ownership and class structure, while British firms remained primarily family owned, reproducing traditional capitalist class structures and elitism. For economists, the market is fairly uniform across space and time, yet sociologists see a fair amount of variation. States, corporations, labor unions, and other organized actors interact through a set of rules and cultural categories called "fields": the market is not uniform but is made up of many different sectors and spheres with their own sets of rules. Like economists, sociologists accept that property and contract are fundamental institutions, but sociologists see complexity: for example, sometimes businessmen *purposely avoid* using contracts as a way of creating trust (Macauley 1963). People are motivated by more than profit and gain but also by self-realization, meaning, justice, status, and simply following routines ambivalently and without asking many questions.

Advances in economic theory

While weaknesses remain, economics has seen some improvement and some ideas of interest. Even if these ideas end up wrong, they have provided intellectual stimulation and made academics aware of issues and problems in contemporary society. I will mention two areas within economics of interest: information costs, and game theory.

New institutional economics (NIE)

One problem with economic theory is that it cannot explain why institutions and organizations exist. If the market is the most efficient form of economic behavior, why do structured, persistent organizations like IBM and British Petroleum exist – why don't managers and employees simply make one-on-one labor contracts with each other? Why the need for enormous, rule-bound bureaucracies with forests of paperwork? Further, what of the problem of information costs? Market theory assumes consumers and producers have near-perfect information – with the corollary that cheating, like inefficiency, should wash out. Yet this is not reality. Ronald Coase and Herbert Simon addressed these issues, and from their efforts new institutional economics was born. NIE has tremendous insights (cf. Simon 1945; March and Simon 1958; Cyert and March 1963; Bates 1988) that economic sociologists respect but challenge, especially for development and organizations. For now, we lay out the basics of NIE. My account follows the logic of NIE's most influential practitioner and theorist, Oliver Williamson (1975, 1985).

According to Williamson, institutions and organizations are "governance structures," formal, rule-bound relations between actors that provide the means to monitor and punish or reward behavior. Governance structures are created when markets are inefficient. This occurs when a situation has three characteristics: (1) information about other actors is costly or unattainable (or imperfect); (2) assets are specific to the exchange at hand and costly; and (3) opportunism is possible and would be costly. "Asset specificity" means that there are large investments that cannot be recouped easily or immediately: for example, millions of dollars invested in building a new factory and purchasing technology to make it operative. Further, these assets are invested for a specific, narrow range of products: for example, a car manufacturing plant cannot be used to make prepared foods or beer if the auto market collapses.

Why should governance structures emerge in such situations? If a large sum of money is invested in "asset specificity," investors have an incentive to produce efficiently and make a profit to recoup their investment. Yet they can be hurt by opportunism (cheating) (e.g. suppliers who deliver goods that are worse or more expensive than they could possibly be – cutting into profits). It might be wholesale or retail purchasers who do not advertise or push the investors' goods with suffi-cient energy or intelligence. In these cases the investors are in trouble: they have invested quite a lot of money into producing a narrow range of goods, and oppor-tunism of these sorts (plus others less benign) can kill their prospects for generating profit (as well as jobs and general social wealth). In this case the market could fail, thanks to opportunism. It is more cost-effective to *control* suppliers or distributors, perhaps by buying them up. This way, the investors now own suppliers and distri-butors and can monitor their activity (for example, by inspections or audits of balance books). This control gives the investors more information and the ability to monitor and punish cheating, reducing the possibility that opportunism will arise and hurt their profits.

The powerful insight here is that markets do not always create efficiency and growth: they may also create the opportunity for cheating and hurt investment and growth. We do not always know who the cheaters are out there, whether among employees or purchasers or suppliers. This incomplete information brings risks to investment and production, and these risks are lowered by gaining as much information as possible (to avoid cheating) and as much control as possible (to punish cheaters). *Control* – power – becomes part of the equation of economic organization, practice, and logic. Much economic sociology accepts this logic but expands upon it, moving away from some of the shortcomings of NIE. Like economic theory, NIE assumes rational choice and efficiency imperatives; these are its Achilles' heel. Organizations or institutions must exist because they are the most efficient – otherwise, some-thing better would come along to drive them out. Yet inefficiencies do persist. Further, Douglass North (1990) pointed out that inefficient laws and organizations might survive because someone gains – say, corrupt politicians or managers out for personal gain at the expense of shareholders or society. Finally, institutions, govern-ance structures, power, and culture have a history that NIE does not usually address – governance structures arise when needed and can change when needed, yet history shows that such change is not always easy, and that change often leads to unexpected outcomes, as we will see in the chapters that follow.

While NIE has created debates and criticisms, it has advanced both economics and sociology. For economists, it provides a more powerful way of looking at *organiza-tions* and organizational dynamics by including power and control (even if in rudimentary form). For sociologists, NIE reminds us that many decisions in the busi-ness realm do involve calculation of costs – in particular costs of information and control – and that surveillance (obtaining information) and capacity to punish are crucial to economic organization (a point forcefully made in other contexts by Michel Foucault (1980)).

Game theory

After World War II some economists and mathematicians began to take interaction seriously and to model it mathematically. Until the 1950s economics focused on the single person in the marketplace – yet markets are made up of interactions. This created an enormous problem for the advancement of economic theory, and game theorists set out to address this oversight. Rather than considering exchange as a one-shot deal, game theory suggests we base our decisions on what we think others will do. This insight began with the work of John von Neumann and was refined and advanced by John Nash – winner of the Nobel prize in economics and the subject of the award-winning film *A Beautiful Mind*.[8] The concepts, logic, and mathematics behind game theory are too complex to present in any brief form here, but we will give a quick overview of what it is about.

Essentially, the costs and benefits to any strategy are set not only by static factors – the cost of resources, for example, or available finances – but also by what other people will do in a given situation, which is not static but dynamic. All players in a "game" consider what other players are likely to do, and this sets their costs and benefits. John Nash claimed that in most interactions there is a "Nash equilibrium," a set of strategies for each player that make the most sense for each player. Even if the *collective* outcome is irrational, the individual strategies are rational. The classic example of this is the prisoners' dilemma: so-called because it is a hypothetical situation involving two prisoners (criminal suspects) who are put in a situation where the logical choice for each individual leads to a conclusion that is bad for *both* parties. Let us consider the following scenario, which captures the essence of the game. Suppose that I (person #1) and another individual (person #2) rob a bank. We use shotguns, and shotgun ownership is illegal, punishable by five years in jail. Bank robbery is punishable by fifteen years in jail. We carry out the crime successfully. We cover our faces and hide the money so that the police cannot in any way pin the bank robbery on us. However, the police suspect us and search our apartments. They don't find money, masks, or other important evidence – but they do find two shotguns. They can send us to jail for shotgun possession only. But the police are cunning. They put us in separate rooms, at the same time, and don't let us communicate. Before our defense lawyers can show up, they make each one of us a deal *individually*: if you squeal on the other person – testify in court that the other person robbed the bank – you will receive only two years for shotgun ownership, not the full five.

The choice before me (prisoner #1) may seem straightforward, but it is not: the *other person* (prisoner #2) is also making a decision *independently*, and I do not know the outcome. The cops let me know I have only a few minutes to decide. I face the situation outlined in Figure 2.2.

What should I do? If both of us keep quiet, we both go to jail for five years. If we both squeal on each other, we both go to jail for seventeen years: the full fifteen for bank robbery and the reduced two for shotgun possession (since we both squeal – part of the deal to reduce the sentence from five years to two). If I squeal and my partner keeps quiet, I only go to jail for two years: the reduction for squealing,

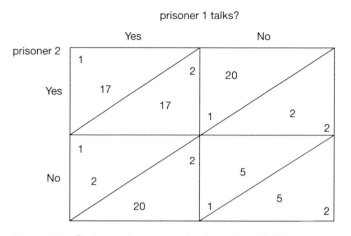

Figure 2.2   Choices and outcomes for the prisoners' dilemma

but the police do not have any means of convicting me for bank robbery. My partner, however, did not squeal and gets the full five years, *plus* fifteen years because my testimony convicts him of bank robbery. If I keep quiet and my partner squeals, the two- and twenty-year sentences are reversed: I get twenty, my partner gets two.

The rational choice for each individual is to *squeal on the other*. Given imperfect information on what the other will do, I am taking a great risk if I keep quiet. It would be nice if we both shut up and got only five years. In addition, this is a *collectively* rational response: the total is ten years (five + five), but the others are twenty-two (twenty + two) or thirty-four (seventeen + seventeen) years in total. This sounds good – but I wonder . . . If my partner is hoping I won't talk, he'll keep quiet – so I *should* squeal and get only two years. Further, if I keep quiet (out of hope for the collectively rational outcome), but my partner squeals, I get *twenty* years. If I talk, I might get only two years, but I certainly avoid the worst individual fate: twenty years. Hence, both I and my partner squeal and get seventeen years. This is the Nash equilibrium – individually rational but collectively irrational.

What about reality? The reality is that we do see the prisoners' dilemma pop up in real life – and not just in police stations. Two important cases are "public goods" and environmental degradation. Public goods are goods and services we all need and use: security (police but also the armed forces), infrastructure (e.g. roads), and education, but we could also include sanitation and utilities (at one time electricity was publicly owned and run). We all use these goods and services, but would we all contribute our fair share? According to game theory, we might not: some of us might contribute voluntarily, but others would *free ride*: they would pay nothing voluntarily, letting everyone else pick up the tab. If enough people free ride, there would not be enough money to pay for road construction, education, and the like – services we all require and benefit from. Not paying is the equivalent of the prisoners squealing: it is rational not to pay if others will pay, because we would get the service for free. Yet if enough people do not pay, there is no service – the equivalent of both prisoners squealing. A rationally individual action leads to a group irrational outcome. This is why states tax us and use the tax money to pay for these services: the state essentially is forcing us to contribute to avoid the free rider problem. A concrete version of this is public television. In the United States, commercial television stations generate income through advertising, but to gain advertising revenue they must show programs that have mass appeal. Specialized programs (e.g. for children, or documentaries) will not have a broad enough appeal to get advertisers to pay for ads. Further, commercial stations in the United States must spend a large amount of time on advertisements to make a profit. Public television must gain revenue to operate from grants from the government or private organizations (such as corporations) or from voluntary donations from listeners. This is why public television and radio stations have pledge drives: to get listeners and viewers to contribute and not to worry about ads or whether programs offend corporate or state interests. In Great Britain, television owners pay a television license fee of over £100 per year to cover BBC operating costs. The BBC does not need as many advertisements and does not have to rely on mass audiences and corporate interests. In Britain the television license overcomes the free rider problem that American public television and radio face – a group rational outcome is achieved by forcing people *not* to free ride.

Another example is environmental degradation. The environment benefits us all: weather, natural resources for producing shelter, clothing, and the like. Ozone holes and global warming can harm us all: rising global temperatures devastate food production and change ocean currents, affecting weather patterns. Ozone holes allow more ultraviolet light to the earth's surface, which can increase rates of skin cancer. It is in all our interests to be environmentally sound: we should recycle as much as possible, and in fact we should consume far less than we do; we should not drive except rarely and use public transportation; we should minimize use of electricity; and so on. Occasional individuals take it on themselves to be environmentally aware – but most of us do not. We are apprehensive of consuming less and making life less comfortable. We are afraid that by consuming less we may hurt our own status standing within society: consumption of goods is part of status hierarchies, and status is important in getting jobs. Further, why should I be environmentally aware if nobody else will be? Why should I sacrifice if nobody else will, and if my individual sacrifice is too small to make a real difference to the environment? Individual rational action again leads to group irrational actions, much like both prisoners squealing on each other.

In fact, the prisoners' dilemma has become a sociological criticism of *neoclassical economic* policies. Economists often claim that the best way to organize production or supply of goods and services is through the market. Sociologists counter that in some cases this may be accurate; but where there is a market and people are contributing (purchasing) voluntarily, the problem of the free rider and the logic of the prisoners' dilemma is not far behind. Economists claim that perhaps we should privatize garbage collection or education; sociologists counter that this will produce inequality and a *collapse* in the quality of these services. Producers and providers will compete for the attention of the wealthy, who are a small minority. The rest of us lose out. This is collectively irrational but individually rational – at least for the wealthy (and for economists who inherit wealth).

Game theory does provide interesting insights and ways of thinking about group behavior. But it is not perfect, and, like economic theory, it has its limitations. It assumes actors are more rational than they often are in reality. Even Nash faced this problem when some economists found that real subjects responded differently from Nash's prediction: they followed rules of fairness, not cold, personal calculation (Nassar 1998: 199). In fact, actors often choose a *role* that shapes what he/she perceives to be in his/her interests and expected behavior in the game (Montgomery 1998). Much game theory is also *normative*: it recommends what the rational, utility-maximizing actor *should* do. It is poorer at actually describing or predicting what people in the real world *actually* do. Prisoners' dilemma-type games do provide insights, but many moments defy it. Identities, networks, and the social construction of expectations do not fit well with economists' game theory. That said, I believe game theory provides important lessons: interaction is *dynamic*, and rules and calculations *must* be addressed in the context of dynamic interactions. Too much economic theory and sociology is static. It may be that sociologists will adapt game theory to culture, power, and social constructions. In this way economics does provide ideas for developing economic sociology; even if we do not accept economists' claims at face value, there is value in listening.

The rise of markets and economic development

Consider seventeenth-century Europe before the explosion of industrial capitalism. A few large cities dot the map – Paris, London, Rome – and hustle and bustle centers on commerce and agriculture. Across Europe small forges produce weapons or basic output for limited use; most people are peasants or serfs[1] who work the land and produce many of their own goods. Some skilled villagers produce specialized goods (e.g. the village smithy), and skills are passed to novices working beside masters. Identity is local, families are extended, and several generations may live under one roof. People survive mostly on what they produce, and many goods passing through cities often do not reach them. Life expectancy is low, infant mortality is high, and literacy is rare. Many peasants do not work for money but exchange goods through primitive barter (payment in kind). They do not travel; the village is their world.

Skip ahead to the late twentieth century. Urban centers have multiplied not just in Europe or North America but also across the globe. Large cities are no longer centers of commerce or royal politics alone: industry or services can now act as the heart of cities and population centers. Peasants migrate to these large cities, living in neighborhoods near their place of work and alongside people from their part of the world; but beyond the neighborhood is an ocean of unfamiliar faces and strange customs of other races and creeds. People work for a wage – for money – which they exchange for needed goods. No barter here. Life is based on formal, cold agreements backed up by the force of the state, not the word of honor of a familiar neighbor or others in the village. Goods are produced in enormous factories, spaces filled with machines and people all acting together, in rhythm, following the movements of the clock rather than the sun and seasons. Generations within a single family are starting to live apart (the nuclear family), and children are less a source of labor (although they earned money early in industrial capitalism, when factories employed women and children).

As the twentieth century opened, immigrants to Pittsburgh produced steel for the new world power, Birmingham and Manchester were Britain's industrial centers, German military power was growing with its industry in the Ruhr, and Russian peasants flocked to textile and munitions factories in St. Petersburg and Moscow. Railroads made travel cheap, and even workers in nineteenth-century Boston could travel to Rye Beach for an afternoon. Infant mortality dropped with better sanitation and affordable medical services. Capitalism's wealth found its way into education through state funding (e.g. scholarships or land grants), endowments by wealthy individuals, or tuition paid by individual students, and the rise in research and mass education aided economic growth. At the same time, the new working class flexed its muscle through strikes and unions. World War I was followed by radicalization of workers' movements in Europe (not unimportant in the Russian Revolution) and the United States.

The first chapters of the story of development are set in Western Europe and North America. The modern industrial economy as we know it – production of goods primarily through the use of technology and inanimate sources of power, all within a single location (the factory) and by a particular class (the working class) – was born in England. Here wool trade wealth, a growing army of cheap labor (e.g. peasants unable to survive in the countryside following Enclosure), and an institutional environment conducive to scientific work and discovery (minimal church interference, developing universities, private property) provided resources and positive incentives for technological discoveries and their application by entrepreneurs (Polanyi 1944; Moore 1966; North and Thomas 1973; Goldstone 2000). As the textile and then other industries began to develop, French elites, long England's main global competition, began to apply similar institutions and organizations, although sometimes imperfectly (Reddy 1984).[2] With increasing wealth from trade, France and England developed a network of colonies that provided captive markets and cheap inputs of raw materials.[3] One set of colonies, those that became the United States, developed industry as well as using English technological and organizational knowhow (e.g. a division of labor, and goods with standardized parts – the future basis for the assembly line and mass production). In the nineteenth century, foreign investment, cheap immigrant labor, protectionist policies for home industries, and an expanding domestic market (including state military purchases) drove the American economy into the global elite. Finally, buoyed up by an increasingly strong state and scientific know-how in its university system, Germany began to compete with France and Britain for the position of top industrial powerhouse.

The economies of the United States and Western Europe continued to grow in the twentieth century, thanks in part to maintaining the lead in scientific expertise and to global structural advantages. However, state expenses for the military (including two world wars and the Cold War) and welfare began to sap economic vitality. Cheaper labor, lower taxes (thanks in part to weaker labor and welfare laws), and more deferential politicians in Latin America and East Asia tempted Western corporations to move production there. First Japan, and then Taiwan and South Korea (the "Asian dragons" or "tigers") began to wrestle into the league of the top economies, and in the 1990s there was talk of a bright future for other Southeast Asian countries. Politicians and pundits alike looked to China as the world's eventual economic superpower. Latin America experienced hopeful growth in the 1950s, followed by decline through the 1970s and 1980s, but after 2000 Brazil was hailed as the new local economic elite. Western capitalism remained resilient, and development of services and intellectual output (e.g. software) continues.

The story of development covers several centuries and the entire globe. It is vast and complex; doing it justice would require several volumes. Instead, in this chapter I try to give a basic overview of some of the more salient issues, arguments, and forces of economic development and growth. There is as yet no theory that has been proven perfect and true, and so debate rages. The goal here is to sensitize the reader to the strengths and weaknesses of different views of development, and to show basic processes of social change over time.

Economists and development

Most economists, at least in their formal work, do not concern themselves much with the rise of capitalism. As we saw in Chapter 2, they take markets as a given and focus more on technical aspects of their ideal model. The typical contemporary economics of development stresses four important factors for growth: liberalized exchange, property rights, a stable currency and prices, and a minimal state that provides basic public goods but does not redistribute wealth on a grand scale. From these foundations, neoliberal arguments favor inclusion in a global market and criticize attempts by states, industries, and citizens to protect their economies through state support of failing firms (e.g. subsidies) or protectionist measures that keep out foreign competition or make it expensive. Economists were most confident of the correctness of their view when East Asian economies burst onto the world scene in the late 1970s. In their view, Japan, Taiwan, and South Korea proved the wisdom of producing for the world market without state interference in the economy, whether through subsidies or outright ownership of industry. (As we will see, they were wrong in this conclusion.)

A few economic historians have taken seriously the question of how market capitalism emerged. To Nobel prize-winner Douglass North, the key to the emergence of capitalism and further development is *institutions*, the formal laws and informal norms that govern economic action and that are embedded in organized power and history. North and Thomas (1973) claimed that a crucial institution was *private property*. The development of property rights in England led to the rise of the first modern capitalist economy. Without stable property rights there was no incentive to invest in large-scale production, for without private property there was no guarantee that an investor would be able to claim the profits for himself and recoup his investment. With stable property rights, investors would plow capital into large-scale production (e.g. factories), which would produce profits, employment, and tax revenue. Property in this way equates individual and social returns – the capitalist, society, and the state all benefit. England developed the first set of stable property rights, and so became the first industrial nation – an accident of institutional history. Other countries eventually legislated property rights, although the stability of these rights varied. Where they were weaker, economic development was hindered. North later expanded his model to include the state and ideology (North 1981) and formal and informal institutions (North 1990). States must be able to defend not only property rights but also the rule of law in general, but states cannot watch everywhere, all the time. Managers, owners, employees, and buyers must also follow the law. Only ideology makes this possible – otherwise, purely calculating rational actors would cheat more often than is actually the case. Buyer and seller at a farmer's market – where police are usually not patrolling rigorously – act in good faith not out of rational behavior, but because they believe it is good *not* to cheat another. In addition, informal institutions – how people really act – can affect economic performance. North (1990) argued that institutions also privilege certain elites; if they benefit and have enough power, they will defend imperfect economies, hurting overall social and economic growth.

What is "capitalism"?

The observant reader might ask just what "capitalism" is, and how it differs from a "market economy" or an "industrial economy" (or industrialization). An industrial economy is an economy based on large-scale production utilizing technology and bureaucratically structured factories. Capitalism versus market economies is a more subtle difference. "Market economy" implies a system in which actors are relatively free in their choice of purchases, dealings, and activities. In a market, we exchange goods and services relatively freely: workers negotiate labor contracts with employers, buyers negotiate prices with sellers (Zelizer 1988). "Capitalism" implies deeper social structures and logics: class society, accumulation and exploitation, authority grounded in ownership of private property, tendencies towards rationalization through formal rules of control and measurement. One way of describing the difference is that "market economy" implies particular structures that permit entrepreneurs and corporations to trade and produce autonomously, while "capitalism" implies a market economy plus its underlying institutions and logics. (For rhetorical purposes scholars often use the two terms interchangeably, and I will occasionally do so as well.)[4]

According to Max Weber (1987 [1923]), capitalism as an economic system is characterized by the following practices and economic organization: production for profit, organized in private enterprise (i.e. founded on private property); minimal barriers to trade (e.g. no barriers based on ethnicity or religion); exchange and value through money rather than barter; minimal barriers to hiring and firing labor (a free labor market); and an environment of calculable law enforced by a bureaucratic state. In the absence of a state willing and able to enforce market laws (e.g. contract, property), entrepreneurs will not invest time and money in economic development. This "ideal type" captures similarities of market capitalism across space and time, although real market economies have important differences. American capitalism involves multiple autonomous corporations, while corporations in Japan and South Korea are more concentrated. However, these same basic characteristics operate in all these countries. The next question that arises is how capitalism emerged.

From this we can address what forces facilitate or hinder market economies – one of the most burning questions of the twentieth century, affecting the lives of every person on the planet. While local markets for trade and production existed throughout time and across space, their integration into a broader country-wide or "national" system (Lie 1992) is rather recent, and it first appeared in Western Europe and then in North America. Why and how did this happen?

Sociology on the rise of capitalism

In contrast to formal economics, sociological approaches look deeper into structures, culture, and institutions across space and time to ascertain *how* market capitalism operates and *why* it emerged – reflecting the intellectual concerns of Marx and Weber. In fact, sociology truly emerged in the nineteenth century in attempts to understand capitalism's functioning and birth. The various answers these early thinkers provided are foundations for different approaches in economic sociology and political economy, and I focus on the three most prominent: Marx and Engels, Weber, and Durkheim.

Marxist theory: classes and dialectics

According to Marx and Engels, history passes through stages, and each stage has its own internal dialectic of class contradictions and conflict that will eventually overthrow the system (except at the last stage, communism) (Figure 3.1). Capitalist practices and structures only come to fruition when supported and developed by the class whose interests it fulfills, the bourgeoisie. Capitalism follows agrarian feudalism, under which the nobility enjoy status – the primary form of social power – and control the land and those who live off of it (serfs). Historically, the nobility exploited serfs by taking either part of their produce or rents (forcing serfs to sell their output on the market). Within the feudal economy city-based merchants accumulated money through exchanging goods, whether agricultural produce or expensive goods. Yet while merchants accumulated wealth over time, even investing it in rudimentary production (e.g. textiles), *status* remained the basis of feudalist social authority. The new bourgeoisie were becoming an economic elite subservient to a different social-political elite. This created class conflict between the nobility and market-based bourgeoisie. In the resulting capitalist revolution, the bourgeoisie overthrew the nobility by destroying their social order and replacing it with political and social systems that encouraged capitalism. Money and property became the primary sources of status and power. Property ownership was sanctified in codified law, no longer subject to the whims of the monarch. Representative democracy eventually emerged as the most useful form of government for the bourgeoisie (as it reflected the logic of money and a larger bourgeois class).[5] In this same dialectical logic, Marx and Engels claimed that the working class would eventually come to see the contradiction between its own interests and those of the bourgeoisie

(a)

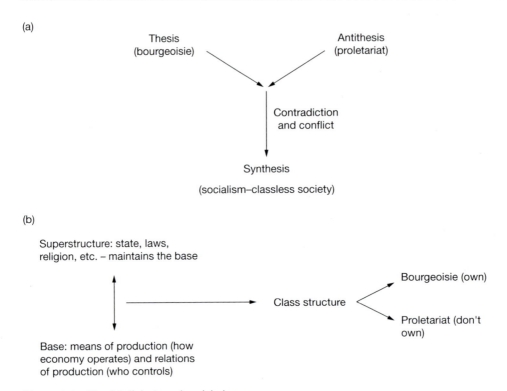

Figure 3.1   Marxist dialects and social change

and capitalism. As evil as capitalism is, it is a necessary phase that creates the technology and wealth required for communism. The proletariat would understand the malevolent nature of private property (as the basis for class exploitation) and use its numerical superiority to overthrow capitalism and impose communism. Free of private property, communism would be class-free.

Richard Lachmann (1989, 1990) challenged the classical Marxist framework. If Marx and Engels claimed that politics and social structure were an *outcome* of economic structure and forces, Lachmann inverted the relationship: capitalist economies and class structures emerged from *political* events, namely elites' attempts to control resources to fortify their political positions. Social elites such as lords and nobles clashed with royal elites and those around them. Both sides realized that power required resources, and the politics and conflict of pre-modern Europe, between crown and nobles (which sometimes erupted into civil wars), was over control of land, taxation and revenue, loyalties of the local population, and the like. When nobles consolidated control over land and labor – which varied (e.g. better in England than in France or Russia) – they had to do something with their resources, and they turned to producing for the market to maintain their economic advantages. Class dynamics were still crucial, but they were not quite what Marx imagined. A social and economic elite that enjoyed privileges from the crown was less likely to develop their holdings (as in France and Russia). An elite suspicious and relatively independent of the crown (as in England) focused on developing what they had to maintain that independence – hence the emergence of capitalism (defense of elite power), yet differences in its form across Europe.

Overall, Marxism suggests several social forces we must consider when studying economies (as well as polities and societies). First is the classic "base-superstructure" framework: the economy (the base) is the root of all social processes, and from the specific configurations of the means and relations of production of the base the superstructure (all other social institutions and structures, supporting the base) emerges. Second, underlying the surface view of society as factories, political parties, and the like, deeper structural forces are at work, shaping how economic organizations and rules develop. Finally, Marxist thought has a sense of confidence: because these structural forces are at work everywhere, the present can be understood and the future discerned. Not that all this has gone without criticism – in fact, Marxism has generated a fair amount of debate, partly because of the political action it suggests. Critiques are far-ranging. For example, Weberians claim that the Marxist conception of "class" is too nebulous and devoid of concrete mechanisms of social control over different types of resources: class power requires concrete social manifestations such as organizations or economic rules (Parkin 1979). Others noticed that the proletarian revolution cannot emerge because of rational action and free riding (Olson 1965). However, the Marxist framework retains insights that we cannot immediately discard. In particular, the logic of accumulation and exploitation, class struggle, the economic base as the determinant of broader social structure may be applied to many different economic, historical, and social issues, from revolutions to gender inequality – and to development (Figure 3.1).

Max Weber: institutions and organizations

Wight (2005) claims that economists misunderstand or take out of context much of Adam Smith's seminal ideas; the same is true of Weber. As I claimed in Chapter 1, too often scholars use Weber to oppose cultural to structural explanations, when Weber in fact saw both structure *and* culture as important. In addition, sociologists too often have taken Weber's early work (especially *The Protestant Ethic*) to be the basic statement of his theory, thus misunderstanding or oversimplifying him (e.g. Marshall 1980). Weber's early work did stress the importance of culture, but this was only his first foray into the issue of the roots of capitalism. While ultimately Weber himself went beyond the Protestant ethic thesis, it is worthwhile recounting it for an understanding of the Weberian logic of historical and comparative thought. We begin with Weber's seminal question: Why did capitalism emerge *where* it did (the West) and *when* it did (by the eighteenth century)?[6] His first explanation was the famous Protestant ethic. He reasoned like this: What social force was unique to (Northern) Europe and powerful enough at this time to generate capitalism? His answer was Calvinism, especially its predestination thesis, according to which only a certain number of people are "chosen" for entry into heaven. However, people were unsure who was chosen or whether they could lose this status, thereby creating psychological stress. People wanted to believe they were chosen, yet they could not prove definitively that they were. People searched for ways to deal with this stress and uncertainty, and an interesting strategy emerged. People pursued *work* as if it were what their lives were really all about, rather than as a mere source of income. Work was good and would keep one in God's graces. Further, those who worked hard did not spend their income lavishly (e.g. on expensive goods) but instead reinvested their income and lived frugally and humbly – God's preferred behavior. People who owned businesses worked hard and invested profits in their businesses.[7] Further, these people devised a way to determine whether one was chosen: God would not let someone who was pious, frugal, economical, and hard-working *fail* (this would fly against God's perfection). Failure in spite of hard, honest, economical work would be left for the imperfect, those destined for hell. Hence, people, especially those in business, not only worked hard for the sake of work and staying in God's favor; they also improved their work to attain success, especially in entrepreneurship, to ease their fears about their fates after death.

This became the driving force for the emergence of capitalism. First, work was no longer simply an occupation or source of wages; it was a *calling*, why one existed and what one lived for. Second, life was frugal; profit was to be reinvested so that the firm could grow, rather than being spent on lavish goods. This became a source of discipline for which capitalism became (in)famous. Third, entrepreneurs and owners searched constantly for ways to improve business. One method was double-entry bookkeeping (accounting showing money coming in and going out), which allowed businessmen to calculate where they were making and losing money, and from this to improve performance and focus on profitable undertakings – improving success. This "ethic" started with Calvinism and spread to Protestantism generally. To compete with hard-working, efficient Protestants, one had to follow their logic. Eventually, this logic of capitalism spread throughout Europe, and later the world, because it was a powerful engine of economic growth. And its roots were forgotten. This was a bitter irony: we work hard to obtain "success," and why? We do not really know – the reasons are lost in the mists of time. This is, to us, how capitalism has *always* operated.

The beauty of Weber's Protestant ethic thesis is its historical complexity and how it demonstrates the importance of ideas (culture) and historical accident, but he continued his historical-institutional exploration. In his mature thesis on how capitalism emerged, *General Economic History* (a set of lectures published after his death), Weber suggested that capitalism emerged in the West because of a particular historical *conjuncture* of institutions, laws, and collective practices. This thesis is not as neat as his Protestant ethic, nor is it as tidy as Marx's class dialectics. Capitalism emerged initially from a set of historical accidents. It was not designed, nor was it automatic or inevitable. The historical roadmap runs like this (cf. Collins 1980; see also Figure 3.2). The Judeo-Christian tradition denied magic and fostered a materialist study of the world. This allowed for the kind of analyses that opened up the way for both study of the world and application of knowledge, and of the legitimation of decision-making based on money. The Reformation helped break down

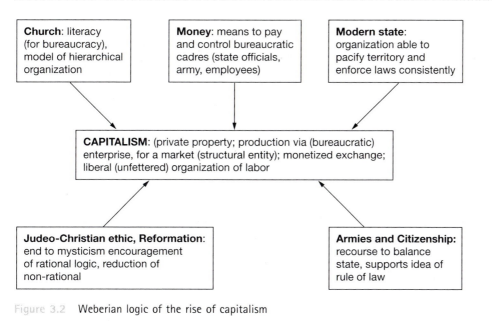

Church: literacy (for bureaucracy), model of hierarchical organization

Money: means to pay and control bureaucratic cadres (state officials, army, employees)

Modern state: organization able to pacify territory and enforce laws consistently

CAPITALISM: (private property; production via (bureaucratic) enterprise, for a market (structural entity); monetized exchange; liberal (unfettered) organization of labor

Judeo-Christian ethic, Reformation: end to mysticism encouragement of rational logic, reduction of non-rational

Armies and Citizenship: recourse to balance state, supports idea of rule of law

Figure 3.2   Weberian logic of the rise of capitalism

Source: Weber (1987 [1923]); see also Collins (1980)

boundaries between different social and ethnic groups, widening the exchange of goods and services and expanding the economy. Education for work within the Christian church provided literate administrators and a model for bureaucratic organization; this was the basis for more competent bureaucratic states (that could pacify territories and administer law), and from there a model for modern companies and corporations that require bureaucratic structure to produce an enormous amount of goods and wealth. Wars bred citizenship as a reward to soldiers who fought. With bureaucracy, this gave birth to the rule of law: citizenship implied rights before the state that political leaders had to obey, and this became a cornerstone to the rule of law – without which an economy does not have either stability or recourse against the state. Coinage (currency) allowed bureaucracies, especially states, to wield administrators and police, maintaining social order; currency also facilitated exchange and production by creating a unit of value. In short, the combination of wars, organizational innovations (bureaucracy and the modern state), flexible group barriers and identities, and acceptance of materialism mixed together and led to the rise of private property (a set of rights, akin to citizenship), modern companies (organizations combining bureaucratic structure and private property), and a logic of rational calculation, all promoted or defended by the power of the state. A new form of economic power and culture was embedded in structures and institutions that emerged from various sources and directions. Once capitalism as a system of economic institutions and practices did emerge, it generated economic wealth and political power: states had a greater capacity to engage in warfare, and emerging capitalist powers carried capitalism with them via gunships and armies.

In other words, capitalism emerged because of *political* events and *institutional* outcomes. A similar logic comes from historian Paul Kennedy (1987). Studying the "rise and fall of the great powers" (Austria, Spain, Britain, France, Germany, Russia, the United States, and Japan), Kennedy notes that Western capitalist countries were the first great powers because their market economies generated enormous wealth and technological innovation that allowed them to excel at war. In fact, it was war that generated capitalism and reinforced it – because when states engage in war, they spend money on munitions. Capitalists provide the weapons for war and make good profit on this venture. These profits from war are reinvested in production of weapons and non-military goods. In the end, capitalism might have emerged in Europe not because of religion but because there was no single all-powerful state, as in China. Instead, there were several states unable to conquer each other. Because they fought continuously, they continuously spent money on weapons – literally investing in economic growth. War, perhaps, built capitalism and spread it throughout the globe.[8] Jack Goldstone (1987, 2000) adds to the cultural and institutional side of Weber's mature story by exploring the impact of the Anglican Church's attitude to science. Rather than interfere in scientific discovery, the Church of England was more neutral; its theology did not see the advance of scientific discourse as contradictory to Christianity, and scientific discoveries (aiding economic development) fit a mechanistic view of the universe of God the watchmaker, with scientific laws (e.g. Newton's laws of motion) part of His creation.

Before *General Economic History* Weber also commented on the workings of capitalist organization (and modernity more generally) in his massive *Economy and Society* (Weber 1978 [1922]). He was wise enough to see that ideas and material resources were *equally* important – the switchman metaphor I noted in Chapter 1. Culture directs the organization and use of resources. He also understood that material interests and culture were not free floating. Rather, they were embedded in and reproduced by institutions, such as complex laws and organizational structures. This attempt to understand capitalist modernity took Weber to organization, and he claimed that two key traits of capitalism are bureaucracy and rationalization. Bureaucracies are organizations with precise, formal rules, routines, and structures that allow their leaders to control and coordinate large numbers of people, by measuring and managing them, from steelworkers to secretaries. There are precise gradations for promotion and pay, and precise rules for reward and punishment. Output is measured in time and output. (In its extreme, such measuring and prescribing work is *micro-management*.) That is, the modern bureaucracy structures economic life (and all life) by placing people into distinct niches with specific tasks and relations to other people; employees are dependent on the organization for material and symbolic resources – wages and status – and this power gives organizational leaders the ability to mobilize massive numbers of people towards a common goal, whether defeating an enemy on the battlefield or in the marketplace. Hence Weber was both in fear and awe of bureaucracies: while they dehumanized labor, taking creative control from the employee (which Marx saw as the root of alienation), they also facilitated the realization of complex tasks and large-scale activity and production. If for Marx the face of capitalist modernity was that of the bourgeois owner, for Weber it was the bureaucrat.

Interestingly, this led to a tension in Weber's work. On the one hand, historical accident is important. Just because capitalism now runs the globe does not mean it always will. Underdeveloped countries may import some aspects of capitalism, but capitalism is a complex set of structures and practices that cannot be created overnight, and creating them is extremely difficult. At the same time, Weber saw rationalization as an inevitable development that would continue on its own: it was an "iron cage" which humanity had entered and would never escape. In other words, Weber saw both historical variation and accident, and ahistorical inevitability. The former survives in contemporary political economy that stresses the importance of the state; the latter was important to modernization theory, which saw development as culture-based and inevitable.

Durkheim, modernity, and capitalism

Emile Durkheim did not develop a specific theory of the rise of capitalism or its operation. Rather, he analyzed modernity generally, of which capitalism was a part – a reversal of Marxism. Capitalism is not so much a specific form of resource control (property) or organization (rationalized bureaucracy) as a result of certain social solidarity. If Marx's engine of economic change was class struggle, Durkheim's was "social density." In his first major work, a study of the social division of labor, Durkheim (1947) claimed that advances in communications and transport technology brought isolated communities together with profound consequences. Earlier in human history, communities were isolated and technologically undeveloped, and people had to rely on themselves for most production. People were jacks of all trades: they all had to have the same basic skills for survival, such as how to build and repair homes, grow crops, and produce basic household goods (such as clothes). Solidarity – the social glue holding people together – was "mechanical," in that people in each community shared the same experiences and skills. This commonality held people together. As communications and transportation brought people into closer proximity – increasing the density of human interaction – people had to differentiate between each other to survive. This went hand-in-hand with urbanization and industrialization. People had to adopt *specific* skills and roles – no longer a jack-of-all-trades but a worker producing or trading specific goods. As a result, people lost the ability to survive on their own and became *dependent* on each other – this was "organic" solidarity of modern society.

While this does not explain specifically how capitalism develops, it does suggest prerequisites for capitalism. In fact, it is safe to say that Durkheim and those who have followed his tradition (especially modernization theorists) focus less on "capitalism" *per se* and more on "industrial society" (see n.4, this chapter), which allows broader comparisons of modern societies. Buttressing the new industrial society was the division of labor and increasing social complexity – the creation of more specific social and economic roles that, coupled with new technology, made large-scale production (factories with skilled workers) possible. This new industrial economy was further underpinned by new values inherent in organic solidarity. Rational action cannot hold a complex industrial society together – this is the "problem of order." Durkheim was generally critical of utilitarian thought (the logic of rational choice and neoclassical economics) and did not see rational choice as the state of human nature (Aron 1965). Rather, the rise and functioning of industrial society (and capitalism) depends on broader social structures and forces of modernity in which it is embedded. Modern industrial capitalism as we know it requires contracts, restitutive law (punishment by fines or in accordance with the crime, rather than extreme punishment for an insult to the collective), money, and some degree of individualism (linked to the division of labor). These facilitate production and exchange which give capitalism its dynamism. Individualist values can also facilitate the kind of rational calculation and maximization of personal gain that drive accumulation and investment – values that Weber located in religion and the Reformation. Put crudely, in villages, people bartered corn for bread; there were no stimuli or foundations for expanding production and innovation dynamically. In modern cities, money, property, and contract created workforces, organizations, and relations for making industrial goods on a large scale. Finally, industrial capitalism can be harmful if it creates anomie, whether through migration of peasants from familiar villages to unfamiliar industrial cities or through the unfolding of individualist logics of self and interaction. Common values, identities, and structures hold capitalism together in spite of itself.

Classical sociologists left a legacy on which future sociologists could build. However, this legacy was not straightforward. Some sociologists drew on early Durkheim and Weber's "Protestant Ethic" thesis, while others turned to Weber's institutional work and Durkheim's later ritual-centered study of religion. From these legacies, three major theories emerged in the twentieth century. The first was modernization theory, drawing on Durkheim and Weber and anti-Marxist in orientation. It was attacked by Marxist dependency and world-systems theory, which in turn was challenged by Weberian state-centered political economy. This was in addition to neoclassical economic theory, which also developed in the course of the twentieth century in the face of the same basic questions of development.

Values of modernity and development: modernization theory

The Cold War rivalry between the United States and the USSR was partly a struggle of economic models. The Soviet side was a crude form of Marxism that promoted state-run, state-planned "command economies" that claimed to foster equality and justice. While the reality of Soviet society was far from this ideal, officially promoted Marxism–Leninism had great power as a critique of capitalist inequality and as an alternative for "Third World" countries – underdeveloped and caught between the "two worlds" of capitalism (the "West") and socialism (the Soviet bloc). Against Marxism's appeal to those less well-off (or to guerrilla fighters), modernization theory was offered as a "non-communist manifesto" (Rostow 1965) providing hope for capitalist (non-Soviet) development.

The basic ideas of modernization theory followed the work and ideas of Talcott Parsons and his students (e.g. Parsons 1951; Parsons et al. 1953; Parsons and

Smelser 1965). Parsons' theory is rich but dense, and I simplify it. Parsons drew his foundation for a theory of development from Durkheim's *Division of Labor* and a limited application of Weber's Protestant ethic and rationalization. From these two sources Parsons and his followers saw social solidarity based on common values. As societies developed, those values, and hence social organization and solidarity, shifted as well. The key issue was how to maintain solidarity and create those values necessary for economic development. Parsons reflected on the differences between "modern" and "pre-modern" societies and devised his famous "pattern variables." While complex in themselves, they boil down to a shift in values, from emphasis on relations of kin and personal trust to those based on impersonal merit and general trust. For Parsons' student Marion Levy (1966), the engine of modernization was advancement in sources and technology of physical power (e.g. for production or transportation) and increasing social complexity. Economic and social complexity require changes in social norms and practices: from particularistic to universalistic, for example. Levy's colleagues, many at Princeton University, tried to use data from Russia, Japan, and China to support the framework (Black 1966; Black *et al.* 1975; Rozman 1981).

On the surface, modernization theory could be persuasive. Growth in the Western world was correlated with a change in values (in no small part from increasing mass education and the inculcation of skills and norms), the advancement of non-elites (e.g. the middle class), and the rule of law. The best fit was between modernization theory and the histories of Great Britain and the United States (or at least of their mythic histories). The theory offered hope to Western politicians and a guide to foreign policy: provide aid and incorporate developing countries into the world capitalist economy, and their middle classes (and middle-class values) would emerge.[9] As well, modernization theory promised to dig beneath national and global economic structures to see just what made them tick: put another way, modernization scholars did not assume structures of class or capital but tried to see just what made people do what they did and how this contributed to growth.

Despite the promise, modernization theory came under criticism in the 1970s. Like much Parsons-inspired theory, its categories and logic were dense and too abstract for much meaningful research. Some claimed that the theory was ethnocentric: it saw in the British and American histories the single model for normal development for the rest of the world. This made alternative experiences illegitimate. In fact, while Catholic values were supposedly antithetical to modernization (due to the stress on tradition, deference to authority, and collectivism), Catholic countries in Latin America such as Mexico did experience moments of growth. Others argued that for modernization theory the ultimate sign of development was consumerism, yet this was a superficial manifestation of norms and institutions (Skocpol 1976). (If consumerism and development went hand-in-hand for America, it was less tightly linked in Europe and especially in East Asia.) That is, rather than compare cases and induce value shifts or the causality of values on development, modernization theorists extrapolated certain broad Anglo-American values to the entire story of global development. As scholars looked closely at non-Western countries, they noticed modernization was far from complete or was in error, especially concerning continued underdevelopment in Latin America and Africa. Out of their experiences two related theories emerged: dependency theory and world-systems theory, which claimed (in opposition to economic and modernization theory) that incorporation into world capitalism was the *source* of underdevelopment, not its solution.

Marxism's revenge: dependency theory and world-systems theory

These two approaches take structuralism and Marxist theory to the global level. In dependency theory, development is situated in *historical* structures (Cardoso and Faletto 1979). "Latecomer" countries (not in the first wave of development) become *dependent* on First World nations for investment and markets, because First World nations have gained better technologies and industrial capacity. World-systems theory (Wallerstein 1974) posits real structural forces and mechanisms that create and reproduce global inequality. Just as such forces arise within capitalist societies, they also arise of their own accord in a global capitalist market. For dependency theory, such forces are not so rigid. There is no global capitalist system, but there are relations of power and exchange between different countries. Dependent countries can emerge from underdevelopment; however, it is difficult to do so. Because it allows more historical variability, dependency theory can be expanded to explain why some countries do grow, and so I focus primarily on this, rather than on world-systems theory.

Dependency and world systems see two types of countries: the *core* and the *periphery*. The core are developed countries with working capitalism and wealth. The periphery are perpetually underdeveloped, poor, and dependent on the core for investment, technology, and economic know-how. (Theorists later added a third category, *semiperiphery*, for countries that were developing and alleviating poverty, e.g. Taiwan or South Korea.) Many peripheral countries were once European colonies (e.g. in Africa). The core have strategic advantages over the periphery. They have capital and technological know-how for research and development or production of industrial or high-tech goods, much of which is locked up in patents.[10] They have finance for advanced educational systems (tax money for schools and universities, funding for scholarships). Core countries enjoy more developed militaries, which they sometimes used to impose their will on the periphery. American political and military influence over Latin America in the nineteenth and twentieth centuries kept most of those countries in line with American economic and foreign policies (Paterson 1979: ch. 3); in 1983 Ronald Reagan sent American troops into Grenada against a supposedly Marxist regime.

While political and economic elites in the core may be aware of these unequal relations and try to manipulate them to their collective advantage, it is a mistake to see dependency as the result of a Western conspiracy. Rather, it is the historical outcome of structural relations. Much as a capitalist country's internal class relations are the natural outcome of such institutions as private property, global relations of inequality come from the unequal distribution of capital – a result of the unequal historical

emergence of capitalism. The forces Weber saw at work allowed European entrepreneurs and elites the opportunity to invest not only in primitive production,
exchange, and accumulation, but also in investment for progress in technology and
knowledge. As their states and economies grew, European armies improved as well.
The quest for resources (e.g. gold, spices) and geopolitical advantage (e.g. controlling trade routes) led European monarchs and ministers to make empires.[11] Peoples
in Africa, Latin America, and Asia found themselves the subjects of Britain, Spain,
France, and eventually Germany. Colonies became both a source of cheap resources
and labor and markets trapped in the orbit of imperial masters. This put the colonies,
once they were independent, at a disadvantage: the mother countries had been
exploiting them for generations, leaving them in a state of underdevelopment and
dependence on Europe.

Direct colonization was not the only path to underdevelopment and peripheral status.
Latin American countries achieved independence from Spain and Portugal in the late
eighteenth and early nineteenth centuries, yet they remained dependent on the core.
This was not because of direct control (American military pressure aside). Latin
American countries sold raw materials such as hides, gold, copper, and even guano
(nitrates for fertilizer and explosives) to Europe and the United States. Some export
profits went to foreign-owned companies – and back to the core. Profits that
remained in Latin America went into importing industrial goods from the United
States or Europe. (see Figure 3.3) Further, states developed in Latin America by
borrowing money from the core – contrast this to states in Europe and North
America, which obtained money from their own populations through taxation and
internal borrowing (e.g. treasury bonds) (Centeno 1997). Both political development
and trade imbalances made Latin America reliant on the core for goods, knowledge,
and finance. Latin American countries tried to escape this through various policies
after the 1930s (I discuss these below) that ultimately led to increased debt and
even greater dependence on the core for finance and for policies to ease debt. In
response, core countries exported the neoliberal model of growth; but "technocrats,"

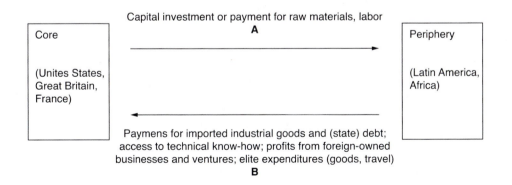

Figure 3.3   How dependency operates

state elites with training and knowledge from the core (especially the United States), accepted the neoliberal creeds of a minimal state and open markets to foreign investment, and imposed them on their own countries. Latin American countries were dependent *intellectually* for models of economic growth (cf. Centeno and Silva 1998).

The power of the dependency model (and by extension, of world-systems theory) is how it uses structure and history to explain the emergence and persistence of unequal development. Structure comes alive through elite interests, historical events and timing, and the logic of capitalism within and between countries. However, dependency and world-systems theories are not perfect. These two theories aimed to explain underdevelopment – but they have a more difficult time explaining how some countries, such as Japan and South Korea (or more recently, China), could move from the periphery to the semi-periphery and to the core. That is, dependency and world-systems theory are less powerful for explaining *variation* in development trajectories and outcomes. Yet even in these cases of development success, dependency still has wisdom: as Evans (1995) notes, despite its enviable growth, South Korean business and state elites still bemoan how their output, for the most part, remains less innovative in contrast to front-line production from American or German companies. Japan was the wonder-child in the 1980s, but it has been displaced by China – for the moment.

Weber returns: institutional and state-centered theory

Dependency and world-systems theory challenged modernization theory, but soon faced their own challenge: Japan, followed by South Korea, Taiwan, and other East Asian "dragons," experienced rapid growth to compete with Western countries. While Latin American countries did experience growth, this slowed by the 1980s, leaving Mexico, Brazil, and others in debt to leading capitalist countries and lenders, dependent on their terms of repayment. This made sense in the context of dependency – but what about East Asia? Neomodernizationists saw cultural values as important to East Asian development (Rozman 1991), but then how could modernization theory handle Latin American stagnation? To make sense of the difference between the two regions' fates, sociologists and political scientists turned to the *state* as mediator of power and relations between a country and the outside world, and as mediator between different organized forces within its home society (Skocpol 1979).

The state did not make its theoretical reappearance in the 1980s: earlier scholars had noted its importance. As we saw earlier, Max Weber noted how states (and formal organizations generally) structured human activity. States can pacify territories and create stability through force and law – the kind of stability capitalism requires. Yet states can do more, as Karl Polanyi (1944) revealed in his classic account of the rise of Western capitalism in England. His main insight was that a market *economy* requires a market *society*: a social system free from institutional barriers to commodification of land, labor, and exchange. Yet according to Polanyi, human beings ground social interaction in fairness and reciprocity. Unfettered commodification and exchange of labor or land are antithetical to human nature (Polanyi 1957). Historically, human beings have not thought of these as commodities bought and sold for money. Further, reciprocity values were embedded in local rituals and institutions such as local welfare and poor relief administered by churches, or local minimum wage laws. Such welfare hindered the market: a minimum wage meant employees were not dependent on capitalists for survival, weakening discipline. Localized welfare also created barriers to exchange: for example, to receive church aid, the poor had to live in a particular locale, restricting the flow of labor. As well, there were no "national" economies. Instead, trade and production were local, contributing to local insulation from broader economies and shocks.

Market society could not emerge organically from Protestantism, middle classes, or a bourgeoisie – the state had to impose it, creating social pain and risking reaction from below (e.g. 1930s fascism). Institutionalized market resistance to a national economy based on commodification had to be broken, and only the state had the force to do so. The result was market dynamism built on increasing wealth for the elite and increasing dependence of all workers on this elite. Polanyi did point out a weakness in this new system: states and the global market were not all-powerful, and sometimes society struck back. For example, the price of bread fluctuated with supply and demand, and when there was too little bread, its price rose. This violated the "moral economy" of laborers and peasants (Thompson 1971), who accepted elite authority in return for subsistence (e.g. cheap bread). Worse yet, as capitalism became a global system and capital moved increasingly across national borders, countries became interdependent. When the Great Depression broke out, its effects could not be contained. As economies went into crisis, society bit back against market forces of commodification that made people functions of money value: they turned to fascism or communism.

Polanyi's story provides a powerful critique of economic theory as well as modernization and dependency theory: markets do not emerge naturally because they are unnatural. They do not emerge from a natural inclination to self-improvement and wealth, nor from a particular set of values. They are creations of the state and its elite allies. The failure of markets or their inability to generate growth must therefore be, at least in part, a function of state capacity. Scholars seeking to explain why some economies developed while others did not could use lessons from Weber and Polanyi. States became the arbiters of economic fates: the world system (like contemporary "globalization") was not so all-powerful after all. This led in the 1980s to a new explanation of capitalist development: state-centered theory.

States and development: growth versus stagnation

Polanyi showed that states matter in general; but what about states and the different trajectories of Latin America and East Asia? How could one part of the world remain dependent while another part of the world outside the core approach the same level of development as that core? State structures, state–society relations, and policy choices which state elites made were crucial to the answer. Latin American leaders set out to shield themselves from the uncertainties and shocks of the global market; East Asian leaders, a few decades later, set out to exploit the opportunities of the global market. Both policies had successes, but ultimately that chosen in Latin America led the region back into dependency. As well, state–society links and relations between states and the outside world differed, fostering independence and growth in East Asia, but problematic development in Latin America.

Policy choices

In the twentieth century two basic models dominated development policies in the industrializing world (cf. Gereffi and Wyman 1990; Haggard 1990). The first was *import substitution industrialization* (ISI). The state, sometimes in partnership with its bourgeoisie and foreign multinational corporations (Evans 1979), invested in producing goods that had been imported (e.g. heavy industrial output, textiles, or automobiles). Internalizing such production would allow the country to retain profits and to buffer itself from instability in the outside economic world. This initially required loans, but eventual domestic growth and profit would repay these loans and lead to further investment and, hopefully, to "take-off" into the First World. The alternative was *export-oriented industrialization* (EOI), in which the state directed production of exports for developed countries. Countries with this policy generally kept their currencies weak to aid exports and hinder imports; sometimes they protected domestic industries against competition through direct and indirect barriers (e.g. tariffs, or requiring hefty quality standards for imports). A partnership between state and business facilitated long-term planning to target potentially profitable market niches abroad. If ISI aimed to shield a country from the global economy, EOI aimed to take advantage of it.

Latin American countries began with ISI and continued along that line from the 1930s, following the shocks of the Great Depression. As developed economies collapsed, their demand for raw materials and production of output collapsed as well, leaving Latin American economies vulnerable. In response both to this global instability and populist demands for economic rewards, Latin American governments sporadically implemented ISI or related policies from the 1930s up until the 1970s. Governments either nationalized industries or contributed heavily to their creation, sometimes owning them outright (e.g. state-owned enterprises (SOEs)), e.g. Mexican and Brazilian state-owned oil companies Pemex and Petrobras. In the 1970s Mexico nationalized its banks and entered the oil industry after the discovery of oil deposits. Economic growth was fairly impressive at times; in the 1950s, Latin American economies grew faster than in East Asia (e.g. around 9 percent in Mexico). However, problems set in. Latin American countries needed to borrow to set up industries, and they continued to borrow over time, especially in the 1970s.[12] So long as foreign (especially American) interest rates were reasonable, governments could cover their debts with income streams or additional borrowing, mortgaging the future. However, two potential problems of this ISI strategy exploded in the late 1970s and early 1980s. To combat inflation at home, the American Federal Reserve raised interest rates. Interest payments on Latin America debt skyrocketed, and foreign investment moved from Latin America to American treasury bills (e.g. government bonds). Latin America now had high debt but weak income. To make matters worse, public ownership trapped the state into financing inefficient companies. Improving productivity would have involved investing in new technology and reducing labor costs – but Latin American states owned these firms, and unemployed employees might vent their anger by voting out politicians who fired them or by taking to the streets.[13] Latin American states were also closely linked to their elites, who demanded state subsidies.

In the early 1980s many Latin American countries were on the verge of bankruptcy, especially Brazil, Argentina, and Mexico. The Reagan administration devised a policy to help out these countries, but it required radical policy changes that included paying off foreign debt, reducing welfare, and privatizing (selling off) state-owned firms. Latin American populations would work harder for less money and lose their firms to foreign owners to pay off debts and attract foreign investment. Chile had begun such a policy much earlier, after the 1973 *coup d'état* that brought Colonel Augusto Pinochet to power. In the 1980s, non-democratic regimes in Mexico and Brazil began implementing "austerity programs" to reduce state debt and bring in foreign investment. ISI had once produced impressive growth, but the combination of debt and inefficient firms that the state could not close led back to dependency, as Latin American countries were forced to open up to the world economy.

Given that their home markets remained weak after World War II, East Asian countries tried some ISI but reoriented to export-oriented economies. While this ran the risk of remaining sensitive to the economic conditions of developed countries (their target markets), it also allowed them to tap those economies' wealth. Japanese companies made a profit if the United States and Europe were doing well, and they could compete on the developed countries' own turf. East Asian industries were newer and eventually had more up-to-date production technology. Wages and labor costs were lower (partly due to a lack of unionization), and welfare expenditures were low.[14] This allowed East Asian countries to produce cheaper goods than Western companies. Also, Japanese, Korean, and Taiwanese companies initially produced for the lower end of the market (e.g. less flashy cars, wigs, and cheap clothes). Profits were later invested in up-market production, and by the 1980s Asian goods were competing with top-of-the-line Western goods. Honda and Toyota cars were once a joke, cheap, lower end cars, but by the late 1980s both were among the best cars and bestsellers in the United States. (Korean auto producer Hyundai followed a similar strategy: cheaper cars at first, and then improving the image with a constantly better product.)

The contrast to Latin American economies was clear. GDP per capita in Latin America slowed by the 1970s but continued to rise in East Asia. In the late 1980s the GDP per capita (gross domestic product per person, a measure of national wealth) was $2690 in South Korea but $1830 in Mexico. Annual GDP growth in South Korea for 1955 to 1965 was 5.1 percent, versus 9.7 percent for Mexico; 1965 to 1980 9.5 percent growth for South Korean versus 6.5 percent for Mexico. From 1980 to 1987 Mexico's growth rate was 0.5 percent, in contrast to a rate of 8.6 percent in South Korea. Not only had South Korea outstripped Mexico; its high growth rate was consistent (Gereffi 1990). Further, other Asian countries were growing: to complement the original dragons were "little dragons" such as Thailand, Malaysia, and even Vietnam. However, East Asian countries were not economic utopias. In the late

1980s the Japanese economy showed signs of strain: bad investments in a real estate bubble and weak transparency of financial institutions allowed bad debt to build up, creating an economic malaise that lasted throughout the 1990s. In 1997 to 1998 a financial "flu" spread through the region, and foreign investors sold assets such as shares and currency, leading to a brief recession in the region.

States and economies: "embedded autonomy"

Policy choices were important, but *why* such policies were chosen and *how* they could be enacted remain to be answered. Elites can clamor for hand-outs, but states do not always provide them. Why? Following Weber's logic, Peter Evans (1995) suggested that the ability of the state to aid growth depends on its relations to society and the degree of a state's "embedded autonomy." In embedded states, officials are closely linked to social actors (such as industrial leaders) and gain a business perspective. This fosters communication of needs and ideas and can potentially help states develop useful policies, as state elites would know business needs and opportunities in the global economy. However, if states are too embedded, they are captured by society. State officials who are also members of the capitalist ruling class can hijack the state for their own aims. Or state leaders are highly dependent on the capitalist elite for their own political survival, perhaps because capitalists supply the money for political parties. States also have degrees of *autonomy*: relative freedom from demands of social groups and relative institutional insulation from social pressures, and the degree of internal *esprit de corps* (collective closeness and identity). A state with high autonomy can do what it thinks needs to be done. If there is too little embeddedness, autonomous state officials might not understand what business really needs, or act against business (and broader societal) interests.

The upshot is that states want enough embeddedness to discover and craft the best policies for growth and equitable distribution of wealth, but they also need enough autonomy to act in the best interests of the country and to avoid capture by specific classes or elites. States also need trained, professional officials with a sense of unity and mission who are able and willing to formulate and carry out policies for the best of the state and society. Creating such state–society relations is far from easy – in fact, it may be more an accident of history. Let us look at Evans' categorization of states, their capacity to make policies, and what kinds of policies we might expect (Table 3.1).

In quadrant **I** (e.g. South Korea, but also Japan), state officials and business leaders are closely linked through networks. Perhaps officials and businessmen went to the

Table 3.1 Embedded autonomy

	High autonomy	Low autonomy
High embeddedness	I	II
	(South Korea)	(Argentina)
Low embeddedness	III	IV
	(India)	(Zaire)

same elite university, or both worked together in business or the state (truer for Japan than Korea). Working together creates networks that allow state and business to exchange ideas, for the state to transmit to business what it considers important social and economic goals, and for business to tell the state what it needs to make those goals work. Yet the state is sufficiently *autonomous*: state officials are tightly linked, they have a close sense of *esprit de corps*, and the state is not very dependent on society (especially elites) for important political resources. The state can undertake what policies it feels are necessary for development rather than for elite wealth alone. As a result, state policies helped South Korea out of abject poverty following World War II and the Korean War.

In quadrant **II** we have a captured state. State leaders in this type of state–society relationship, as in the case of Argentina (but much of Latin America in general, and perhaps the United States as well), are closely networked with social elites, perhaps even dependent on them for necessary political resources (e.g. campaign contributions), and perhaps even part of them (the political elite comes from the social elite and shares its interests and identity). The state is *too* embedded in society and does not have sufficient independence or autonomy. In this case, more likely than not state policies will serve the interests of the elite, or of certain segments of the elite. For example, the state is more likely to continue to subsidize companies that are inefficient and draining the state of finances that would be better used elsewhere.

Quadrant **III** is the mirror opposite of quadrant **II**. State officials have sufficient independence but are poorly linked to business and society. The two sides do not communicate well and may be disdainful of each other: officials look down on businessmen as mere traders, while businessmen regard officials as petty bureaucrats. State officials think they know what is best for society when they do not, and state policies are of little help to business. In India, computer science students used state scholarships to study in the United States. India's bureaucracy was so disdainful of business that these students remained in the US and contributed to American IT development (Evans 1995).

Quadrant **IV** is the predatory state. State–society links are weak, even antagonistic: business sees the state as a predator, and state officials see society and business as sources of easy money (e.g. through bribes or taxes). Further, the state has weak *esprit de corps* and professionalism, and state officials engage in corrupt activities rather than enforcing policy and the rule of law.

Why was South Korea so lucky? World War II and the Korean War played prominent roles in some explanations. Korea's agricultural elite were decimated by Japanese colonialism – this is the class that often blocks commercialization of agriculture or development of industry (Moore 1966; Haggard 1990: ch. 3). Latin America's agricultural elites, untouched by war, remained intact. Not that the scene was perfect in the 1950s. After the Korean War, state–business links were rife with corruption (Amsden 1989). State funds (often from American support in the face of the threats from North Korea, China, and the USSR) were diverted to elites' pockets to build economic empires that contributed only to personal fortune. A military *coup* in 1961 replaced President Syngman Rhee with General Park Chung Hee, and Park began to clean up the house. The *chaebols* were told to become engines of economic growth (Amsden 1989). As well, South Korea had Japan to look up to as a model of successful post-war development (Fajnzylber 1990). Even this story has still not been picture-perfect. The *chaebols* suffered from global oscillations and corruption, and some pundits believe that the Korean state subsidized too many inefficient firms. Military dictatorship led to social mobilization (students and workers) against the regime, and the threat of North Korea (perhaps soon in possession of nuclear weapons) persists.

Development: lessons and the future

As I write this chapter, China's economy is the marvel of the world and China is exporting not only clothing but also capital. A Chinese firm offered to buy the bankrupt British auto firm MG-Rover. Chinese managers are investing in oil and other natural resources in Latin America and Africa to keep their economic machine running. The Chinese middle classes continue to grow, sending their children to foreign universities and driving more cars (contributing greenhouse gases). Meanwhile, Brazil and India – also large countries in terms of territory and populations – seem ready for take-off into growth, despite histories of underdevelopment. Both are recipients of investment by American companies, both have potentially large internal markets to make that investment pay off (although both also have a large proportion of their populations in poverty), and both are strategically placed in Latin America and the Asian subcontinent. Both countries have cheap but increasingly skilled labor and access to foreign investment and foreign markets. Western countries look on in amazement, some satisfaction – and even some fear. How long before China has enough wealth to become a serious competitor to the United States and Europe – not only with its economic might, but also with a military machine fed by that economic growth?

For other countries, the future does not seem so rosy. In 2005 Gordon Brown, Chancellor of the Exchequer in Great Britain, proposed that developed countries erase Africa's debts, as African countries spent too much income servicing debts to Western countries and aid organizations. African governments would have to improve their own investment climates by reducing corruption and improving law and order. In light of this chapter's narratives and theories, one might think that Brown's hopes have a weak chance of success. Yet despite criticisms, neoliberal claims about benefits of the world market cannot be discounted – some African economies have benefited from China's spectacular growth and thirst for oil and other raw materials. Perhaps sacrificing some political autonomy for profit or investment is not necessarily a bad thing. The issue is finding the optimal situation – where interdependence, cooperation, and overall growth go hand-in-hand, where economic growth across nations is not a zero-sum game. Such have been the *claims* of classical and neoclassical economics – whether they can be the norm is a different question.

One can ask how much legitimacy all our theories have in light of the evidence of development. All have some insights, or else scholars would not have proposed and developed them in the first place. The truth is complex: each theory captures some aspects of reality, and each is tied to organized groups whose material, symbolic, and ideological interests these theories serve. Neoliberal policies favor those with capital: not only wealthy individuals, but also managers of multinational corporations or large investment funds that gain from free global markets and weak states. Neoliberals rightly point out the importance of foreign investment to development, yet this misses aspects of economic power. Foreign investors may not build a factory and the infrastructure around it (e.g. roads) in Mexico or Nigeria; rather, they may buy shares in existing firms, and if the Mexican or Nigerian governments do something investors do not like, the investors can sell their shares quickly and take their money elsewhere. This is known as *capital flight*: capital enters a country in such a way that it can be taken out again quickly. Developing countries must be careful with their policies – not only to provide a stable environment for investment, but also not to do things that, no matter how inconsequential in the end, offend foreign investors such that they leave and take their capital with them. In short, neoliberal theory slights the negative side of foreign investment and liberalized markets: governments have less leverage *vis-à-vis* investors, but it is governments, not investors, who are more responsible for the well-being of their people. Modernization theory, too, can hide the darker side of development. It serves those who exalt Western values and can be a façade for policies. Consider China: while growth helps China's military, leaders of such countries as the United States claim development will also create a Chinese middle class sharing its Western counterpart's democratic and civic values. Dependency theory can galvanize resistance from those who feel exploited – peasants and workers in developing countries, and intellectuals who champion their causes.

There are still intellectual reasons to continue to take these approaches seriously. While modernization theory suffered from ethnocentricity, avoidance of power and an ahistorical logic, it did point to the importance of culture. Peter Berger (1991) proposed testable propositions of "neomodernization," scrapped the teleological view of the original theory, and focused on variation in outcomes. Dependency theory has also survived as state-centered institutional theory, to cope with variation (dependency in Latin America versus development in East Asia). While some variations in this approach use rational choice to address policy choices, there is room for cultural categories, logics, and conceptions of legitimacy. Neoliberal theory has been problematic. In the 1980s economists looked on Japan, Korea, Taiwan, and East Asia generally to claim that their model was correct – but more in-depth research showed how East Asian development depended on strong, active states (Wade 1990). If a country opens up its market to foreign influence and reduces the role of its state in its economy, then foreign investment *may* follow – but it may not, and if it does, it may render that country less capable of handling global economic shocks or setting its own domestic policies autonomously. In fact, some scholars claim that neoliberal policies actually lead to greater inequality and social breakdown, rather than general societal enrichment (Gray 1998).

Table 3.2 summarizes four basic approaches to development. All differ on basic questions, as well as on how they conceptualize growth – for example, is power

Table 3.2 Basic overview of major theories of development

	Neoclassical/neoliberal theory	Modernization theory	Dependency/ world-systems theory	State-centered theory
Central issue	Economic growth (aggregate)	Development of economy and polity	Power and Domination	Variation in development paths/outcomes
Major variables	Macroeconomic factors (e.g. inflation), relative costs (labor, materials, capital)	Values	Class control of resources	State structure and relations to society, outside world
Obstacles to goal	Institutional barriers (e.g. tariffs), insufficient capital investment (due to bad tax laws)	Traditional values that denigrate individualism, merit, entrepreneurship	Weak position in the world market vis-à-vis developed economies and classes	Incoherent state, lopsided state–society relations (low integration, capture)
Outlook	Rosy if politicians understand the value of free trade and open markets	Rosy in the long term: all will modernize	Gloomy: expect consistent domination by "core" capitalist classes/countries	Variable, but right state–society and state–world balance tricky
Role of state	Should provide basic public goods and law enforcement, and little more	Promote social order and proper, modern values	Usually help reproduce inequality: captured by local elites and threatened by foreign capitalist elites	Central: mediates relations between classes and between country and world system
Question most feared?	"Development for whom?"	"Why don't all countries have American structures and opportunities?"	Where did East Asian dragons come from?	And what of non-structural forces (e.g. culture)?

assumed or explicit, or is equality crucial to their explanation or an assumed outcome of "correct" development? All provide different policies, from minimal state pressure, to a focus on education of certain skills and values, to confronting (perhaps futilely) the global economy. All four continue to provide insights, but to understand variation in development we must continue to innovate, using existing insights.

This discussion of development has encountered a variety of social forces at work: state structures, policy choices, historical accidents such as when a country industrialized, position in the global market and structure of global power, and the like. Political and economic elites have had choices, even if these choices came with costs and obstacles. Two lessons stand out: countries must be lucky in their position in the world system and world history; and countries must be lucky enough to have coherent states able to guide their economies through the waters of the global economy. States remain at the center of the picture, and so we must examine more closely how states operate and their policies.

4 The state, public policy, and economic organization

For most of us, Washington, London, and Moscow are distant, yet what happens in these seats of power affects our lives. Public policy may seem distant, technical, far from democratic politics, shaped by policy wonks and bureaucrats. Yet the state is *the* dominant social organization, and its actions – "public policy" – shape our lives. American presidents raise or lower taxes and send the country to war – affecting prices, investment, interest rates, and jobs. States decide whether a firm is a monopoly, shaping consumer choice. Some states invest in or own companies, while others avoid direct ownership and let market forces sort things out. Perhaps the most visible policy is welfare. A minimum wage might raise labor costs and consumer purchasing by giving money to those with too little to spend. European welfare targets the middle class as well as the poor: cheap education and medical care that lower middle-class Americans dream of. When Britain's Labor Party reintroduced university tuition in the late 1990s (universities were free), working-class children began to worry about the cost of university education. We must investigate *how* public policies emerge – and why, contrary to economists' expectations, they *continue* to be different in different countries.

This chapter aims to understand how states make policies and how policies affect economies, while debunking the myth of "best policy." I do this through comparisons and histories to see *why* different countries developed different policies and whether one country can adopt another's policies. American welfare is relatively weak, yet coexists with high profits and labor productivity. French policy is kinder to employees. Japanese policies encourage lifetime employment and informality (real business is done in sushi bars outside of public scrutiny). This made it difficult for Japan to extricate itself from economic problems of the 1990s, yet it also made Japan's economic miracle possible. The American government cannot realistically adopt most French or Japanese policies because it is illegitimate (and illegal) for the state to meddle so closely in the economy. France and Japan's states do meddle in the economy because, historically, their states were stronger than their societies. In the United States, society was strong enough to limit state actions to regulating the market.

Efficiency, competition, and "regression to the norm"

First let us look at the economists' perspective. As we saw in Chapter 2, economists see economies as markets, where competition is at work and efficiency is the ultimate engine of change and stability. Those firms that survive are, logically, the most efficient (or else they would not have survived) – and economists believe the same is true for public policy. Policies that create inefficient economies will lead those countries to be less productive than countries with efficient policies. Competition is international – between national economies as well as firms – and efficiency should hold for policy. Only countries with a large quantity of important resources (e.g. oil) can temporarily avoid competition and efficiency.

According to basic economics, policies, like economic structures, follow *regression to the norm* (recall this from Chapter 2). Economists believe there is one set of most efficient policies, just as they believe there is one most efficient form of production or exchange. As countries compete, winning policies stand out. Other countries must follow suit or suffer worsening economic output, lower standards of living, and even unemployment as firms leave for better countries. Economists think this is so because *comparative advantage*, like competition in general, is central to their theory. David Ricardo suggested that countries begin with "factor endowments" that provide comparative advantages, such as certain types of raw materials. Countries should follow their strengths to survive market competition. If Country A has forests and Country B has oil, Country A should make furniture and Country B should produce oil and petroleum products. Country A would have to import oil to make petroleum products, and the transport costs alone would make their chemicals more expensive than those made in oil-rich Country B. Country B would be foolish to make furniture, since they do not have the raw materials (forests) – they would have to import timber, and *then* compete with Country A's cheaper furniture (cheaper because Country A does not need to import timber). Different countries' positions in the world market depend on their factor endowments. It is best to let markets work through the invisible hand rather than through state intervention. The best state is minimalist, and the best policies are those that let the market work at maximum efficiency. (Keynesianists see an active state as necessary to economic health. I return to this later.) The problem is that endowments can be created. Japan and South Korea have limited natural resources, yet they became economic powerhouses. They did not rely on natural evolution in a market – their states actively created the foundation for international competitiveness through policies that economists still find abnormal (cf. Porter 1990).

Countries not only show variation in policies – that variation *continues over time*. Regression to a norm occurs only through real force and pressure, for example, when international organizations such as the IMF and World Bank force developing countries to adopt certain policies in return for financial support. These persistent differences scream out for attention, but first we must examine the state and how it acts in the economy.

States and economies

Public policy is a matter of states; we must briefly examine the link between states, social actors, and economy. *Institutions* are important to state behavior. Electoral rules, provision of resources, and state structure shape state power and independence to act. The more open the state is to society, the more groups can "capture" it. The American government is run by elected officials and their appointees are indebted to business elites. French officials work their way up the bureaucratic ladder and are less indebted to outsiders. They feel less pressure and have some insulation from society. In Japan, officials work their way up the ladder and retire early, leaving the state for private corporations. This creates working links between former officials and colleagues still in government, and allows feedback between business and government – but officials do not owe favors to business (Colignon and Usui 2003).

Culture shapes public policy by defining the state's legitimate, natural role in the economy. Americans historically want some state *protection* but not state *control*. The French, and to a lesser extent the British (more recently), see state control as sometimes more natural than private ownership.[1] Powerful arguments use culture to explain policy differences across countries. *Classes* cannot be ignored, as the structural locations of owners, managers, and different employees shape interests and policies they demand. Classes in this context are not unitary. For example, industrialists are more likely to favor tariffs to protect industries, while raw materials producers will be against tariffs that might provoke other countries who buy their output to enact their own protective measures.[2] But class location shapes *general* interests and does not explain policy preference alone. *Organizations* – corporations, political parties, organizations of interests (e.g. business lobbies, labor unions) – collect and coordinate resources (money, manpower), contribute to political parties, bring people into the streets to protest (something French farmers are adept at), and so on.

Different theories call on these variables in different ways. Marxist approaches privilege class. Weberian approaches refer to organizations and how institutions provide opportunities to influence states. Neo-Durkheimian approaches focus on culture and institutions. Our job is to understand how these variables affect states and policies, what insights these explanations provide, and which explanations work best.

The state's ability to act in the economy

States are powerful organizations, in no small part because, as the givers and defenders of law, states control the use of violence. Yet state leaders, whether kings or presidents, cannot do as they please in the economy. Instead, there are social forces that constrain states, and sometimes even influence state actions. The state's natural degree of autonomy has been hotly disputed. Marxists see states constrained by capital and forced to serve the interests of capitalism. Weberians have been kinder to states. While states are concerned with economic health and development (states need money, from taxes or borrowing, to pay for police and soldiers), state elites also have power over life and death because states control violence. Weberians ask what determines the amount of power a state has and why state leaders make the decisions they make. Generally, sociologists and political scientists have focused on how *structures* and *institutions* determine state freedom and what states can, and must, do. The degree to which state elites (not just presidents and prime ministers, but also junior ministers and senior civil servants) owe their jobs to outsiders financing elections reduces state autonomy from society and the capacity to act independently.

Pluralism

In pluralism, the state is an arena, rather than an organization in its own right. In this arena representatives of different social groups congregate and articulate the different visions, needs, and demands from society (Alford and Friedland 1985). Decision-making operates through debates and negotiations between representatives in the legislative and executive branches – for example, senators and congressmen negotiating with each other and the president, Members of Parliament negotiating with each other or with opposition parties, lobby groups persuading legislators on behalf of their interest groups (e.g. businesses), and so on. Those groups that can garner the most votes have the strongest impact on policy-making. Such influence can come from having money – as is the case for corporate lobbies that contribute heavily to political parties. It can also come from mobilizing a large number of voters who may punish representatives for not voting their way – as is the case with unions. Policies adopted thus reflect the balance of mobilized people and money in politics.

Instrumentalist Marxism

Following the logic of Marx and Engels' "Manifesto of the Communist Party," instrumental Marxists see the state as the "executive committee" of the bourgeoisie.[3] The ruling class exerts strong *direct* influence on the state, either through economic clout (campaign contributions to parties and politicians) or through networks between the ruling class and state elites (Miliband 1969). Heads of parties and governments are likely to come from the ruling class and will have their class's interests at heart when making policy. This approach may seem a little simplistic, but it does ring true in some historical moments. Domhoff (1998: chs 4, 7) claims elite participation shaped American welfare policies under Roosevelt. C. Wright Mills (1959) conjured up the evil spirit of a "power elite" – heads of politics, the economy, and the military – sometimes allied and sometimes competing but always coordinating political decision-making. The presidency of George W. Bush gives at least superficial support to instrumentalist Marxism. The strong ties between Bush and members of the business elite, through his vice-president Dick Cheney, proved profitable to certain corporations, whether in energy policy (drilling in Alaska, dealing in electricity in California) or in rebuilding post-war Iraq (Haliburton).

Structuralist Marxism

A more nuanced Marxist approach does not see states as directly controlled by *individual* members of the ruling class. Instead, state leaders think independently, but they realize that the survival of the state (and their own elite positions) depends on healthy capitalism and a capitalist class willing to invest and produce. Healthy economies provide jobs for the population and keep people happy and calm, and healthy economies provide tax revenue that states can use to purchase weapons and survive in geopolitical competition (e.g. wars). Thus state leaders will cater to the needs of capitalism and the ruling class to keep the economy running. Interestingly, this suggests that states can act *against* interests of *capitalists* if this is necessary *to save capitalism itself* (Poulantzas 1978). Capitalists' interests may be short term and harmful to long-term capitalist survival, and so the state must take action that saves capitalism, even if this runs against the interests of capitalists. Take one Marxist explanation for the rise of the welfare state. Capitalists – individuals owning industrial property – should not like welfare because it requires high taxes to pay for welfare policies and empowers employees (e.g. allowing unions, providing for an eight-hour work day and safety regulations). In fact, capitalists usually fight welfare laws. If capitalists so dislike welfare, how did welfare policies ever get through governments and become policies? The answer: without welfare, employees would suffer during economic downturns and become radicalized, perhaps radicalized enough to organize and demand the replacement of capitalism with communism. Capitalists are too short-sighted to see the dilemma, but state leaders are not so short-sighted. They can enact welfare legislation to keep employees happy. Capitalists may not make as much profit, but workers are happier and capitalism survives.

Weberian approaches: opportunity and "state capacity"

Marxist approaches were popular in the 1970s but came under attack when it became clear that "ruling classes do not rule" and that state leaders do not think only about capitalism when formulating policies (Block 1977b). Studies of welfare states discovered that welfare was *different* in different countries *that had similar capitalist economies*. If European and North American countries all had capitalism, why did they have *different* forms of welfare, and why did their welfare states emerge at *different* times (Skocpol 1980; Weir and Stocpol 1985)? Instrumental Marxism could not explain why welfare should even exist – since welfare hurts capitalists' profits and power. Except for a minority, what elite would willingly allow redistribution of wealth through higher taxes on corporations and high income? Structuralist Marxism did offer an explanation for welfare: state leaders were saving capitalism from economic crisis and the ruling class's lack of long-term vision. Yet *variation* and *timing* – different welfare policies at different times – continued to evade Marxists.

The new paradigm emerging in the 1980s focused less on capitalists and more on states. Taking a page from Weberian thought, the new approach to state policy assumed that the state could have autonomy, but that autonomy varied over time, depending on historical circumstances (e.g. when corporations or elites had power or when they were weak). Further, the new approach focused less on classes and more on corporations and organizations – elites and classes really had no power outside of their organizational bases, and so it made sense to focus on what organizations existed, what resources they had, what alliances their leaders made, and where their interests lay. The key variables were state structure and the different linkages between states and organized groups, from labor unions and farmers to different factions within the capitalist class (e.g. agricultural elites, different industrialists). The result was a framework that could be applied to welfare (Skocpol 1992), economic development outside the West (Haggard 1990), economic reforms in Western capitalism (Zysman 1983; Hall 1986) – some of which we discussed in Chapter 3.

At present, the Weberian view is dominant. The inability of pluralism to adequately address power, and the inability of Marxist perspectives to provide explanations about state behavior and variation, have left the Weberian approach as the strongest understanding of how states and public policy operate. States are organizations with limited resources that must negotiate with social actors, whether corporations or trade unions. But states do not base their authority on force alone: they also wield legitimate authority and symbolic power (Bourdieu 1996), i.e. the authority to define legitimate actors in the polity. Equally, states are constrained not only by resources and structure but also by "political culture," conceptions of normal politics. In short: states can act autonomously, but their power is variable. State leaders must negotiate with or around other elites and account for legitimacy in their social context. We can be fairly confident that states are not simply reflections of class interests and power (the Marxist view) or of coalitions of voters or of some general, negotiated "majority view" (pluralism). When states set policies they are constrained by their structures, as we have just seen, and they are also constrained by culture: by the political culture of the society in which they are embedded, and in legacies of past policies.

Policy regimes: a cross-national comparison

States are partly constrained by what they have done: this is "path dependency." Past policies create a pool of knowledge and relations among state and societal actors – we know best what we have done. Further, if past policies achieved success, they become seen as accurate representations of reality, much as discoveries in physics and chemistry that lead to new insights are believed to capture aspects of physical reality (Dobbin 1994). These policies are embedded in rituals, structures, and other manifestations in the state: contained in bureaucratic procedures or in the experiences, knowledge, and beliefs of state officials who will hesitate to adopt radically different policy styles because they would seem unnatural, illegitimate, and unknown. Thus we can say that states have styles of policies or "policy paradigms" (Hall 1992): a particular set and type of public policies and a logic underlying them as a whole. These paradigms develop over time, but not smoothly, and they persist until a major shock forces elites to call policy logic into question. This is a *branching point*: like the growth of a tree or bush, there is a moment when policy styles can suddenly change and grow in a new direction. However, branching points are limited, and policy regimes do not change in any old direction. Instead, they are constrained by *political culture*: a set of fundamental principles about "normal" and legitimate political institutions and practices. What is important is where a political culture locates *sovereignty*, the ultimate source of political authority. Sovereignty is sacred, and state leaders trample on sovereignty only at their peril.

Within their own histories different countries have developed their own political cultures. This is strongest among developed countries. (Dependent countries may find that their political culture is trumped by the demands of the IMF or the United States.) In this section I turn to several countries' policy paradigms (Table 4.1). I begin with the American model, whose logic followed American political hegemony to dominate the logics of such economic bodies as the International Monetary Fund, World Bank, and World Trade Organization. A crucial point is that all of these policy styles coincided with economic growth. We cannot say for certain that one model is the best. If the American model best promotes entrepreneurship, the Japanese and German models certainly led to growth. In the 1960s scholars thought French policies were the wave of the future; in the 1930s the American model was far from optimal.[4]

The American model

The American model of public policy is best described as minimal state interference in the economy, and then only to defend fair pricing and competition (Dobbin 1994). The American policy regime as it has been for over a hundred years was different not long after the birth of the nation. In the first fifty or so years after independence, the federal government was rather weak and not particularly involved in the

Table 4.1 States and policy models

Model	Sovereignty	Basic nature of policy regime
American	Communities	Enforce price competition, prevent monopolies
British	Elite individuals	Protect entrepreneurs but let the economy run itself (pre-1945); provide for social justice and redistribution of wealth by state technocrats (post-1945)
French	Nation	Direct investment and development; direct and harness the market for general social development
German	Corporate entities (state, business, unions)	Protect capital and labor, promote long-term technological development for national good
East Asian	Political elite/state	"Economic nationalism" and a (relatively) strong state role in directing the economy

Note: cf. Dobbin (1994); Piore and Sabel (1984)

economy. But *local* states, such as New York or Pennsylvania, were more active. Originally, states aided in the financing, ownership, and control of canals (Roy 1997). Governors and legislators argued that local states should set up canal companies, help finance and run them, and support them when necessary. Canals would improve transport and economic infrastructure, aiding the economy. In the first half of the nineteenth century, local states continued their activism and got involved in railroads. The costs of constructing and maintaining rail lines, trains and wagons, and stations made railroads an expensive venture. Some states (New Jersey, Ohio, Pennsylvania) got involved in setting up railroad corporations. They provided capital and attracted private financing by promising that investors would be liable only for what they invested (limited liability). Corporations were born as legal entities at this time, only they were *semi-public*. Local states such as Pennsylvania and Ohio were investors and owners alongside private individuals. Like individuals, states took on debt to build railroads. Boundaries between "private" and "public" were blurred (Roy 1997) in a way that would seem abnormal today. Ironically, the modern corporation was created by American states – by the mid-nineteenth century it would be anathema to think that a state *should* be a corporate owner.

Branching points soon led to changes in the American policy regime. American political culture locates sovereignty in the *community*,[5] and economic policies and organizations must not harm them. Initially, states were heavily involved in railroad corporations to help communities develop. First, state investment would spur railroad construction faster than the market could, and railroad transportation would help local economies. Second, by actively participating in corporations (as part owners), states (led by elected politicians) could guard the public interest against private greed by controlling corporate policies directly. However, a counter-argument emerged: state involvement in the economy would create serious problems. State officials would be *corrupted* – they would put their own interests ahead of the public, and the temptation for politicians to take kick-backs would be too great (Dobbin 1994: ch. 2). Further, state officials would not be competent at running businesses, and this would hurt growth. This counter-argument became more convincing after problems and scandals with railroad investments. Railroads were not always profitable in the 1830s. In the 1837 recession, local states were close to bankruptcy because of these investments and had to raise taxes (Roy 1997: ch. 3). This provoked the anger of the voting public, and some states, such as Ohio, drew up new laws forbidding state involvement in the economy. In Pennsylvania, participation in the building and running of railroads led to instances of corrupt state officials. The response was to set up laws forbidding state participation in the economy.

This story may have ended here and been different from the situation today – we might still have had large organizations but not with the same structure or functions. However, New Jersey law permitted monopolies and oligopolies, granting charters to one or a few groups to finance and run canals and railroads using private investment. This led to a backlash from anti-corporate groups – but these groups *lost* the political battle in the New Jersey legislature. This provided the foundation for the rise of the American corporation, an event I return to in Chapter 5. This new organizational form commanded enormous amounts of capital, and by the end of the nineteenth century corporations were powerful entities. Owners and managers bribed or influenced governments for favorable laws, and they were buying up competitors or merging with them to reduce competition. Regardless of why they did this, monopolies and oligopolies raised the specter of corporations using market power to dictate to consumers and communities. This perceived threat to democracy fueled the Progressive Movement, which demanded limits to corporate power. Its crowning achievement was the Sherman Anti-trust Act, which forbade cartels and monopolies.[6]

Overall, by the twentieth century the American policy regime had come into being – it was taken for granted as the natural social order, institutionalized through laws, procedures, and assumptions about why those laws and procedures exist. Monopolies and market control were anathema. Free markets, trade, and competition were considered to be the natural form of the market; anything else was a deviation that threatened both economic growth and democratic and community politics. The American state would not interfere in markets as European or Asian states would, for example, directly commanding investment or owning firms. The American state would step into the market to maintain market competition. In the global market, the American government has been at the forefront of pushing open markets, although at times it has also reverted to protectionism (for example, under George W. Bush). Even American welfare was not as intrusive as in Europe: unlike its European counterparts, the American state did not provide cheap medicine or education, but gave monetary aid to those who needed it (e.g. scholarships or Medicare/Medicaid to the poor or elderly). At its most intrusive, the American state regulated the economy, such as controlling the flow of money on Wall Street, or limiting the number of airline flights or radio and television stations. In the 1970s, American voters tired of social instability (e.g. crime, protests, and contention over Vietnam) and economic stagnation, and voted Ronald Reagan into the presidency. Reagan dismantled some state regulation of the economy, freeing up the flow of capital investment and airlines, for example. He also increased military spending, which expanded the budget deficit. Overall, however, Reagan maintained the American policy regime of a minimalist state protecting market competition – a model that those after him would maintain as well and promote to the rest of the world.

The British model

The British model shares traits with its American cousin but also has differences, especially since the end of World War II. In the British political culture that emerged after that country's civil war, individuals were assumed to be rational beings with innate political rights (Greenfeld 1992: ch. 1). States could not trample on these rights. In particular, the *elite* were the most important and protected Englishmen. Not only were they the most rational because they were the most educated, industrious, and enlightened; but also, because they owned land or other means of production (early small factories), they had an investment or stake in the country's well-being. Where American policy located the engine of economic growth in collective entities such as corporations, British policy located the engine of growth in industrious, rational, elite individuals: *entrepreneurs* (Dobbin 1994: ch. 4). The role of the state was to protect entrepreneurs by allowing them to organize – cartels were legal in Great Britain – and by sheltering them from hostile forces. One way to foster protection was through trade regulations that sheltered the Empire from external competition and gave advantages to homeland producers and entrepreneurs. Generally, this protected the traditional family-owned firm – unlike in the United States, British firms were primarily family owned (Chandler 1990), and the British policy regime protected the rational (elite) entrepreneurs that made these engines of industry the driving force behind British capitalist power.

The British model of public policy and the state changed after World War II. The state took over the rational elite that had been the fulcrum of political culture and policy: the state elite, not the aristocracy, knew best, echoing the state-centered political logic of the Continent and Enlightenment and redressing centuries of class inequality and promoting overall social justice. The Labour government nationalized nearly one-fifth of the economy (including key sectors such as railroads and roads, aviation, coal, iron, and steel) and created the National Health Service. In the wake of wartime devastation (not so long after the trauma of World War I), only the state could invest and coordinate the enormous amounts of capital and other resources (including manpower) necessary to rebuild Britain. Structurally, the state could enter and shape the economy as it could not have done earlier. As well, the Labour Party's ideology of state provision and coordination (resonating with class tension in British society)[7] was sufficiently popular to broader (non-elite) masses that the Labour government could push through its program. Until World War I, suffrage (the right to vote) was restricted along class lines: the working class and the lower classes generally could not vote. (Only those with a stake in Britain – i.e. an investment – would have national interests at heart, or so the argument went.) Lower classes were already mobilizing around issues of class interest and social justice. In Britain, parties historically have had a strong ideological identity. Unlike in the United States, where parties based their legitimacy on delivering public goods to neighborhoods, British parties grounded their legitimacy in class-based ideology (Katznelson 1985). The Labour Party was dedicated to social justice and empowerment of the working and lower classes, and one particular policy was state control of industry in order to protect employees and guarantee social justice. Thus, the combination of victory and sacrifice in two world wars, the need to repair the country, and the legitimacy of social justice issues led post-war governments until the 1980s to champion state-led control of the economy and welfare as a reward to its citizens for their sacrifices in two world wars and as a symbol of an enlightened state and society. This was not a total shift away from the former policy regime; the state did not interfere directly in all aspects of the economy, or play the role of auditor rather than commander. However, for ideological and geopolitical reasons, the state no longer trusted entrepreneurs to generate wealth or social well-being. Overall, post-war structure and party ideologies shifted British pubic policy towards a stronger state role in the economy.

This state-centered welfare model persisted while Britain's position in the world economy declined, leading to another shift in policy logic under Margaret Thatcher and the Conservative Party after 1979 – a combination of pro-market ideology with a strong state presence. Britain's central position in the world economy began to unravel after 1945. American aid was premised on Britain opening up the Commonwealth to American trade (Block 1977a), and British firms could not hide behind the trade barriers of the Commonwealth. Until the 1970s the United Kingdom could work on capital amassed over centuries of economic domination of the globe; but the price of rebuilding and of welfare, coupled with increased competition from the Untied States and Europe, as well as from rising stars in East Asia, made this model untenable. After decades of empire, such decline was painful. Welfare, state ownership of industrial sectors (railroads, telecommunications, oil), and labor policies created high taxes and red tape. By the 1970s Britain was a shadow of its former self, and the sudden rise in oil prices and competition from East Asia hurt the profitability of British industry. The burden of a strong state became too great. Further, the 1970s was a decade of conflict, culminating in the "winter of discontent" (1978 to 1979), when various unions (fire unions, garbage collectors) went on strike.

Thatcher claimed that she wanted to unleash entrepreneurship and private initiative to save the British economy. She did legislate some liberalization – for example, freer movement of capital and investment – returning to the classic British policy of oversight at arm's length. However, at the same time she created a new policy regime of strengthening state control, particularly in organizations of the welfare state. Rather than rely on competition to force doctors or universities to become more efficient and deliver better services, Thatcher and leaders after her *increased* state control – depriving professionals such as doctors and university professors of much autonomy and forcing them to follow state plans and goals supposedly in line with market logic (Gray 1998).[8] Bureaucracy expanded in the National Health Service and the educational system, and formal powers were transferred from doctors and professors to bureaucrats and committees. New systems of evaluating performance were created, using quantitative measures – e.g. the Quality Assurance Assessment (QAA) test of pedagogical effectiveness (which academics protested was an enormous paperwork burden that measured little) and the Research Assessment Exercise (RAE) to review faculty publications and rate departments and universities.

Tony Blair, Gordon Brown, and the Labour Party came to power in 1997 but did not reverse Thatcher's policy logic. While Labour increased investment in public services, especially in the National Health Service, state control of public services also increased. Privatization had a bad image – partly due to the fiasco of railroad privatization – yet nationalization was not back on the agenda. The Bank of England (the UK's central bank) was given autonomy to set interest rates, continuing the market-oriented policies of the Thatcher era. Competition was encouraged, although under the watchful eye of a regulatory state – a state not regulating economic activity *per se*, but rather the *implementation* of that activity (e.g. requiring a battery of tests for putting new goods on the market, or continuing to guard labor rights). Finally, the state did not provide the same protection of home-grown entrepreneurs that it had provided decades earlier – partly because of the pro-market ideological shift, partly because of Britain's links to the European Union (with its demands for freer trade).

The French model

In France, the state is the primary player in the economy, often directing corporate policies (cf. Dobbin (1994) on railroad policy) or owning and controlling firms (Zysman 1983). Until recently the French model involved the creation of "champions," enormous private or state-owned firms that had a near-monopoly position inside France's domestic market – protecting them from domestic competition – so that they could compete effectively on the *world* market. The French state's involvement in the economy was far greater than in the United States or Britain. In the French perspective it is illogical to let self-centered, profit-seeking entrepreneurs run the economy when it is clear that the state has society's best interests at heart. The ideology of the United State's and Great Britain posits that entrepreneurs help society when they work for themselves.

In the French logic the state is the ultimate guardian of social interests and represents a collective identity of "nation" (Greenfeld 1992: ch. 2).[9] Entrepreneurs have only their own interests at heart and cannot be trusted to provide maximum gain to society as a whole. In France, political ideology rejects this. The French state has consistently defended its strong role in the economy by reference to its mission of guarding the general public – something that the American states does, so it claims, by *staying out* of the economy except to enforce anti-monopoly laws and fair pricing policies (Dobbin 1994: ch. 3). Only those who are called to work for the state and trained appropriately can be trusted to make the best decisions for the country's economy and overall well-being. Hence industrial development follows general state plans. This does not mean that France does not have a capitalist economy. The state may own or heavily regulate firms, but private enterprise is indeed encouraged – it is simply not given the same freedom as in the UK or US. In return for this loss of freedom, French firms often receive subsidies or other support from the state to help them remain competitive in the face of external competition. But the state-centered model has proved sturdy, and efforts to lessen state participation in the economy have never dislodged the state from its central role. Even attempts to privatize the French economy and sell off state-run firms and services ran into implementation problems (Hall 1986).

This paradigm emerged from France's political history. Put briefly, France's history is the history of empire, war, and political conflict, and to survive, the French state had to centralize and strengthen its control over the population – not only politically but also economically. Out of the need for a strong state in order to survive geopolitical competition, bureaucrats – first to the French kings and later to elected leaders – put interests of "state" as most important, because the state was the ultimate expression and defender of society. As the state developed, a collective identity linked initially to the Catholic Church developed as well. Catholicism's strong sense of collective identity dovetailed with France's emerging national identity: as the wit of the day put it, the French were the defenders of the true faith, and the French king was more Catholic than the Pope. The king identified himself and his ruling family with the collective "nation," but over time the state – an organization that outlives individual human beings – came to replace the king as the representative and center of the nation (Greenfeld 1992). Over the centuries leading up to the modern age, these tendencies had two effects. The first was the creation of groups interested in a strong state – state officials and bureaucrats, members of the court, political parties, an elitist educational system – and auxiliary social groups dependent on the state (e.g. the nobility or workers). Groups such as peasants, artisans, workers, and capitalist owners calculated their own strategies based on a strong state: workers went on strike against perceived capitalist injustices, but in France's polity aimed their demands at that strong state (Tilly 1986). Education of technocrats and elites assumed a strong state, and training (e.g. in economics) assumed a strong state in policy models. Thus, in collective political practices, the French grounded strategies of economic growth and organization and political contention in a strong state, encouraging it to remain strong to address investment, workers' rights, and so on. The second effect was that France's state-centered policies coexisted with economic growth that made France a world power – much as happened in Great Britain and the United States. French leaders and the public assumed that their policies held the key to truth.

Thus the state participated actively in the economy, not only to encourage economic development but also to *direct* that development in routes dictated by state needs. This included such important economic projects as the construction of canals and railroads in the eighteenth and nineteenth centuries, and the development of nuclear power and the automobile industry in the twentieth century. Hence France's policy regime favors state power and participation, in contrast to the state's arm's-length, referee role in the United States and ambiguous position in Great Britain. Such a strong state role might seem abnormal to the Anglo-American world, but France's track record suggests this perception is flawed. After World War II the French economy was heralded as a "miracle," and some scholars believed that the French model of state-centered investment and planning was the inevitable future (Shonfield 1965). After the shocks of increased oil prices in the 1970s, French firms restructured and the French economy recovered from inflation faster than the United States or Great Britain (Zysman 1983). (The same was true for Japan's state-centered economy.) French health care and railroads remain among the best in Europe. France's problems – including a budget deficit that contradicted the demands of integration into the euro zone – are not necessarily an outgrowth of a central state role (such problems occur elsewhere). However, French employment rules are among the more stringent in the developed world, leading to labor market inflexibility. As a result, youth unemployment in 2006 was around 23 percent, and up to 400,000 French expatriots (mostly young) had moved to Great Britain for work more easily obtainable in the UK's more flexible labor market (*Guardian*, April 8, 2006: 21).

The German model

In German public policy, the state plays a strong role of economic coordinator (stronger in the Nazi era). Historically the German state shaped social and economic institutions partly because it was a "latecomer" to industrialization, and partly due to the nature of state–society relations. Unlike in Britain, the emergent bourgeoisie was weaker and more willing to give the state a wide berth in politics, while pursuing economic and cultural ends (Blackbourn 1984). At the same time, "Germany" emerged from Prussia, in which the state and rural elite (the Junkers) were closely linked through state service. As a result, the German state and elite were closely linked through networks and through relations of dependency, made stronger by the "marriage of iron and rye" in which Otto von Bismarck provided state protection and investment to industrial and agricultural elites. (In a sense, Germany combined British social elitism and French *dirigisme*.) Pro-working-class social democracy was well developed in Germany. Bismarck launched one of Europe's first welfare states to make blue-collar workers loyal to and dependent on the state, and Social Democrats were a beacon for workers' parties. Overall, state sponsorship of elites and workers created a "corporatist" structure: strong state–society relations, with the state taking a leading role *vis-à-vis* even private organizations.[10] After World War II the German state retreated, but the corporatist legacy remained; her policy paradigm is oriented to facilitating growth, competition, and cooperation through these organizations.

Following this, two organizations in particular had strong roles, with the state's blessing: *banks* and *trade unions* (Piore and Sabel 1984). Banks historically have played a larger role in financing firms and taking part in their decision-making – very different to the United States and Great Britain, where banks generally provide short-term loans and do not participate in corporate decisions. This reflects the *timing* of German industrialization. Capitalism and industry in Great Britain, France, and the United States developed earlier (the eighteenth century), and these countries had time to accumulate capital, technology, knowledge, and organization. As a latecomer, Germany did not have this luxury: it had to industrialize quickly to survive geopolitical competition. The state and banks had to take the role of the weak bourgeoisie to build industry (Gerschenkron 1962). Because banks invested large sums over the long term, bankers had an interest in seeing how loans were used (so that firms would repay them). Lending banks took positions on firms' boards of directors. This created networks that made it possible for German firms to react together, quickly, in the face of economic shocks (Zysman 1983).

German unions also play a crucial role in economic organization. Part of state-led welfare and corporatism involved legalizing unions and working-class political parties. While unions and parliamentary parties did not have ultimate decision-making power, they were still respected on the shop-floor once legalized. German industrialization before World War I was oriented partly towards military production, and so German industry oriented to specialized industrial output – requiring skilled labor capable of adapting to producing new types of goods. While German industry moved away from military production after 1945, the legacy of organized, skilled labor remained. Coupled with the importance of banks, the German economy stressed long-term (bank) investment in specialized production. State policy no longer protected industry and agriculture as it had before 1945; but it did protect the ability of banks to engage in long-term relations with business, and it has encouraged the maintenance of a skilled labor force (unlike Western trends towards deskilling of labor to drive down wages). Following the long power of unions and social democratic politics, German policies encourage employees' rights, including welfare support and labor laws (e.g. about working days). Because German policies coincided with economic growth after World War II and especially in the 1970s and 1980s,[11] those policies came to be seen as the correct path to success and provided a German policy regime – one that, in spite of its success, has not received the same attention for emulation as its partner in post-war success, Japan.

East Asian models

East Asia emerged from the 1970s as dynamic economies due to strong states, policies, and embedded autonomy. Yet there is no single East Asian model; state–society relations and policies *differed* in the region, and policies show as much variation as similarity (cf. Hamilton and Biggart 1988). I will focus on South Korea, Japan, and Taiwan, although there are second generation dragons (e.g. Malaysia, Indonesia, Vietnam), and of course China.

The paradigm case for East Asia is Japan. Japan's economic structure is similar to Korea's, except the state is not as strong. The Japanese business groups, the *zaibatsu* (renamed *keiretsu* after World War II), were formed after the Meiji Restoration in the 1870s, when a new elite took power to direct Japanese economic and military development to ward off the threat of Western imperialism in the nineteenth century. This elite encouraged industrialization, giving birth to the *zaibatsu*, industrial empires centered on financial institutions or trading houses. Following World War II, the *zaibatsu* were not dismantled as originally intended but were left in place to help Japanese post-war economic development – and to avoid the emergence of communism. Relations between business and state are close in Japan, coordinated formally through the Ministry of International Trade and Industry (MITI) and informally through close personal networks between the state and business. Formally, the MITI coordinates economic policy and aids the *keiretsu* in development strategies. However, the MITI does not have the same power as Korean ministries. Rather, it helps provide protection from foreign competition and the development of plans and resources for meeting those plans (Johnson 1982). This helps Japanese firms compete in the world market and cooperate at home, both with each other and with smaller firms that provide necessary supplies and inputs. Informally, state officials retire early and then move into non-profit organizations or businesses, to work as consultants by using their networks to the state (where they once worked). This is *amakudari*, "descent from heaven" or from the state into the private sector. This has created a close network between state and society that allows for communication and the development and implementation of economic plans (Colignon and Usai 2003). All this has helped Japan to develop into the second-best economy in the world. The policy regime that emerged was one where the state plays a strong supporting role in the economy, but does not direct it (as in Korea).[12] On the other hand, state support is greater than in Western economies, and only France comes close to Japan's close links between state and business. Japan's economic success not only convinced Japanese policy-makers and business elite that their policy model was the correct, natural approach to economic growth; it also convinced other countries in the region to emulate Japan's policy paradigm (a strong state and economic nationalism) (Fajnzylber 1990).[13] As in the United States or Great Britain, Japanese policy-makers and elites *reified* their policy model as true economic laws.[14]

The South Korean state directs investment and has a strong say in policies pursued by the *chaebol*, large corporate empires that collect firms in various fields. This followed the post-World War II political landscape in South Korea. Following Japanese colonization, World War II, and the Korean War, South Korea was laid waste, and only the state remained strong enough to maintain social stability. Agricultural elites were weakened by the Japanese occupation, and Korea had yet to industrialize and develop a true capitalist elite. The Korean state – a dictatorship for much of its post-war history – encouraged the growth of industry, but state–society relations were corrupt. The South Korean state was potentially the most powerful force in society, but it took a strong-willed leader to make use of that power, to force the *chaebol* to focus on general economic growth. (As we saw in Chapter 3, American funds and General Park Chung Hee's regime also encouraged growth.) This propelled South Korea into the ranks of the developed world. Only corruption and the 1998 crisis in Asian currencies spoiled Korea's run of economic fortune. This history bred a policy regime and state structure in which the state directs economic growth, interacting with business groups like the *chaebol* to determine the optimum path for the best economic development and then providing financing and direction to help the *chaebol* fulfill state economic plans (Evans 1995).

Relative to these two, Taiwan's state is more hands-off (although not as hands-off as the American state). While the Taiwanese state has owned a few important firms – in areas such as steel and petrochemicals – it mostly encourages the growth and development of numerous small firms, for example, promoting exports through tax credits. This stems from the post-1949 politics of the Taiwanese state and the KMT, the ruling party that fled mainland China after losing the revolution and civil war to Mao's communist army (Hamilton and Biggart 1988). The local population was wary of their new KMT rulers – Chiang Kai-shek's KMT was noted for corruption during its rule on the mainland before World War II – and to gain popular acceptance, Chiang ruled with a light fist. Taiwan remained a non-democratic, single-party state, but that state acted benignly, aiding social development rather than controlling it directly. This legitimation enabled the ruling party to remain in power, but it also set the policy logic: a state leading by example rather than by control, encouraging economic development but not directing it – what Robert Wade (1990) has called a "governed market."

According to Gary Hamilton and Nicole Biggart (1988), East Asian policy models emerged initially from states' needs to legitimate their authority, rather than from any concern for efficiency. Following the Korea War, the South Korean state needed to legitimate its strong, centralized control over society not only to rebuild South Korea, but also to keep its citizenry constantly prepared for military action – the defense of the homeland from a possible sudden invasion by North Korea (as happened in 1950). The South Korean leadership used Confucian meanings and rituals that stressed paternalist authority and collective discipline: the state, like a father, was head of the "social household" and deserved respect and authority. In return, the state (like the father) was to ensure provision and direction. This justified a strong state, and this strong centralized power spread to the *chaebol*, also highly centralized around banks or financial institutions and family run. After World War II, the Japanese state tried to rebuild while avoiding the dictatorial militarism of Japanese imperialism since the 1870s. After 1945 the American administration in Japan allowed the emperor to remain the overall Japanese leader, but the emperor was more a *symbolic* figure: real power was concentrated in the bureaucracy. But this symbolic image provided legitimation for the state and a model of authority for firms and policy: the state would be a central, important figure, but it would lead through consultation with the elite, rather than dictating and organizing them (as in South Korea). In Taiwan, the KMT, insecure in its legitimacy, drew on Confucianism, but rather than utilize the strong paternalist image used in South Korea, the KMT used the image of the benign father who sets an example through provision and good behavior. This legitimated the regime and the role of the state – provider at arm's length, allowing autonomy for society. Further, Taiwan shared the culture of mainland China, including the importance of family relations – and so Taiwan shared China's historical proclivity for small firms united through family bonds. This overlapped with a paternal but benign state whose policies encouraged but did not directly control economic activity.

Policies: change and continuity

These accounts of policy regimes show that states' policies differ, and that differences persist over time. Different policies have been successful at different times. This might suggest that once it emerges, a policy regime is imprinted on a national economy and does not change easily. As Dobbin (1993, 1994) points out, this is often the case: experiments in the 1930s with different policy regimes were short-lived in the United States and Great Britain, and the French policy paradigm has been fairly consistent since before the French Revolution (1789). Part of the reason, Dobbin argues, is that if policies create growth, state elites, professionals (economists or technocrats), and others who contribute to national discourse credit the policy logic with success. They then develop theories of economic success based on the experience of their policies. The American economy grew with little state interference (except for trade tariffs) – and so American economists, business leaders, and state officials theorized that growth was linked to a minimal state. The French economy grew with vigorous state involvement – and so French intellectual and state elites theorized that an active state is key to growth. When French or American leaders face new problems (economic decline or uncertainty, for example), they turn to policies and informal rules of thumb that they know – and these are the historical lessons from their own policies.

In sociological terms the logics of French, British, American, or other policies are *institutionalized* in discourse, knowledge, and general understandings about the objective laws of the social universe. The logic of policies becomes academic models (such as neoliberalism) that are taught to students and professionals, who carry that conception of "normal" economy and policy back into the public sphere and the state. At the same time, policies shape states. As states face new issues or problems, they expand on existing policies because states can only expand on the organizational structure that they have. The American state would have a difficult time following a French policy model because the American state is not as centralized as the French state. To implement a French state-centered economy, the American state would have to increase its own size and power *vis-à-vis* society. However, this would threaten entrenched interests: for example, of corporate elites who would lose power and income (to taxes to pay for the enlarged state), to local communities and citizens who would fear greater state power. Alternatively, French citizens have been reluctant to allow their state to leave the economy: French citizens want a state that answers to them. French business is private and answers only to shareholders, but the French state (a democracy) answers to its citizens. Citizens have more power over the economy – and thus over their own jobs and well-being – if their state retains economic power.

But change can occur as well, and this usually requires a shock that has two effects: it jolts the system and suggests that policy itself created serious problems, and it weakens elites who would otherwise fight to defend their own interests. As we saw, World War II weakened elites in Great Britain, allowing the state to expand into the market, but a more striking example is Russia. There have been some continuities to economic policy in Russia – namely a strong state. However, Imperial Russia did recognize private property (although it was weaker than in the West). The Soviet regime did not recognize private property or autonomous exchange: the communist economy was totally coordinated by the state and the Communist Party. This was a different type of policy from that in Imperial Russia. What made the change possible was that World War I led to the Russian Revolution and the collapse of the imperial Russian state and political system. The Soviet communist economy survived until the late 1980s. Economic weaknesses and the need to face Stalinist crimes prompted Mikhail Gorbachev to introduce political and economic reforms (*glasnost'* and *perestroika*), but these led to ethnic unrest and rebellion that brought down the USSR in 1991. From the rubble of the Soviet Union, "Russia" emerged with new leaders dedicated to eradicating communism and introducing capitalism – and so private property and autonomous exchange were introduced once again. When these policies created a corrupt super-elite ("oligarchs") and when the state defaulted on its debt in 1998, state policies shifted once again when Vladimir Putin became president in 2000. He strengthened the state, reigning in oligarchs and local political elites. The lesson: change is possible but it is not easy.

One important question is whether the European Union can overcome different policy paradigms and encourage an integrated European policy logic. At present, the EU has not been able to do so; EU rules and monetary union (the euro) constrain states, but only in a limited way. There are limits on budget deficits, although in 2003 France and Germany broke this rule. One problem is that the EU does not have real power. "Europe" is not a single state with its own police and army (the ability to enforce rules) but a confederation of sovereign states. The proposed

European constitution may give some power to the EU – in particular, regulation of labor and trade, as well as European Central Bank interest rates – but at present it appears that sovereign states will retain much of their authority. The EU's real power is the hope that when one country violates the rules, other countries will sanction it. If this remains so, the EU will have limited power to impose a single, unified policy regime across Europe.

Global policy paradigms: Keynesianism, monetarism, and welfare

So far we have looked at policies in *national societies* and domestic forces shaping them: state structures, state–society relations, and political culture. Different countries can also share aspects of logics of public policy. This may be either because different states face the same problems and copy each other, or certain ideas become shared by influential scholars or public figures in several countries, and the same policy ideas spread (Hall 1989). For example, following the Great Depression, capitalist countries adopted welfare and state intervention in the economy. Different states intervened in different ways and with different welfare policies, but *all* still intervened. In the 1970s, when Western capitalist countries suffered inflation and stagnant growth, privatization of state-owned firms or services and cutting back on welfare became shared policies, even if actual implementation differed. The British privatized more than the French, and the Americans had the least to privatize.

These two examples were part of two broader policy trends that swept capitalist countries: Keynesianism and monetarism.[15] I focus on these two policy logics for two reasons. They dominated the twentieth century and we face their impacts today; and while monetarism is in vogue, it has serious weaknesses that have caused economic problems, and so a variant of Keynesianism may return.

Keynesianism

Keynesianism – the economic thought of British economist John Maynard Keynes – began as a critique of *laissez-faire* economics and minimalist states (Keynes 1936). Keynes noted problems of economic theory, such as "wage stickiness" (slow wage responses to market changes) or that markets do not automatically correct themselves efficiently. Take the Great Depression: as the business climate worsened, investment and purchases dropped; as these dropped, the business climate became worse still. Recessions and depressions are generally of a cyclical nature, but usually an economy bottoms out and business leaders begin to invest and purchase once again, convinced the economy will eventually improve. In the Great Depression the market was not correcting itself sufficiently quickly, resulting in continued mass unemployment and dislocation. In Europe, the Depression radicalized workers to left-wing politics, which frightened the middle classes into right-wing reactionary forces, including fascists.

In response, Keynes championed state intervention in the economy in such times of stress: "counter-cyclical activity" or spending. When economies go into decline, states should spend more, even if this means borrowing money, to make up for absent market demand. Whether putting people to work constructing parks and highways or buying goods (grain or weapons), the state is injecting money into the economy, helping to provide profit, stabilize the economy, and improve the business climate. Eventually, business leaders will feel confident about investing and purchasing, and the state can spend less and pay its debts.

Keynesianist economists and political scientists see active state intervention extending beyond counter-cyclical spending to improve market demand – it is a regular feature of modern capitalism. Michael Piore and Charles Sabel (1984), for example, claim that modern capitalism follows a "mass production paradigm," in contrast to the "craft production paradigm" of earlier eras. In the craft paradigm, skilled artisans produce specialized goods at a high price. The drawback is that output is not cheap or affordable by the mass public, but these artisans can react quickly to changes in the economy. (According to Piore and Sabel, Germany's craft legacy helped German firms adapt to economic changes in the 1970s and 1980s.) Mass production means mass output of similar cheap goods – the McDonald's hamburger is a classic example – but this requires large investment in factories. To encourage such massive investment, an economy must be stable so that factories can produce *constant* profit and investors can eventually receive profits. This requires that the state stabilize the economy by providing buffers from economic shocks. Crucial buffers include: a supply of cheap food so that workers do not need constant wage increases; a constant supply of oil and energy to keep production costs low and constant; a constant supply of cheap labor (usually minorities) that can be hired and fired quickly in response to rises and falls in market demand; and a stable currency to maintain stable global trade. Keynesianism provided the legitimacy and tools for these buffers. This is more than simply buying goods to keep up demand during a market slump; it is active intervention all the time. States keep stocks of oil and grain in reserve, so that if there is a sudden deficit or price rise in food and oil, the state can release these reserves and bring prices down. The alternative is instability. If prices suddenly rise for food, workers will demand higher wages, leading to higher prices for goods, leading to more wage demands – a "wage-inflation spiral." If energy prices go up, prices of other goods increase, which also feeds the wage–inflation spiral. (The wage–inflation spiral is likely to be stronger if workers are unionized.)

As mass production emerged and faced the ultimate test of instability during the 1930s, developed states created these Keynesian buffers, but only piecemeal and incompletely, without realizing the broader logic of their polities. This system began to unravel in the 1970s (Piore and Sabel 1984: ch. 7), when American grain reserves were sold to the USSR, oil-producing countries organized OPEC and increased the price of oil (reducing its supply), countries withdrew from the gold standard (which anchored currencies and kept exchange rates stable),[16] and civil rights movements attacked discrimination of ethnic minorities who had been the reserve of cheap and temporary labor. The result was "stagflation": economic stagnation along with inflation. Keynesianism and state activity were blamed, although the real problem was the abandonment of the incomplete Keynesianist system by reducing these buffers. Stagflation was incomprehensible, since growth should have occurred with inflation (which might have reduced the positive impact of growth). Capitalist policy-makers faced a dilemma.

Monetarism

Monetarism posited that the best economy was an economy free of states, and it stepped into the breach, promising to end stagflation and improve the economic climate. Keynesianism legitimated state deficit spending, but this generated several problems. Politicians were as likely to spend too much in good economic times as in bad – a form of political bribery, such as providing welfare to keep the poor quiet or providing profit to firms whose owners and managers were networked with politicians (as in military-industrial firms). An activist state will not just spend money; it will also increase its regulation of the economy, perhaps to the point of hurting business. In 1970s stagflation, state activism was badly wounded by monetarists. The most noted enemy of Keynesianist thought was University of Chicago economist and Nobel laureate Milton Friedman, who claimed that an activist state did not only waste money and hurt competition – it also hurt freedom (Friedman and Friedman 1980). A strong state hinders individual choice and autonomy. A strong welfare state has too much leverage over citizens. A state that provides free housing, education, and medicine helps citizens – but it also disempowers them by making them *dependent* on the state for important goods and services. In contrast, a market encouraged competition (and efficiency) and also empowered people both as consumers and citizens. In a market the consumer is king, served (supposedly) by business. This justified ending state intervention and unleashing the market everywhere possible.

That the Friedmans' claims were over-simplistic or even wrong did not limit their appeal, especially in the United States and Great Britain. Monetarism appealed to an elite that wanted increased control over their investments or their own firms and to keep a larger percentage of their profits. In this way monetarism became a tool for foreign investment: the promise of minimal state interference. This appealed not only to the American government, but also to technocrats in developing countries, especially Latin America (Centeno 1996). But monetarism perversely appealed to non-elites. In the United States, liberalism came under attack in the 1970s, accused of supporting rogue elements who would not look for a job unless forced to do so. Welfare criticism was couched in racial language as well: from Nixon's "law and order" platform to Brooklyn Italians and Jews who once supported liberalism but were annoyed at blacks intruding into their schools and neighborhoods (Rieder 1985), welfare came to be seen as a redistribution of wealth and autonomy from (hard-working) whites to (less hard-working) blacks. (That welfare and liberalism helped whites, e.g. provision of unemployment benefits or collective bargaining, was forgotten.) While monetarism is not inherently racist, its anti-welfare logic fit the new anti-welfare politics of the 1970s, and it was easy for Ronald Reagan to combine the two. In the United Kingdom, anti-welfare racism broke out with debates over asylum seekers in the 1990s. Margaret Thatcher, John Major, and Tony Blair could not embrace monetarism as could Reagan. Keynesianism and welfare were too strongly embedded in British social life. Privatizing medicine was one step removed from a real economic revolution, and the rhetoric of class and social justice remained powerful despite Thatcher's attacks (e.g. on nationalized industries or trade unions).

If monetarism caught on in the United States, Great Britain, and Latin America, it was weaker on the European continent. But Europe does not share the market individualism of Anglo-America; corporatist states and class identities are far stronger and have deeper histories, and it is no surprise that monetarism was more foreign to policy paradigms there. The French state formally embraced privatization but implemented it slowly and incompletely (Hall 1986) – partly because of the state's traditionally strong role in economy and society, and partly because privatization and neoliberalism were seen as "punishment" rather than paths to efficiency, freeing managers and entrepreneurs to enrich themselves. In Germany, the power of trade unions and the Left prevented a full turn to monetarism; the German economy was also on the move in the 1970s and 1980s, and there was less impetus to trim welfare and labor rights. (State ownership was also less extensive than in Britain or France.) Further east, post-socialist economies embraced various forms of monetarism, especially shock therapy, because they had little choice: this was the condition for receiving foreign aid, and post-socialist leaders desperately wanted to signal legitimacy in the eyes of Western elites. Despite economic stagnation, Japan resisted advice to open up her economy, end lifetime employment, and examine banks' finances. Japanese state–business relations had created the post-war economic miracle, and monetarism flew in the face of Japanese success and legitimacy.

Evaluating Keynesianism and monetarism

Both policies attempted to address the pressing issues of their day: the Depression and unemployment, and economic stagnation. Both had some success addressing their perceived problems, but neither policy was an outright success. Keynesianism suffered two major flaws. First, it justified deficit spending that government leaders did not constrain to market downturns ("pork-barrel politics"), expanding budget deficits. Second, to work effectively, Keynesian policy needed to be expanded and maintained, especially reserves of labor and resources. Monetarism has flaws as well. The biggest is that organized power and inequality is outside the theory. Taking markets at face value, monetarists assume that with a minimal state and maximal freedom allowed to corporations, economies will grow, and everybody will benefit. Corporate growth should lead to expanded production, meaning more employment and better wages for employees.[17] Further, corporations are ultimately market players, and so they must address consumers' needs. In monetarism, consumers ultimately hold power – yet monetarism made inequality worse (Gray 1998). The rich got richer, the poor poorer, and those in between did not always see much real improvement. Corporations are no more consumer-friendly, and corporate power has grown. Many economists suggest monetarism is not only successful but natural

– and many economic publications (e.g. *The Economist*) follow this line to some degree. Social problems should correct themselves in a free market. That this remains more a claim than reality has not stopped many economists harping on tight budgets, minimal welfare, and global freedom of trade and capital. There are gains from free trade, but markets work best for the majority when balanced by other social concerns.

Comparison of welfare policies

To make sense out of the different approaches to state-society relations and policy, and to highlight the national differences in policy styles, I turn to a policy common to industrialized, modern economies: the welfare state. Here I look briefly at differences between American and European welfare to highlight the difference between state–society relations and policy logics in the old world and the new. American and European welfare policies do have fundamental differences that reflect state structures and policy logics: a decentralized state with a hands-off policy regime gave birth to a limited American welfare state, while more centralized European states with proactive policy regimes gave birth to more comprehensive welfare in Europe. The American version is "maternal" (Skocpol 1992): policies guard the weak (e.g. the poor, unemployed, single mothers). Families receive food stamps or Medicaid only if they fall below a certain threshold of income and assets. Federal Stafford Loans are available only to low-income students, and financial aid at universities is need-based, doled out on the basis of parental income and assets. In short, American welfare aims to prop up the lower end of society and enable them to get out of poverty, although provision is often far from adequate. In contrast, European welfare is "paternalist." While the less well-off may receive benefits, welfare is granted to *all* members of society. Free or low-cost health care is available to anyone who desires it. Tax benefits are geared towards lower income families, but other monetary benefits are available to all: for example, a child allowance of approximately £15 per week is available to *all* new parents in the United Kingdom. University education, like medicine, was once free at the point of entry to all citizens, although lack of state funding meant that students shouldered an increasing portion of the cost of their studies, more and more often through private loans. Compare this to the United States: students receive scholarships or student loans and graduate with a massive debt – but this is taken for granted as a privilege and investment in one's future. In the UK, cheap higher education is seen as a right for all and an investment in *society*'s future.

A major difference between European and American welfare histories is the role of the state. In the United States, independent social groups and the autonomous courts played a strong role in shaping the form which welfare policies took. Courts in Europe have much less autonomy than those in the United States. Further, states are relatively more centralized and insulated than the American federal government. A history of constant warfare, feudalism, and elitism created states that relied on their own trained bureaucrats rather than outside groups for policy advise (Anderson 1979).

Decision-making power over the use of finances and other resources resided with trained civil servants rather than with party officials (Katznelson 1985), because states developed before political parties. In the United States, parties were more mature when civil service reforms were enacted. Further, the American state grew dramatically only after the two world wars, when the Democrats and Republicans were well established.[18] Therefore, European welfare policies were designed by politicians and bureaucrats *within* the state. European states responded to pressure, but not to immediate pressure from voters, as in the United States. Rather, state officials responded to perceived threats (high unemployment, mass discontent). American politicians produced welfare policies that responded to voting groups – such as war veterans or Southern farming interests (Quadagno 1988).

Unintended outcomes: states and informal economies

So far I have assumed that the consequences of state policies are usually intended. This is not always the case, and perhaps the best illustration of this is the *informal economy*. This also relates back to the subject matter of Chapter 3. One assumption of development is that growth and generated wealth are legal: accounted for, relatively transparent for investment or taxation. However, we should not ignore activity and wealth in the shadows – in illegal or quasi-legal areas of the economy sometimes called black markets, gray markets, or shadow economies. Black markets are infamous for such goods and services as drugs, prostitution, contraband, and gambling, but other forms of economic activity may be illegal as well – for example, driving an unlicensed taxi cab around New York or moonlighting as a repairman for cash "on the side" (unreported income). While measuring the size of the shadow economy across the globe is difficult, some estimates put forward a sizeable figure (Becker 2004: 18–21). In Latin America, more than half of urban employment is in the informal economy, contributing around one-fourth of the region's GDP. In Africa, more than 60 percent of urban jobs and nearly 80 percent of non-agricultural work are in the informal economy. In Asia, anywhere from 40 percent to 60 percent of jobs (depending on the country) are in the informal economy, making up around 40 percent of GDP. In these areas, the percentage of women in the informal sector is greater than that of men.

What is the informal economy and why does it exist? Some approaches consider informal economies to be marginal to developing economies (i.e. they are older, "traditional" production) or the results of capitalist exploitation (cf. Becker 2004: 10). These views suffer from key defects. First, informal economies are far from marginal and in some areas have been growing (e.g. Latin America in the 1990s), and informal business activity is far from "traditional" (agricultural). Further, business elites subordinate lesser producers through formal means or market mechanisms such as subcontracting. The key question is why activity is "informal" to begin with, and here we run into states and laws, and how they make costs of activity high. In short, *states* create informal or shadow economies (and black markets) in two ways. First, they *categorize*, defining what is legal/legitimate versus illegal/illegitimate: requiring licenses to practice medicine or sell drugs, for example. Second, state licensing and general regulation, the markers of legality, impose costs that may be so high as to drive people into informality. If a taxi license costs $10 and requires a one-page form, cabbies will invest time and money for the license. If the license costs $1000 per month and requires a ten-page form with several documents (e.g. driver's license, doctor's certificate of health, passport or other proof of citizenship), many cabbies will see this as costly and will risk working illegally. This is what Hernando de Soto (1989) found in Peru's informal economy. People living on the margins did not have the time or money to apply for the many licenses needed to run taxi services or sell goods, so they did their work anyway, hoping they could bribe a police officer who might discover them. They put food on the table and sometimes expanded business – if successful enough, obtaining formal licenses.

Informal economies suggest entrepreneurship that either runs against a society's current morals (e.g. as in the sex trade) or suffers from excessive state regulation – perhaps because state leaders really feel the need to regulate the economy, or perhaps because they see licenses as an easy way to make money.[19] In the second case, informal economies and state (over)regulation that breeds them create paradoxes of informality (Portes 1994), including further criminalization of the economy and inefficiencies that drain the economy of investment. Because informal economies are illegal or quasi-legal, informal entrepreneurs cannot use the law to defend contracts, property, and security. The police are likely to arrest them, and so they must pay predators or pay for informal protection, such as the Mafia. In fact, while stereotypical Mafia activities include prostitution, drug trafficking, and gambling, the Mafia also act as enforcers when formal legal organizations do not: from defending simple contracts in Italy (Gambetta 1993) to defending exchange and property in post-socialist Russia (Volkov 2002). States can clear up informal economies by increasing police activity, but this may use up capital better spent on education, health, and infrastructure. Alternatively, states could reduce and streamline taxes and regulation to what is absolutely necessary (e.g. reasonable health and labor codes) and encourage entrepreneurs to leave the shadows. This has been the argument from neoliberal economists, and here economists have something to teach sociologists. States might help create just, honest markets, but they can interfere with honest attempts to make a living and contribute to the economy.

Comparisons, evaluations, conclusions

Policy-making is a complicated process, and these paradigms capture parts of reality. But which captures reality *best*? In the 1950s pluralism reigned supreme; in the late 1960s and 1970s pluralism shared the spotlight with variants of Marxism. By the 1980s Weberian sociology returned, and at policy studies currently combine insights from Weber and Durkheim: from Weber an appreciation of the state as an independent actor and the role of organized power; from Durkheim the appreciation of culture in shaping policies by constraining policy-making to what is known, normal, and legitimate – policy is constrained by state capacity (state structure) and totems of what is sacred and profane in society.

State centered, market centered, and mixed: a comparison

Scholarly debates do not end with competing explanations about roots and forms of different countries' social policies and welfare states. They extend to *effectiveness* of policies. Different policy models were linked to growth. The American state provided tariff protection against foreign competition and stimulated the economy through deficit spending and military purchases. But the American economy is freer relative to other economies – allowing growth but also bubbles (such as the late 1990s). The British state has been more *laissez-faire* than many others, even allowing cartels, and for much of its history it has remained wary of regulating the market. Only with two world wars did the British state actively intervene in the economy. The results have been mixed – but how much of Britain's post-war decline was due to red tape and how much to the loss of an empire and global hegemony?

One problem with debates over Keynesianism and monetarism, or between the different policy regimes, is that ideology often interferes with analyses. Left-learning scholars and pundits prefer the state to regulate the market for the benefit of the less well-off or for the majority. This attracts Leftists to Keynesianism's safety nets and state activism. Those who distrust states (as incompetent or tyrannical) are more attracted to monetarism; pundits who see inequality as natural and even justifiable find in monetarism an "objective," "scientific" means to defend a minimalist state and maximal social authority for elites. Business managers often prefer monetarism because it legitimates corporate power and autonomy; bureaucrats and academics prefer a stronger state partly because it promotes their interests.

We often ask what kinds of policies are "best," but this begs the question of "best for whom?" It is easy to say that one's favorite policy benefits everybody, but policy pundits generally make this claim. The truth is that even if everyone benefits under a type of policy, some groups in society benefit more than others. Strong, interventionist states in Europe and Asia managed to create greater social equality than in the United States, Great Britain, or Latin American countries that imposed monetarist policies. (See the list of Gini coefficients, a measurement of socioeconomic equality, in Table 4.2. A score of 0 indicates perfect equality; 100 indicates perfect inequality. This is not an indication of socioeconomic development *per se*.) American society was lucky to experience many decades of economic growth, while interest groups could shape policies to their benefit. Since the rise of monetarism this has benefited the upper 20 percent of society; the gap between rich and poor has increased (with the middle class suffering since the mid-1970s as well). In Europe, Leftist parties have championed the less well-off, and state bureaucrats can implement some form of provision for the needy. But social democratic, pro-socialist ideology has a stronger hold on European populations than in the United States, where there is no true "Leftist" party and where socialism has not enjoyed much popularity (even before the Cold War and the "threat" of communism).

Economists believe there is one best path to growth and overall social health, and that is through the free market with minimal state regulation. But the empirical truth is that no single policy regime and state structure has led to constant growth.

Table 4.2 GINI coefficients for countries analyzed, plus others for comparisons

Country	Gini coefficient and year
*United States	40.8 (2000)
*Great Britain	36 (1999)
*New Zealand	36.2 (1997)
France	32.7 (1995)
Germany	28.3 (2000)
Sweden	25 (2000)
Japan	24.9 (1993)
South Korea	31.6 (1998)
*Mexico	54.6 (2000)
*Chile	57.1 (2000)
*Brazil	59.3 (2001)
India	32.5 (1999)
Pakistan	33 (1998)
Egypt	34.4 (1999)
China	44.7 (2001)
*Russia	31 (2002)

Note: Data drawn from United Nations (2005). Countries with an asterisk (*) are those which in the past two decades have had primarily monetarist policies.

American policies allow for entrepreneurs and innovation to emerge – due to minimal state interference and a greater promise for entrepreneurs to reap profits from their work. Yet European and Asian policies and their active states provide investment and greater long-term vision. However, the risk in European/Asian policies is that state and business elites should forecast what their societies will need in twenty years' time. If they are wrong, twenty years of investment will lead to little benefit. At least America's relatively free market allows for rapid innovation and change if circumstances worsen. But weak states and free markets also encourage inequality.

Perhaps the real lesson is that growth is a function of innovation and investment and gaining a market niche. These result from historical luck as much as policy, and many policies provide both aids to growth and equality as well as obstacles. Some policies have failed miserably: for example, state socialism of the Soviet model helped the USSR to industrialize in the 1930s, but the costs in human life and investment were enormous. Current British policies promise greater equality as well as growth, but the red tape involved – emerging from state insecurity and distrust over professionals' ability to work honestly – made it difficult to deliver those promises. France's railroads and health care are costly but work fairly well; in other areas (e.g. agriculture), state leaders have found it difficult to change or extract themselves from the current situation. The world still awaits a "best" policy, and for now there are still rich and poor, booms and busts, and development continues apace. It would be foolish to expect homogenized state structures and policies anytime soon.

5 The heart of the economy

Organizations and corporations

Twenty years ago, large multidivisional corporations were the heart and soul of developed Western economies. They employed millions of blue-collar laborers and white-collar managers and professionals who worked for most of their lives in one or two firms. Blue-collar employees were probably unionized, and corporations provided pensions and local social support (and health care in the United States). By the 1980s, firms were diversifying their activity beyond traditional core areas, sometimes deindustrializing in the process and shedding employee benefits. Blue-collar workers were shed to reduced labor costs; by the 1990s white-collar employees and middle managers were "downsized" as well to make the firm "lean and mean."[1] Unions were on the retreat after attacks from states and from cheaper, non-unionized labor forces abroad. Smaller software, information technology, and "dot-com" firms, with small numbers of educated employees, advanced technology and spurred the American stock market. The large corporation that once ruled the world with armies of employees and pools of capital seemed to have been over-taken by smaller companies that adapted to the changing market.

What happened to the corporation and modern economic organization? This is an important question for today's youth. These organizations *are* work; their formal rules and informal structures provide security, wages, and benefits. Their structures have changed, from the M-form to the multi-layered subsidiary to small firm networks (see Figure 5.1). Yet no other issue in economic sociology is drier: theories and narratives are often debated in rarefied air of elite universities with advanced statistical techniques or jargon that many sociologists cannot (or refuse to) grasp. We cannot ignore these important stories and debates. My goal is to make sense of organizations and competing theories. Economists and sociologists do battle again; the economic logic remains seductive even if, empirically, it is weaker.

The economists' view: organizations, markets, and efficiency

Economics is in an odd position *vis-à-vis* organizations. Economists cannot avoid large corporations and small firms, and they are often called on to evaluate a firm's

(a) *M-form*: example of DuPont; cf Chandler (1962)

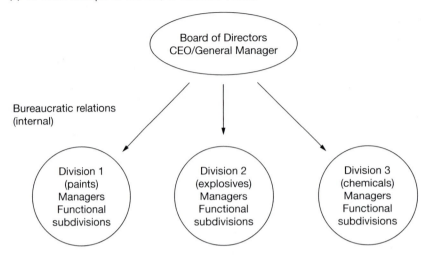

(b) *Multi-layererd subsidiary form*: divisions become independent entities; Prechel (1997)

(c) *Small firm networks*; Perrow (1993)

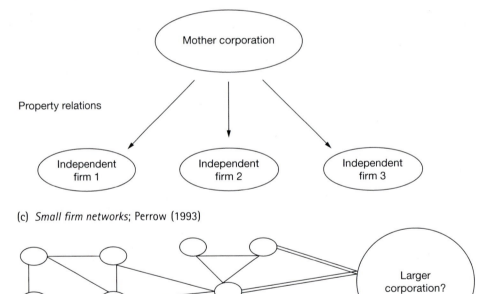

Figure 5.1   Corporate and organizational structures

value to determine share price or recommend investment strategies. Despite the numerous models to evaluate market value and forecast economic trends (or to try to do so), economic theory, ironically, has difficulty answering why firms exist at all in the forms they take. As we saw in Chapter 2, neoclassical theory assumes a market of rational individuals exchanging or competing with each other; economists are less successful in explaining organizational strategies and structures. First, they assume those organizational forms that survive are the most efficient or receive non-market help (e.g. state subsidies to inefficient firms). Second, they assume that market-based individual exchanges are the best form of economic activity. An economy is just individuals and choices; the corporation or factory is just a large number of individuals with individual labor contracts and jobs. They do not have "emergent properties."[2] Why should organizations like corporations exist, when "spot markets" of temporary labor contracts are better? Why should IBM or British Petroleum outlive human beings? Yet organizations do exist as more than mere collections of people. They are rituals, rules, collective identities that are "reified," considered to be real just like human beings. At the same time, economists do see organizations as more than individuals: just as individuals "maximize utility," firms "maximize profits." Yet this misses the rules and practices of organizational power and function.

New institutional economics (NIE)

To overcome these shortcomings, some economists created a subfield called "new institutional economics" (or sometimes "law and economics") which views firms as sets of rules that shape costs. NIE was born when John Commons (1934) and Ronald Coase (1937) suggested that the effect of laws on costs had to be addressed in economic literature. Many years later, Alfred Chandler and Oliver Williamson took up the challenge. A key scholar in the field, Chandler argues that the modern corporation emerged from the need to coordinate mass production and distribution over large territories. The first modern corporations were American railroad firms (Chandler 1977), whose managers faced a daunting task: coordinating activity involving expensive equipment (trains and lines, offices, goods in transit) across a large swath of the American continent. Until then, most companies were small manufacture (e.g. textiles) or trade, and father–son teams managed day-to-day work. Production was housed literally under one roof; sons accompanied ships along rivers to trading points. Railroads were costly, and managers had to ensure that trains ran and were as full as possible. Professional managers, also born into this "corporate revolution," created organizational structures that divided tasks such as sales and maintenance of trains and track to assistant or "line" managers. Not only did line staff perform specific, coordinated tasks; they also reported information about costs and sales to top managers. With this information, managers could coordinate activities across wide geography.

In the twentieth century, the corporation evolved into the "M-form" (multidivisional form) when industrial firms faced further challenges of coordinating information and production (see Figure 5.1). The DuPont chemical firm grew, producing munitions during World War I, but the expanded firm was difficult to coordinate (Chandler 1962). To cope, DuPont managers restructured their firm so that different product lines became mini-firms answerable to the overarching DuPont organization. In this "M-form," each division had its own managers of sales, procurement, development, and the like. This made coordination easier, as each division was responsible for its product line. General management had to worry only about general policies; the specifics of producing paint or explosives were left to separate divisions and managers who knew their products and markets. When some DuPont managers left the company, they took their new-found M-form with them. Later, General Motors institutionalized the M-form for the American economy and the developed world.

As we saw in Chapter 2, Oliver Williamson (1975, 1985) claimed that organizations are a means to defend investments against risks of opportunism. If the spot market transaction is more efficient, employees' immediate tasks and rates could be consistently negotiated at a market rate – similar to "temp workers" or outsiders contracted for one job. Yet organizations such as corporations are more stable, and employees have more general tasks. Why? The answer, Williamson claims, is in Coase's "transaction costs." While "transaction" has a more complex and abstract definition, for our purposes it is an exchange between two people or groups. A transaction may be potentially costly for participants, and to reduce costs – especially the risk of opportunism – actors create *governance structures*: rules to control economic action. Generally, Williamson suggests three basic forms of transacting: spot markets, contract, and organizations; the latter two are governance structures. Three variables determine which form actors use: whether a transaction is a one-time deal or repeated; "information asymmetry"; and sunk costs (investments not immediately recoverable). For making cars, sunk costs include the factory (land, buildings) and technology. Williamson also assumes the threat of "opportunism with guile" – not everybody cheats, but some do, and badly. Now we have the tools to explain why a firm exists. If a transaction is a one-time deal, I exchange money for a good. If a deal is repeated but I know how the other will act, or sunk costs are low (so that cheating is not costly), I will use a contract. If the deal is repeated – say, a supplier will constantly provide needed inputs (e.g. to build cars) – I become dependent on that supplier. If sunk costs are great, I have more to lose. Finally, if I have imperfect information about my supplier, I do not know whether he will cheat, provide substandard goods, or gouge me with higher prices than need be. My solution: buy my supplier. Property rights give me control and access to my supplier's books and factory, reducing the problem of information. I can then avoid cheating and reduce the risk to my investment.

Related to transaction cost economics is *principal–agent theory* (Alchian and Demsetz 1972; Jensen and Meckling 1976). The "principal" owns resources (e.g. capital, the firm), and the "agent" is contracted to administer that capital in the owner's absence. The usual example is an owner or shareholders versus managers who run day-to-day operations. Owners and shareholders have many holdings and are too busy to run any one firm, and they also may not have the knowledge to run their holdings. They hire managers to run their property – assuming that managers will work hard and competently. NIE alerts us to a potential problem: the principal has no guarantee that the agent will act in the principal's interests. The incentive to cheat is always present: what is to stop a manager from manipulating data (e.g. performance statistics) to make owners think the firm is doing well or to mask the manager's theft of assets? (Sociologists do not always consider opportunism.) Two general strategies have emerged over the "principal–agent problem." The first is complex monitoring mechanisms, such as constant reports and paper trails about the agent's use of resources. Managers may need permission to use a firm's resources (e.g. for travel), or they may need to submit constant, detailed reports about the firm's performance to an independent auditor. An alternative strategy is to link the agents' and principals' interests. The manager may receive shares in the firm as part of her salary; as a shareholder, her incentive is *not* to cheat.[3]

Institutional economics approaches also point out the importance of rules by demonstrating their perverse effects. If rules shape costs and thus action, then rules that are perverse to market competition and efficiency will produce perverse and inefficient practices. One is *moral hazard*, more popularly called "the tail wagging the dog." In moral hazard, rules for solving a problem either make that problem worse or create another problem. For example, investors may be concerned about opportunism and want to monitor managers and employees with constant detailed reports. However, not all organizational activity can be measured by check lists (cf. Wilson 1989), and so this ends up wasting time and effort. To survive and get promoted, employees and managers make sure their activity conforms to required reports, *not* to producing quality output. They produce for the bureaucratic apparatus, not the market or consumer – the tail wags the dog. A classic example was the Soviet economy (Berliner 1957; Nove 1977), which I discuss in Chapter 7. Detailed Five-year Plans and myriad bureaucratic rules and reports on production and organizational routine encouraged Soviet managers and employees to produce for Plan reports – even if this meant that output was worthless or even fictitious! Another example of moral hazard in operation is the current situation of state monitoring of public services, such as higher education, in contemporary Great Britain, to which I return later.

Institutional economists used these cases to suggest that politics and economics should not mix much; yet why do such perversities continue? Why does the market not bite back? Here we must move away from the "economics" logic of institutions. Douglass North (1990) suggests that perverse outcomes persist because elites gain – maybe not profit or economic growth, but personal gains such as power or prestige. Sociologists in the "neoinstitutionalist" school suggest that legitimacy and politics are as important as profit and markets, and this drives moral hazards. However, we must not discount NIE's insights. (In a sense, much economic sociology is a response to NIE.) Overall, the lesson of new institutional economics is that *control* is central to organizational structure and operation. Economics sociologists do not necessarily deny this, and it is one area of overlap between the two camps. What sociologists do debate is whether governance structures and worries about opportunism are the whole answer, and whether there are deeper structural, institutional, cultural, and historical forces that shape *how* people perceive such issues as opportunism and cost, and *what kinds of tools* they have available for constructing organizations.

Sociological explanations: institutions, states, power, and culture

Sociologists do not deny the importance of competition or efficiency, but neither do they privilege them. Broader structural forces and cultural conceptions are important as well, shaping what managers think to maximize or how to do so. This is one reason why "moral hazards" survive: they are "hazards" to economists, for whom markets are objectively about profit and efficiency. For sociologists economies have subjective, cultural totems, just as religion and politics do, and "hazards" are components and outcomes of social forces underlying economic structure and practice – including organizations.

Organizations as structured class power and capitalist logics

In the basic Marxist logic, firms reflect the demands of capitalism: exploitation and control of labor, accumulation of profit, and production of surplus value. One drawback of Marxist sociology is that it does not address variation in organizational strategy and structure; in this theory, different organizational forms are less meaningful than the fact that they transform materials into goods and extract labor power from employees. However, Marxist approaches provide useful insights and issues for examination, especially concerning how class power permeates and shapes organizational structures and processes, and the ideologies that legitimate and propagate them. Two key ideologies and organizational logics were Taylorism and Fordism. Both aimed to increase productivity and profit at the expense of employee autonomy. Both made use of observation, measurement, and control of work habits, including employees' actual movements. F. W. Taylor (1911) noticed that efficiency was low because employees were either lax or inefficient in going about their jobs. His solution was the organizational ideology called scientific management (or Taylorism). A key feature of this was "time and motion studies." Managers would photograph workers at work and measure the time they spent in movement. They would then change how employees worked to reduce time wasted – improving productivity and profit. This may sound innocuous, but it was not. First, Taylor assumed that employees would work inefficiently ("soldiering") – because they were free riding or were not sufficiently enlightened.[4] They had to be measured and controlled; real autonomy and decision-making were with managers and engineers, who had scientific knowledge of how to run the firm. Yet at the same time, an important part of the program was giving employees a cut in the profits as a material and moral incentive. If a firm's profits increased, part of it should go to employees' wages. Alas, managers usually ignored this part of Taylor's recommendations (Bendix 1974).

Fordism was an extension of Taylorism, embedding Taylor's efficiency logic in a physical structure, the assembly line. Not only are workers observed and controlled;

their labor and work is strongly linked to the technology of production, suggesting that efficiency improves not only with better arranged work but also by replacing human skills with machines (a process of "deskilling"). In addition, workers were not only an input (labor) but also potential buyers of a firm's output. Managers had to take an interest in their employees' buying power and desires, justifying a degree of managerial paternalism. For this reason, managers at Ford Motors and General Motors struck deals with their unions in the 1950s to improve workers' pay – extra wages might go towards purchasing a Ford (or GM) automobile. In Fordist analyses with Marxist overtones, rigorous organizational structures of observation, measurement, and control exist to aid in the accumulation of capital. Managers who implement Taylorist or Fordist schemas are following the logic of capitalism: maximize exploitation to maximize profit. Some neo-Marxists added that Taylorism and Fordism aimed not only to control but also to deskill employees, further reducing their labor power (Braverman 1974). This deprived employees of their bargaining chip which they had *vis-à-vis* owners and managers: labor power. A skilled worker is difficult to replace, and that worker can threaten to take away his skills by leaving or going on strike. Lesser skilled workers are easier to replace.

In the past twenty years some scholars have talked of a "post-Fordist" economy: rigid, rule-bound structures of work and production are replaced by flexibility and employee initiative. This was a response to Third World competition and the potential for communications technology to allow employees to work beyond the physical confines of the assembly line. By the 1980s business success required flexible work to aid innovation and change in a firm's output – which the large, bureaucratic Fordist organization did not facilitate. Further, by the 1980s manufacturing was moving from the developed to developing countries (cheaper labor, lower taxes, and access to foreign markets), and the service sector was taking up a greater share of Western economies. Service industries do not work well with an assembly line structure – and so employees were given more autonomy. On the surface, this may sound like an improvement over scientific management's fetish for control, but it came at a price. If post-Fordist employees gained autonomy, they lost the paternalist support of managers and unions (service industries are less likely to be unionized). Employees were also slaves to product and profit targets: how they worked to achieve these targets was unimportant, even if that meant working overtime without additional pay. Finally, the growth of a "target culture" and personnel departments meant post-Fordist employees were still being measured. If they reached targets in a specified time, they received bonuses and possible promotion; otherwise nothing, even if plans and targets were a function of bureaucratic committees and not market demand. Here Marxist and Weberian analyses run together: the logic of profit, accumulation, and exploitation remain paramount, driving the shift from Fordism to post-Fordism (exploitation through the assembly line or profit targets), with bureaucratic rationalization influencing *how* logics of capitalism are implemented.

In Marxist-inspired studies of structures of work and production, the organization is the empirical focus, but the real explanation involves deeper structures and logics of exploitation, accumulation, and profit. The organization is a puppet of these logics, as are the state, schools, and other institutions. This explanation has some power:

a few basic logics potentially explain much of the complex economic structure and their functions in which we work. Yet disembodied logics of capitalism are meaningless without cognizant actors: in other words, we need to consider more proximal (local) forces such as the organization and its politics, as well as other structures such as fields and states (which have political as well as economic interests). Further, such Marxist logic may explain why work everywhere seems the same; it cannot explain why work in different places and times varies. Japanese and German workers are encouraged to develop skills, take advantage of flexibility, and interact with managers to innovate new products or work procedures (Piore and Sabel 1984). British workers (until recently) felt less of the pressure of unemployment than did American workers. All these systems are capitalist, yet their organizational and work dynamics also differed. To understand that, we have to turn to such forces as niches and fields, and the state.

Weberian and neo-Weberian views

For Weber, capitalism and modernity inherently meant bureaucracy. Modern organizations such as firms and factories, states, and armies are bureaucratic. Two driving forces are behind the rise and dominance of bureaucratic organizations: rationalization and concentration of resources. Both are forms of power, and both have different effects on how organizations operate and on their surrounding economy.

Rationalization

A current popular thesis is "McDonaldization" (Ritzer 1993), which follows Weber's claim that modernity generally and capitalism in particular are a project of rationalization. Chandler noted much the same about the rise of the modern corporation: complex structures were a means to obtain information about production and sales for making better decisions, reducing costs, and improving profit and market survival. According to this thesis, economic activity – work and production of goods and services as well as those very goods and their consumption – are increasingly standardized, measured, and controlled. A McDonald's hamburger is the same everywhere, which is a key to success. Travelers may not know about local food, but they know McDonald's. This is because McDonald's has a tight, detailed set of rules and procedures that cover their activity: the type and amount of meat in a hamburger (usually centrally supplied and controlled by the corporation), the process of cooking, how employees should dress and greet customers, and so on. Thus, McDonald's provides the same standard meal everywhere, giving the consumer *certainty*.

Rationalization is not limited to life inside the firm: organizations impose rationalization beyond their formal structural boundaries. The most visible version of this comes from the state. Social security or National Insurance numbers, registration (e.g. for driving, medical care), and the like are all part of the state-led project of classification and control. In censuses the state offers classificatory schemes such as "ethnicity," and we choose our own "identity." In this way the state gains a better picture of its society and shapes it. But rationalization is not limited to the state: firms as well classify and rationalize consumers. Consider marketing, which turns individuals into complex data sets which firms try to manipulate. A contemporary example is cards that supermarkets offer customers: we fill out a form with basic information about ourselves, and we receive a card swiped at check-out that may offer discounts on certain items. The store is rationalizing us, collecting information: what groups of goods we buy, at what time of the day and month, if they are on sale, and so on. This way, managers know how to place goods (what we are likely to buy together), to whom to send what kind of advertisements, and so on. Such rationalization may seem more innocuous than Taylorism – but it is also intrusive and a subtle form of control. Supermarket managers are discovering patterns of behavior we ourselves may not realize and using this knowledge to maximize sales and profit without our overt knowledge.

This thesis is similar to that of neo-Marxism and Fordism. Even in a post-Fordist world, with employees subject to fewer specific assembly line-style controls, employees must meet standards of work and output, reducing the gains of flexible work. However, there is one subtle difference. Fordism/Taylorism and neo-Marxism generally see a smoking gun: managers and owners out to maximize profit at the expense of labor. In Weberian rationalization, measurement and control are not merely for the sake of profit; it is part of the grander attempt to create certainty. And we are not entirely sure why we do this; we may argue that rationalized production improves efficiency and profit, but we think this way only because we are wearing cultural blinkers. In fact, more flexible, less formally rationalized labor may ultimately be more efficient by providing flexibility and involving employees in seeking out new strategies and discovering and addressing problems (cf. Piore and Sabel 1984). Managers, owners, financial advisers, state officials, and even citizens are caught up in Weber's "iron cage" of increasing rationalization that is of our own unconscious making.

The rationalization thesis has much to recommend it – but it is not without criticism. No system of rationalization and control is perfect, for no system of information is perfect, and no schema structuring behavior leads to absolute, objective efficiency: it is likely that there is no "best practice" that can be imposed for any length of time. Rationalization assumes stability and certainty, but reality is too complex to control through such means. The McDonald's hamburger and work procedures are ideal types; in any system there are spaces for maneuver and hiding (Foucault 1977; Scott 1990). What the rationalization thesis points to is the *tendency* of the modernity project to classify, measure, and control, to fulfill a set of goals. Behind rationalization are actors with different individual goals and degrees of competence; rationalization does not move forward on its own account, and as we will see with neoinstitutionalism, rationalization may be more illusory than real.

Corporations, states, and power

Modern organizations are not only about complex rules and coordination: they are also about controlling large amounts of resources, including money and people. While Weber was fearful of the dehumanizing effects of rationalization, he was also in awe of the capacity of modern organizations to mobilize large numbers of people, money, and materials for complex goals (producing cars or conquering countries).

Charles Perrow (1986) argues that sociologists should focus primarily on organizational power, for organizational elites wield vast resources against states as well as employees. Put simply, organizations *are* power, and organizational strategies and structures reflect how their leaders accumulate and use power. Some scholars of elites, in fact, focus their analyses on institutional and organizational positions: elites or the "ruling class" are not those with the most money but those who sit atop large organizations (e.g. Dye 1990). Organizational power can alter the interests of organizational leaders, so that elites design rules and pressure states for their own interests rather than those of the organization – what Robert Michels (1959) called the "Iron Law of Oligarchy." For example, American coal-miners' unions won miners concessions, but union leaders also exploited their members, sometimes as badly as employers (Gaventa 1980). We may see this in our own workplaces, where managers impose new rules or strategies that serve them as much as the health or goals of the firm.[5]

Corporate power is at work not only with firms but also *vis-à-vis* outside entities such as governments. Corporate leaders can wield leverage against states to gain advantage. The most obvious is contributions to political parties, which make politicians dependent on corporate managers and shareholders. But organizational influence is not limited to such direct relationships. More indirect (but equally powerful) influence is the threat to relocate, taking away contributions to the local economy such as employment and purchases of goods and services. Corporations can threaten to take their business elsewhere if local politicians do not pass favorable policies and legislation. Multinational corporations use this tactic against underdeveloped countries, demanding favorable (low) taxes in return for providing employment – which, as low paying as it is, is still employment. Even in the United States, large organizations use the threat of exit. Automobile firms, such as Honda and Saturn, "shopped around" states and municipalities in search of the best combination of taxes, infrastructure, and labor costs. Like death and taxes, organizational power seems unavoidable, and is probably greater than we realize.

An example of the impact of organizational power on laws and from there on organizational structure came from the 1980s. Prechel (1990, 1997) argues that changes in business law and corporate structure (in his case study, for the steel industry) demonstrates that state policies can reflect and augment class and corporate interests. After decades of state regulation and increasing corporate debt (with the threat of bankruptcies – antithetical to corporate *and* government interests), CEOs and corporate shareholders lobbied the government to reduce state interference in business, and they found in Reagan a president whose quasi-libertarian ideology intersected with their interests. Judges became more lenient to mergers, less likely to apply anti-trust legislation. Legislators altered tax laws to allow corporate restructuring and give corporations greater leeway to exploit markets and employees to maximize wealth and minimize accountability. The Economic Recovery Act of 1981 made tax credits more advantageous to corporations and liberalized capital flow within corporations – further liberalized in the Tax Reform Act of 1986, which removed the tax burden for restructuring assets and capital flows within a corporate structure. The result was a change from the M-form to a new structure more advantageous

BOX 5.1   POLITICAL ELITES AND ORGANIZATIONAL INTERESTS

The relationships between corporate and political elites are infamous but usually more subtle and complex than assumed in usual public rhetoric. Consider the presidency of George W. Bush and corporate America. Vice-president Dick Cheney worked with Haliburton, and while networks may have helped Haliburton receive government contracts for work in Iraq, so did Haliburton's expertise and capacity in oil technology. President Bush had close relations with the managers of Enron – yet the Enron scandal became Bush's scandal, forcing him to push through legislation to clean up accounting and transparency procedures.

So long as elections are costly affairs, money for them must come from somewhere – if not the state, then from private contributions. Individuals can usually contribute only small sums, whereas organizations – from corporations to unions – have deeper pockets and more discernable policy interests (lower taxes and regulations, or improved safety rules and wages). In addition, we cannot forget that political parties are large organizations; politicians who run as a Democrat or Tory receive backing, in return for which they must ally themselves to some extent with that party's political ideology and policy interests (not always exactly those of constituents). In Great Britain, the Labour Party was accused of selling places in the House of Lords (the unelected chamber, with oversight power over bills passed by the House of Commons) in exchange for loans to the Labour Party. This reinvigorated the debate over whether the state should fund all major political parties so as to reduce dependence on wealthy individuals and corporations. In the United States, campaign for finance reform was temporarily on the agenda in the late 1990s. Rather than state funding, the idea was regulating who could contribute money, and in what amount, to political parties and campaigns.

When considering corporate power and local governments and communities, we should not restrict ourselves to business firms alone. Sport is as much business as "sport." In the 1990s, both the Pittsburgh Pirates (baseball) and Steelers (football) wanted new stadiums – not a single multipurpose stadium, but individual baseball and football stadiums, to replace the aging Three Rivers Stadium. Both teams claimed they needed more seating, better facilities, and luxury boxes to attract corporate clients – only this way could both teams bring in enough additional revenue to compete for highly paid players. Both teams proposed that local government finance the new stadiums. While local opinion was relatively favorable to a new football stadium – the Steelers have been iconic in Pittsburgh, especially since the 1970s – the local population was less inclined to fund a new stadium for the Pirates, whose fortunes (and, perhaps, management) had not been stellar in recent years. Pirates owners and management threatened to take the team elsewhere; this would not be the first time a sports team had left its home town for a new city and new stadium (Baltimore Colts to Indianapolis; Cleveland Browns to Baltimore; Montreal Expos to Washington, DC). Pittsburgh mayor Tom Murphy proposed using local taxes to fund the stadium (plus a new convention center), but voters in surrounding counties rejected the proposal. Murphy turned to "Plan B," which also involved taxation – but he did not put it to a vote. Corporate sports interests won in Pittsburgh, where once steel firms reigned supreme.

to managers and shareholders: the more decentralized "multilayered subsidiary form," (MLSF) (cf. Prechel 1997) (see Figure 5.1). Unlike the M-form, which housed all divisions within one corporate body, in the MLSF corporate divisions were spun off or restructured as independent or semi-independent entities, owned and controlled by a mother firm, with financial firewalls in between all entities to limit accountability and legal/financial responsibility (e.g. bankruptcy). Managers and owners were less responsible for organizational failings but still profited from successes. The MLSF also made it easier for corporate owners and managers to extract surplus labor from employees. Former subdivisions became legally independent firms, facing the market on their own, forced to compete and to balance their own budgets with less chance of subsidies from the mother corporation, which was easier when all subdivisions were under one roof (sometimes called cross-subsidization). In short, a new type of corporate organizational form emerged because the American government was more receptive to corporate pressure in the 1980s; organizational elites benefited from new policies. Organizational power triumphed.

We cannot understand economies without referring to organizational power. William Roy's synthesis (to which I return below) suggests as much: business elites convinced New Jersey legislators to expand the legal rights of corporations, which then gained so much economic power that they could keep pressing politicians for benefits (e.g. lower taxes or accountability). It would be fair to say that the corporation created itself: not capitalism *per se* or functional needs of efficiency or "modernity," but rather concrete organizational elites created an organizational form that enhanced their power and ability to pursue their interests. The importance of organizational power and interests, in contrast to broader, vaguer "class forces" or "modernity," is clear in the history of a massive federal project in the 1930s, the Tennessee Valley Authority (TVA) (Colignon 1997), designed to produce both cheap electricity and employment in Depression-era America. How the TVA was designed and developed – not always according to the original plan – cannot be understood without studying specific ideologies and networks of organizational leaders in the TVA, the federal government, and local governments and businesses. As alliances shifted, so did the balance of power over the TVA; because of the particular coalition that won, the TVA was more business-friendly than intended.

Organizations as "myth and ceremony": neoinstitutionalism

A recent approach to organizations is "neoinstitutionalism," which began as a response to economic theory and to population ecology. The driving question behind population ecology was: Why do organizations have different structures? Population ecologists (e.g. Hannan and Freeman 1989) referred to evolution: organisms survive and reproduce if they adapt to the environment, and the same holds for organizations. To survive, an organization must fit in with consumers and suppliers. Because goods and services, consumers, and inputs (steel versus food) are not the same, food-processing firms and automobile firms face different environments, and they have different organizational structures and procedures. Firms with the most efficient (or perhaps effective) fit survive to produce and sell. In response, neoinstitutionalists noted that organizational structures also showed certain *similarities*, and that many of those structures were not always economically rational. To explain homogeneity and seeming irrationality, neoinstitutionalists turned to legitimacy, culture, and fields. Drawing inspiration from Durkheim, Pierre Bourdieu, and Anthony Giddens (among others), neoinstitutionalists see organizations not just as formal rules and structures but also as collections of rituals and categories, such that they are also "myths and ceremonies." Looking at real behavior, neoinstitutionalists made two discoveries about rules and practices: managers follow the lead of other managers as much as markets, and organizational structure is a fig-leaf with less impact on work and production than was assumed. In other words, there is a sociological rationality to organizations that does not always correspond to business rationality.

The brief example of the British Leyland Motor Corporation shows how organizational (and business) dynamics are often far from economically rational while having a sociological rationality.[6] After World War II, British auto firms were losing ground to larger foreign conglomerates, especially American giants Ford and General Motors, and the French state was encouraging massive "champions" (cf. Chapter 4). Following this trend, the British state encouraged mergers to create a British automotive champion. In 1965, Rover and Alvis merged, and Rover was bought out soon after by truck-maker Leyland. Meanwhile, the British Motor Corporation had acquired Austin, Morris, and MG. In 1968 these two corporations merged into the British Leyland Motor Corporation. However, the different divisions within this conglomerate acted like the independent firms they had been until recently. Triumph designed a car that could have used the engine from another Leyland producer – yet they did not. British Leyland managers did not necessarily want to integrate, and by 1974 – six years after the super-merger – British Leyland was under threat of bankruptcy.

How do sociologists explain widespread, economically irrational behavior? Where economists ground behavior in rational action, neoinstitutionalists claim people want to control risk and uncertainty; in the jargon, they are "uncertainty minimizers." Managers and owners are usually not out for maximum profit; rather, they want a constant income stream that is sufficient to pay debts, maintain production, and invest. Second, neoinstitutionalists turn to Durkheim's insights on religion: structures are rituals that instill and reproduce meaning. Organizations are now sets of rituals – and so culture and *symbolic* resources (especially legitimacy) are as important as money. Firms need money to operate; but if investors and other market gatekeepers do not think a firm is playing by the rules – it does not have appropriate structure (e.g. no human resources department, old-fashioned technology) – they will not recommend that people invest in or buy from that firm. The state or professional organizations may investigate or withhold certification.[7] Managers must adopt legitimate strategies and structures, and to do so they follow each other as consumers. There are many consumers with diverse interests, but there are a limited number of other producers. Given costs of obtaining information, it is easier for managers to watch or talk to each other (White 1981). This does not mean that competition is absent, but it is influenced by managers' shared understandings of legitimate strategies. Managers and owners feel compelled to follow fads and appear legitimate or "in the loop," even if these fads do not bring significant or lasting gain (e.g. 1990s down-sizing to reduce labor costs and give firms higher profit margins and stock dividends), or if this deprived them of people with important skills.

Neoinstitutionalists then embed uncertainty minimizing and legitimation in a broader context: not the market, but the *field*. A field is a community of organizations that share an identity, usually linked to what they produce – the field of American auto producers, for example, or of universities and colleges. Managers watch others inside the field to see what is legitimate and to negotiate competition. Intense competition, such as undercutting each other through severe price wars, leads to uncertainty. To avoid this, field leaders, usually the most powerful firms, provide a template of legitimate strategies and structures, and they punish those managers who challenge principles of the field (sometimes by ganging up on the deviant and undercutting their prices).[8]

Fields and isomorphism

Paul DiMaggio and Walter Powell (1983) identified three ways in which shared strategies and understandings spread through fields: they called these "isomorphisms" ("isomorphic" means analogous).[9] One is "coercive isomorphism." When organizations depend on another actor for capital or other resources, they become obliged to adopt policies or structures in return. An example is non-profit organizations (e.g. museums) that rely on the state for money. State committees are more likely to fund non-profits with "proper" activities, structures, and ways of reporting activities (DiMaggio 1991). In Great Britain the state funds universities, and in return it demands highly documented procedures, such as complex and detailed reports to prove that departments are doing what officials in London consider proper, e.g. offering choice and "marketable skills"; monitoring quality and objectivity through formal internal reviews and double marking of papers and exams (a second lecturer checks a colleague's marks) and external examiners (professors in another university who check students' grades and exam questions). Departments submit materials on research activity for the state-run Research Assessment Exercise, which awards rankings and money to a department and its university.[10] Much as they dislike these cumbersome requirements, lecturers cannot avoid them because there is no alternative to state funding; all English universities adopt uniform bureaucratic procedures, even if these add little value (Willmott 1995; Underwood 2000).[11] Similar coercive isomorphism is present in Britain's National Health Service (Harrison and Ahmad 2000).

A second mechanism is "normative isomorphism." Organizational managers adopt similar strategies because they have similar backgrounds and ideologies, knowledge, and training. Such managers view business environments in a similar way and devise similar tactics. It is not necessary for all managers in a field to have shared backgrounds and ideologies – only that a sufficient number do, after which other isomorphic mechanisms kick in (e.g. mimetic, the next form). For example, many firms in the United States adopted new ways of thinking about corporate structure, from identifying with a general range of output to identifying the corporation with a financial bottom line, regardless of what the corporation produced. This change

occurred because a new generation of managers with MBAs or training and experience in finance departments was taking the reigns of management from an older
generation trained in sales and marketing (Fligstein 1990).

The third form is "mimetic isomorphism" (Table 5.1). In this form, managers in a
field face a shared dilemma. If one member happens upon a solution to that dilemma,
others follow suit because this seems to be a way out. An example comes from
the automobile industry in the 1930s. Ford was the automobile leader, and it
produced a limited number of cars. In contrast, General Motors was born through
a series of mergers that just happened to create a mish-mash of different auto
models: Cadillac for wealthy car owners, Oldsmobile for the upper-middle class, and
so on. When the Great Depression hit, most consumers could not afford cars – a
dilemma all auto manufacturers shared. This was nearly fatal to Ford, but not to
GM: wealthy Americans could still buy Cadillacs or Oldsmobiles. By an accident of
history, GM found a solution to the common dilemma: diversify output, and if demand
for one product collapses, others might still sell and help the firm survive. Other
auto manufacturers followed suit (Fligstein 1990).[12] Another case of mimetic isomorphism is university education. When field leaders in the Ivy League (Harvard, Yale)
and "public Ivies" (University of Chicago, University of California at Berkeley) adopt
such programs as seminars and "core curriculum" or a research focus for faculty,
others follow the prestigious leaders to avoid abnormality.[13] Even states can follow
mimetic isomorphism. To develop quickly and avoid the fate of neighboring China
(carved up by European powers), Japanese elites in the nineteenth century copied
civil service, post office, educational, and other systems from Britain, Germany, the
United States, and other Western powers (Westney 1987).

Fields and organizational structures: "conceptions of control"

While managers may think of profit, they also aim for stability, certainty, and legitimacy in the eyes of the state, investors, other managers, and even consumers. To
create stability, managers within a field adopt similar strategies and structures – but
these change over time. How so, if market competition and efficiency are not the

Table 5.1 Forms of organizational isomorphism

Isomorphism	Logic of spread of organizational form
Coercive	*Resource dependency*: organizations adopt forms imposed by those that control needed resources (money, legitimacy)
Normative	*Shared norms and values*: managers with similar educational and occupational biographies and experiences
Mimetic	*Shared problem*: managers adopt seemingly successful solutions, especially if linked through networks that can spread more concrete information on new solutions
Competitive	*Access to consumers*: organizations adopt forms and strategies that increase appeal to consumers (not unrelated to coercive isomorphism)

Note: cf. DiMaggio and Powell (1983)

only major forces at work? To explain different organizational change over time, Neil Fligstein (1990, 2001a) combines field dynamics (including isomorphisms) and culture. He claims that at any point in time, fields are governed by a "conception of control," a common set of principles to reduce competition and uncertainty. Since the late nineteenth century, America has had five conceptions of control over production, sales, and structure. Change in a conception of control stems from three sources. The first is a shock to organizational health, such as the Great Depression or increasing corporate debt in the late 1960s and early 1970s. The second source of change is "institutional entrepreneurs," elites with resources (e.g. money) who are outside fields and not subject to field control. Corporate raiders were one example of "entrepreneurs" (Hirsch 1986). The third source of change is the state. As we saw in Chapter 4, states have "policy logics" that they periodically enforce by passing new legislation that makes former conceptions of control problematic and forces field leaders to devise new rules and strategies for the field.

The initial conception of control (late nineteenth century) was creating cartels: groups of firms agreeing on prices, turf, and tactics to minimize competition. Managers who violated the norm of collective price agreements became victims of vicious price competition. However, political activists and some politicians perceived this not as tactics against uncertainty but as a corporate threat to consumers and communities; Congress passed the Sherman Antitrust Act to outlaw cartels. This forced firms to shift tactics. The next set of principles was the manufacturing conception of control. Managers focused on a limited line of goods – the classic example was Ford's Model T – and the mass market for those goods. Managers sought security through vertical integration: purchasing suppliers and even distributors (e.g. from extracting iron ore to making and distributing steel or cars) to control as much of their business as possible against poaching by other firms.[14] This conception of control brought stable production and income until the Great Depression, when relying on a limited line of goods could lead to ruin if that niche market dried up – as nearly happened to Ford. In contrast, General Motors did not fare as badly because GM managers accidentally devised a new conception of control. As noted earlier, GM provided the template for diversified output. GM's success in the face of the Depression legitimated the sales and marketing conception of control: it was a solution to a shared problem.

By the 1950s this conception of control dominated American industry. It allowed firms to avoid risk and competition: competitors would not only diversify products, they would also differentiate their products from each other so that consumers could buy both. As American workers' purchasing power increased, this was a viable business strategy. To make it work, firms had to merge or purchase other firms to diversify and expand output. However, mergers and acquisitions required capital, and corporate debt increased. By the late 1960s and early 1970s, with stagflation and high oil prices a serious problem, this debt became a nightmare. In response, boards of directors promoted managers with financial backgrounds and outlooks, and this led to the financial conception of control. Firms were no longer identified with particular output (e.g. steel or cars); they were identified with profit. This made it legitimate to expand beyond core businesses. US Steel, once the world's leading steel-maker, reorganized as holding company USX, with US Steel now a subsidiary. USX diversified to increase its profits and market value, and its main purchase was Marathon Oil. National Steel became National Intergroup and set about acquiring insurance companies, eventually selling its steel businesses to employees or Japanese firms.

According to Fligstein (2001a: ch. 7), a new conception of control emerged in the 1980s: the shareholder conception of control (Table 5.2). By the 1980s corporations held assets (e.g. property and land) that gave them a market value higher than their formal share prices indicated. Corporate raiders bought firms' shares and sold off these assets for enormous profits. To fight raiders, managers improved share value by down-sizing (releasing employees and middle managers) and focusing on short-term profit to improve share value – keeping shareholders happy and proving that managers were doing their job (maximizing share value and shareholders' assets). Now corporations are not product or profit as much as assets; strategies involve maximizing short-term value of these assets for shareholders, not the firm *per se*.[15]

We must be careful, however, not to give too much power to fields and isomorphism. Meyer and Rowan (1977), co-founders of neoinstitutionalism, noted "decoupling," or what we normally call "going through the motions": organizations adopt strategies and structures but do not give them real importance in everyday organizational life and work. Changes are cosmetic. Back to British universities:

BOX 5.2   THE FATE OF WEIRTON STEEL

Weirton Steel is the center of the economy and identity to Weirton, West Virginia (my home town), located in the Ohio Valley (once the heartland of America's steel industry). Weirton Steel was once one of the country's most important producers of tin-plate and rolled steel, and it was one of the main constituents of National Steel. Weirton Steel was the town's largest employer. Good working relations between management and the union meant decent wages and labor peace, and the company and its employees prospered in the 1950s, 1960s, and 1970s. Employees enjoyed paid vacations, good medical insurance, and support for local infrastructure. Symbolically, the town's original high school (later junior high school) and until recently the high school football field were located in the shadow of the company's blast furnaces. In the late 1970s, Weirton Steel hit hard times. Higher prices for oil and competition from imports primarily from Japan hurt the company's profitability, and in the early 1980s National Steel considered expanding its business beyond the steel sector, now in trouble. National Steel managers considered spinning off Weirton Steel, and then they accepted the idea of employee ownership (ESOP). Following a massive PR campaign by the union and Weirton Steel managers, the employees bought out the company from the parent National Steel, but this did not improve its situation significantly. Employment continued to shrink and high school graduates could no longer count on a job at the mill – with the result that children left after graduation, increasing the average age of the town. After 2000 Weirton Steel faced the threat of bankruptcy. National Steel, meanwhile, sold off its other steel companies to Japanese steel corporations.

Table 5.2 Neil Fligstein's "conceptions of control"

Conception of control	Basic era	Basic logic at work
Manufacturing	1900–1930s	Firm identified with production of core set of goods. Reduce uncertainty by securing production; mergers with suppliers (secure supplies) creates vertical integration. Managers rise through production.
Sales and marketing	1930s–1960s	Firm identified with a broader set of a family of goods (e.g. household products). Reduce uncertainty by avoiding direct competition. Mergers with producers of similar lines of products helps avoid competition. Managers rise through sales and marketing.
Financial	1960s–1980s	Firm identified with profit, regardless of activity. Reduce uncertainty by investing in sure profits. Mergers with profitable companies available for purchase. Managers rise through finance.
Shareholder	Late 1980s–	Firm identified with share value. Reduce uncertainty by avoiding competition via diversification. Mergers with companies with valuable assets but low share value.

Source: Fligstein (1990)

bureaucratic procedures check educational practices and procedures, but in reality university lecturers fill out massive mounds of paperwork to paint the picture the state wants to see. They try to teach and write as they once had (although the RAE (c.f. p. 73) diluted research quality). The state may want new practices, but university lecturers go through the motions without implementing the entire substance of what the government wants. This is a form of resistance: appearing to comply, while really not doing what is demanded.[16] Thus it is unclear how much organizational change is real and how much is cosmetic – draining time and money, but not so important to how firms really work.

Class plus institutions: William Roy's synthesis

In his study of the rise of the modern corporation, Roy (1997) brings together insights from Weberian and neoinstitutionalist theory. From Weber he notes the importance of classes, not in the Marxist sense but as groups controlling resources (cf. Chapter 6); the corporation was created and enforced by a new financial class that controlled (but did not always own) investment capital. From Weberians Roy also acknowledges the importance of the state: its laws shaped corporate structure and endowed the category "corporation" with the same legal status and symbolic importance as physical individuals. Finally, Roy sees neoinstitutionalist isomorphism at work: once the state created the corporation and a new financial elite emerged, that elite used coercive isomorphism to force the spread of the corporate form, leading to the birth of various fields and conceptions of control.

Roy attacks Chandler's thesis by showing that the most capital-intensive industries were not the first to adopt the corporate form. Growth and productivity were not well correlated with adopting the corporate form. If efficiency gains do not explain the rise of the corporation, what does? Roy sees the real reason for the sudden explosion of the corporate form in historical contingencies of power, property, and institutions. Property provided rights of control over organizations and resources, backed by the state. Property emerged from relations of power between elites and states, which in turn reshaped power relations by creating a new class of financiers and institutionalizing new rules of organizational control. As we saw briefly in Chapter 4, local states and entrepreneurs worked together to construct canals and then railroads. Entrepreneurs by themselves could not raise sufficient capital to fund railroad construction, and leaders of states such as New York, New Jersey, Ohio, and Pennsylvania saw railroads as a stimulant to economic growth. However, critics attacked the state–business partnership as a possible source of corruption and tyranny, and painted state officials as incompetent in business. Events in the 1830s seemed to bear them out: Pennsylvania and Ohio financed railroad construction and found themselves in debt when the business cycle dipped downward, leaving the states unable to make enough money to repay railroad debts. News of corruption also surfaced. While Pennsylvania and Ohio backed out of state–business partnerships, events took a different turn in New Jersey, where state government did not invest public funds in canals or railroads. Instead, it granted charters to a select few companies, and critics lost to pro-business interests who saw strong business as good for tax revenues. In 1875 the New Jersey legislature passed new laws giving the corporation, a private organization, the legal status and rights equivalent to those of an individual. The corporation became an organization with property embodied in shares that could be owned by many different people. Because of the "full faith and credit" clause in the American constitution – what is legal in one state must be recognized as legal in others – the law bred the modern corporation.

This was the legal side of the story. There was also the interaction between class and institutional dynamics for the rise of the corporation (Roy 1997: ch. 5; also Chandler 1977). Before the Civil War and the expansion of the railroads, Wall Street was not particularly important. While risky, investment in shares of railroad companies could provide large profits for speculators out to buy shares and sell them quickly at a higher price in the hopes of huge profits in the railway boom. Money to finance railroad construction and to purchase shares flooded in from American elites and from Great Britain. This vast amount of capital investment entering the stock market propelled Wall Street to prominence, and with it brokers and financiers who managed that money. By the end of the nineteenth century, industrial finance no longer came from isolated wealthy families or partnerships; it came from Wall Street financiers. They preferred the corporate model, with its bureaucratic structure (better information on organizational performance) and freely traded shares allowing speculation. An entrepreneur who wanted financing needed the financiers' approval – and they demanded the corporate form. This was coercive isomorphism: financiers enforced the corporate form that they assumed to be normal and served their interests.

Cross-national variation: different organizational forms

I have focused primarily on the American case in this chapter, in part because the modern corporation was born in nineteenth-century America. The rise of the corporation coincided with the rise of American economic and political power. That rise was helped by cheap immigrant labor, the flood of investment from abroad and from profits generated at home, protectionist policies supporting American industry, a growing domestic market hungry for food and steel, and later by production of armaments for European and American armies in World War I. The incredible growth of the American economy served as a model for other countries to follow (mimetic isomorphism): success and capital investment spread the corporate form across the globe. Yet organizational strategies and structures are not entirely the same everywhere. We have run across some aspects of cross-national variation in Chapters 3 and 4: different development policies and different policy paradigms and state–society relations created variation in corporate structures across countries. Take British and German corporations (Chandler 1990). In the late nineteenth century, the German state saw advantages of the large American corporation, especially raising capital and achieving economies of scale. An industrial latecomer, the German state was active in economic development, including the concentration of capital in banks and industry (Gerschenkron 1962). The German state encouraged large, capital-intensive corporations, with investment in research and development as well as production (aided by the growth of the German educational system), and local German states (the *Lander*) participated in shareholding, much as American states had in the early nineteenth century. Through the twentieth century two types of firms predominated in the German economy: larger conglomerates with close relations to banks, and smaller firms with narrower production, often family owned. The market for shareholding is more restricted than in the United States, although relations with banks are closer and more long term, providing the investment that in the US comes from share or bond offerings on the stock market.

In contrast, British corporations began as family owned, reflecting Britain's status as the first industrial nation, with capitalism generated and nourished by capital from wealthy families or elite partnerships. These wealthy elites created "corporations" to limit their liability in the case of debts or business failure, but the fear of losing control over organizational wealth led these elites to constrain majority shareholding (and sometimes total shareholding) to their families and partners. This meant families retained authority and profits – but it also limited the amount of capital available to invest, restricting size and ability to expand. In contrast, American corporations invited outsiders to purchase shares, and German corporations could invite banks into long-term investment partnerships, increasing the capital available for investment in production and expansion of production and markets. According to Chandler, this greater capital availability gave American and German corporations an advantage over their British competitors and allowed American and German firms to catch up with and overtake British firms, and the British economy, in the global market by the twentieth century.

As we saw briefly in Chapter 4, East Asian countries, in contrast, had two contrasting organizational structures: large and concentrated (Japan and South Korea), or small and networked (Taiwan). The Japanese *keiretsu* and Korean *chaebol* are centralized, with different multidivisional companies united around a bank or financial organization and producing in different sectors. Capital and production are more concentrated here than in most Western economies; the landscape is (relatively) closer to oligopoly.[17] In Japan, the *keiretsu* (the post-World War II form of the *zaibatsu*) is a business group of different large companies, organized around a bank or financial institution, in which members own shares in each other (facilitating cooperation and coordination). The *zaibatsu* began as family empires in the late nineteenth century, after the Meiji Restoration brought a new elite to power and the state began investing heavily in industrialization and economic growth (for military reasons but also to avoid the fate of China – colonization by the West). The American occupational administration dismantled the *zaibatsu* after World War II, but afterwards many reformed around financial institutions rather than families. Some forms were horizontal working relations between large enterprises, while others were more hierarchical structures of smaller and larger firms, with the smaller firms sometimes involved in manufacturing industrial components and with relations between large and small firms. These relations are often based on subcontracting, with both sides interacting closely rather than at arm's length (as a market model assumes). This means that links between *keiretsu* members are not as strong as in the *chaebol*; member firms have more autonomy and relations are often more horizontal, but there is sufficient structure to facilitate coordination of production and investment. The Japanese state also encourages competition between *keiretsu*.

In the South Korean *chaebol*, large companies in different areas of production are structured around a central holding company or financial institution, with relations tighter and more hierarchical than in the *keiretsu*. These *chaebol* dominate Korea's economy: in the 1980s, fifty *chaebol* produced around 80 percent of South Korea's GDP (Hamilton and Biggart 1988: S59). The typical *chaebol* was born during the Japanese occupation or after World War II. As we saw in Chapter 3, a business elite gained from the Rhee regime's largesse; Park Chung Hee's military regime forced *chaebols* to produce national wealth. Close links with the state facilitated targeted investment and production, and the centralized structure helped *chaebol* coordinate investment and production for foreign markets. (See Figure 5.2 for a typical *keiretsu* and *chaebol* structure.) While the *chaebol* were heralded for leading Korea out of poverty into the ranks of the developed world, problems of corruption set in in the 1990s, revealing the dark side to tight hierarchy with limited transparency and external accountability (e.g. to differentiated shareholders).

In contrast to the landscapes in Japan and South Korea, most companies in Taiwan are small firms, and Taiwan's corporate landscape resembles scores of "small firm networks" (see Figure 5.1). The typical family firm does not have more than 300 employees or enormous assets (in the 1980s often no more than $20 million) (Hamilton and Biggart 1988: S60; Wade 1990: 67). Companies do not continue growing as production and profit improve. Rather, as the typical firm grows, it eventually splits into different but linked smaller firms instead of consolidating as a large structure. For example, a relative of the original firm's owner will take over the new firm. Thus, rather than large corporations or corporate empires as in the United States or Japan, Taiwan has many smaller firms networked together by dense formal and informal linkages of personal/family relations.

Alternative to the formal organization: "networked organization"

The corporation dominates global capitalism, yet historical dominance is fleeting. Are we seeing the end of the corporate form? Taiwan's economic success suggests alternative structures can also work. The bureaucratic corporation was not without criticism: bloated corporate bureaucracies were not adept at maneuvering with economic changes.[18] After economic (oil) shocks of the 1970s, corporations were burdened with large labor forces, debts, and myriad formal rules. The future seemed to be flexible production and "small firm networks" (Perrow 1993): small firms working together through formal contractual relations and informal personal networks, with support from local governments. If the market rewarded flexibility, managers and employees of smaller firms, more vulnerable to market competition but able to adapt more quickly, would be productive and survive.

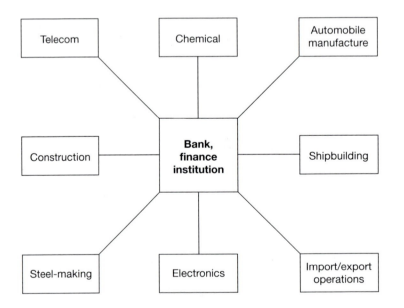

Figure 5.2   General structure of a generic *keiretsu* and *chaebol*

Note: In the *keiretsu*, interorganizational relations are looser and often based on reciprocal ownership. In the typical *chaebol*, relations from the center to components are more centralized.
Source: Author's compilation from various business and academic sources.

While this seems to make sense from economic theory – spot markets as natural organization – firms are still part of the picture. Small firm networks are not "markets," but neither are they the large, vertically integrated corporations of the past, such as US Steel or General Motors. Walter Powell (1990) challenged the assumption that economies were either large firms or spot markets; there was this intermediate form that was "neither market nor hierarchy," densely networked small firms more structured than pure markets but more decentralized and informal than bureaucratic organizations. Small firms working in biotechnology or information technology (e.g. in California's Silicon Valley or Massachusetts' Route 128) pooled capital and know-how to cooperate on innovation and production (Powell *et al.* 1996; Saxonian 1996). Success was possible because networks provided trust and cooperation. People who know and trust each other can come together more easily for joint work (if they share interests in that work), and the network relation eases working together: the actors already know each other and can negotiate strategies and disagreements informally. Networks avoid inefficiencies of red tape and formal rules that can hinder production, while overcoming distance and short-term vision of atomized market individuals. Further, networks help overcome information costs – a general feature of network relations. If one firm wants to set up a joint venture to produce a good (because it cannot produce it alone), there may be many potential partners. Which partner to choose? Those other firms run by strangers are unknowns: what are their managers' abilities and preferences, and what is the possibility of cheating? Information about potential partners who are in one's network chain – known directly or through other friends and acquaintances – is more accessible, reducing the cost of seeking out a partner. One need only work through one's network chain and begin negotiations – and the joint venture is underway.

Networked small firms do not always have the capital that larger corporations can muster, although the value generated through public share offerings of dot-coms and similar firms in the late 1990s suggests that small firms, in the right sector and the right time, can do so. In manufacturing, smaller firms have to work together to cover different areas of production usually needed to produce shoes or computers. Sometimes small firms are in one region, such as Italy's Po Valley, where local government provides financial incentives and helps create cooperation to reduce risk. Other times small firms are located in different countries. For example, the laptop I am working on was not constructed by one firm in one country; components were produced and the entire laptop assembled in different countries (e.g. Taiwan, Malaysia, Japan). The same is true of my clothes. This is a case of "commodity chains" involved in the manufacture of many goods: production and assembly of components in different areas become a finished good for the global market (Gereffi 1994).

Small firms generally involve more intense interaction that aids flexible work and innovation (if managers take advantage of this). They also usually do not have unionized labor, which gives many a "sweat shop" quality: squeezing workers for lower wages. As well, small firms do not require capital outlays that larger factories, with large labor forces and amounts of machinery, require – low start-up costs or start-up costs spread across many firms allow investors to take risks. While small firms linked through commodity chains are an important part of global production, however, we should not slight the large corporation. Small firms often work for larger corporations, such as IBM, General Motors and Ford, or The Gap. Networks allow entrepreneurs of newer products to pool know-how and production; but large-scale mass production requires larger, more stable structures. While networks are important, reports of the death of larger organizations are premature. It may be wise to recall an insight from American economic history: if the majority of Americans worked for small firms, larger factories and corporations bought from those small firms or produced the wealth for clients of those small firms.

Work and organizations

I end this chapter with that side of organizations most important to us: *work*. We think of organizations as hierarchies of structured authority, with bosses the main expression of organizational authority – but there is more to the picture than this. If capitalist firms exploited and accumulated, they could also give employees more than wages. Larger companies once shielded employees from markets through unions and internal labor markets that gave workers some stability and a basis for fair play. An *internal labor market* (ILM) is a formal gradation of work within an organization (e.g. "working up the ladder" from one job to the next). American ILMs and unions developed and emerged in the first decades of the twentieth century (cf. Jacoby 1985). In the nineteenth century, shop-floor foremen were managers' agents, directly observing and controlling employees. In the 1920s and 1930s foreman authority declined: unions and personnel managers criticized foremen for arbitrary use of authority, and in response to criticisms and to increase their control of labor, company owners and managers implemented ILMs and accepted the legality of unions. This turned large companies into microeconomies of sorts.

ILMs and unions provided some security for employees of larger industrial firms. An employee could complain to a union representative about unfair work practices, unions could mobilize members to agitate for better pay and working conditions, and ILMs gave employees a sense of stable progress in their careers. As well, larger American corporations provided benefits such as paid vacations, cheaper insurance (cheaper because firms or unions could obtain lower group rates), and pensions – benefits that in Europe are usually provided by the state.[19] Despite complaints of exploitation, employees in such large companies did not face the full rigors and uncertainties of a pure labor market. Managers also gained: ILMs and unions helped reduce labor conflict and turnover (employees leaving), enhancing stability of production, productivity, and profit. Not that all employees enjoyed these advantages. Employees at smaller firms, as well as women and non-whites in low-status jobs, either had no union or ILM support, or ended up in dead-end jobs within ILMs. This led to a "dual labor market": a labor market for better skilled (white male) workers, who ended up in advantageous jobs and positions within ILMs, and a market for less skilled, lower status labor (often done by women and non-whites) without such a security blanket (cf. Sabel 1982).

By the 1970s this began to change, as foreign competitors provided cheaper goods in part because of lower labor costs and mass production and mass markets became more unstable (Sabel 1982: ch. 5). ILMs and unions now meant relatively higher labor costs, a disadvantage in the increasingly global marketplace. In response, American companies began reducing benefits, and service companies and newer manufacturing firms tried to avoid having unions. Unions went into decline, and internal labor markets were changing to more flexible but insecure modes of employment – not just target-based work and rewards of post-Fordism, but also temporary work (temp workers) and outsourcing of jobs, rather than constant employment of people to deal with those tasks. Partly this is the politics and ideology of neoliberal economics: unions and ILMs interfere with the free market in labor and the logic of capital accumulation. Firms are judged more on the immediate share value than in the past, where sales, market position, and output were once equally important. This is not only the case in the United States. British companies are starting to follow suit. European countries are now engaged in debates over more flexible hiring and firing policies. In March 2006, the French prime minister announced a new law giving employers more flexibility in hiring and firing younger employees, thereby loosening up the labor market. Students responded with sporadic riots throughout March, and French president Jacques Chirac scrapped the law. Whether West Europe can maintain generous job protection for employees (in the face of higher unemployment) remains to be seen.

As smaller firms have become more important to the new service-based economy in the developed world, employees find themselves under more stress and uncertainty without ILMs or unions. By their very nature – production of goods or services through human effort as much as technology, importance of networks, relations dictated as much by face-to-face interactions as by formal rules – small firms offer flexibility and perhaps greater creativity. This may not be entirely realized everywhere; by the nature of their size, face-to-face interactions and authority (what Edwards (1979) calls "simple power") make personalities and competence of small firm managers more important than in larger firms, where employees tend to be shielded by multiple layers of leadership. Further, the "creative potential" of small firms depends on the sector they are in: work in small firms providing secretaries is likely to be less interesting and autonomous than work in small software firms.

Despite Powell's claim that small firms and networks are not a pure market, small firm production is closer to the market "norm": unions and ILMs mitigate competitive pressures. One increasing trend in employment demonstrates the new market logic in operation, undercutting the stability and structure of the past: the temp worker, prominent primarily in the service sector. "Kelly girls" were once the occasional low-level clerical staff (almost always women) hired on a temporary basis by firms for the needs of the moment: replacements for employees temporarily away from the job (e.g. illness, vacation) or additional labor in moments of increased business. In a drive to be "lean and mean," firms have reduced labor costs by relying more on temporary workers and reducing core staff. Temporary workers receive lower wages (usually by the hour rather than a set salary) and no benefits such as insurance. Temp workers increase labor flexibility: they can be hired on an as-needed basis.[20] If this is good for the profit margin, it is not so good for temp workers, who usually have no idea when work will be available and for how long. He or she has no effective recourse (such as a union) against an unjust boss or unjust labor practices (except for serious violations of labor law). Sick days and vacations mean lost wages. Every assignment means getting used to a new firm – people, practices, organizational culture – and the realization that personal relations made will likely end when the assignment ends. In short, the temp worker is truly labor as a machine, not as a human being with social as well as financial needs.[21]

I have simplified the structure of employment to highlight structural changes and the logics of the economy in flux: the reality is more complex, as some firms take advantage of temp workers while others do not and both types of employees work side-by-side (Parker 1994). Yet this stark simplification does show the emerging logic of the post-industrial economy in the United States and Europe. While flexible work may be one face to the new service-based, post-Fordist economy, insecurity and stress (even for salaried employees) is the other face, with employees becoming more replaceable and interchangeable, like machines. Firms increasingly have two types of employees – the permanent employee and the temp worker – reinforcing the split or dual labor market of long-term, skilled employees versus lesser skilled temp workers. (The latter can be a threat to the former, increasing stress of meeting targets.) How long this state of affairs will persist is difficult to say: one can be a pessimist and see this as the market's cold logic victorious, or one can see this as one cycle of economic history. At one time, industrial workers were non-unionized and treated as cheap inputs; but then unions and ILMs emerged. The service economy does not lend itself so easily to unionization: as we saw in Chapter 4, mass production requires a fairly stable labor force manufacturing at a stable pace, which gives managers an incentive to support labor stability. The service sector has less affinity with mass production and more with craft production (except for the occasional large firms, e.g. the accounting firm Price-Waterhouse). Yet history has a way of repeating itself; one can imagine a future in which temp and service employees, tired of insecurity, low wages, and no benefits, manage to organize into unions. One sees forces for both futures at work; we must wait and see which triumphs, when, and how.

Conclusion: organizations and the modern economy

While networked production and post-Fordism spread, the formal organization is alive and well, at least in the multinational corporation (MNC). Since the 1970s the number of MNCs has increased from 7000 to 40,000, and exchange across suppliers and producers within MNCs makes up nearly half of all global trade. A small number of MNCs dominate production of important sectors such as oil, aviation, and automobile manufacture (McMichael 2004: 100–1). Many small firms networked in commodity chains are ultimately dependent upon MNCs for investment and purchases. While MNCs have nominal relations with a homeland – place of its birth and corporate headquarters – MNCs also have loyalty to profit, market share, and share value. While

BOX 5.3 TEMP WORK

Yesterday you finished two weeks of computer work at a small local firm. Your job ended because the employee you replaced returned from sick leave, or because that particular job was done. You made a good impression, so there is hope of returning there on a more permanent basis, but you no longer hold your breath. You get anxious the following day, wondering if a phone call will come to say that your services are needed again at another small or medium-sized firm, hopefully close enough that you can get to it with public transportation or on foot if necessary. If the call does not come today, then it is another afternoon of cleaning, watching television, or working on your résumé and searching through the job ads.

Such is life for many temp workers. This "occupation" is less and less marginal to the American labor market – and this model may be spreading across the developed world. In the late 1990s, Manpower deployed approximately 1.5 million people to temporary jobs each day – a respectable number of "employees" for a single operation. In the 1990s, temp agencies increased their profits (Manpower made $7 billion in 1995) and began specializing in the kinds of temp workers they employed and deployed to client firms. Where temp agencies once provided low-skilled manual laborers (e.g. cleaners and janitors), they now provide more skilled workers, such as accountants or people with IT skills. By the mid-1990s temp workers made up almost 2 percent of the American labor force, and were growing. Temp agencies were also growing in Europe. While their employees accounted for only 1 percent of European labor, firms themselves hire temporary workers *directly*. In the Netherlands, temp workers were around 3 percent over the overall labor force, and growing. Businesses have many advantages in hiring more and more people from temp agencies on a temporary basis: fewer costs for benefits, training, and even hiring. Temp workers provide employment flexibility and can help firms get around laws: the fewer permanent employees, the smaller the firm, and the fewer state regulations apply. Temp workers can also help break unions.

This may not seem all that attractive to temp workers themselves, except for certain people who prefer short-term contracts and wider experience – for example, students during summer vacation. Not only are the material rewards small, but the psychological impact cannot be ignored: temp workers often feel they have secondary status or no real importance to the firm they work for at that moment. This has led to some hope of unionization. While temps are a disperse group – among the most fragmented employees – there is a precedent: American farmers. There is also the possibility of existing unions offering associate status as a way both to revitalize existing unions and to extend collective bargaining and benefits to this growing segment of the labor market.

Source: "Full-time Activity," *The Economist*, November 5, 1996;
Joseph H. Foegen, "'Temp' Workers: Ready for Unions?"
Business and Economic Review 46 (July–September 2000); Michael Sivy,
"Temp Workers Deliver Permanent Profits," *Money* 23 (June 1994).

they do not have the same power as states – MNCs do not yet have formal armies – they are still powerful organizations, and their financial clout influences state policies in the developing world. While workers in Detroit and Sheffield might be forgiven for thinking that corporations are in decline – where are the once plentiful corporate jobs in these cities? – those jobs are scattered across the globe, in places with cheaper, non-unionized labor and weaker, more dependent (or corrupt) governments.

Organizational strategies and structures are more than profit-oriented reactions to costs of production and opportunism. And while organizational resources create and nurture elites, organizations are (usually) not just toys of the elite. Instead, as we have seen, organizations are embedded in broader contexts: from logics and class relations of market capitalism to fields of power relations and cultural constructs among similar organizations. Organizations also embed: we are embedded directly or indirectly in organizations when we work for universities or large corporations, or when we work for small firms that are networked to other small firms or that supply larger corporations. While the intellectual legacies of Adam Smith, Marx, and Durkheim do provide important insights into organizations – the importance (but not domination) of efficiency, class, and culture – perhaps ultimately Weber was right: modernity is organizational rituals, routines, and meanings, that reproduce structures, power, and meanings of efficiency, class, and culture. When we imagine an economy that is not made up of organizations, then either we will have regressed to an era long gone, or moved on to a new stage in human social development – a real post-modern era.

6 Economies, inequality, and mobility

Economies and inequality are inevitably intertwined. Inequality results from the unequal distribution of access to status and material or symbolic resources, which are limited and not easy to generate. It takes money to make money – the poor do not have the means to escape poverty. Economic structures are not "innocent bystanders" in this story: structures and logics of economic organization, recruitment, reward, and reproduction give advantages to social groups with disproportionate resources and power, such as control of property and decision-making. Managers and owners receive higher wages than employees and a cut of profit; males and whites are more likely to have better or more powerful jobs and higher wages than women and non-whites. Structures of inequality, in turn, shape the economy. If white, middle-class males hold economic power, hiring white, middle-class males for elite positions will seem natural. This discrimination may be due to personal prejudices – men with low opinions of women, whites who believe non-whites are inferior. Discrimination may be "institutional," embedded in or an outcome of impersonal rules. Until recently, professional sports and sports reporting were male-dominated: physical activities were the domain of the physical sex, men. News executives believed few would take women's sports or women reporting on sports seriously, and they feared viewers would reject the combination of women and sports.

While inequality takes many forms, there are three essential axes or dimensions of inequality in the modern world: class, race/ethnicity, and gender. "Class" refers to shared structural position – a simple definition that hides conceptual complexity. "Race/ethnicity" refers to groups with perceived social identities: "African-American" ("black"), "Hispanic," "Jew," and so on. These are not biologically objective: genetic differences between "races" are incredibly small and insignificant, and in reality "race" or "ethnicity" matter because we assign meanings to these categories and assign the categories to people.[1] "Gender" is a set of inherent qualities and assumed behaviors that people of different sexes (biological traits) are assumed to have. Men and women are assumed to have different roles in the economy as well as society, given assumed traits and abilities. Some biological traits of the sexes do matter in the economy; for example, women physically bear children, and this cannot but affect how they work – although the way states and corporations react to this is socially constructed through our assumptions about normal roles and behavior in the economy.

Changes in inequality and the economy do not happen naturally, although economic theory tends to suggest there are rational market reasons as to why inequality exists. If a female manager brings greater returns to the firm than a male manager, then she should be hired, or else the firm is not acting to maximize its profit. If women are consistently turned down for men in the executive world, then, according to the theory, men must bring greater returns. One can extend this logic to race/ethnicity and class. Yet this explanation runs around the very point of stratification in the economy – economies have logics of class, race/ethnicity, and gender (e.g. a "gendered economy") that give status to certain actors (e.g. white males) and reward their practices, identities, and cultural capital. Change is more likely to come from active political mobilization that forces either a change in laws (e.g. anti-discrimination legislation or hiring quotas) or in corporate behavior (e.g. threats to boycott discriminatory firms). Yet this may not be enough: laws addressing inequality and discrimination (whether personal or institutional) might be seen as illegitimate state inference with a working economy. As we will see, this has made gender equality difficult: women must act like men to make it in the corporate world, which reproduces the status of males and their stereotypical behavior (e.g. macho image, being cold and tough).

One theoretical lens we will use to examine stratification in the economy involves *capital*: social resources which actors have and can exchange for rewards or status. Recall the various forms of capital: economic (money or its equivalent), social (networks and image), cultural (symbolic knowledge and knowledge of appropriate practices), and human (skills). Capital begets more capital: one can invest money in the stock market or a business and make profit; one can invest social capital (networks) and cultural capital (social skills) in training for and seeking a job, and receive economic capital (high wages at good firms) in exchange. Institutions structure access to and exchange of capital, and people control these institutions. Hence, to understand economies and inequality, we must move beyond the simpler picture of prejudiced white males running an economy to their advantage. As often as this may happen, it does not account for how widespread and constant inequality is, nor does it explain the reasons for successful (or unsuccessful) change in patterns of inequality.

Class and economy

I begin with the most classic form of inequality: class. The precise nature of "class" is not without dispute. Some sociologists take a light view of class, equating it with "occupation." While this has the advantage of making measurement easy – just ask a person about his or her job and relate this to pay and authority – it gives short shrift to mechanisms that create and reproduce stratification. To most Marxists, "class" refers to relations to the means of production. Classes are people with a similar relation to economic resources and power. That class which owns and controls economic property is the ruling class. Other classes are subordinate: to survive they depend on the ruling class for jobs. This sense of class is rather abstract

– it is not a direct relationship between individuals, but rather an indirect relation-ship through relations to capital. Individuals are under the spell of their class location; classes act *through* individuals. Consider an individual worker. He is not controlled by any single owner – he can switch jobs. However, all he has is his labor power, so he is powerless *vis-à-vis* the owner *class*. The bourgeoisie *as a class* owns the means of production (factories), while the proletariat *as a class* sells its labor power to the bourgeoisie in return for wages. These wages do not equal the full value of their labor, creating *exploitation*.

The Weberian concept of "class" differs somewhat. Rather than relations to the means of production (ownership), Weber defined class as position on and relations to the market. Industrial owners remain a class, as does the proletariat, but we can now think of financiers as a class – those who control the flow of capital invest-ment. We can also talk of different classes of producers – importers and exporters, agricultural and industrial elites – and different laborers (e.g. skilled versus unskilled industrial workers versus agricultural wage laborers). The strength of the Weberian conception is that it allows us to account for social groups that do not fit Marx's schema. Professionals such as doctors, lawyers, and enterprise managers have social status and high wages but they do not own any real means of production. To Weber, they share a similar position on the market: they create rewards by selling knowl-edge to consumers at a premium (managers sell knowledge/labor to owners; doctors sell medical knowledge/labor to patients).[2] This helps us to understand the rise and fall of classes.

While the Marxist and Weberian conceptualizations of "class" have many similari-ties, there are also interesting differences. The first is that for Marx, economic structures create classes: institutions of resource control (i.e. property) create groups that share structural locations, sources of power and profit, and interests. In the Weberian schema, classes create economic structures: economic institutions provide opportunity, but classes ultimately are political creatures that gain social closure over some resource. Classes create themselves. Another difference concerns the centrality of exploitation or closure (Tilly 1998). In the Marxist logic, classes are about exploitation: either the exploiters (who control the means of production) or the exploited (whose labor power maintains the economy). In the Weberian logic, exploitation is not necessarily absent, but neither is it necessary to class. Professionals capture the returns to credentials and knowledge; while they exchange this knowledge for rents (e.g. fees in the marketplace), they are not necessarily making their profit from exploitation. Doctors may have secretaries whom they exploit, but the secretaries do not produce the good or service – the doctors do. Professionals, in a sense, exploit themselves, but thanks to social closure they gain from this self-exploitation. Thus one way of differentiating between the two that I will use to structure the discussion on economy and class is the following: in Marx, economies shape classes, whereas for Weber, classes shape economies. I use the examples of class boundaries and mobility (or its difficulty) to show how economies shape classes, and of the rise of professions to show how classes create themselves and shape economies.

Economies shape classes

Economic structures, institutions, and policies give resource access and opportunities to restricted groups. This need not be static: economic change can reshape the class landscape and make class boundaries less rigid, more open to entrance and exit. However, at the extremes – the elite and the underclass – boundaries may be less permeable. The elite are an elite because they are few and control powerful resources (property, massive amounts of capital); they want to keep boundaries tight. The underclass by definition have few resources; until modern societies are truly meritocratic, their advancement out of poverty faces difficulties, for they start with little cultural, social, or economic capital to begin with. Research on class boundaries and mobility is rich in quantitative and qualitative data and methods. I will not address the methods and data, for that discussion would be too technical and is best left for other studies (or the original studies themselves).

Class mobility

In the twentieth century, sociologists tried to refine categories of class or class-like social stratification. A popular approach took the basic Weberian idea of class and Durkheim's logic of social complexity and the division of labor. Scholars in this tradition equated "class" with "occupation," and they proposed hierarchies based on the income and education or income and status linked to a job. While this slighted the complex mechanisms of class formation and power, it did facilitate research on mobility and showed that modern capitalist societies were not as mobile as popularly believed. Grouping occupations by similar tasks, education, and rewards – professionals, skilled laborers, unskilled manual laborers, agricultural laborers, and so on – sociologists explored mobility between parents and children (usually fathers and sons).[3] Mobility studies would show whether class boundaries were rigid or permeable. As often happens, the results were mixed and debates not entirely resolved, although a few insights were obtained.

The first major statement of social mobility came from Seymour Martin Lipset and Hans Zetterberg (1959), who claimed that mobility patterns should be the same in all industrial countries. Industrialism has a logic of rationalization and functional needs (e.g. merit): farming becomes mechanized, factories develop requiring skilled blue-collar and white-collar labor, and the logic of an industrial economy demands that education and skills, not family status and connections, dominate mobility. This thesis was a little too optimistic; class and family background still mattered (Grusky 1983), but there was mobility. Blau and Duncan (1967) discovered that, in most cases, American sons' jobs were at the same level or one level higher (or sometimes lower) than their fathers'. The great American dream of rags to riches remained a dream, but modest upward movement was possible. Was this true for other industrialized countries, or was the United States exceptional? Lipset and Zetterberg claimed it was not, yet research showed different *observed* patterns of mobility: proportions of sons who were better off than their fathers varied across developed countries.[4]

Featherman, Jones, and Hauser (1975) proposed a revision to Lipset and Zetterberg (later known as the "FJH hypothesis") that explained differences but also showed similarities. Industrial countries still had similar mobility patterns, but there were differences *elsewhere* in social structure that accounted for difference. A modern industrial economy was still much the same everywhere. Featherman *et al.* and other scholars in the 1980s (e.g. Grusky and Hauser 1984; Hauser and Grusky 1988) differentiated between two components of mobility. Industrial countries had fairly similar patterns of *circulation mobility* (or *exchange mobility*) because they shared the same basic economic structure. While this over-simplifies the process of "industrialization," it still contains an important truth. As a country industrializes, more jobs are created in industry, while mechanization of agriculture means fewer jobs in farming – children were pulled from the farm to the factory. Sons of skilled laborers found factory jobs (perhaps more skilled than their fathers') or expanding white-collar positions as managers or in the service sector as industrial economies expanded in the 1950s and 1960s. (The expanding welfare state also provided white-collar work for the sons of working class men, especially in Europe.) This accounted for the same *core* mobility. Differences in the overall observed pattern came from different structural and cultural starting points. A country whose population had a greater percentage of peasants at the start of industrialization would have different overall numbers of farmers' sons moving into factory jobs, for example.

Debates continued after the initial FJH hypothesis. Grusky and Hauser (1984) used a larger data set and complex statistical methods to test FJH. They discovered that class "inheritance" – a son in the same class as his father – was strongest for farming and white-collar positions. (This does not mean that farmers' sons always stayed on the farm; rather, sons of bankers, managers, and steel workers were not likely to become farmers.) The blue-collar stratum is the most permeable. Farmers' sons move into blue-collar jobs with some ease, but blue-collar sons may remain blue-collar or dragged into white-collar jobs by economic expansion (e.g. in management or the service economy) or education. Grusky and Hauser (1984) also claimed that the FJH hypothesis worked for lesser developed countries and that policies were more important than assumed.[5] Not that FJH and its followers were without criticism. Using the same data but different means to measure mobility, Slomczynski and Krauze (1987) claimed to find even greater variation and that a country's policies and institutions mattered more than FJH allowed. In Europe, Richard Erikson and colleagues (Erikson *et al.* 1979, 1982, 1983; Erikson and Goldthorpe 1987) discovered variations in mobility across European countries: whether one's class origins mattered depended on educational and economic policies. Mobility was more fluid in Sweden than in France and England, for example. In wider studies of European countries, Erikson and Goldthorpe (1987) discovered that even this core of circulation mobility showed variation, despite substantial similarities. Again, different policies mattered (e.g. more meritocratic education in Sweden).

It may seem odd that there are as yet no definitive answers about mobility patterns and the rigidity or permeability of class boundaries. Can't we just count how many sons have the same or different jobs as their fathers? No – this misses the deeper complexities of mobility. A growing economy will create mobility – if there are more new white-collar jobs than white-collar sons, the new hires must come from somewhere – but this hides just how class operates (which circulation mobility is supposed to address). Getting at circulation mobility is a difficult task involving probabilities (e.g. advanced loglinear models) and making sure that the data from different countries are comparable (no easy task!). Still, this research has given us insights into economies, class, and mobility. Yet if structural changes in the economy pushed and pulled children away from their parents' classes, something still kept many in place – especially among the poor (not addressed in these statistical studies because they were not counted in the data sets). To address this we must turn to mechanisms of *reproduction* rather than mobility, for which ethnography and qualitative methods have provided powerful insights and brought Marx and Weber back into the picture.

Obstacles to mobility: cultural capital, education, and reproduction

If economies are based on efficiency and competition, merit should be central to hiring and rewarding. Firms want the best managers and employees regardless of race, gender, or class. Yet why does class reproduction persist – why are managers more likely to come from middle- or upper-middle-class backgrounds? There are several answers. One is that lower classes are, by the whim of nature, less suited to the tasks and rewards of higher-status professions. This is "Social Darwinism," a nineteenth-century ideology defending elite privilege (Bendix 1974) that does not withstand scrutiny, even if one still hears its echoes in discourse. A second answer is that class background shapes available economic, social, and cultural capital. Institutions of recruitment (education and work) have a class-biased logic: the value of class capital is not equal. While the best-known and respected work on inequality and capital is that of the late Pierre Bourdieu, he was not the first to note the class bias to education and recruitment.

Let us focus on education: supposedly, it trains students equally (more or less) and rewards the brightest and hardest working, helping them to get the best jobs. This is not entirely inaccurate – but it is not the full picture. Critics of capitalist society claim that just as capitalist logics permeate states, religion, or the police, they also pervade education and functionally reproduce class differences (Bowles and Gintis 1976). Schools and universities have bourgeois logics that reward bourgeois practices and punish working-class identities and practices (Willis 1977). That bourgeois logic is bureaucratic and non-manual: desks, homework and written evaluations involving mental tasks, a movement from concrete objects to abstract concepts. White-collar children respond favorably to this because it fits with their class environment. From their white-collar families, neighborhoods, and social worlds, they have a more developed vocabulary for expressing abstract thoughts (Bernstein 1975). Much as white-collar children might complain about school, they live with it because it is familiar. For blue-collar children, the white-collar world of education is unfamiliar and even threatening. Physical work and masculinity are devalued: "shop" classes are lower status, sometimes in separate locations. Coarser language, more natural and less threatening in the working-class world, is punished. These children have three possible paths. They can adapt sufficiently to survive and pass, perhaps with advancement over their parents' status (escaping the working class). They can fail to adapt and not do well in school; white-collar jobs with any status are now harder to obtain. They can also rebel. Willis' (1977) "Lads" did this: talking back to teachers, making fun of better students, and skipping school were not "deviance" but class resistance. They succeeded in resisting, but then they were rejected by the educational system, ending up with too few skills to leave the working class.[6]

This Marxist critique of education and merit has insights but also oversights. The biggest problem is *how* class operates. Just why do working-class children feel out of place in school? Not all working-class children do badly; there is more to one's success in school than simple class background. *How* class matters depends on how it bequeaths social and cultural capital. A blue-collar child with white-collar friends, or a blue-collar child who is observant and cunning enough to understand how education operates (even if she does not use sociological jargon), can play the system and succeed. Here Pierre Bourdieu and his followers have added to our insights. Children with highbrow social and cultural capital achieve better grades and access to better schools and universities, get more out of their education, and get better jobs (DiMaggio 1982; DiMaggio and Mohr 1985). The white-collar logic of education fits with their *habitus* (one's strategies, interpretations, and knowledge), and they are better able to form strategies for survival and advancement. White-collar children have cultural capital that fits better with the logic of white-collar work. When the time comes for hiring, highbrow social and cultural capital – diplomas from well-respected universities, good grades in prestigious disciplines, knowledge about politics, the arts, and good wine, letters of recommendation or informal recommendations from respected advisers or parents' friends – can gain one access to jobs in prestigious firms.[7] Class, status, and achievement in education and work are related through concrete mechanisms involving how one exchanges one's available capital for educational and occupational success.

Elite schools provide their students not only with technical knowledge but also cultural capital – this gives them access to elite positions and jobs. This "class function" of schools and cultural capital is more apparent in Europe. In France, pre-university education at elite *taupe* schools rewards knowledge of subject material, but teachers are even more rewarding of grace under pressure. Homework assignments are almost physically impossible, involving a staggering amount of reading. Teachers will ask students questions in oral discussions or written exams, and they expect answers that are correct – but that also sparkle with wit and the appropriate turn of phrase (Bourdieu 1996: Part II, ch. 1). Grace is more important than detail. Only clerks to the elite to need know detail – their job is to brief their superiors. Future leaders – the best students of the *taupe*, who then (with good grades) go on to the elite French universities (*grandes écoles*) – must be able to field a question which is not their specialty and provide graceful, witty responses: form over substance. This is the stuff of images and politics. Oxford and Cambridge are similar, and the "Oxbridge" model continues to be important in Britain: courses are individual meetings with professors and grades are based on final examinations, where students are expected not only to regurgitate material but to do so in a way that shows grace and wit. Even elite American universities have a hint of this. Consider the "core curriculum" at Harvard University, which requires that students have a well-rounded education. Why should a future chemist or lawyer learn the intricate history and technical detail of Beethoven's symphonies? Certainly this rounds a person out – but it also provides cultural capital that may be exchanged in the future for status.

One can see class and cultural capital at the other end of the class spectrum. Jay MacLeod (1995) studied two groups of boys in an inner-city slum. The "Hallway Hangers" were white, from dysfunctional families that lived for many years in low-income housing projects. The "Brothers" were black, had not lived long in the projects, and had father figures. Both groups went to a local underfunded school and faced the "achievement ideology": the American creed that everyone is res-ponsible for his/her own fate, and that failure is one's fault alone. The Hangers, like Willis' Lads, were disrespectful of school and authority. They saw through the façade of the school to its underlying logic of class violence: their parents had not done well, and so to respect school and work hard was a rejection of their mothers. While they suspected deeper forces were at work keeping them down, they did not have in their *habitus* the theoretical ability to see through the achievement ideology; and in any case, who would listen to lower class delinquents who deal drugs, put no effort into school, had run-ins with the law, and were generally disrespectful to others? The Brothers had more hope in their futures: they felt that their parents had failed in life because of past discrimination that, while not absent, was weaker in America thanks to civil rights. The Brothers were more disciplined, put more time into their studies, and respected others.

In the end, neither the Hangers nor the Brothers went far in life. Here MacLeod's two groups provide a fascinating contrast. The Hangers were rebels, the Brothers respectful of education and social mores; the Hangers were white, the Brothers black; the Hangers had no ambitions in school, while the Brothers did (although both groups aspired to some achievement). Both groups had difficulties obtaining jobs. Both failed in their quests for mobility: here we must look for a similarity, which is *class and its cultural capital*. They did not have the networks to get decent first-time work (except in local pizza parlors). Employers did not want to hire kids from the projects because of the reputation (fair or not) for poor work and unlawful behavior.[8] In the local school, teachers tracked the Hangers to vocational-technical jobs, but the students put little effort into them. The school was more rewarding of the Brothers, but not much more: underfunded and undermanned, teachers could do little more than hold the line and try to provide basic foundations in reading and writing. The police were already wary of blacks (thus of the Brothers), and the Hangers' behavior did not enamor them to the men in blue. In short, economic and social structures reproduce inequality through cultural capital. If one has too little cultural, social, and economic capital to succeed in school, one's chances of mobility are limited. If one's school does not provide adequate capital, its students face obstacles to mobility. It takes capital to make capital.

Elites and institutions: interlocking directorates

In Chapter 5, we saw briefly how the rise of the corporation created a new class of financiers. This is not the only case of economic institutions creating or facili-tating class structure and power. Sociologists such as G. William Domhoff and Michael Mizruchi had studied "interlocking directorates," networks of corporate executives who sit on multiple, overlapping boards of directors. Control of the corporate form is through shareholding and boards of directors (who own shares outright or represent shareholders). However, these elites are not restricted to sitting on one or two boards of directors: they can sit on many. Further, there is no law against the same people sitting together on more than one board. Together, these are the two defining features of interlocking directorates. In his review of research on this phenomenon, Mizruchi (1996) notes that interlocks run throughout the American economy (but also exist in other capitalist economies), but there is still much we do not know about them. Interlocks provide the possibility for elite collusion – this structure brings elites into contact with each other, and provides the possibility for collective action such as reducing price competition. However, it is uncertain that interlocks lead to collusion all that often, nor is it clear that elites create interlocks *in order to collude*: interlocks are more likely to occur randomly or for other reasons that are less harmful to market competition. For example, companies may invite representatives of banks to sit on boards. Because the number of major banks is limited, this is likely to lead to one person sitting on several boards. One possible reason for this is that companies feel they can get easier credit with such people sitting on their boards. As well, several companies may invite a small number of well-known, respected entrepreneurs or corporate managers to bring legitimacy (cf. isomorphism in Chapter 5) and signal to investors that a firm involves people of unique competence who would not associate with illegitimate firms.

If these are disparate reasons for interlocks, they have one important side effect: enhancing elite connectivity and the ability to act (Zeitlin 1974; Domhoff 1998). Interlocks aid the spread of information and ability to coordinate strategies – whether corporate strategies, investment, or tactics *vis-à-vis* the state (e.g. welfare or taxes). Note that this is not the same as collusion against market competition, although interlocks may help spread new strategies (isomorphism) to avoid destructive price wars. In short, institutions of capitalism and corporate ownership shape class structures: through the interlocks they facilitate, capitalist institutions of boards and shareholding bring elites into closer proximity with each other, enhancing class identity and the potential for elites to mobilize their resources.

Classes shape economies: the case of American doctors

While economic institutions and structures create opportunities from which classes emerge, it is not always inevitable that classes *will* emerge. Sometimes class actors must take the initiative to capture a resource and create rewards: classes shape economies. If a "class" gains enough sense of its collective identity and interests, and if it can organize control over a particular resource (a near-monopoly position), it can set its own rewards and even shape the marketplace to its advantage. A clear example is the history of the American medical profession (Starr 1982). American doctors are the most respected and rewarded profession, with high status, authority, rewards, and autonomy. The structural-functional (and economics) explanation is that jobs more important to society (e.g. doctors) must have better pay to attract the hardest working, most competent people (Davis and Moore 1945). This is wrong.

First, the comparative record: consider two developed countries, the US and the (former) USSR. Doctors in the latter had far less wealth and status in their own society than their American counterparts. Second, the historical record shows that doctors *created* their own authority and rewards by organizing control over medical knowledge and then shaping access to the market of medical care – a history in which they beat the state, hospitals, insurers, and trade unions. American doctors in the early nineteenth century struggled to make ends meet; theirs was not a high-paying, high-status profession. Doctors trained in European universities were jealous of their European counterparts who made a living as personal physicians to the aristocratic elite. These "trained doctors" (as I will call them) competed with "lay doctors" who had "hands-on" training with older lay doctors – learning by doing.[9] This competition was the heart of the problem. Were there fewer doctors for many patients, competition would be less, cooperation would be easier, and wages would be higher.

One way to reshape the medical labor market was to limit the number of people allowed to practice medicine. In the early nineteenth century trained doctors pushed for licensing laws, with licenses requiring a specialized education. Medical schools began to emerge: not the grand institutions of today, but money-making vocational schools for basic training. Medical education was a business, and the new medical degree was, in practice, not really a sign of rigorous, quality training. Further, states wanted money from licenses – so what if doctors were no good? Medical schools were loath to enforce licensing – this might put them out of business. The idea that a small group of doctors should monopolize knowledge also ran afoul of democratic culture. Just as all shared political authority in the fledging American republic, they also believed that all could share knowledge (e.g. learning and practicing medicine by reading books) (Starr 1982: Book 1, ch. 1).

Despite this failure, doctors still had one tool: the patient–client relationship. To survive, doctors tried to get patients and keep them by cultivating a personal rela-tionship. Doctors made house calls without complaint; they stressed that in a one-to-one relationship the doctor knew the patient's history, helping diagnosis. This gave patients an advantage – doctors needed them. After the 1870s, the context shifted. The primary force behind this change, as part of general modernization and industrialization in America, was the coming of *science* as a totem of truth and authority: it unlocked the secrets of the universe and transformed the world. Along with this, universities changed, adopting the German format of integrating research and teaching. Medical schools at elite universities (Harvard, Johns Hopkins) adapted the new form, and in the field of universities this new format spread. Doctors with formal education at research-based universities gained status that other doctors did not have. This made an MD from a university with rigorous research credentials a powerful tool of authority *vis-à-vis* patients. They would use this tool in combat with organizations, but first doctors had to organize – which happened with the emer-gence of the American Medical Association (AMA). The AMA promised doctors corporate identity and a means to promote interests. Yet the AMA needed to orga-nize its members, which it did through malpractice insurance. This insurance was expensive, but the AMA got cheaper group rates for members. It offered a carrot and stick: join the AMA and follow its guidelines, and receive affordable malpractice insurance. Resist, and lose (Starr 1982: Book 1, ch. 3).

Now doctors could take on those who would capture them. Companies and unions wanted to run medical care because this gave them leverage *vis-à-vis* workers: owners or unions could control doctors and offer cheap medicine in return for worker loyalty (to the firm or to the union). Insurance companies and hospitals were businesses, and they wanted to control doctors to help control costs and survive in competition. After World War II, the American federal government wanted to introduce a state-sponsored system of cheap medical care for everyone, as in Europe. Doctors successfully resisted them all and set their work and rates independently. How? Once the AMA took a united stand to keep doctors independent, AMA doctors could use their patient–client relationship. Hospitals and insurance companies made money from patients, but doctors referred them to hospitals and insurance companies in the first place – and patients trusted their doctors more. The same was true with the government's attempt to create a national health care plan: doctors mobilized a lobby campaign targeting patients and Congress. Who did patients trust: a cold bureaucratic state (or insurance company or trade union), or the doctor who has personally tended to one's health for years?[10]

This extended discussion of Starr's detailed study makes an important point: classes create themselves. British historian E.P. Thompson noted that the English working class "was present at its own creation" (Thompson 1963: 9), emerging not only from structural relations (property and industry) but also from workers' own class identities. Doctors or workers might see themselves as men, blacks or whites, or as particular kinds of doctors or workers (fragmenting "class"). Instead, political and organizational histories create class identities and power. With no AMA, American doctors might have been captured by the state, as happened in Britain or socialist countries, or by companies, as happened to engineers.[11]

The challenge of class and economic sociology

What is happening to classes in post-industrial societies? The answer depends on how one defines "class." In the Marxist sense, deindustrialization might reduce the proletariat – but what of the service class? In a Weberian logic, "class" cannot disappear unless structured power disappears or material and symbolic resources become infinite. Post-industrial societies will have "classes" too: different groups will continue to compete for status and authority in the marketplace. Those classes may be fragmented, but they are there – if they gain a sense of collective self, they can become status groups as well. Temp workers share a particular (powerless) market position – why not speak of them as a class? One challenge of economic sociology is to expand class analyses as economic structures shift, to discern new classes and their potential bases of power or issues of protest, and to understand the relation between classes and the politics of economic change.

Another important challenge to economic sociologists is to come to grips with the slippery term "class" and decide on a common conceptualization. Debates over the meaning of "class" are not what they were in the 1970s, but that debate was never truly resolved. It is probably clear that I prefer the Weberian definition: it adds a political dimension, expands the power of analysis (i.e. beyond property-owning or industrial classes), and permits the study of how classes can shape economies. This Weberian idea of "class" is not quite the same as "occupation," especially when Weber's concept of status group is added to the mix. "Occupation" is a legal or academic category, and while such categories can influence people's identities, they are not the only factor involved: we must account for organizations and general economic structures, as well as politics. If we approach class from a Weberian perspective, we can also begin to better understand and merge class analyses with our next dimension of economic inequality: race and ethnicity.

Race, ethnicity, and economy

For reasons of ideology, status competition, exploitation, and economic and political power, some groups have labeled others as a particular race or ethnicity that is different from the norm and subject to lower status and control. Even as these beliefs have weakened, different "racial" and "ethnic" groups have different positions in the social and economic hierarchy.[12] Past histories of discrimination (e.g. against Irish or African-Americans) mean some groups have fewer resources – lower wages or cultural capital, dwellings in bad neighborhoods with worse schools – and face obstacles to mobility in the marketplace. Not that this is permanent: some groups made progress, such as descendants of Irish immigrants to the United States or of Indian immigrants to Great Britain. The story of race and ethnicity in the economy is not straightforward, and logics of race/ethnic discrimination and of class reproduction interact.

Race and ethnicity in the American economy

Race and ethnicity in the American economy and inequality stem directly from histories of migration and power relations. For race, the history of slavery – too complex for this book – is crucial. While white Europeans were brought over as indentured servants, a contractual labor relation of service in return for payment of debts, the majority of forced labor "migrants" (against their will) were "black," of African descent. The slave-trade went to more than the American colonies (e.g. to Brazil and Caribbean islands), but in the American South slave labor became a mainstay of tobacco and cotton. Even the end of slavery and emancipation of blacks did not lead to much improvement. In the South, Jim Crow laws kept blacks in the position of second-class citizens, often unable to vote (or terrorized into voting for the white elite) and with too few opportunities to escape low-paying sharecropping (where landowners leased land to agricultural laborers at onerous rents). When mechanization of agriculture drove blacks north and northern industrialists brought in blacks as non-unionized labor against white-dominated unions, the situation was not always better. African-Americans ended up in locales with weaker economies or in low-skilled manual labor, for example, janitorial services. However, African-American "enclaves" in the north were more hospitable to political mobilization that became one root of civil rights (Piven and Cloward 1979). Civil rights legislation against racial discrimination paid off: by the 1960s and 1970s, occupational and wage inequality were dropping, and younger African-Americans' life chances on average were closing in on those of average young white Americans, even in the South (Fossett *et al.* 1986). However, in the 1980s and 1990s these gains began to stagnate or even reverse: the income gap between whites and blacks actually grew marginally worse.

Like racism, ethnocentricity – ethnic discrimination based on beliefs that one's ethnic group is superior to others and ethnicity-based social closure – exists as well, although here immigration rather than slavery plays a role, one that does not create uniform disadvantage, for some ethnic groups have done better than others. The white English, Protestant elite played on status differences – primarily religion (Protestantism of the dominant English and Catholicism of the subdued Irish) and cultural capital – to portray immigrant Irish as lesser people available for cheap labor but little more, which they institutionalized in the existing educational system (Collins 1975). Immigrant Chinese and Jews faced restrictions on education and employment – such as infamous university quotas against Jews – that restricted the former to low-skilled, low-paying manual labor (including railroad construction) and the latter to wholesale and retail exchange in particular locations (such as New York City). These restrictions were repealed only around World War II. As immigration and labor laws were liberalized (e.g. more liberal immigration after 1965), more migrants entered the United States. Discrimination did not end – while Irish-Americans had improved their standing, thanks in part to gaining control over political machines and occupations (e.g. politics and the police in Boston), Latinos, especially Mexicans, faced the stereotype of unskilled welfare cheats. However, more important to ethnic inequality was capital and structural integration with the broader (white) population. This led to ethnic communities and enclaves: structural divisions, where particular ethnic groups live, work, and do business together, not fully integrated with the surrounding social and economic context. This is not always a bad thing – ethnic communities can create opportunities to make up for disadvantages of discrimination of low levels of cultural and social capital.

The impact of discrimination and racial-ethnic politics is clear in the data. African-Americans suffer worse rates of single-parent families, infant mortality, drug use, arrest and incarceration, life expectancy, and health than white Americans. The average wage is approximately three-quarters that of whites' wages; median income for African-American families in the 1990s was approximately 60 percent that of whites'. If we add ethnicity, the picture is more complex. Some ethnic groups migrated to the United States at the right time (post-civil rights) and with the right capital to help them in the labor market. Those groups that, as a whole, migrated to the United States with low cultural, social, and human capital had less to offer to the economy – truly Marx's proletariat with only physical labor to offer. While Mexican migrants usually did not have sufficient educational credentials or much money, Cuban migrants to the US following Castro's take-over came with money and education, and South Korean migrants after 1965 often had higher education

and even managerial experience (Aldrich and Waldinger 1990). These differing histories of race and ethnicity create the following picture of inequality: I list median family
income and percentage of that social group in poverty for the year 1989 (Waters
and Eschbach 1995: 423). The average white family income was $37,630, and 10
percent of white families lived in poverty. The numbers for blacks were $22,430,
and 29 percent in poverty; for Mexican families, $24,119, and 26.3 percent; for
Cuban families, $32,417 and 14.6 percent. Chinese, Korean, and Japanese families
were better off: their median family income and percentage of families in poverty
were $41,316/14 percent, $33,909/13.7 percent, and $51,550/7 percent, respectively.
Worse-off were Native Americans ($21,750/30.9 percent) and Cambodians ($18,126/
42.6 percent).

Despite gains made in the 1960s and 1970s, economic trends in the 1980s began
to harm inequality for non-whites, in no small part due to deindustrialization in the
North, the rise of non-unionized labor in the South, and the new information-based,
high-skilled economy of the 1990s. Employment inequality between blacks and
whites recently is greater in the North than in the South and West. Why? The
economy in the West and South has been more vibrant than in the North – meaning
there are more jobs available. Further, firms in the South and West are smaller and
less likely to be unionized. Larger firms have more capital and can pay higher wages
that attract whites, and so managers have less need to employ lower paid non-
whites. Unions restrict managers' hiring authority, and so managers are more likely
to use formal educational credentials for hiring – favoring whites (Cohn and Fossett
1995). African-Americans with unionized jobs were not much better off with northern
deindustrialization in the 1980s and 1990s. Latinos had not worked as much in unionized, industrial labor; they took non-unionized, lower wage jobs in the growing South.
In the new economy of the 1980s and 1990s, lesser educated blacks and Latinos
did not fare so well, while Asian immigrants had human capital that fit with the
demands for higher skills (e.g. in information technology). (Keep in mind that "Latino"
is a wide group: e.g. Cubans, Puerto Ricans, Mexicans.) Overall structural changes
such as deindustrialization hurt the black–white employment gap; migration exacerbated the employment and wage gap between whites and Latinos (McCall 2001).

What these data make clear is that the economy is run by whites, for the benefit
of whites: the American economy has a racial and ethnic component. Certainly prejudice has been and remains present, but this is only part of the story. As a 1992
report by the Federal Reserve Bank of Boston noted, African-Americans (and Latinos)
have greater difficulty obtaining mortgages: they are more likely to be rejected, even
taking into account class factors such as lower average income. (Part of this stems
from related factors, such as the inability of African-Americans in worse-off neighborhoods to get housing insurance required for mortgages.) Due to slavery and
successors in Jim Crow laws, generations of African-Americans for the most part
have had little cultural and human capital for mobility up the occupational ladder
into better neighborhoods with better schools for their children. Some ethnic groups
have been able to realize the "American dream" that may have attracted them to
the United States in the first place, while others continue to struggle.

BOX 6.1 A RACIALIZED ECONOMY

In the 1980s, a popular television comedy starred Bill Cosby as a well-off gynecologist (Clifford Huxtable) with a happy, healthy, upper-middle-class family. On the one hand, this suggested that African-Americans had "made it," both economically and symbolically. There were enough cases of successful black professionals, and enough of a thaw in race stereotypes and relations, that a successful black professional could be the basis for a successful sitcom. At the same time, this image hid a reality of many African-Americans still stuck in the lower status jobs, in no small part due to their class background and limited social and cultural capital. In this situation, hard work and dedication to studies might not be enough to guarantee more than modest mobility. The unemployment rate for blacks is higher than for whites: depending on the data source, perhaps as high as 10 percent overall and up to 30 percent unemployment for African-American youth (Rogers III 2004). Starting salaries are lower for African-American youth, even if starting positions are similar (Cancio *et al.* 1996). African-Americans are under-represented in higher status occupations: 3 to 4 percent of doctors, lawyers, and engineers were black in the 1990s. Blacks were under-represented in politics, and only with the recent Bush administration have *two* African-Americans (Collin Powell and Condoleeza Rice) held important cabinet positions. This unequal access to economic rewards (good jobs or wages) are linked in part to education, where a significantly smaller percentage of African-Americans complete a college education. This is part of racialized society and economy. If blacks are over-represented among the underprivileged, they start out with less than average capital – reproducing a racialized American lower class. Affirmative action was supposed to cut around this, and it has worked – Collin Powell admitted that it was helpful to his career. Affirmative action helps open doors – but it cannot get people to those doors. As Jay MacLeod (1995) pointed out in his ethnographic study of two groups of underprivileged boys, underprivileged youth (regardless of race or ethnicity) need *investments* in cultural and social capital early in life – not only from families, but also from schools and neighborhoods. This may make possible more Huxtables, Powells, and Rices.

Ethnicity and the economy: ethnic economies and ethnic enclaves

Ethnic identity and boundaries are cultural, but they can become embedded in economic structures: dense networks of production and exchange limited to a particular ethnic group and the regions they inhabit. When an ethnic group is restricted from access to the mainstream economy due to low skills or prejudice, that minority may be able to create its own economic community called an "ethnic economy" or "ethnic enclave" (Light and Karageorgis 1994). In an ethnic economy, management, ownership, and labor remain within that particular ethnic group, although customers may be outsiders. An "ethnic enclave economy" is a special case of a more concentrated and densely connected venture: firms and activities are physically bunched together in a particular locale, there is greater than usual interdependence between firms, and owners and managers generally employ only their own co-ethnics (Light and Karageorgis 1994: 649). Not all ethnic communities develop non-trivial ethnic economies: the various American Chinatowns (New York, San Francisco) are ethnic economies, but the distinctly Slavic neighborhoods in Pittsburgh and Chicago did not develop ethnic economies – these immigrants and their children worked in factories. (That they were white Europeans helped integration but not status.) Ethnic minorities outside the labor market have to be entrepreneurial, opening their own businesses and relying on labor from immediate families. Not all ethnic groups are equally entrepreneurial: Arabs, Chinese, Greeks, Italians, Jews, and Japanese are among the more entrepreneurial in the United States; Cubans, Latin Americans, and Western and Central European ethnic groups are less entrepreneurial; and Mexicans, African-Americans, Vietnamese, and Puerto Ricans are less entrepreneurial still, although this is not a mark of lethargy but of integration (no need for entrepreneurship) or structural obstacles (Light and Karageorgis 1994: 649). For example, Jews created an enclave in Manhattan (Lower East Side), while Chinese immigrants flocked to Chinatowns – this created a critical mass that helped provide labor, capital, and general advantages of dense network structures. Ethnic groups that immigrated with or gained social and cultural capital (e.g. European migrants) also had an easier time than other ethnic groups maneuvering within the American economy and setting up their own shops (Aldrich and Waldinger 1990).

Ethnic entrepreneurship has particular characteristics. Firms tend to be small, and in fact only 20 percent of minority-owned firms in the United States have any employees – that is, four-fifths of ethnic entrepreneurship involves self-employment (Light and Karageorgis 1994: 661). Dense networks in ethnic communities and economies provide advantages to business. They can facilitate raising capital: these networks create trust and reciprocity ("helping our own") for loans, not only from other co-ethnics (friends and family) but also from local banks. Dense networks help facilitate cooperation (although not necessarily collusion) to overcome the free rider and help all entrepreneurs do well. For example, Pakistani clothing makers in Manchester (UK) meet regularly to discuss prices and exchange, in order to avoid deadly price wars; South Koreans in Los Angeles use networks to control more than one-third of the local market for beer and wine (Light and Karageorgis 1994: 661). Ethnic entrepreneurs often survive by providing for co-ethnics' tastes (something they would know better than other ethnic groups), or they take over niches and sectors that are abandoned: e.g. going into urban food service as larger firms leave the area, opening small shops as white shop-owners retire or abandon the fight against WalMart (Aldrich and Waldinger 1990).

Cross-nationally, ethnic economies and enclaves are more prominent in North America and Australia than in Europe. This is due to general state policies. America and Australia have histories of ethnic pluralism, although liberalization of immigration and work expanded only after World War II in the United States, and Australia is currently experiencing heated political debate over migration (partly linked with asylum seekers). Both American and Australian economic policies are generally pro-free enterprise, which is essential to small-scale entrepreneurship. Even if there are regulations and restrictions, the general direction of policy is to encourage small-scale business. In contrast, some European countries constrain employment and entrepreneurship by immigrants. For example, more stringent and restrictive labor laws in Europe increase the costs of opening and operating a small business (regardless of one's ethnic status), and a migrant to Germany must wait eight years to receive a residence permit before he or she can open a business (Aldrich and Waldinger 1990).

Race and ethnicity: class in sheep's clothing?

Why do race and ethnicity seem to matter anymore? This seemingly innocuous (or naïve) question stems from the roots of race/ethnic inequality. We cannot discount discrimination: despite anti-prejudicial legislation, discrimination survives. Pager and Quillian (2005) compared surveys of employers with their actual practice, using black and white men with virtually identical backgrounds (including ex-offending), and discovered that employers were more likely to hire white than black ex-offenders (and less likely to hire ex-offenders than is suggested in surveys). In 1980 and 1994, Britain's Commission for Racial Equality carried out studies in which a white and non-white male, with the same characteristics, applied for the same job. The white men were twice as likely to get an interview than the non-white men (Commission for Racial Equality 2006). So long as it stems from discrimination, this form of inequality is truly racial/ethnic. However, discrimination does not explain inequality entirely; neither does it explain discrimination that is not based on racial or ethnic prejudice, i.e. not giving mortgages to non-whites, not because they are non-white, but because of other factors. This is "institutionalized racism": institutionalized, routinized procedures that in and of themselves are not overtly prejudicial still have outcomes that are discriminatory on the basis of race or ethnicity. Yet this does not clarify the issue. Original discrimination creates a class dynamic: African-Americans, denied economic, cultural, and social capital through slavery and Jim Crow laws, have little to pass down. After World War II, inner city blacks faced disadvantages not entirely from prejudice – although some employers (including black owners) distrust and will not hire black males. As William Julius Wilson (1997) shows, the problem is that they also lack sufficient money or skills to move to better locales (e.g. the suburbs) or to invest in education or their own ethnic economies. Inner-city whites are just as much at risk: they too lack the economic and cultural capital to get out.

In short, while racial and ethnic inequality may *begin* with discrimination, it persists because of class logics as well. Blacks brought in as slaves were exploited; that exploitation was justified by racist ideology, according to which blacks were a different race in need of control. Irish and Jews as well faced hostile ideologies, although they were white Europeans and not slaves, and so American anti-Semitism and anti-Irish prejudice were not so stark. (In contrast, German, especially Nazi, anti-Semitism was more developed and extreme: Jews were an inherently hostile, dangerous race.) Facing structural and ideological disadvantages, these non-white groups did what they could: Jews, the Irish, and later Asians formed ethnic economies and improved their economic and cultural capital, such that they could use social liberalization through civil rights and other legislation to enter the "mainstream." Other groups, such as many Latinos and blacks, remained structurally disadvantaged. What began as race and ethnicity became class dynamics with racial and ethnic faces. However, social forces take another turn. Because some non-whites remain over-represented in the lower classes, policy-makers and cultural elites (e.g. journalists and academics) who dominate discourse interpret these class dynamics as *racial or ethnic* dynamics (Figure 6.1).

An example of this dynamic is best seen in affirmative action. Affirmative action was supposed to address the class roots of ethnic and racial (and gender) inequality: give less well-off non-whites (and females) better jobs and wages than their parents had – even if this meant giving them jobs over better-qualified whites – and they would gain and pass on social and cultural capital to their children, leveling the playing field for that next generation of whites and non-whites. Yet affirmative action generated a backlash that strengthened racial categories and assumptions, that hid the class dynamic at work (cf. Rieder 1985). After the 1960s, many whites felt punished for being white: if they gained from their racial/ethnic advantage, visiting the sins of the father on the son understandably evokes outrage. Political elites picked up on this, politicizing affirmative action and issues of race and ethnicity – hiding class dynamics and creating the potential for political backlash.

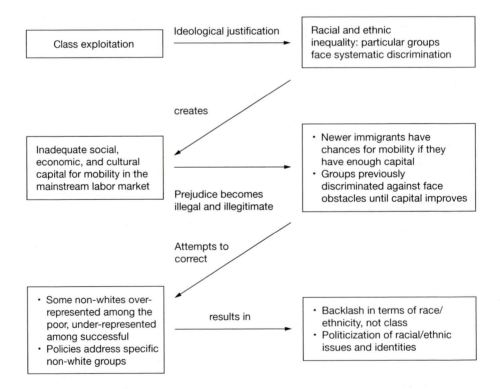

Figure 6.1   Race/ethnicity and class dynamics

Race and ethnicity in European economies

In Europe, race and ethnicity have a more complex history: ethnicity is linked to the rise and fall of nation-states, and race is linked to the Atlantic slave-trade and to pseudo-scientific justifications of nationalist claims and identities. The English identified the Irish as a different, lower race; but the Irish were white, European, and Christian, and English political liberties softened the racial difference. On the Continent, racial discourse persisted, strongest in Germany (cf. Greenfeld 1992; Goldhagen 1996). Difficulties in forming a German country to correspond to strivings of a "national" German people (the national identity existed before the country) were explained through national and racial differences: the French, English, and Russians did not want a German country, and they were aided by non-German elements hostile to the German people, namely the Jews. Central European Christianity had anti-Semitic tones that made the Jews out to be a separate people, and with the coming of scientific discourse, this difference became seen as "racial." This race-based anti-semitism grew under the Nazis and exploded in the Holocaust.[13] The experience of the Holocaust gave strength to legislation against hate speech and hate crimes or overtly discriminatory politics – although the 1990s saw a return of right-wing anti-ethnic politics in such leaders and organizations as France's Jean-Marie Le Pen or the British National Party. While such *political* discrimination and inequality was combated, racial and ethnic inequality persisted and took on new structural form following World War II – later fueling right-wing xenophobia. Since the 1990s, Britain's ethnic issue has taken on increased significance: tensions between whites and non-whites have increased, partly due to politicization of migration and asylum seekers and the emergence of small but vocal far-right factions.[14]

Given the historical importance and strength of nation-states in Europe, the politics of exclusion and migration vary across countries; we cannot quite talk of a "European" pattern of racial and ethnic inequality and economic participation, and so I will focus on individual countries. Let us begin with ethnicity and inequality in Great Britain. Britain did not have the same history of slavery that the American South had; until the post-World War II period, class was more salient to stratification. Instead, Britain had immigration. While migrants supplied cheap labor from the second half of the nineteenth century, the greater need for labor and the disintegration of the Empire brought an increased flux of migrants to the United Kingdom from India, Pakistan, Bangladesh, and the Caribbean following World War II. (Chinese migrants came later.) These migrants arrived with different degrees of human capital (skills and knowledge of English), class-based cultural capital, and family structures, and like migrants everywhere, they settled into different parts of the country. Indian and Chinese families integrated more easily into British society, using or augmenting their human capital and that of their children, many entering the Civil Service. Migrants from Bangladesh, Pakistan, and the Caribbean had less human capital, took lower status jobs, and ended up in regions that were later badly hit by economic decline and deindustrialization (e.g. the North and West). In fact, around 70 percent of British non-whites lived in the eighty-eight most deprived areas.

The interaction of migration, capital, and economic structure contributed to ethnic inequality, which has remained fairly stable over the past fifty years. According to British government data for 2002, Indians and Chinese have done well; Indian migrants' descendants improved educational credentials, and second- and third-generation British-Indians entered the Civil Service or other professions. Bangladeshis, Pakistanis, and Black Caribbeans fared worse. While 77 percent of the employable white population have work, only 59 percent of non-whites are employed. While 70 percent and 67 percent of employable Indians and Chinese have jobs, 45 percent of Pakistanis and Bangladeshis and 60 percent of blacks overall have work. Employment rates for whites and non-whites are closest in the South, except for London. In the "rust belt" of northern England the disparity is worse: in Yorkshire the employment rates for whites and non-whites are 76 percent versus 55 percent. White unemployment in 2002 was 4 percent but 8 percent for non-whites. Unemployment for men and women was 10 percent for Black Caribbeans, 8 percent for Pakistanis, and 11 percent for Bangladeshis (but 16 percent for Bangladeshi men alone). Bangladeshi and Pakistani men were more likely to end up in low-status, dead-end jobs: 52 percent of Bangladeshi men worked in restaurants; 13 percent of Pakistani men worked as taxi drivers. In consequence, three-quarters of Pakistani and Bangladeshi families had less than half of the average family income (after housing costs); 43 percent of Indian families and 30 percent of white families earned less than half of the average family income (after housing costs). Overall, low human capital, life in deprived areas (providing substandard housing, employment, education, and overall investment in economic, human, and social capital), and continuing discrimination have added an ethnic dimension to British inequality (Commission for Racial Equality 2006). While the decline in industry and rise in services seemed to helped employment for all ethnic groups, inequality persisted, in part because Pakistanis and Bangladeshis did not fair well in the new service economy (Iganski and Payne 1999).

On the European Continent, the problem of little useful data makes comparative analyses of racial and ethnic inequality (and class inequality as well) difficult (Crouch 1999: 157).[15] Not that ethnic inequality is not present: the current politics and economics of race are linked to increases in asylum seeking and migration (made possible by liberal European Union human rights rules) and to the long-standing tradition of *gastarbeiter*: "guest workers," laborers from foreign countries coming to Europe for temporary or low-wage jobs that native-born peoples would not or could not fill, acting as a pool of cheap labor.[16] Germany, France, the Netherlands, and Belgium had the largest inflows of migrants. Yugoslavia and Turkey were principal sources of migrants, due to civil war in one and lack of equivalent economic opportunity in the other (Rex 1998). Post-war *gastarbeiter* arrived in Germany from Turkey; Algerians migrated to former colonial master France. *Gastarbeiter* arrived with few economic skills and low cultural capital (e.g. language). Often, they lived in lower class neighborhoods not well integrated with the majority population. Political policies could also hinder their chances for improvement. In Germany, citizenship laws involve ethnic blood-lines (*volk*); *gastarbeiter* could not gain citizenship and had tenuous rights to remain in the country. In France, citizenship is "color-blind." Policies require integration through discarding differences (e.g. Muslims girls are not allowed to wear headscarves in public schools). This has not stopped ethnic inequality. Because of the status of their origin (non-German, French colonial or former colonial subject), migrants did not have initial capital or access to mobility. They may not have encountered the same obstacles as African-Americans, but the result was similar: perpetual lower status. This created ethnic tensions and even riots (e.g. in France, November 2005 – see Box 6.2). Race and ethnicity exist even when not publicly discussed.

Race, ethnicity, and economy: the challenge and the future

The fault line in American politics has been race; ethnicity will follow when white Americans cease being the majority by the mid-twenty-first century. In Europe, non-white immigrants and higher non-white birth rates mean that multicultural societies are a reality – and Europeans are bracing themselves for the onslaught of rhetoric from Left and Right, white and non-white, politicians and activists. The Netherlands, once among Europe's more liberal countries, has increased restrictions on immigration. French and British politicians and commentators talk more about integration into a common identity, although just what that common identity is remains unclear. Underneath this politics is economic structure: ethnic under-classes tired of poverty or unequal access to mobility, or successful ethnic groups arousing the ire of less well-off whites, or anti-immigrant groups in the United States and Europe accusing non-whites of abusing the welfare state or taking jobs away from whites.

The challenge for economic sociology is to get a better picture of racial and ethnic inequality, to determine just when it is a class phenomenon and when it is a racial/ethnic phenomenon, and to propose means to deal with the politics of economic division. The American solution, to the extent that there is one, is free enterprise: let non-whites work their way up the socioeconomic ladder. While this hides effects of cultural or social capital, it also allows opportunity: an ideology of free enterprise does allow ethnic economies to develop and, in many cases, provide returns to their inhabitants. The European solution has been more political, when ethnicity and race are discussed: either to promote multicultural tolerance, or to force a common identity. These *political* solutions, however, do not always provide the *economic* (material) capital that non-whites may need to improve their social position. Here economic sociologists should disentangle the political and the economic, the class and the racial/ethnic, to dislodge the assumptions of elites and non-elites – and hopefully to provide workable suggestions to facilitate true meritocracy.

Gendered economies: glass ceilings and second shifts

We now turn to our third axis of inequality and the economy; gender. Studies of occupational stratification often leave out gender – yet, when inserted into analyses, gender is almost always prominent. If one examines the typical status hierarchy of jobs, one sees women clustered towards the bottom (middle management,

BOX 6.2 ETHNICITY AND RIOTS IN FRANCE

In November 2005, riots broke out in a Paris suburb and began to spread across the nation. Over 10,000 cars were destroyed; rioters attacked or vandalized over 500 public buildings (including schools); the police arrested nearly 5000 people. The majority of those rioting were Muslim second-generation immigrants from north Africa. The riots were triggered when two young Muslim men, thinking the police were chasing them, entered an electrical substation and died of electrocution. The fuel for the riots, however, was material deprivation – not religion or Muslim identity *per se*. While the politics of Muslims and non-Muslims following September 11, 2001 has become a source of tension in Europe, economic inequality is the constant reminder of ethnic "exclusion." If unemployment in France is around 10 percent (20 percent for youth), unemployment figures for French Muslims (most of whom are non-white immigrants) may be around twice that level – while Muslims make up around 10 percent of France's population, they are more likely to live in France's deprived neighborhoods, with poor infrastructure and educational resources. And such deprivation is not recent but rather goes back several generations: inherited underprivilege. France has an ethnic dimension to inequality and its underclass, except that French political elites, like others on the European Continent, do not want to talk of ethnic and racial issues or divides. Yet state policies do not seem to be addressing the situation, and may be making it worse. State intervention in the economy (e.g. support for a minimum wage, limits on hours worked per week, strict rules for hiring and firing employees) has kept expansion of jobs and employment relatively low *vis-à-vis* the American, British, and other economies. Those minor reforms which the state has pushed have done little to open up the labor market, instead creating a dual labor market of more privileged employees supported by labor laws and lesser paid, lesser protected employees on temporary contracts. Poorer neighborhoods of state-constructed project housing are on the outskirts of Paris; they do not have the same infrastructure or architectural beauty, and they house large numbers of non-white poor. (Marx and Engels noted that class consciousness and solidarity derive from workers living at close quarters. The same logic can work for other underprivileged social groups.) Their addresses hurt their employment chances in the same way that they can hurt lower class Americans (MacLeod 1995).

Rather than address issues of ethnic-based economic inequality (or ethnic-based divides generally), politicians engaged in posturing. President Jacques Chirac stressed France's glorious history and scrapped labor law reforms after (white) youth protested. While some politicians realized the need to integrate non-white minorities into French society and improve their social situation, Chirac stressed that laws and institutions should remain color-blind: addressing ethnic and racial inequality and division without noting it. (Thanks in part to the formal integrationist policy, the French government does not recognize racial or ethnic difference in laws and reports.) The French cultural and political elite are white Europeans; police harassment in these "ethnic ghettos" has exacerbated tensions and feelings of exclusion.

Sources: "Be My Guest," *The Economist*, October 8, 2005; "An Underclass Rebellion," *The Economist*, November 12, 2005; "France's Failure," *The Economist*, November 12, 2005; "After the Riots," *The Economist*, December 17, 2005. Online via Business Source Premier. Available HTTP: <http://www.economist.co.uk> (accessed April 3, 2006).

self-employed service, clerical and food service, routine clerical work), men towards the top (upper-level managers, professionals, and owners, and also the industrial working class) (Reskin and Roos 1990; Andes 1992). While gender inequality is seemingly apparent, it is also in many ways the trickiest to analyze, since race and ethnicity offer distinct groups and histories of economies, politics, and migration: one can track discrete actors and organizations that shaped these different social groups' inclusion into economies. Gender is more subtle and runs deeper into everyday practices, but it is there: as Scott (1986: 1067) suggests, gender is a core element of modern social relations and of relations of power. With gender, the waters are far muddier: while we can see particular individuals and groups in action, such as the National Organization for Women, the general practices that reproduce gender roles and relations run deep into the very fabric of individuals' own practices, roles, and everyday beliefs. Gender roles are reproduced in the firm and the home, on the street and in the boardroom. This is not simply because people may be openly prejudiced. Gender and the economy is more than a story of sexist male managers. Rather, we have to look at socially constructed gender roles, what Bem (1993) calls the "lenses of gender" – and the gendered logics of how economic rules and organizations operate – the kinds of behaviors, practices, and roles that are rewarded, and why.

An investigation into the gender gap in pay in Great Britain (Women and Work Commission 2006) showed that today the average working woman earns from 83 percent to 87 percent of an average working man's wage, depending on the statistics one looks at – although in the 1970s the gender gap was 35 percent. In Great Britain, women now make up 33 percent of managers (versus only 1.8 percent in 1974), yet the top 100 British firms do not have a woman CEO (*Observer*, February 26, 2006, p. 4). The Women and Work Commission suggested several roots to this inequality. Women often end up in jobs with worse status, pay, and chances for promotion – a "ghetto" of sorts. Women's work experience has a worse fit with demands for high-status jobs or promotions: typically, women spend less time in work, have career interruptions (e.g. giving birth), and engage in more part-time work early on. Their qualifications do not always fit in with occupations rewarded with good wages: female students are more likely to get degrees in English, the arts and design, psychology, and sociology, whereas male students are more likely to study business, physics, economics, and math in their pre-university and university education. This is not because women's skills are inherently inferior; rather, economic institutions are gendered. Finally, women in Britain start with lower pay than men, and their salaries do not improve as fast as men's. This is despite the fact that British girls get better A-level and pre-A-level grades, and their educational and occupational aspirations are no lower than boys'.

On the European Continent, women have received help from European Community directives for equal pay and equal employment opportunity. This does not mean equality was achieved, however. Women's participation in the labor force did increase, from around 30 percent of women working in 1970 to nearly 40 percent in the 1990s for Europe as a whole, but individual countries' rates varied (Glasner 1998: 93–6): Denmark had over 50 percent participation in 1986 (declining in the

1990s), with Britain, France, and Portugal not far behind and women in Ireland and Spain participating the least (less than 40 percent in 1992). In the 1990s nearly three-quarters of working women were in the services sector compared to half of all working men, and women were more likely to have lower status jobs, especially in countries with higher women's participation rates (Glasner 1998: 98). Meanwhile, wage differentials persist, although women's wages have increased faster than men's (Crouch 1999: 164).

The story in the United States is not so different. According to Bielby and Baron (1986), employment patterns demonstrate persistent and systematic gender inequality. For example, if men and women have the same basic organizational tasks or occupations in the same company, they are likely to have different job titles; men's titles have higher status and authority. Yet businesses do not gain from this – there is no trade-off of efficiency for inequality (if human capital is equal). In fact, women may work *harder* at their jobs than men do. Bielby and Bielby (1988) tested a claim by Gary Becker (1981, 1985): women's pay and positions are lower than men's because they put less time and effort into work. This is so, supposedly, because husbands and wives decide on a rational division of labor: the workplace is his domain, the home is her's.[17] Not so. Even if women invest less *time* than men – perhaps because of family and a "second shift" of home care (see below) – they put as much or more effort into their jobs as do men. Women's lower positions and pay are not due to less effort. Bielby and Bielby conclude (1988: 1056) that, given the greater effort that women put into work to offset perceived biases, employers would be rational to discriminate against *men*.

Gender has a long but varied history in economies (Tilly and Scott 1978). In agricultural and early industrial economies of Europe, women worked alongside men (and children) in fields and factories. Their labor was equally valuable for growing crops or bringing in meager pay. While men dominated peasant households, women performed many useful jobs, and organizing the home was paramount to survival. With industrialization, women were as poorly paid as men, but men gradually came to dominate the shop-floor, leaving women to tend children and the home. The work they could get was low-status and low paying: maid, assistant. This led to a division not only of labor but also of rewards. Men's work had *exchange value*: for their work in factories, men received money they could use to buy food, clothing, and other material benefits. Women's work had *use value*. The reward for this work was in the output which was used or consumed: dinner was eaten, tidy beds slept in, clean floors dirtied again, children safe. While this work was as important as men's – men paid the rent and women kept the abode livable – she could not redeem the fruits of her labor at the store. When she had to go to the store, she depended on her husband for money. Because men monopolized the work that had exchange value, and because exchange value was necessary in the marketplace, men gained the upper hand in the distribution of resources.

Women did not remain subservient in the West. Women's liberation movements emerged, sometimes as temperance movements (in the United States the infamous Molly Pitcher – but also in Ireland) and sometimes related to pro-welfare movements led by upper-middle-class women (as in the United States) (Skocpol 1992). But this was not all – other forces and events changed the social and economic structures and gave women below the upper classes the opportunity to begin participating in the world of labor. One important event and force was *war*. World Wars I and II made it possible – in fact, necessary – for women to work in factories in non-trivial positions. The reason was simple: men were fighting at the front, and there were too few men at home to produce enough munitions. Women were recruited to take their men's places in factories – hence the famous image of "Rosie the Riveter," muscular (i.e. a masculine, industrial trait) and volunteering her labor for the war effort. In an ironic twist of gender history, men shot each other, and women returned to work to manufacture the bullets they used. When both wars ended, informal movements to "get men back to work" and to "get women back home" emerged – but not all women wanted to give up the position of earning their own keep. The combination of women's liberation movements from above, and the feeling of emancipation offered by wartime employment from below, created the ideas and their receptivity that helped propel women's rights.

Despite this, gender inequality persists, and it is uncertain how deep gains have taken root. While women's equality seems better institutionalized in Europe thanks to stronger traditions of social democracy, in the United States the post-Reagan swell of conservatism and religious fundamentalism may threaten some of those gains (although women's real gains may be greater in the United States). Gender issues are not so strong on political agendas in the era of welfare roll-back and international terrorism; while global women's movements got their ideas a fair hearing in UN organizations (e.g. UNIFEM) in the 1990s, "security" became more important after 2001, and issues of women's rights and equality became more muted in the discussions of United Nations organizations for international development.

"Gendered economies"

An economy is gendered when logics of economic and organizational institutions and practices have assumed gender behaviors. One way this works is when criteria for evaluating behavior (i.e. to decide rewards) have gender qualities and an assumed hierarchy. Take Western business. Desired behavior includes confidence and strength, the ability to be cold and bold, and a drive to "win" in the combat of business competition. These are traits that tend to reflect contemporary masculinity: a desire to win at great cost to oneself rather than accommodate, hard-nosed calculation of the bottom line rather than consideration of a broader range of factors (e.g. personal satisfaction), competition and victory rather than negotiation and cooperation. Acker (1990) sees gendered economic logics at work in organizations. If one reads rules and procedures for work, pay, and promotion in a typical firm (or in academic work on organizations), one sees abstract, gender-neutral descriptions. However, says Acker, men and women populate these jobs on an unequal basis. Women fill one set of positions, men another – and managers (unconsciously) evaluate these positions and award higher status to positions populated primarily by men. The formal, gender-neutral hierarchy is not divorced from gender. Further, the logic of tasks, task fulfillment, and promotion has a masculine feel to it: images of work are gendered. Star employees devote all their time to the job, with little time for outside activities (except those that still involve the job, e.g. after-hours networking). What of procreation – having and raising children? As important as this is to the survival of humanity, the star employee cannot split time with the family. Hence, as Acker argues, the time logics of work and procreation are contradictory, not complementary: the logic of employment is male. Dress codes are inherently male; women feel the need to ape men's "power" image (e.g. the "power skirt" akin to the "power tie"). In interactions, men are perceived to act while women provide support; in speech, men are more likely to interrupt women than the reverse.

Just as class and race/ethnicity interact with economic structures and practices, so does gender: a gendered history deprived women of capital and imbued economic structures with gendered logics. Because our identities historically had a gender component to them, the institutions we humans have devised also have a gendered component, especially in expectations of normal, legitimate behavior. Even if women have money to study at Harvard Law School, do they have cultural capital – knowledge and ability to demonstrate "proper" appearance, vocabulary, and practices – to fit in as high-powered lawyers in high-powered law firms or to overcome the assumptions of proper gender roles in such a profession? (Not that this doesn't happen – over the past few decades women have infiltrated men's professions, such as medical or legal, although they do not yet make up half of doctors or of lawyers in all developed countries.) Often women do not get this far: they feel drawn to particular jobs and roles that seem normal for women, or because they see little chance of success in male-dominated fields.[18]

How a gendered economy reproduces inequality

It is one thing to use statistics to show that women populate the lower rung of occupations. Without mechanisms that produce this inequality our discussion is incomplete, and so we turn to *how* gendered economies operate. The general mechanisms involve structural and cultural capital available to women, as well as assumptions of normal roles and behavior. Consider structure. One force reproducing gender inequality is networks (cf. Davies-Netzley 1998), which are important for recruitment and promotion. Someone in a senior position takes a "junior" under his or her wing and trains them in formal and informal skills needed for success, goes to bat for him or her in organizational politics, and passes on resources (e.g. information, good projects). If women are under-represented towards the top of the status scale, they do not have an "old girls' club" akin to the "old boys' club" for their use. In the perfect gender-neutral world, this would not matter: men and women would create networks based on utility or friendship regardless of the other's sex. Alas, this is not the ideal world; work is gendered, and men and women tend to network with other men and women. Women must network with men; but this becomes difficult when those networks are underpinned by gendered activities, such as playing or watching sports (squash or baseball), evening activities (going to bars after hours),[19] or talking about or engaging in "sexual conquests." Our assumptions about gender roles and related behavior acts on the art of networking. If men dominate a job, there are fewer women with whom aspiring women can network or who can take them "under her wing." Yet even having powerful people inside their networks has less of a pay-off for women than for men. These powerful people are less likely to invest in women than men, or in other words are less likely to "go to bat" for women than for men (McGuire 2002). Not all networks are equal: even network relations are gendered.[20]

On the cultural side, assumptions about normal gender roles reproduce inequality and a gendered economy through hiring: who gets hired for what kinds of jobs, in what kinds of firms. Back to women sports reporters. This is not unusual now – although women still occupy the lower status positions (e.g. engaging athletes on the sidelines in superfluous discussion, rather than calling the game from the booth for most of the broadcast) – but before the 1990s "women" and "sports" did not mix. How could a woman understand the men's world of physical contact sports, such as football (American or European)? One might argue that the world of cultural production is heavy on marketing, while law firms should hire the best quality employee. Even this is not so: in her study of law firms' hiring practices, Gorman (2005) discovered that men were more likely to be hired than women if character-istics desired in the new employee were more "masculine" – ambitious, assertive, business skills, energetic, independent, leadership – and the reverse if desired qualities were "feminine" – cooperative, emotional, verbally oriented, sympathetic (Gorman 2005: 726). Further, the presence of women partners increased the prob-ability of women hires at lower levels, but not necessarily for promotions or hiring above the entry level. That is, law firms coded desired employee traits in gendered logics that *were not formally spelled out* in applications or evaluations of candidates. Rather, they were more subtly embedded in the way employers thought about their particular law firms and the jobs the new employees were supposed to do.

These are general structural and cultural mechanisms that reproduce the gendered economy in everyday practice (Figure 6.2). Let us turn to how they play out in more general manifestations of gender inequality in the economy: the jobs women receive, obstacles to promotion within organizations, second shifts, and forces for change.

Women's jobs

Part of institutionalized gender inequality stems from the work that women are offered. Women are more likely to occupy lower paid, lower status jobs than men – women are statistically over-represented in the worst jobs. The classic case is in dentistry, where nearly all dental hygienists are women. This has sometimes been called a "ghetto": like the original meaning of the word, an occupational ghetto is a low-status "site" which is difficult to escape. This may be so for some jobs because of the images of work and the gendered traits of men and women: jobs that are harder, more rigorous, or colder are considered men's jobs, whereas work that involves caring and nurturing or jobs that are more emotional are available for women – based on the supposed rational–emotional dichotomy of men versus women (Bem 1993). Alternatively, the demands of a job might conflict with child-birth and raising a family – and even if the latter can be shared, biology still intrudes when it comes to bearing children. Jobs that require constant "face time" in the

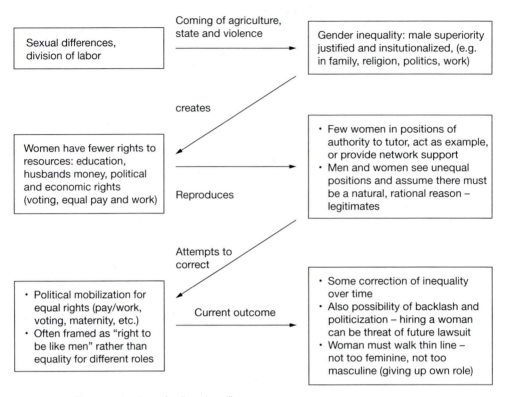

Figure 6.2 The reproduction of a "gendered" economy

office or on the road, and time in the run-up to birth, birth itself, and recovery after-ward come into conflict. Thus, employers may be less willing to hire women for such demanding (but materially rewarding) jobs – or women may avoid them for fear of the choice they will have to make. Finally, cultural and social capital and demonstration may be in operation. A job that is mostly male dominated is less likely to inspire girls and young women to aspire to that job: they have fewer female role models or women with whom they can network, and they may feel they are less likely to succeed than in a job that is dominated by women. So long as gender is important to our identities (and it shows no indication of going away), this is a significant part of (self)recruitment: women will be less likely to go into fields that are mostly male dominated. Given that, historically, good jobs were male dominated, women have long faced these obstacles of accumulating enough social and cultural capital (networks, role models, comfort) to break through the gender barrier and make the number of men and women equal in work.

To illustrate, let us take the example of education. Women are more likely to teach at lower levels (kindergarten and primary school), while men are increasingly repre-sented the higher one goes up the educational ladder. In itself this might be innocuous, except for two points. The first is that the early years of education are academically "softer" and lower status: more about basic skills and socialization versus the "harder" and more rigorous subjects (physics, chemistry) at the end of pre-university education, where men are more likely to make their appearance. In universities, we find men making up the majority of most departments, especially in the higher status sciences, law, medicine, and business/economics. Women are clustered in the humanities and, interestingly, sociology. Not surprisingly, the gender composition of students tends to reflect the gender make-up of the faculty: more women than men in sociology, more men than women in economics or engineering. Women who want to go into education will be drawn by role models and networks to the lower rungs of the ladder or particular disciplines. Let us go further with a concrete example of Masters' degrees awarded in 2002 to 2003 at the University of California – San Diego (Table 6.1).

The logic of gender and education resembles the status ladder in organizations' ILMs: not only are women concentrated towards the lower-level, dead-end jobs, they are less likely to be promoted within ILMs than men. At the lower rungs of the ladder women are secretaries, while men might be accountants or other assistants. This gives men greater chances for eventual promotion; on the other hand, one has little chance of eventually becoming a manager by starting out as a secretary. Generally, the best such women can hope for is to become the senior secretary in a firm – unless she moves to a different firm. Before the civil rights movement and legislation of the 1960s, personnel departments would follow formal or informal rules and assign women to less important jobs because of the assumption that men needed better jobs to support their families; in other words, women's work was a luxury. This does not mean that gender inequality appeared with ILMs: as jobs became more routine and less prestigious, men gave them over to women. For example, in the early decades of industrialization, men and women worked together in factories; but as status and wages for skilled laborers increased, men came to dominate. The same is true for secretaries: as one reads nineteenth-century literature (American and British), one sees that businessmen's personal secretaries were

Table 6.1 Gender and Masters' degrees for a sample of departments, University of California, San Diego, 2002 to 2003

Degree program	No. men receiving degree	No. women receiving degree
Chemistry and biochemistry	28	16
Mathematics	16	4
Physics	14	2
Computer science	29	4
Economics	0	6
Political science	7	5
History	7	4
Literature	2	12
Teacher education	9	70

Source: From publicly available data: HTTP <http://www-ogsr.ucsd.edu/reports/graddata/03Fall>

other (younger) men. Only with the advent of the typewriter, when secretarial work became more routine and deskilled, did women come to dominate this profession. As ILMs developed in the twentieth century, they were imbued with the gendered logics of the economy and the firms in which they were embedded. By the same measure, as equal rights legislation has taken effect, personnel departments and ILMs may have helped women come closer to equality: these are precisely the organizational departments and rules that respond to and (imperfectly) enact formal laws inside the firm.

Glass ceilings and glass cliffs

If a woman is hired into a non-trivial, higher status job, the next gendered issue that arises is promotion. The key to promotion is the appearance of success: demonstrating that one has capacities to do more demanding but better rewarded tasks. Women face the challenge of demonstrating capacity *as women*: just as children from the working class must work harder in school to show they are worthy of obtaining good grades and jobs (because of cultural capital), women must work harder than men for rewards. This is because two barriers confront women: the infamous *glass ceiling* and the less famous "glass cliff." The glass ceiling is a metaphor for an invisible barrier to advancement: there are no formal rules prohibiting women from obtaining top positions (e.g. CEOs), yet they are statistically under-represented. There are many fewer women than men in managerial positions, especially among top managers and CEOs. In the United States, for example, women have been badly under-represented in managerial positions; only by the 1990s did they make up over one-third of managerial positions, although their average earnings were approximately 60 percent of male managers' average earnings (Andes 1992: 233). In Great Britain, there are no women CEOs among the top 100 British corporations. The is due to women's lack of cultural and social capital, or a bad fit between the capital they have and that which is needed for promotion to the highest levels of management. Men do not usually sit around and say, "We can't hire her because she is a woman." Instead, they might not consider a women candidate for promotion because she is not a team leader or does not fit in personally – perhaps because she tries too hard to act like a man or comes across as too aggressive (more natural to men than to women in the usual cultural stereotypes) – or because she does not seem tough or decisive enough (because she may seem too feminine), or because of fear that she may take time off to have children (or has done so and has generated some resentment). Or they do not even consider promoting her because of her lack of capital: her network of allies and support does not extend to those men making promotion decisions.

The glass ceiling can come alive in women's own accounts of efforts and obstacles encountered in the rise to the top. They do not always face blatant sexism: rather, they may run afoul of assumptions about roles and the reasons we experience what we do in working life – to what we attribute success or failure. In her interviews with men and women managers in California, Davies-Netzley (1998) noticed that women and men have different perceptions of their experiences with what it takes to be successful and gain promotion. While men stress hard work and ability, women add the importance of networks (with all the problems of creating usable networks) and maneuvering around assumptions of gender roles: not being too feminine to appear soft, but not being too masculine to appear "butch" or a "bitch." Civil rights legislation, and the growing awareness that women bring human capital and talent to organizations, has helped reduce the glass ceiling. There is also another way around this informal obstacle: jumping between firms (Yamagata *et al.* 1997). A woman who faces a glass ceiling in her own firm can go out on to the job market and try to find a job at a relatively higher position in another firm. That is, the glass ceiling is not universal; it is *organizational*, because the mechanisms of gender inequality tend to work through everyday economic interactions – those of organizations that make up the economy.

The glass ceiling hypothesis is not without controversy, however. Baxter and Wright (2000) contend that glass ceiling effects are fairly weak in the United States, Sweden, and Australia. They specify that the glass ceiling should mean that upward mobility becomes increasingly difficult for women as they go up the organizational ladder: empirically, we should see smaller and smaller percentages of women managers as we go further up. They do show that there is a *general* gender gap in management – more men than women. In the United States, once women get into the important layers of management, their chances of promotion are not much different from those of men. In other words, there is a glass ceiling to the first layer of "real" management (where managers have real decision-making authority over company policy, not over its implementation – the role of middle managers). Once women overcome this, they are not that much worse off than men. In Sweden and Australia, however, there may be a more systematic and rigorous glass ceiling effect: women do face increasing difficulty each step up the corporate ladder. However, Bihagen and Ohls (2006) suggest that in Sweden women face their greatest challenges entering at the lower rungs of corporate management, and that as they go higher they face fewer obstacles.

A new discovery is the glass cliff: women may make it to top positions, but then they are over-represented in firms that fail (Ryan and Haslam 2005). Firms in financial trouble for deep-seated structural and procedural reasons (e.g. out-of-date procedures or technology, lack of human capital) require major changes to secure loans or investment and survive. One way directors of these firms can signal willingness to accept radical change – and thus attract support – is hiring a woman to be CEO. The firms then receive some capital, but unless the woman leader can address the firm's serious problems – unlikely, given the hurdles women managers face and given that previous managers could not save the firm – failure is likely. A woman gets her chance – at failure. Hence the metaphor of the glass cliff: "glass" because the social forces behind it are not formal rules; cliff because it is failure produced not by the woman's individual abilities but by broader social forces.

The "second shift"

When women returned into the labor stream after World War II, they did not exactly trade the home for the office or factory. In fact, they were burdened with both.

This is called the "second shift." Like men, working women have a "first shift" at work. But they then usually have to fulfill household duties: shopping, caring for children (or organizing child care), preparing meals, keeping the house clean and in order, and so on.[21] This is the "second shift": it is like work, only at home, and often with little help from husbands. This is particularly prominent among white-collar families, where the woman holds a full-time or near full-time white-collar job that requires at least forty hours of work a week, if not more. Arlie Hochschild (1989) studied several married couples to address just how husbands and wives dealt with the second shift, and she made an interesting discovery. She asked her subjects about their political ideologies – liberal, moderate, or conservative – and then conducted in-depth interviews with these husbands and wives. In the liberal households the women were allowed to work in whatever job they liked, but their husbands did little to help them. The men labeled themselves liberal by letting their wives work, but they then turned around and claimed that if she exercised her right to work, that did not reduce her duties at home – using feminism against feminism, it would seem! Conservative husbands were less liberal with their wives' careers, but they were more willing to help out around the house – but not because they had any sympathy for the second shift. Rather, the women played on their husbands' conservative stereotypes. Wives would act helpless and appeal to their husbands for help; husbands would see them as the typically helpless female and help out around the house – justifying male superiority to themselves but also helping reduce their wives' second shifts. Relationships in the liberal households were strained; the husbands helped little, either citing her freedom of choice or choosing chores that allowed them to hide (for example, spending time in the garage or shed tending to or repairing the power tools).

Certain occupations and technologies have helped alleviate some of the stress of the second shift. Consider female real estate agents (Wharton 1994). These women had an easier time managing dual roles as wage-earner and home-maker because the real estate business allowed some flexibility in working hours: while these women had to work on weekends and evenings, they also had time free during the day to do many of the errands running a household requires (e.g. taking children to school or the doctor's, going to the supermarket). Computers and mobile phones also added to flexibility: these women could work at home and even when out running these errands; for example, discussing tactics and sales or dealing with colleagues and clients via the mobile phone while with children (at home or out).

Change in gender and the economy

Yet despite this history of gender inequality, there are glimmers of hope for equality: women in industrialized countries made gains. In economic theory, gender inequality should disappear as women become better educated and gain useful economic skills, unless there are good economic reasons for it to persist (Epstein 1992). Women have become better educated, yet inequality persists. Markets do not objectively, automatically reward particular skills – status and rewards come from *political* actions that help groups secure rights and resources. If this was true for doctors and lawyers, it is likely true for women as well. And in fact it is: if women have made gains in wages and access to education and jobs, it is not because the "market" has finally rewarded them, but because activists (men and women) fought long and hard for the chance to equal the two sexes' market opportunities. In a study of gender inequality in several developed countries, Wright *et al.* (1995) discovered that the best predictor of improved gender equality was the strength of political movements for women's rights. The smallest gap in organizational authority between men and women was in the United States and Australia; the largest was in Japan, and the gap was greater in Norway and Sweden than in the United Kingdom. This is possibly because women's movements were strongest in the US, UK, and Australia. Women's movements have been weak in Japan, and social democracy in Norway and Sweden is oriented towards welfare goals rather than advancing individual gain (i.e. improving women's positions and rewards in the workplace).

The challenge of gender and economies

For all the history of gender inequality and the data I have presented above, one part of the overall picture is clear: change towards equality has been afoot in recent decades. This should encourage men and women who invested in civil rights. Rather than the dreaded fear that quotas would reduce efficiency and productivity by favoring less qualified women in the name of gender politics, women's movements for equal rights have brought women closer to parity with men without sacrificing economic productivity or growth. Women's movements were initially about political and social rights: the right to vote, the right for more equal social status with men (e.g. in the case of divorce, or violence). As women gained on these fronts, they turned to employment. In the United States, the battle for equal rights was long and drawn-out, and not always victorious – the proposed Equal Rights Amendment was allowed to die before enough states could ratify it as a constitutional amendment. Yet as African-Americans benefited from civil rights, so did women. However, we should never be blind to what might be lost when something is gained. As women enter the workforce alongside men, has this increased labor competition helped reduce real wages over the past thirty years? More husbands and wives work today to earn for their families what the male earner could, on his own, fifty years ago. But what effect does this have on families or children's well-being? Does more daycare provide the equivalent to parents' love?

If trends continue, women will eventually attain equal jobs and pay. However, the road will not be easy. Debates over maternity leave face obstacles from managers (who face increased labor costs) and the occasional disgruntled co-workers who see maternity leave as discriminatory against those who do not have children. Patriarchy in everyday life will not die a quiet or quick death, and so we should expect that the gendered economy will not disappear so quickly either: organizations, work, and employees' relations will still have a gendered logic to them if this logic appears in the outside world. As well, the second shift cannot continue in its present form without some change in assumptions and relations between men and women. Unless women are content to bear the burden, that contradiction will be resolved only by regressing to unequal gender relations once again, or rethinking masculinity and what it means to be a "man." However, this may not be such a foreboding issue. As women demand the right to work and have a family in the face of dis-gruntled co-workers and employers, fathers have slowly taken up the cause. In Great Britain, where labor law permits two weeks' paternity leave and requires that certain organizations allow flexible hours for working men and women with children, fathers have increasingly changed their working hours to devote more time to their chil-dren: from 2002 to 2005, the percentage of working fathers choosing flexible working hours rose from 11 percent to 31 percent according to a government report. To do so, fathers were not only changing their hours, they were sometimes changing their jobs (Curtin 2006). An increased focus on the work–family relationship is possible only because of a focus on women's roles as wife, mother, and employee. Analyzing and addressing gender in the economy can bring benefits not only to women and mothers, but to men and fathers, and children as well – not a bad spill-over effect.

7 The great experiment:
Markets in the shadows of socialism

In 1991 ethnic contention, economic chaos, and political conflict brought an end to the Soviet Union, breaking it into fifteen newly independent countries in desperate need of reform. Political reform (where it took place) aimed to create democracy, with mixed results. Economic reform allegedly aimed to create vibrant market economies, but this experiment in post-Soviet market-building has been more complex than originally imagined. After a decade of collapse and corruption (the 1990s), Russia saw economic growth after 2000 thanks to the high price of oil. Petro-dollars mask decrepit technology, problematic practices, and value wasted in unnecessary production.[1] In Belarus, the state subsidizes industry in Soviet fashion, maintaining employment and output – but Belarus relies heavily on cheap energy from Russia. The Baltics benefited from foreign investment, while Ukraine suffered incoherent reforms and corruption. East European countries, once Soviet satellites whose loyalty was assured by the Red Army, had reasonable success creating market economies and growth – but they had more experience with economic reform and proto-market structures, and they were willing to become economic satellites of the West.

On its own, the story of post-socialist economic change demands scrutiny, but for our study of economic sociology these countries provide a laboratory to examine the (re)birth of capitalism and the nature of embeddedness. If economies and radical economic change, like that in Russia and other post-Soviet economies, are embedded in wider social and political structures and practice, then we should observe *social friction*: conflict over or resistance to policies and outcomes, confusion over implementation of reforms, and persistence of previous practices (known as path dependency). One can see the importance of embeddedness by contrasting the sociological approach to the analyses and reforms proposed by two important camps of economists who studied or even participated in the reforms: neoliberal "shock therapy" and the "gradualist" alternative. Both share assumptions of neoclassical economics, but they differ on some points. Shock therapists believed change should be rapid: laws underpinning a market economy could be legislated speedily, and the new regime of free trade, bankruptcy, reduced subsidies to firms, and private property would quickly induce market behavior (Lipton *et al.* 1990). Gradualists claimed there would be a lag between new laws and behavior – learning a radically new system takes time – and reforms, especially privatization, should be slower (Murrell 1991, 1992).[2] In contrast, economic sociologists and some political scientists were more cautious. Some suggested political changes could make states less able to enact market laws and even increase corruption (Solnick 1998). Others focused on how exchange and privatization were shaped by networks between local and federal state officials, enterprise managers, and emerging financial elites. Finally, a small group of scholars focused on culture, power, and everyday practices, claiming that creating capitalism in post-socialist countries, as in Western Europe centuries before, was a social construction of new economic legitimacy, practices, and authority – a recipe for confusion and conflict.

The overall result of post-socialist market-building has been mixed: success in some cases, failure in others, muddling through in yet others. To capture the entire picture of these various countries would take several books, and so I will focus primarily on Russia, although at the end I will turn to other countries' experiences for contrasts and lessons. In particular, the comparison between Russia and China is instructive to understanding economic change. To truly grasp the enormity of this experiment, we must first understand the experiment that preceded it: the attempt to create communism, which left legacies that current Russian (and Polish and Ukrainian) political and economic actors confront every day.

The Soviet economy

In the 1930s the capitalist world was mired in the Great Depression. In the Soviet Union, not only factories but entire industrial cities (e.g. Magnitogorsk) were being built, in an economy without private property or entrepreneurship, where production and exchange were coordinated by the state. While Soviet production was far from efficient and output was not always useful – much was poor quality or fictitious – at least there was growth and employment. (The extent of repression only became truly known following Stalin's death in 1953.) By the 1980s, the Soviet economy was on the verge of crisis. Productivity was stagnant, agriculture was an enormous black hole sucking up money, technology was aging, and the military drained money and manpower. Minor reforms under Leonid Brezhnev and Yurii Andropov brought little improvement. The last Soviet leader, Mikhail Gorbachev, took increasingly radical measures that led to chaos and helped bring down the USSR.

Logics of the Soviet economy and the coming of crisis

All economies go through cycles, and the Soviet economy was no different. Its crises emerged from particular Soviet structures, institutions, and logics. The Soviet economy shared traits with Western capitalism, such as bureaucracy, planning, and rationalization of production and exchange. However, anti-capitalism at the heart of Soviet ideology and practice produced significant differences, even in how bureaucracy and rationalization operated (Kornai 1992; Kotkin 1995). One logic was the absence of private property. In Marxist thought, abolishing private property ends exploitation. In theory, all Soviet industrial property was owned collectively by the working class and was administered by the state (controlled in theory by the pro-letarian Communist Party). The reality was that workers were exploited by the Party elite. Another logic was micromanagement and planning, manifested in the Five-year Plan. Like a religious totem, the Five-year Plan, and yearly and monthly plans, were sacred to state planners and Party leaders. The key measure of meeting the Plan was quantity of output (e.g. tons of steel, square meters of plate glass, number of shoes). Only by fulfilling these targets could managers retain or advance their status. Whether consumers (individuals or other enterprises) could actually use these goods was ultimately less important than producing them, for by claiming that the USSR produced more steel or shoes than the United States, without having unem-ployment, the Soviet leadership could claim they had the superior economy.[3] A final logic was paternalist provision, including the absence of unemployment and provi-sion of goods and welfare benefits through enterprises. Soviet ideology was pre-dicated on providing "cradle-to-grave" welfare. Enterprises provided their workers with apartments, vacations, medical care, daycare for their children, and other consumer goods they could not buy on the market – because there was no private "market" and many goods were in short supply (e.g. cars). In some regions, large enterprises also supported local infrastructure (e.g. roads, schools, hospitals). Enterprise managers and Party leaders traded this financial burden for legitimacy and power – workers were dependent on the enterprise for provision and employ-ment that they could not find in the (non-existent) private market.

These logics fulfilled propaganda but contributed to economic problems. The absence of private property, profit, and autonomous exchange contributed to severe ineffi-ciencies. Planners in Moscow, not firms trying to appease consumers, planned what goods would be available. Measurement of enterprise success was not profit, P/E ratios, or share price, but rather fulfilling physical output. This led to a situation of the tail wagging the dog. Managers did not often think about whether their output was useful to other firms or consumers – they simply did what the state wanted, i.e. produce quantity. This resulted in seemingly irrational situations as sheets of plate glass or iron nails so large that few other enterprises could use them, even though the sheer weight meant fulfilling the output target (Nove 1977). Without private property and profit, enterprises relied on subsidies from the state – they could not sell shares or make and keep profit for future use. The state could not allow inefficient enterprises to go bankrupt because this would bring unemployment, and so the state sank money into enterprises with little return on investment. Following the paternalist logic, enterprise funds went to employee provision (apart-ments, cars) as well as production. The state provided cheap bread – leaders knew how bread shortages triggered the French and Russian Revolutions – and Soviet youths used cheap bread as soccer balls (real soccer balls were hard to find) and farmers used it to feed their pigs. This was an inefficient use of resources: too much cheap bread, too few soccer balls and pig feed.

Left on its own, the Soviet economy provided for its citizens. If they did not have the goods Western consumers enjoyed, they had practically guaranteed jobs, shelter, and basic necessities. While this created welfare values that would interfere with market reforms in the 1900s, it also bred economic problems by the 1980s. Cold War competition meant the increasing need to innovate – but the Soviet military could not keep up with American technological advances due to incentives *against* innovation in design and production. Innovation risked missing production targets, which managers could not afford. In addition, the Soviet economy could not feed its population; in the 1970s and 1980s, the USSR had to import grain. While oil prices were high in the 1970s, the Soviets could use petro-dollars (oil profits) for imports, but in the 1980s the price of oil dropped as Western nations adopted energy-efficient technology and OPEC nations pumped out more oil (partly to punish the USSR for invading Afghanistan) (Kotkin 2004). The arms race, dwindling petro-dollars, and inefficient industry and agriculture led to a near-crisis situation. When he became leader of the Communist Party in 1985, Mikhail Gorbachev set out to reform the economy. His initial steps were non-structural, for example, increasing discipline by reducing the availability of alcohol (to which Russians responded by brewing their own moonshine, *samogon*) and enforcing work schedules (e.g. raiding movie theaters in the afternoon to find people who were supposed to be at work). Gorbachev turned to more ambitious reforms that began to free up the economy from state control. He gave autonomy to enterprise managers and legalized small-scale entrepreneurship (cooperatives and then small independent firms). To go further, Gorbachev had to attack the massive state bureaucracy by introducing political reforms, from easing censorship (*glasnost*, "openness") to opening up elections to non-Communist competitors. This allowed the emergence of challengers, from Boris Yeltsin (president of the Russian Federation) to leaders of ethnic enclaves and republics (e.g. Ukraine, the Baltics). This also allowed challenges from non-communist movements in East Europe, which heralded the end of communism.

Revisiting the birth of capitalism: post-socialist market-building

After the end of communism in East Europe in 1989 and the Soviet Union in 1991, political elites turned to pressing needs: creating new, stable political systems (such as democracy); redefining identities (e.g. "nations"); constructing effective states, the rule of law, and civil societies; and building dynamic market economies to reverse the degeneration of the final years of Soviet socialism. Not all leaders followed the same paths: Belarus under Aleksandr Lukashenko remains eerily Soviet – a dictatorship and strong state presence in the economy. Others successfully liberalized polities and economies (e.g. the Baltics, Poland, Hungary). While the rapid and radical experiments of post-socialist countries to create their own new modernities is too complex for one chapter, I focus on market-building and economic change mostly in Russia.

Russian economic reform after the collapse of communism

Gorbachev's economic reforms, called *perestroika* ("restructuring"), decentralized economic authority from Moscow to the regions, enterprises, and small private businesses. Enterprise managers gained more freedom to produce outside state planning; cooperatives were legalized as small, autonomous organizations setting their own prices and buying and selling fairly freely. By 1990, Gorbachev and reformers spoke of private property. These reforms did not improve economic performance – if anything, radical and not always coherent reforms led to opportunism and confusion. As the state lost the ability to monitor and control economic activity, opportunism emerged (Solnick 1998). This included the emergence of organized crime (*mafiia*) and managers laundering state subsidies into personal profits (Kotkin 2001). By 1991 consumer goods were even rarer than in the 1980s.

Once the USSR disappeared, Russian president Boris Yeltsin and his chief reform adviser Yegor Gaidar instituted radical reforms to improve the economy and to end the state's control over the economy. Following the tenets of neoclassical economic theory and shock therapy, there were three main components to market reforms: liberalization and creating market discipline, privatization, and monetization (Table 7.1). All three were considered foundations to the workings of a vibrant market economy and economic growth: they would provide both the freedom and incentives to private investment and efficiency, and they would provide mechanisms to enforce discipline and to punish economic inefficiency and waste.

These reforms had mixed results, at best. Some sectors grew, especially those in raw materials extraction and export. Electronics, metallurgy, and textile sectors suffered initially (although metallurgy recovered somewhat after 2000). Private banks appeared overnight, with some accumulating wealth quickly – much of it from the Communist Party, the state, or foreign aid (Hoffman 2002). A new super-elite called the "oligarchs" – similar in some ways to America's nineteenth-century robber barons – gained control over these finances and traded political support for Yeltsin for ownership over potentially lucrative sectors, especially oil, but also nickel and palladium. These oligarchs used economic and political reforms to their own benefit, harming economic health and democracy in the process. Further, the state continued to expend finances on public services, from medical care and teachers to daycare. To cover these expenses, the state floated government debt – like American treasury bonds – but unfortunately, tax collection was so corrupt and inefficient that the state

Table 7.1 Dimensions of post-socialist economic reform

Liberalization and discipline	Freeing economic activity from state control, encouraging market discipline: competition, bankruptcy
Privatization	Creating private property and incentives to responsible use of capital
Monetization	Creating a stable, strong ruble to facilitate exchange and embody market value

could not pay its debt. This pyramid of state debt exploded in August 1998, when Yeltsin's new prime minister, Sergei Kirienko, announced a default. Immediately the value of the ruble dropped five times against the dollar (leading to a burst of inflation) and the financial system froze up, with some major banks going bankrupt. After becoming president in 2000, Vladimir Putin pushed through additional reform legislation, tightening up bankruptcy law, cracking down on some tax evasion, and generally attempting to bring order and stability to politics and policy-making – a necessity for capitalist investment. More than anything, rising oil prices and oil profits helped Putin's Russia improve, further encouraging foreign investment in Russian shares despite the recent 1998 crash.

The liberalized economy versus the state, mafiia, and shadow economy

This area of reforms aimed to promote the rise of efficient, competitive private business by reducing barriers to market entry. This involved legalizing private enterprise and creating foundations for private exchange, and enforcing discipline through bankruptcy and freeing up prices (encouraging competition and market value). This included reducing state subsidies to firms, which now had to sell goods if they wanted money to pay wages and bills. Liberalization was perhaps the easiest area of reform, since it involved freeing up prices and allowing private entrepreneurs to open their own firms. (Granted, this involved massive bureaucratic paperwork for entrepreneurs.) Private firms did open fairly quickly in the early 1990s: from 14,000 cooperatives in 1987 to 270,000 registered firms in 1991 and around 877,000 in 1995 (OECD 2002: 76). They supplied goods and services once lacking or difficult to obtain in the Soviet era, and they provided work and wages to those workers let go from or leaving low-paying state-owned firms. However, reforms and the state created or allowed market obstacles or distortions: from corruption and the *mafiia* (organized criminal bands), to shadow and virtual economies of production and exchange unreported to the state and tax authorities.

The predatory state and the shadow economy

As we saw in Chapter 3, state regulations of business can create shadow economies; the Soviet and post-Soviet economies are no exception, and this was a prominent feature of the Soviet economy. In fact, because private, entrepreneurial activity was restricted or illegal in the Soviet era, the Soviet economy ended up with a vast shadow economy, from theft of building materials, cotton, or oil, to working in the evenings for additional rubles or a bottle of vodka (Grossman 1977) – except for the legalized sale of food grown on private plots and occasional artisan work, private enterprise was *de facto* shadow economic activity (or else the police stopped it). The post-Soviet economy also had a shadow economy, but not for the exact same reasons. Private activity was allowed, but taxes were draconian. Between value-added taxes, taxes on *gross* income, and other various fees, honest managers or entrepreneurs might end up paying close to 100 percent of their net profit in taxes (Gustafson 1999; Ryvkina 1999). Much of the shadow economy is normal everyday business unreported to the state so as to avoid tax. This may be as simple as a repairman working in the evenings for hard cash – something that happens often enough in developed market economies – to complex deals, in which firms buy and sell real goods and services while reporting fictitious, cheaper deals to the tax police.

One part of the shadow economy is the "virtual economy." Here exchange is based not on money but on *barter*, exchange in kind, often undocumented to avoid taxes. Inefficient firms that produce goods which nobody wants cannot survive by making a profit – they make none from the goods they produce (bad quality, no market demand). However, they need raw materials, energy and electricity, transportation, and enough goods and money to remunerate employees. So managers of these poorly-off firms barter their goods to firms that supply them, such as natural gas, electricity, and railroad monopolies (Gazprom, UES, Russian Railroads). Clifford Gaddy and Barry Ickes (2002) asked just why these large, profitable firms that supply inefficient firms continued to do so, when this reduces their profit: why accept barter for electricity or gas, when UES and Gazprom can sell electricity and gas to firms that pay hard cash? And not only were Gazprom, UES, and others not making rubles – they were actually *losing* in these deals. The poorly-off firms were offering goods at a barter value higher than the ruble value in the market (see Figure 7.1.) Thus Gazprom, UES, and others were losing twice over: losing rubles, and gaining bartered goods at a higher "virtual" price. The upshot: in the barter deals of the virtual economy, Gazprom, UES, and the railways were subsidizing inefficient, market-failing firms, just as the state had once done. For this reason Gaddy and Ickes call this a "virtual economy" – virtual because it is outside the market, with value and exchange based not on money but on kind, like a premodern economy.

Why would Gazprom trade gas at below-market prices for goods at above-market prices? First, most of these firms support the regional infrastructure and safety nets for local populations: they provide employment and support local schools and hospitals, and supply other social services (e.g. daycare). Many Russian firms, especially those in the military-industrial complex, are so inefficient and their goods so uncompetitive that they should, by all rights, go under. Were they to go bankrupt and disappear, local welfare would vanish as well. Local politicians use threats of political instability to convince Gazprom to engage in barter. Second, enterprise managers use networks to local political and economic elites to ask for favors. In the Soviet system, managers used networks and favors to survive; this practice still persists as a powerful business ethic. Third, given the draconian tax burden, it makes little sense to have profit – simply to make enough money to pay expenses. Gazprom and UES might lose profit bartering with inefficient firms, but this also reduces their taxes.

Ultimately, the shadow and virtual economies persist because this is the model of a normal economy bequeathed from the Soviet era that the state helps keep alive. Reliance on networks, working in a non-monetary format, eluding the state as a matter of course (like a vast game of cat-and-mouse) were central to Soviet economic normality (Hass 2005). In addition, high taxes provide an incentive for firms to stay

Firm A sells gas, electricity, transport, or other necessary good. The value is 10 rubles per unit. Firm B is inefficient. It produces a good (e.g. textiles, cement) at a market value of 5 rubles per unit. (This is the value on the global market, as sold by efficient competitors.)

Assume Firm B needs one unit of gas/electricity/transport. Assume Firm A needs one unit of textiles/cement.

In a **market economy**, the exchange relation works as follows:

One unit of gas/electricity: B pays A 10 rubles

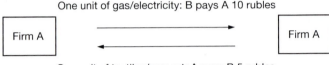

One unit of textiles/cement: A pays B 5 rubles

In the **virtual economy**, A and B barter their goods as equivalents:

One unit of gas/electricity

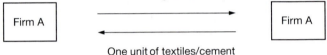

One unit of textiles/cement

In the market economy, A comes out ahead: it spends 5 rubles but gains 10, a profit of 5 rubles – on which it must pay taxes. Firm B is 5 rubles in the red and eventually goes bankrupt because it is inefficient. In the virtual economy, both sides even out. Firm A makes no profit, and in fact loses doubly because it is not selling that gas/electricity to another firm for money – but it also has less tax to pay. Firm B stays alive.

Figure 7.1   Barter, value, and the virtual economy

Source: Gaddy and Ickes (2002)

in the shadow of the virtual economy. Yet once the state has levied its tax burden, it cannot collect taxes. This is partly because the tax inspectorate, like many state departments, is underfunded and understaffed. It is more rational to prosecute a few major cases for a large tax debt and fines than to prosecute many smaller cases (Yakovlev 1999). Many tax inspectors also accept bribes. Local state authorities keep the virtual economy going by ignoring it or encouraging it, because it keeps local voters employed. To banish the shadow and the virtual economies the state first needs to clean up its own act by reducing corruption, improving the skills and organization of state employees, and then proposing taxes that are fair and at reasonable rates.

The stories of virtual and shadow economies are important for several reasons. First, they demonstrate the centrality of the state in setting up formal versus informal exchange. Second, they show that actors will – as economists claim – improve gain (if not maximize it), going beyond the bounds of the law if necessary. Third, as we saw in Chapter 4, informal economies are not documented before the law and cannot be defended by law – aiding criminal entrepreneurs in the business of protection, the *mafiia*.

Exchange, contract, and mafiia

Enforcing contracts in the West is not easy – court backlogs, lawyers' motions, and the like drag out the process. Russian courts were full as well, but there were other obstacles. First, formal contractual exchange was not an everyday practice to Russian managers and entrepreneurs. True, there had been Soviet contracts, but these were essentially terms of production and shipment dictated by the state. They were not negotiated freely by producers and purchasers themselves, as in market economies. Private businessmen had to learn how to draw up contracts, which was not always easy (Hass 1998: ch. 4). For example, early contracts did not always take into account contingencies, details of exchange (e.g. pricing, delivery), or penalties for contractual violations. Not only did private businessmen have to learn how to draw up contracts: they also had to learn how to defend them. Suppose I paid a firm to deliver office supplies – what is to stop them from not delivering, or from closing up shop and reopening under a new name?[4]

One way to guard exchange was to rely primarily on networks and buy/sell with people who one knew or had worked with before (Hendley *et al.* 1999, 2000). This provided two important advantages. First, there was a known history: one had an idea of whether they could trust another, especially from working with them in the past. Second, one could hold another's reputation hostage in the network structure. If an acquaintance violated an agreement, I could tell this to our common friends and acquaintances, smearing that other person's reputation. Given the importance of networks to survival in the Soviet era, actors naturally turned to them in the 1990s – and so reputation became a powerful tool to defend exchange. Many managers who I interviewed in 1994 and 1995 said that this was one of the most powerful forces against contract violation: fear that word would spread that "so-and-so" is dishonest and others should not do business with him/her. The state's own incompetence also encouraged reliance on networks. By using networks actors could set up elaborate business dealings and keep from reporting them to the tax authorities (Yakovlev 1999).

However, reliance on networks for structuring business had one disadvantage: they limited the number of potential clients and buyers. If acquaintances could not or would not buy one's goods or services, that person was in trouble, as several entrepreneurs admitted to me in interviews. When they had to deal with strangers, there were two other tools to help defend exchange and contract. The first was prepayments (Hass 1998: ch. 3). Managers of firms large and small began to demand that buyers pay at least 50 percent of the price for a good or service up front. This served two functions. First, the prepayment was a hostage creating an incentive for both sides to follow through on the agreement. The producer would receive the full sum only by producing the good or service; the buyer had paid part of the price, creating an incentive to pay the rest. Second, prepayments provided capital to help production. Inflation in the early 1990s meant that most Russian producers lacked sufficient money to begin a production run, and prepayments provided some start-up capital. Prepayments became such a normal part of post-Soviet business that Russians sometimes demanded them of foreign clients, who were trustworthy and could pay – who then became annoyed and decided not to deal with Russians (as occurred at a private publisher I studied in 1994 to 1995).

Another means of enforcing exchange, and defending the firms generally, was *mafiia*. Not simply mindless thugs, the Russian "mafiia," like organized crime everywhere, is a business of selling protection and dealing in violence (Gambetta 1993). While criminal groups existed in the Soviet era, some even in the Communist Party, they were not oriented to business and profit *per se*. The new business-oriented *mafiia* emerged with Gorbachev's reforms. New private cooperatives and small businesses needed protection or could act as fronts for laundering money, giving the new generation a chance to emerge (Handelman 1997). Soon different *bandit* groups developed rituals for working with businesses – offering protection in return for "fees," for example (as in the United States or Italy) – or for working with each other to avoid turf wars or handle conflicts between *mafiia* clients (Volkov 2002). *Mafiia* were not usually welcome partners – as businessmen told me, "The best bandit is a dead bandit" – but they could offer protection against other predator *mafiia* and could help defend contractual relations by using the threat of violence against opportunistic clients who might renege on an agreement – something the state was supposed to do but often did not or could not. While *mafiia* demanded money from businesses under threat of violence (known as racketeering), at least they provided this service, unlike the state, which also took money (taxes). As another businessman once told me, the worst *mafiia* was the state!

Learning new practices

In the Soviet era, managers produced what Moscow planners commanded. In the 1990s, managers suddenly had to decide what to produce, at what cost, for what market – a sudden increase in the quantity and quality of managerial decisions. This was a radical change in economic logic for which managers and entrepreneurs who were trained and socialized in the Soviet era did not always have appropriate skills and human capital (Blasi *et al.* 1997). Now firms had to produce for consumers, which meant trying to figure out just who their consumers were or should be, what they might want, and how to produce it (or to convince consumers to buy their products). Learning this new market logic quickly, after decades in the Soviet economy, was difficult. While managers and entrepreneurs adopted some logics and practices fairly quickly, others were overwhelmed by ingrained Soviet practices, kept alive by surviving Soviet-era laws and organizational structures, and by interaction with others who also continued to follow Soviet, non-market logics.

One example of continuity of Soviet practices in the post-Soviet era was in strategies of sales and production (Hass 1997, 1999, 2005). In the Soviet era, the name of the game was production for the state and the Five-year Plan, not for consumers. Managers needed inputs to produce their quotas, and so the state and suppliers were a firm's real target (Verdery 1995). Managers understood how to obtain deficit supplies, negotiate Plan targets with ministers and bureaucrats, and get employees to produce at the end of each month to meet monthly output quotas (or to falsify documents accordingly). This required knowledge and skills related to the enterprise's technical capacities and the politics of the Plan; it did not require knowledge of deducing consumers' wants or how to attract their money. When state control of production and exchange ceased and state subsidies declined, managers suddenly needed to find consumers and sell to them to make money and pay wages and debts. Enterprise managers understood this all too well – but it was more difficult to adopt and implement a radically different practice that oriented production and sales to the demands of the market. Just what is a firm's "market," and how does one interact with it? Seemingly simple, this was actually a difficult task, as stories of creating "marketing" divisions show. As early as 1993 post-Soviet Russian firms were creating marketing divisions, following the advice of Western consultants and business literature. However, these marketing divisions followed a Soviet logic: sell what was already produced according to a firm's technical plans and mission (as set up in the Soviet era). Assistant managers for production, accounting, and supply – important in the Soviet era – still had more status than assistant managers for sales and marketing. Marketing directors and general directors often talked of their new tasks as trying to sell goods – but there seemed little consideration about what goods consumers wanted. Marketing, in short, was not about discovering market demand – it was about selling what a firm had already produced, as it had done for decades before market reforms were enacted.

The problem was that learning a new logic was more than simply opening a marketing division or a general director taking a few seminars in marketing. Rather, it involved changing multiple practices of sales and production for many managers and employees – changing how the post-Soviet firm, *as a collective*, did business. This also meant changing the status hierarchy within firms, something that many non-marketing managers resisted. As well, a general director who admitted the inability to learn marketing was admitting inability to lead in the new era – and so managers often did not show bold initiative in radically changing their own practices, as well as those of their managerial teams. When learning did occur, it was more likely to be among newer or younger managers; both had greater mandates for change and could more easily admit the need to learn (and to change managerial teams), and younger managers had less socialization and experience in the Soviet era, making learning easier. Finally, learning the new logic of marketing and sales was complicated by financial strains and burdens. Firms could not easily retool or spend money to hire foreign marketing consultants. They also needed to sell goods quickly and make money to pay their bills. Finally, inflation depressed general consumer buying power; where were marketing employees supposed to find consumers with money anyway?

In short, change in structures, practices, and strategies of exchange were not limited to defending contract, avoiding the predatory state and *mafiia*, and moving beyond networks. Economic theory assumes that market exchange – a simplified form of marketing skills and practices – is a natural proclivity. While exchange in its crudest, simplest form may be, modern economies are neither crude nor simple, and successful exchange beyond the corner store requires more sophisticated techniques, which themselves must be embedded in organizational practices, procedures, and hierarchies. These do not magically appear because a government, like Russia's in 1992, adopts market-oriented laws and policies. Rather, capitalist exchange must be learned by the actors themselves.

A general lesson of remaking exchange in post-Soviet capitalism is that practices, foundations, and defense of buying and selling do not emerge automatically or naturally follow dictates of business efficiency. Rather, they depend on the actions and capacities of the state, actors' own preconceptions of normal exchange, and existing expediencies. Past practices and knowledge interact with contingencies and actors' own negotiations and creativity.

Privatization: the politics of property

A powerful criticism of the Soviet economy was the absence of private property. Apart from this institution there were no owners with interests tied to efficiency, productivity, profit, and growth; instead there were inefficiencies and waste. Post-socialist privatization had three goals. The economic goal was to create incentives for efficient use of capital: owners (in theory) would be careful about investment and would be more active in seeking profit. The political goals were to sell state-owned firms for profit (to bring in money to the budget), and to deprive the state of economic power of property ownership. If the hope was to promote economic growth, the reality did not always follow. Recall from the discussion of corporations in Chapter 5 that property is not apolitical or innocuous: property and power structure each other, leading to new classes and shaping resources and interests. The rise of the American corporation was a political affair; the creation of private property in a few short years meant that post-socialist privatization was bound to be politically muddled and contentious, and that privatization would not be the panacea automatically leading to a vibrant, competitive market economy. While privatization did help growth, it also created conflict – including hired killings over property ownership – and soured Russians and East Europeans over market reforms that were supposed to be the dawn of a new era.

Politics of privatization

The hopes pinned on privatization were harmed by the lack of capital to invest in private firms and by the politics of privatization. Both were linked. The politics of privatization occurred at two levels: that of the enterprise and of elite politics (especially around the Kremlin). In the Soviet era, managers were agents of the state – they did not own enterprises, but they ran them as their own bailiwicks. As Soviet and post-Soviet reforms began, managers remained in charge of enterprises, but they often saw privatization as a threat to their authority: a new owner might buy the enterprise and replace old managers, and so managers set out to use privatization to gain control over their firms. They used two populist elements of Russian privatization. The first was vouchers. To make privatization palatable to his people, Boris Yeltsin decreed that each Russian citizen would receive 10,000 rubles-worth of vouchers that could be exchanged for an equivalent amount of shares. Average

Russians would participate in the creation of capitalism and become owners, holding a stake in their economy's future. The second element of populism was that 51 percent of shares in industrial enterprises would first be offered to employees, with the remaining shares sold later to outsiders. Using these two policies, managers mobilized their workers, playing on the threat that outsiders would buy the firm and begin massive lay-offs. To workers, the current Soviet-era manager was a known evil, and workers often sold their shares to managers or gave them proxy voting rights. This was "insider privatization" – insiders (managers and workers) gaining a majority of votes in newly privatized firms. This had two effects on growth and investment. When managers and workers bought shares, they did not have additional capital to invest in their firms – in other words, they were owners who could not invest in modernizing technology. (Some outside buyers also used vouchers to purchase a firm without investing "real" money.) Without investment capital, they could not modernize to compete with imports or to export goods, and they survived by retreating from the market, reducing expenditures to a bare minimum and producing enough to pay a fraction of wages (King 2003). In addition, managers and employees were as interested in saving their jobs as improving performance, which might require reducing labor (Soviet firms employed too many workers). Thus an informal alliance emerged: workers supported managers, who tried to avoid laying off workers (Afanas'ev *et al.* 1997).

Elite politics also warped privatization. Not all Russian firms were inefficient destroyers of capital and value. Some were potentially lucrative – especially in oil, natural gas, gold, ferrous and non-ferrous metals, and others in natural resource

BOX 7.1 OLIGARCHS AND POLITICS: FROM YELTSIN TO PUTIN

Oligarchs were Russia's richest and most powerful men in the 1990s. They gained their wealth in the late 1980s and early 1990s through various financial schemes, such as holding state money (e.g. from customs' duties) and speculating on currencies and raw materials. They then bought shares in diverse firms during privatization. Some (Khodorkovskii, Potanin) gained considerably through the loans-for-shares policy, in which the state exchanged its shares in lucrative firms (e.g. Yukos and Sidanko) in return for loans to cover the state debt. The oligarchs won the auctions and augmented their enormous wealth due to an alliance with Yeltsin and his regime, including Anatolii Chubais, who oversaw privatization. Chubais viewed the oligarchs as a counterweight to the potential return of the communists: with property in private hands, the communists could not rebuild communism (state control over property) should they return to power (Hoffman 2002). Some oligarchs milked their empires for personal profit; a few others devoted time and energy to restructuring their holdings, implementing Western methods of transparency, accounting, and planning. One was Mikhail Khodorkovskii, who gained several oil firms that he merged into oil giant Yukos. Oleg Deripaska has Russian managers who gained business training in the West; Kakha Bendukidze restructured his empire so that different engineering firms became more integrated, working together to provide clients with a range of assorted products and services.

However, politics intruded. Vladimir Putin became president due to support from the oligarchs and Boris Yeltsin. After his election in 2000, Putin turned against Boris Berezovskii and Vladimir Gusinskii: both controlled media empires that were potentially critical of the state (especially the war in Chechnya). This cowed the other oligarchs up until 2003, when Khodorkovskii showed political ambitions, including criticizing Putin, contributing money to various political parties, and claiming that he would one day enter politics. Putin and his regime attacked Khodorkovskii and Yukos for tax fraud – while letting other oligarchs escape with simple audits and requests to pay taxes. Khodorkovskii was convicted of tax fraud and jailed in 2005. Yukos, once a Russian success story, was emasculated, and state-owned Rosneft took important Yukos assets in return for the tax debt – and Putin's state began building empires of state-owned enterprises (e.g. oil, gas, aviation).

The most important oligarchs in the 1990s and early 2000s are the following:

Oligarch	Empire (lead company in **bold**)
*Boris Berezovskii	**LogoVAZ** (auto dealership); Russian Aluminum (later sold to Abramovich); Aeroflot; Sibneft (oil); *Kommersant* publishing house, Channel 1 (main television channel)
*Mikhail Khodorkovskii	**Menatep-Rosprom** (investment company); Yukos (oil); Russian Textiles Consortium; firms in chemicals, metallurgy, construction
Roman Abramovich	Sibneft (oil); Russian Aluminum (later sold to Deripaska)
*Vladimir Gusinskii	**MOST-Bank** and **MOST-Group** (investment company); NTV (television), various important newspapers
Oleg Deripaska	**Basic Element** (aluminum extraction and reworking, including Russian Aluminum)
Kakha Bendukidze	**United Heavy Machinery** (engineering, electricity generation, including such firms as Izhorskie Factories and Uralmash)
Vladimir Potanin	**Uneximbank** and **Interros** (investment company); Norilsk Nickel; Sidanko Oil and Sviazinvest telecom (until 1998), NLMK steel, ZiL (cars), Perm Motors, Mikrodin finance, various firms in chemicals, railroad and transportation, exports, print media
*Aleksandr Smolenskii	**SBS-Agro** (bank); confectionaries, media
*Vladimir Vinogradov	**Inkombank**; confectionaries, steel
Mikhail Fridman	**Alfa-Bank** and **Alfa-Group** (investment company); Tiumen' Oil, various firms in cement, chemicals, construction
Anatolii Chubais	**Unified Electricity System**; monopoly electricity grid, local electricity generation and distribution
*Rem Viakhirev	**Gazprom** (natural gas monopoly); domestic gas complex (reserves, extraction), banks (e.g. National Reserve Bank), media (newspapers and television investments)

Note: * Lost many holdings under Putin due to arrest or flight from Russia, leaving position, or negative consequences (e.g. bankruptcy) following August 1998 default and ruble crash.

extraction and reworking. Yeltsin held these firms until the mid-1990s, when they were supposed to be carefully privatized at high prices. However, politics intruded. Yeltsin's reforms brought pain to average Russians, and economic stability was slow in coming. Yeltsin's popularity suffered, and it seemed that the communists might win the 1996 presidential election. Yeltsin needed powerful allies who could fund his campaign, and he used these natural resources firms to cut a deal with the emerging financial elite. His government would sell these firms to these "oligarchs" at rigged auctions at low prices. The oligarchs would support Yeltsin's campaign and regime following the election. And so in late 1995, in the infamous "loans-for-shares" auction, Yeltsin's government sold off these firms to the oligarchs, who then made super-profits. Rigged privatization and the collusion of the Kremlin and business elites delegitimated Yeltsin's market reforms as a ploy for managers and elites (and some foreigners) to plunder Russia, rather than make its economy healthy once again.

In general, privatization could aid growth by attracting investment and giving new owners the power to bring in younger, market-savvy managers and make decisions more in tune with demands of the world market (OECD 2002), but it could also impair market mechanisms, for example, by hindering transparency. David Stark (1996) called this "recombinant property." In Hungary and the Czech Republic, managers purchased shares in each other's enterprises, so that for any group of firms there was no immediately discernable legal owner responsible for performance. In Russia a similar tactic was the use of shell companies distantly controlled by enterprise owners, or offshore companies in Cyprus or other havens outside the reach of Russian law. This tactic helped managers and owners funnel money into personal accounts, avoid accusations of monopoly,[5] and create a firewall against tax authorities and creditors – real money and authority was hidden in these shadow "daughter firms." This brings to light an important point about post-socialist privatization: mechanisms for *transparency* were absent or not enforced, creating legal shadows that hindered the functioning of a working market economy. Transparency is crucial because it alerts investors to potential risks and rewards, and shows relations of money and property (to combat fraud and oligopoly). Instead, managers and new owners used the lack of transparency to create empires and fortunes or to avoid the financial consequences of their decisions.

Privatization in different countries

Variations in privatization policies across former communist countries reflected different debates over the ethical, legitimate, and effective aspects of privatization. According to Stark and Bruszt (1998: ch. 3), debates in Eastern Europe had four dimensions: the role of foreign participation (should foreigners be allowed to invest capital and know-how but also gain control of firms); should privatization be spontaneous or controlled (letting workers and managers privatize on their own initiative versus the state directing the process, with different threats of corruption and ethics at stake); should owners be institutional or natural (investment groups versus real individuals as the primary purchasers of property – the former had more capital but also a greater chance of corruption); and should ownership be concentrated or dispersed (letting a few groups or many citizens buy the majority of property)? No position was perfect. For example, natural and dispersed ownership would invite citizens to partake in privatization, but it would mean less capital for investment. Only institutional investors had such capital, and they wanted to purchase many firms, concentrating capital in a few hands – which reformers wanted to avoid to legitimize capitalism. One additional dimension that arose was setting the value of state-owned assets: would the price for privatization be set by state commissions, in negotiations between the state and potential buyers, or through a market mechanism such as an open auction?

The debates were not resolved in the same way in different countries, leading to different privatization policies (Stark and Bruszt 1998: 88–100). In eastern Germany – the former East Germany, incorporated into West Germany after 1989 – a special state commission set the value of assets and sold them to corporations for money. In the Czech Republic, citizens (rather than corporations or investment funds) used vouchers to buy state-held assets, whose value was set in auctions. In Hungary, corporations – often the firm up for sale – were the primary purchasers, and a firm's workers had the first chance to buy their firm at a value set by independent auditors. In Poland, citizens used vouchers to purchase shares (as in the Czech Republic), but as in Hungary, workers had the first chance to buy their firm. Asset value was set through bargaining, and workers would turn over their shares to "asset managers" who bought and ran the firm in the employees' name. The Russian case combined many of these elements. In the first stage, employees could buy half the shares with vouchers and money; enterprise value was set by a special committee. In a second stage various individuals and groups bidded for the remaining shares from the state, for money only.

Privatization was far from automatic in countries where vast amounts of property were state owned, asset value unclear, and property not fully legitimate. Privatization as well was not simply creating incentives for productivity and investment – it was redistributing property away from the state to someone, but to whom? Generally, managers and elites networked to the state gained control over property and over benefits such as profits (when there were profits) and organizational authority. This lesson was clear to everyone: to workers who wondered who really ran their firms, to managers and owners who sometimes tried to assassinate each other in attempts to gain control of enterprises, and to local and federal governments who used privatization as a means to gain political support. Privatization was inherently about reorganizing the landscape of economic and political power. Economists did not miss this, but they did downplay it – missing the forest of power for the trees of efficiency.

Monetization: market versus virtual value

Monetization means that value resides in a symbolic unit of currency that others trust to hold value: I work hard to earn dollars and trust that a supermarket clerk will accept them for goods, and that the dollar's value will not drop overnight (i.e. from $2 for a coffee to $6 for the same coffee tomorrow). When a country experiences inflation and even hyperinflation (50 percent or more inflation *per month*, as happened in Russia and other former Soviet countries in the early 1990s), people lose faith in their currency.[6] Monetization also requires removing competing symbols: local currencies different from the national unit, and non-currency exchange such as barter. Russia had a national currency, the ruble, which suffered from problems inherited from the communist era, and from the weakening of the state and destabilization of the economy. The communist ruble was not convertible with foreign currencies, and its value on the black market was always lower than through official state channels. As citizens and entrepreneurs had little faith in the ruble's real value, enormous "dollarization" occurred. Entrepreneurs and citizens exchanged rubles for dollars as a surer store of value than rubles or even bank accounts, and some stores and firms required payment in dollars.

A stable ruble was supposed to facilitate exchange, make Russia less dependent on outside currencies and countries, and facilitate tax payment. The creation of national economies requires states strong enough to enforce a national currency. Unified national economies, as in America or Mexico, use a single currency (the dollar or peso) only because the state supports that currency. Russian monetization was not so straightforward. As the Soviet economy unraveled, its institutionalized symbols of value (money) unraveled as well. Monetization faced two powerful obstacles: state weakness and private actors' resistance. Actors may use money to buy and sell because it is convenient – but what currencies do they use? In the Soviet era (pre-1991), only special tourist stores accepted foreign currencies; after 1991, higher-end private stores began to accept dollars or Deutschmarks. This was part of the dollarization of the economy. In response, the government passed a law decreeing that from 1994 all exchange be in rubles. This did not eradicate competition to the ruble, however. Stores simply quoted prices in dollars, payable in rubles – and they invited banks to open exchange points inside or near their stores. Russians continued to hoard their savings in dollars rather than in rubles and ruble-denominated bank accounts – banks' savings were wiped out by inflation in 1992, and banks remained notoriously unstable – literally hiding their personal worth in cupboards or under bed mattresses. The state's real tool to enforce a single currency was tax payments – make people and firms pay taxes in rubles, and they would trade or work for rubles. However, the capacity of the state to enforce tax payments was hurt by competition between Moscow and its regions. So long as Moscow remained too weak to enforce tax payment, the dollar and Deutschmark remained Russia's real currency.

State weakness was compounded by private actors' resistance. If we accept that money is not an inevitable, natural expression of value, then it follows that actors may use different means to code value and facilitate exchange. In fact, the 1990s saw the explosion of what Viviana Zelizer (1997) calls "multiple monies," the expression of value in multiple means (Hass 2005). As noted above, one alternative was foreign currencies. Dollars were the favorite, although people stored value in Deutschmarks and, later, the euro. Some small firms, such as restaurants, would use a stand-in currency called an *uslovnaya edinitsa* (*u.e.*, conditional unit): a fictitious currency that was equal to that day's exchange rate for the dollar. For example, a restaurant might change 5 *u.e.* for a meal, payable in rubles at a rate of 30 rubles per *u.e.* This maintained stability – firms did not worry that inflation would make them change their price lists, because the price in *u.e.* was stable and all they had to change was the ruble–*u.e.* rate.[7] This may seem trivial, but it sent out a powerful symbolic signal: the ruble was not worthy of social trust. Another form of value and exchange was wechsels (*vekselia*), formal IOUs. An enterprise would use electricity, but if it could not pay, it issued wechsels, or IOUs, to the local electricity supplier. The electricity supplier would then hold the wechsels, awaiting payment, or sell them to someone else at a discount (for a lesser monetary value). This way the enterprise got its electricity, the electricity supplier got some money, and a third party got the chance to recoup the debt later. (The same worked for water utilities or banks.) Enterprises racked up enormous wechsel debts to banks and utilities, and one would think that eventually utilities and banks would wise up and stop playing the game – except that operational enterprises meant voters were employed, and so local governments were sometimes active in encouraging these wechsel chains (Woodruff 1999).

One alternative means of embodying value and facilitating exchange – the function of money – was "virtual" value in the "virtual economy." Recall that here agents bartered goods rather than bought and sold them for money. This means that the real value of the goods bartered becomes equal. So far, so good – except when one of those sets of goods is worth *more* in the broader (global) market. For example, Gazprom, UES, and railroads barter gas, electricity, and transport with inefficient firms for low-quality goods. The goods are nearly worthless on the world market, but the gas and electricity are not. What Gazprom, UES, and others are doing is actually reducing their monetary (market) price when they barter, and inflating the exchange value of the worthless goods. In other words, Gazprom would be better off buying goods from market producers and selling their gas at a higher price. Were the virtual economy marginal, this would not be a problem. When barter involves up to 40 percent of Russian firms, there is a significant second economy based not on money but on negotiated barter – "virtual" rather than market value – that upsets monetization.

The lesson of monetization is that the embodiment of value does not emerge naturally from "market" forces. Rather, it comes from a complex interaction of state and private actors. We think of monetary confusion as inherent in developing economies – yet Russia is a "First World" country, with nuclear weapons and, despite its recent history, much human capital and productive capacity. That this kind of country could experience confusion over its money and monetization screams out just how economies are socially, and politically, constructed.

Impact of market-building reforms

Despite shortcomings, market reforms have produced some positive results. Private enterprise has tapped the skills and drive of a creative, educated labor force, reducing the problems of deficit goods and services that plagued the Soviet economy. Some countries, such as Poland, Hungary, Slovenia, the Czech Republic, and the three Baltic countries (Estonia, Latvia, and Lithuania) gained a modicum of economic stability and development, aided by trade with and eventual entry into the European Union. Azerbaijan and Kazakhstan enjoyed oil wealth, which since 2000 Russia has benefited from as well. Others, such as Bulgaria, Georgia, and Armenia, have been damaged by conflicts inside or near their countries: Bulgaria's economy was hurt by civil war in traditional trading partner Yugoslavia, and Georgia and Armenia suffered internal strife. Belarus and Ukraine were slow in implementing economic reforms, and in fact Belarus retains much of a Soviet-style economy, with the state owning or subsidizing large industrial and agricultural enterprises. (The post-socialist wonder is China, to which I turn below.) Post-socialist market reforms have created wealth, but not everyone benefited (Table 7.2).

Yet we cannot evaluate post-socialist economic change in terms of GDP change alone. The distribution of money, authority, and opportunity has a broader impact on everyday life, and to get a fuller sense of just how profound this change has been – just as profound as the birth of Western capitalism over a century ago – we must turn to other facets of the economy and society in the post-socialist world. Again, I turn to Russia for this wider picture.

Table 7.2 Recent economic trends in selected post-socialist economies

Country	Approximate GDP growth (year)		
	Early 1990s	Mid–1990s	Post–2000
Russia	–5% (1991)	–2.6 (1995)	7.3% (2003)
Ukraine	–9% (1991)	–23% (1994)	10% (2003)
Belarus	–1% (1991)	–10% (1995)	
		11% (1997)	7% (2003)
China			9.1% (2003)
Poland	–7% (1991)	7% (1995)	1.8% (2002)
Hungary	–0.5% (1982–1992 average)	1.5% (1995)	
		4.9% (1998)	3.2% (2002)
Czech Republic		2.4% (1994–2004)	3.7% (2003)
Bulgaria	–8% (1991)	3% (1995)	5% (2002)
Kazakhstan	–11% (1991)	–12.6% (1994)	
		1.7% (1997)	9.5% (2002–04)
Estonia	–13% (1991)		
	–22% (1992)	5% (1995, 1998)	5% (2003)
Latvia	–12% (1991)	–32% (1992)	–1% (2005)
		5% (1998)	8% (2003)
Azerbaijan	–23% (1992)	–11% (1995)	10% (1998–2004)

Source: Generated using data from the World Bank, Country Briefs. Online. Available HTTP: <http:www.worldbank.org> (accessed March 20, 2006); The Economist Intelligence Unit. Online. Available HTTP: <http:www.economist.com> (accessed March 20, 2006).

Crime

While we have already seen the rise of *mafiia*, crime has increased in other ways as well, aided by corruption within the police and the state more generally. Russia's market-building project has been redistribution of resources, and sometimes the stakes are high. Competition over these assets has not been restricted to legal means: hired killings have been a black mark on post-Soviet Russia, whether of managers, bankers, entrepreneurs, or journalists reporting on corruption. In 1993 and 1994, bankers were being killed every month, usually as they were arriving home at their apartments. The situation became so bad that in 1995 the head of the bankers' union suggested a three-day bank strike over the seriousness of this threat to bankers' lives. He was killed soon after. More everyday crime, such as theft or muggings, increased as well, heightening the sense of insecurity that contributed to Putin's positive image as a strong hand of discipline and social order. Even the police have taken part in everyday crime. One cannot read the *Moscow Times* for long or talk to foreign travelers without hearing first-hand accounts of police or other officials "shaking down" foreign businessmen or tourists. The police might stop a foreigner to check documents. While one officer frisks the individual, the other checks all documents. If there is money in a wallet, the search ends; otherwise, the individual might be threatened with a trip to the police station to verify that person's visa – unless he or she pays a "fine" on the spot (for what infraction is never clear). A more infamous form of corruption comes from traffic cops. Traffic cops have been known to pull over drivers of foreign cars for "routine" checks or "infractions" of traffic rules; the driver can go through a laborious court process (perhaps losing his or her license temporarily) or pay a "fine" on the spot, which likely stays in the traffic cop's pocket.

Inequality and the standard of life

While oil wealth helped alleviate some of Russia's inequality, the story of the market transition was not pretty. While average Soviets did not enjoy the same standard of living as the average Westerner before 1991, most Soviets were not poor and did have access to reasonable medical care and to a roof over their heads. After 1991, inequality increased. State-owned firms could not pay high salaries, nor could they pay them on time. Some regions benefited more from liberalized trade, while others stagnated. Cities dominated by the military-industrial complex faced hard times in the 1990s, while those in oil, finance, or politics (e.g. some regional capitals) eventually saw improvements. While different statistical studies gave different figures, the received wisdom was that around one-third of the Russian population lived near the poverty line (less than $100 per month) – although this might under-count wealth unreported in the shadow economy. Further, wealth was concentrated in a small elite: *thirty-six* individuals held a quarter of Russia's GDP (*Moscow Times*, May 13, 2004, p. 5). While a middle class has been emerging, it is concentrated in Moscow and St. Petersburg, and mobility is linked more to networks and patronage than to ability and human capital (Gerber and Hout 1998). Educators, from primary schoolteachers to university professors, have been losers in the transition, their salaries low and sometimes only partly paid by the state.

BOX 7.2   HIRED KILLINGS IN RUSSIA

Hired killings over business were no longer shocking by the mid-1990s in Russia. A few noto-rious cases grabbed media headlines and created martyrs, but these are the few among the many. In the first half of the 1990s working in a bank could be hazardous to one's health. Banks meant money, which attracted the attention of organized crime and corrupt people within the state; not giving out a requested loan might lead to a hazardous outcome. The stereotypical method of killing was for the assassin to wait in the entryway to the victim's apartment. In many Soviet-era buildings one could hide underneath the badly lit stairwell and await the victim's return home. The cost of an assassination depended on the victim, but rumor had it that in 1994 a routine killing could cost around $10,000.

The usual reasons for assassinations were conflicts over profits or property: perhaps a manager refused to sell his shares to a prospective outside owner, or a businessman had not settled his accounts with his *mafiia* protection. At other times one invited trouble by investigating the murky side to business. Journalist Dmitrii Kholodov was killed in 1994 when a bomb went off as he opened his briefcase. He was, at the time, investigating corruption in Russian army groups formally stationed in East Europe. In 1995 popular television personality Vladimir Listev was killed, supposedly over resistance to particular transactions in the world of elite television. Popular Petersburg politician Galina Starovoitova was killed for reasons that remain unclear. Some journalists and scholars believed she was killed for her reform politics; others believed she was killed over business affairs into which she strayed unintentionally. None of these three murders – or many others – have been satisfactorily solved.

This aspect of Russia's post-socialist market reminds us chillingly and tragically that econ-omies are, in the end, not just about profit and productivity – if this is the case, it is so in the West, where, after centuries, states and societies have developed and enforced particular rules of the game. Yet economies are as much about power, since money and property are simply forms of power – and it is unsurprising that conflict follows the redistribution or generation of property and profit, especially when the economy is wide open, as in 1990s Russia.

This is inequality as distribution of wealth; but the impact of economic change and inequality goes beyond mere wage data. Consider health. In the mid-1970s, the average male life expectancy began to plateau and threatened to decline – an em-barrassment to a "workers' paradise." In the economic turbulence of the 1990s, life expectancy worsened. While women could expect to live on average to the age of 73, men could expect to live to only 62 at the best count – some other reports in the late 1990s claimed that the average male died before the age of 60. Part of this is due to bad habits such as fatty diets, drinking, and smoking – the aver-age Russian consumed half a liter of vodka each week – but part was due to the stresses of economic dislocation and the decline in the medical system from under-investment. Infant mortality was nearly twenty deaths per 1000 live births – far higher than for developed countries – and in 2006 the estimated death rate was higher than the birth rate – 9.95 births per 1000 versus 14.65 deaths. Even migration from neighboring countries did not help: Russia's population actually *declined* by 0.37 percent in 2005 (CIA 2006).

Gender

Soviet women were quite familiar with the second shift, and the post-Soviet era was little different. If anything, the gendered economy has become more sinister. Women were hit hard in the 1990s, being more likely to lose their jobs than men: not only from direct firings, but even as a result of maternity leave (e.g. coming back to work after having a child to discover that there was no longer a job to come back to). One insidious and tragic outcome of gender and the transition is the rise in prostitution, at times with the knowledge of the girl's parents or mate, especially following the economic crash of 1998. The squeeze on finances damaged employment, and this fed into prostitution.[8] In some families the mother would lose her job and the father would find his wage in rubles nearly worthless, and one way for the family to survive was to let their daughter work as a prostitute. In other cases, young girls in vocational training found themselves without money to continue their studies and their chances of employment after graduation reduced, leaving them little choice but to enter the shadow economy, sometimes as prostitutes. Women came from the regions to Moscow and St. Petersburg to enter the prostitution trade, out of necessity rather than desire. At some highway stops outside Moscow, groups of girls would wait for a "john" to drive up. They would parade before his headlights as he negotiated with a "pimp," often an elderly matron. Women from Eastern Europe and the former USSR have also been drawn into the international sex trade. They may sign up for "programs" to study or work abroad – and criminal ringleaders take their passports in the new country and force them to work as prostitutes. More legal are "mail-order brides." Innocuous forms of this trade involve internet dating, but there have been elaborate package deals, with Western men flying to Moscow to engage in social events, eventually choosing the woman they would like to marry. (In this case, the woman has the right to refuse the man's proposal.) The lawyers work out the details, and the women wait at Western embassies for their visas – something this author saw several times in the American Embassy and Consulate in Russia.

For prostitution and mail-order brides, these women, especially young girls, have been commodified in an extreme fashion. The post-socialist market transition has done this through two effects. First, economic instability and dislocation gave girls a choice: for some, alternatives to prostitution were too costly or had too little chance of success (e.g. textiles jobs in 1998). Some girls entered the trade unknowingly, as in the global sex trade. Second, market-building in post-socialist Russia, as in early capitalist England, is a project of commodification, attaching a price to labor and human beings. Russia's experiences remind us of this side to economic history had we forgotten it.

Racism and xenophobia

Competition over scarce economic resources can spark or fuel ethnic rivalries, as political debates over immigration and asylum-seeking in West Europe and North America clearly show. Russia is little different. The conflict in Chechnya is well-known, but this is not the sole case of ethnic tensions in Russia. As marketization

BOX 7.3 A SIMPLE SOCIOLOGICAL INVESTIGATION OF PROSTITUTION IN ST. PETERSBURG, RUSSIA

In August 2001, as I was finishing yet another research trip to St. Petersburg, I was riding around the streets with my wife's friend and her boyfriend Sasha, who worked as a chauffeur. Because of this he was familiar with the streets of Petersburg, and he often spent "off-time" driving around looking for people in search of a lift (for which he would receive a modest sum). As we drove around after 11:00 in the evening, we noticed a young girl standing under a street light at a bus stop. Sasha remarked that she was a prostitute. We did not believe this, and so he turned the car around. She was no longer there, although we had seen no bus pass by. Of course we remained skeptical, and so he proposed an informal sociological study. First, he drove us along the southern section of Nevskii Prospekt, Petersburg's main and central street. In this section, between the main railroad station (Moscow Station) and the Moscow Hotel, young girls stood at nearly every bus stop. Sasha noted that this was a main area where prostitutes worked – the proximity to the railroad station and an important hotel, where willing johns were likely to be out in numbers. He would slow the car down, and the girls as a group would suddenly try to look inside our car to ascertain what we might want. Sasha then decided to take the investigation more "in-depth," much to my nervousness. He parked the car across from the Moscow Station, and after a moment an elderly matron came up to ask our business. My acquaintance began to negotiate – conclusive proof of the trade afoot – and the matron called to a few girls to approach the car so that we could get a look at the "goods." (At this point I and Sasha's girlfriend successfully convinced him to end the experiment.) From a sociological perspective, what was interesting (and tragic) was not only the existence of prostitutes in such less than seedy (and central) parts of the town – but how there were ritualized practices for exchange in the sex trade.

in Russia began, some ethnic Russians began to suspect non-Russians, especially darker skinned Azerbaijanis or others from the Caucuses, of "stealing" Russian jobs. (Skin tone was not insignificant: some Russians referred to Azerbaijanis as "blacks.") Non-Russians did build their own businesses (e.g. in small trade) through ethnic communities and networks, and they sometimes became targets for populist measures. Moscow mayor Yurii Luzhkov occasionally ordered the police to patrol small kiosks, stores, and traders near railroad stations. If the police found a person who did not have proper documents giving permission to live and work in Moscow (the infamous, and not entirely legal, *propusk* of the Soviet era), they would threaten that person with arrest or deportation (Humphrey 2002: 49–50). Ethnic tensions in the Caucuses, especially in Chechnya, only fueled racism. As well, many *mafiia* were non-Russian (e.g. Kazaanskie and Tambovskie groups in St. Petersburg), only strengthening the image of non-Russian businessmen as criminal. Jews also came in for subtle attack. Many oligarchs had surnames of Jewish extraction; whether any were practicing Jews was never clear, although a few did obtain Israeli passports. Putin's prosecution of such oligarchs as Berezovskii, Gusinskii, and Khodorkovskii could not but tap into latent anti-Semitism (even if unintended).

The pain of the market transition also added to xenophobia by the end of the 1990s. While Russians looked to the West, especially the United States, with interest and curiosity, and perhaps even possible friendship, relations were more sour by 1999. Not only had NATO bombed brother Orthodox Slavs, the Serbs, in Yugoslavia in 1999; the painful transition had been promoted by Western governments and organizations such as the IMF and World Bank. To those more inclined to conspiracy theory, it could have seemed that the goal of economic "advice" was not to help post-communist Russia, but rather to bring her to her knees.

A post-socialist success story: China

While Russia was in a mess, China was an economic success. (Civil rights and political freedoms are another story.) After Mao Zedong's death in 1978 and a brief power struggle, Deng Xiaoping became the uncontested leader of the Chinese Community Party, and he abandoned Mao's communist dogma. He announced "four modernizations" – improving agriculture, industry, science/technology, and defense – and "four cardinal principles" including hegemony of the Communist Party and socialist ideology (formally). Rather than antagonize capitalist countries, Deng used *détente* (working relations between communist and non-communist countries) to attract investment. He opened up agriculture, encouraging peasants to work for themselves and produce for the cities. In short, he introduced a market economy for foreign investment and agricultural production; these, rather than state-led heavy industry, would drive China's growth. By 2005, China's insatiable appetite for oil and raw materials drove up prices for these commodities in the world market. It was no longer a question of "if" China would join (and overtake) the world's economic powers, but "when."

Where Mao's Stalinist methods had failed miserably – Mao's collectivization campaign and Great Leap Forward created the largest famine in human history (an estimated 30 million deaths in 1959 to 1961) – Deng's worked. As China's economy opened up in the 1980s, Chinese leaders used business relations through Hong Kong (until 1997 a British colony) to improve foreign ties. With cheap but increasingly skilled labor, economic zones on the coast catered for foreign investment. With political stability, China was ready for growth. And grow it did: from 1984 to 2004, China's GDP increased by *six times*, and in 2004 China contributed *one-third* of the world economy's overall growth (World Bank 2006b). In 1984, China's GDP was $256 billion; in 2004 it was nearly $1654 billion (World Bank 2005). Not that China's picture is perfect: industry dominates services, poverty and corruption persist (the state has targeted rural poverty through income policies rather then education), the currency remains undervalued (giving Chinese goods artificially lower prices abroad), and growth is based on exports rather than domestic consumption (World Bank 2006a). Yet change has occurred. For example, a new law on corporate governance may enhance transparency and property rights, increasing discipline over managers (World Bank 2006a).[9]

Why was China successful, when Russia – which has more natural resources and, at least when it began market reforms in the 1980s, a more educated and skilled labor force – languished? Several differences are significant (Shirk 1993). The first is that unlike the Soviet and Russian states, the Communist Party and state elite maintained a grip on political power. Under Gorbachev, leaders of the Soviet army quickly became disillusioned with policing the country against ethnic mobilization (Beissinger 2002), and even the post-Soviet Russian army has been hesitant to maintain order (except for such flashpoints as Chechnya). The Chinese military was more proactive in maintaining order, as the June 1989 crackdown on protest in Tianenman Square showed. State and political coherence have been equally important. Gorbachev and Yeltsin implemented democratic as well as market reforms; Deng and his heirs implemented only market reforms while maintaining a communist dictatorship. This gave the regime the power to implement whatever policies they felt were needed, while using repression to maintain social order without worrying about backlash or accountability from voters or regionally elected elites. If Russia's democratic record is questionable, its human, civil, and democratic rights are better than in China. Put another way, scholars have debated whether countries can have both democracy and growth (cf. Huntington 1968); the Russia–China comparison does not paint an optimistic picture.

Similarly, different reforms and degrees of state coherence led to different fates. To implement economic reform, Gorbachev had to attack the state bureaucracy; to gain political power, Boris Yeltsin had to let regional elites take political authority. Deng Xiaoping had a more propitious context for reform. The Cultural Revolution (1966 to 1976) weakened the state bureaucracy: Mao Zedong and young Red Guard activists engaged in constant campaigns assaulting the status or physical security of "enemies of the revolution," including Party members, bureaucrats (even the elite), and enterprise managers. When Mao died in 1976 and Deng consolidated his political position, the state bureaucracy, including economic ministries, was already fairly weak. Deng simply went around Beijing directly to local enterprise managers, negotiating over reforms. To maintain his advantage over his opponents, Deng encouraged local managers to enrich themselves – to be entrepreneurial and make profit, even if this meant that managers of *state-owned* firms were acting as *owners* (which they were not). In return, they would support Deng's leadership. This political deal laid the foundation for growth. In a sense, Deng was allowing a form of corruption or rent-seeking – managers acting as owners – but this gave them the incentive to improve or expand production.[10]

Another important legacy of Russian and Chinese socialism was agricultural production and the peasantry. Stalin destroyed the Soviet peasantry in collectivization in the 1930s: land-holding peasants were forced to join state and collective farms (*sovkhozy* and *kolkhozy*), large agricultural bodies where peasants worked as laborers (an agricultural proletariat).[11] Over time, ambitious children of collective farm workers left for the cities – a "brain drain" of ability and human capital out of agriculture. State and collective farms remained firmly in the grip of bureaucratic leaders. Further, Russia's collectivization took place in the 1930s; when Gorbachev wanted to reform his economy, there were few alive who remembered the art of agricultural entre-preneurship. In China, collectivization was a partial failure: while there was collective work and ownership, the regime had to allow a degree of decentralization and peasant autonomy (Weede 2002). Soon after Mao's death, Deng introduced agri-cultural reforms for a peasantry that still had some memory of autonomous work. Families gained responsibility over a plot of land, were allowed to sell a portion of produce (after providing a certain amount to the local production team), and could reinvest profit as they saw fit. In 1985 the state stopped taking produce and signed contracts with peasant farmers. Agricultural produce in cities was priced more by the market than by the state, encouraging further peasant entrepreneurship. As a result, in 1978 to 1988 agriculture grew by more than three times – providing food to the cities and money to peasant farmers, who could now buy industrial or other goods from the cities.

Yet another difference between Russia and China was foreign investment. Deng's regime quickly opened up China to foreign investment by setting up "Special Economic Zones" in the East, mostly along the coast. The state provided customs and tax benefits to investors, and the central state's monopoly control over exports was broken up. Finally, the state released much of its control over the value of its currency, giving Chinese goods an advantage in foreign markets and further encour-aging foreign companies to invest in producing inside China. Foreign companies and governments responded favorably – more so than to Russia. China was a source of cheap labor; Russia was still a suspicious country. Not surprisingly, this was a legacy of the Cold War. The Soviet Union had been the West's main competitor; China had been a danger in the 1950s and 1960s, but Western paternalist attitudes – a legacy of nineteenth-century colonialism, when Western powers looked on China as in need of direction – made Western investors and governments more inclined to deal positively with China.[12] In addition, an enormous Chinese diaspora – ethnic Chinese who settled abroad, in the United States, Malaysia, and Europe – were sending money to relatives in China, some of which found its way into small-scale entrepreneurship.

In comparison to Russia – and even Latin America – China had a propitious set of circumstances, especially a recently unified country, structured political authority, and a sufficiently powerful military not at odds with the civilian authorities. Pro-devel-opment policies such as coastal economic zones preferential to foreign investment, cheap labor, and a potentially enormous market (after adequate growth) were too much for foreign multinationals to resist. While China's economy is a powerhouse, this does not mean that all is rosy there. Several issues and social forces could break out and damage Chinese growth, politics, and social fabric. The first is that which ripped the USSR apart: ethnicity. China is not ethnically homogenous, and Tibet remains a potential problem and sore spot for China's image abroad. (Tibet was forcibly incorporated by military conquest.) China's economic growth is concen-trated primarily on the coast. Inland, there is more poverty. Ethnicity and poverty coupled together are a potential time bomb. An important business practice in China is *guanxi*, personal networks.[13] Like strong ties and weak ties, *guanxi* provide both information and patronage, which are particularly useful for obtaining good jobs, arranging business deals (obtaining capital, structuring exchange), and working with the ubiquitous state bureaucracy (Bian 1997; Yang 2004). As much as *guanxi* greases the wheels of commerce, it can also hinder the workings of formal law and contribute to corruption – which remains endemic, so much so that the Tianenman demonstrations were partly a popular response to this.[14] Banks and state-owned enterprises remain inefficient and far from transparent; the vibrant private sector supports this area, maintaining employment (as gradualists proposed) but also a structural time bomb. China's leaders set out on a risky course, which so far has paid dividends – but for how long?

Lessons of post-socialism for economic sociology

In 1989 a revolution of sorts broke out in Eastern Europe and the former USSR, and its echoes reverberate – not only for Russians or Poles, but also for social scientists, including economic sociologists. I suggest the following are among the most important:

- The relationship between markets, politics, and growth is complex. Poland has democracy, a market economy, and economic growth. China has authoritarianism and even greater growth. Russia's economy tanked under Yeltsin's pseudo-democracy but has healed somewhat under Putin's quasi-authoritarianism. Vladimir Putin's sometimes anti-democratic policies are an attempt to rebuild state power and economic strength, but they also hearken back to pessimistic beliefs from the 1970s that development requires "bureaucratic authoritarianism" – a strong, non-democratic state to create social stability, political order, and social discipline to attract foreign capital and allow industrialists and elites to accumulate and invest (O'Donnell 1973). Add in China and one wonders if growth and democracy can go hand-in-hand: they did for the United States (although real democratic rights were limited, especially to non-whites and women), but recent developers do not have America's historical luxuries. Yet one sees growth *and* democracy in Poland, the Czech Republic, and Hungary.

  Certainly oil helped Russia, cheap labor helped China, and access to nearby investment and markets helped Poland. Politics is not everything – but neither can it be ignored. The view that "all good things go together" of shock therapists is too simple, but so is the bureaucratic-authoritarian model. What seems to matter more is *how* democracy or dictatorship operate. If there are stable structures of authority that create both discipline and means of defense and recourse, then markets can grow: states, managers, and workers are constrained to act within certain rules while being able to defend basic interests (tax collection, contract, basic wage, and safety rules). If authority is compromised, opportunism and confusion – and economic inefficiencies – threaten. The post-socialist challenge is creating state structures and state–society relations conducive to growth and social order as well as freedom.

- Market-building and economic change are socially embedded. While this has been an important theme of this entire book, nowhere does it come across more powerfully than in the story of post-socialist change, especially in Russia. Change did not follow the dictates of competition and efficiency; rather, it followed the influences of power and culture embedded in institutions, practices, and structures. Privatization and financial liberalization meant the redistribution not only of property and money but of *power*; small wonder privatization and finance were corrupt and led to conflict, including hired killings. Even finance was problematic – as the discussion of monetization revealed, business actors do not automatically gravitate to a single, shared currency as the unit of value and exchange. They play games with rules, structures, and practices – perhaps to thrive, perhaps merely to survive.

This suggests that a market-building project depends on the social context in which it is embedded. The more non-market or anti-market the context, the more difficult the market project will be and the more likely reforms will face resistance or be deformed as actors take advantage of new rules or, equally likely, fail to understand them completely. Recall *decoupling* from Chapter 5: organization change does not go very deep into firms because of resistance and persistence of older practices. In a sense, post-socialist change (especially in Russia) is a case of decoupling on a societal dimension. In short, economies are not independent of other social forces – in theoretical jargon, non-economic factors are not *exogenous* in the real economic world. Reformers (Western, Russian, Ukrainian) cannot legislate what they wish and assume that, with a little force, it will change society. More likely, society will change or challenge the reforms. Were reformers and their Western supporters more cognizant of this – not merely paying lip-service to the banality that voters and people matter, but really considering the complexity of social relations in economic practice – perhaps more propitious reforms would have been proposed, which was not so far from what gradualist economists were shouting in the early 1990s.

- Fundamental change is a cultural project. An approach such as neoclassical economic theory, that sees economic change and growth basically as legislating property, free trade, and efficiency, takes an *instrumental* view of institutions as straightforward formal rules that automatically create desired behavior. But institutions and economic reality are more complex; they are produced and reproduced by everyday practices of business actors, state officials, employees, and consumers. Changing an economy means changing fundamental practices, rituals, and meanings. Like the birth of capitalism and modernity, post-socialism is a *cultural project*, a social *reconstruction* not only of laws but also of people's assumptions of economic normality. Privatization was not just legalizing property ownership; it was creating and imposing a category ("property"), meaning ("ownership"), and authority (rights and limits of ownership) where property had once been *anathema*. Or take "entrepreneurship": what is an entrepreneur? Someone dedicated to business because of personal gains, including creative freedom? Or someone who gets rich quickly by speculating on currency or oil and using networks to steal from the state? I heard both theories in my fifteen years studying Russia. Vladimir Putin could attack oligarchs because they broke the law (not difficult, given Russia's convoluted legal system) and because people wanted this. Russia has the time-honored conflict of a market economy (calculation, commodification, profit) versus a moral economy (equality, non-commodification, social values). Can the Russian state impose a market society today, just as happened in England centuries ago? Economic change is an attempt to come to grips with historical legacies that cannot be wiped away by laws alone; legacies and new laws combine into amalgams. Post-Soviet Russia will resemble both the Soviet system and that Western market capitalism which was (problematically) imported after 1991.

Neoclassical theory is more normative than descriptive; if it has problems telling us how the world works, should we trust its recommendations?[15] If this is the case, post-socialist economic change suggests the importance of economic sociology. Rather than assuming behavior is universally the same, sociologists see behavior and practices as embedded in particular histories, power, and culture. This suggests that neoclassical economic theory, with its assumptions of strict rational action and its oversight of power and culture, is fundamentally flawed. No surprise: neoclassical economic theory has become part of the cultural project of modernity, including post-socialism. Perhaps the greatest lesson of post-socialism – and a major theme of this book – is that we in the West, who dish out advice freely, need a serious re-examination of our assumptions, knowledge, and limitations.

8 Brave new world? A critical examination of "globalization"

A major buzz-word today is "globalization." Political leaders invoke it to justify opening markets or reducing taxes and welfare to make their economies attractive to foreign investors. Protestors invoke "globalization" to blame profit-centered MNCs for world poverty and ecological disaster (e.g. destruction of rainforests, global warming). Globalization leaves MNCs and capitalist elites free from accountability because states will not prosecute them: there is no global state to do so, and any country that tries to reign in business will find investment has fled for somewhere else. So, do we live in a "runaway world" of global capitalism (Giddens 2002), where local and global mesh into "glocal" (the enmeshing and interdependency, or perhaps obfuscation of local and global economic forces)? Or is this as much myth and hype over a return to an historically normal state?

In public rhetoric on globalization, one sees faith or fear – faith that a global market will bring growth and wealth for all (eventually), or fear that a global market will be unruly and destructive or the final blow to equality and justice. As manufacturing moves from developed to developing economies, it seems that workers in the United States or Europe face what populations in Latin America or Asia have long known – powerlessness in the face of mobile capital and dependency. Economists sometimes claim that low-skilled employees in the developed world will feel the most pain, as firms move low-skilled work abroad (cheap wages) or replace it with robots – but how long will it be before firms move *high-skilled* jobs to counties with lower wages? If I am American, I feel at home in much of the world – with little difficulty I can find McDonald's, MTV, and CNN. If I am British, I feel the onslaught of Hollywood and the angst of seeing American imports such as *Friends* and *Will and Grace* take the place of British sitcoms. French leaders have tried to stop the tide of American cultural hegemony by demanding equal opportunity for French culture as well as the purity of the French language from foreign linguistic imports.[1] At the same time there are forces against globalization. Sometimes these are open resistance and local rebellions – that in Chiapas, Mexico is probably the best known, but re-emerging populism in Latin America appears to be a counter-reaction as well. Other times they are a subtle recognition that all things foreign are not so hot – as for Russian consumers of candy, who rediscovered the quality of their own chocolates *vis-à-vis* Twix and Snickers and created Russian soap operas to compete (fairly successfully) with Mexican, Argentinian, and American imports.

Globalization is an important topic, but studies, analyses, and claims about it are untidy at present. Before we add yet another monograph or data set, perhaps we should take stock of what globalization might be and problems in existing frameworks. Thus, in this chapter I do not attempt a full-blown examination of data on globalization: there will not be myriad graphs or tables on world trade, tourism, or export of cultural goods (such as Disney or MTV).[2] I will not do so because our concepts shape the kind of data we look for, and where we look for it. Rather, I want to suggest that thinking over "globalization" remains muddled and incomplete. We need to add many fundamental concepts to the picture; states and institutions of power, important in previous chapters, remain mostly absent in globalization studies. For example, data on global trade is not necessarily meaningful, except to suggest that we buy and sell more with each other if it is not put into the context of power. Instead, I hope to give the reader critical thoughts about issues we must address to make sense of the "new" economy and whether it is really so new. If it is not new, perhaps we inevitably face the same problems, even catastrophes, of the past; if it is new, we had better figure out what good and bad may await us.

The muddles

The problem with globalization discourse is that it suffers from an empirical and an intellectual muddle. First, the empirical muddle: evidence for and against an emerging, integrated global economy is far from unambiguous. Certainly trade has increased, and production chains spread beyond individual countries. Cars and computers are no longer made in one country. Honda is a Japanese automobile firm, but it assembles cars in the United States; American car manufacturers produce components in Latin America. The typical Barbie doll is not made in a single country; its component parts are made throughout East Asia, using forms from the United States. As we saw earlier, commodity chain production and outsourcing and subcontracting through small firm networks have increased. Tourism is booming thanks to cheaper flights and accommodation and middle-class wealth, and more middle-class children (especially from China) are going abroad for at least one year of university education. After deregulation in the 1970s and 1980s, capital has flowed more freely between countries, and states cannot ignore the judgments of currency speculators and corporate investors. Currencies and shares are traded twenty-four hours a day; while traders sleep in New York, trading goes on in Hong Kong, and vice versa. Asian investors subsidize the American state by purchasing treasury bonds – if they decide this is bad business the American government is in trouble. There is a greater flow of goods and services across borders, and what happens in one part of the world affects other areas. This is the story *for* a global economy – but it is only one part of the story. In contrast, a country's borders still act as barriers to exchange of goods and services, even for integrated production such as cars – even if two countries have formal agreements for free trade and share language or other customs. (That is, the symbolic presence of a border *on its own* reduces exchange.) There is little convergence of tax rates despite the seeming force of global competition to do so (Rodrik 1998). As we saw in Chapter 4, leading industrial countries maintained distinctly different policy norms, and this shows no sign of diminishing. In 2006 the French state proposed merging France's gas companies Gaz de France and Suez into another national champion – this following the Russian state's purchase of a controlling block of shares in gas monopoly Gazprom. European countries are again stressing national ownership in the face of mergers between companies from different countries; economic nationalism is not yet dead.[3] Some states have also played foreign markets to their advantage while others have not. East Asian countries left the periphery because state leaders could play the global market skillfully while protecting themselves. Latin American economies have been dependent on developed countries, in part due to a "triple alliance" of states, national elites, and foreign corporations (Evans 1979).

The second muddle is intellectual, where three crucial weaknesses move through arguments and analyses. First, the term "globalization" itself remains imprecise (Kellner 2002). What is "globalization" or a "global economy"? Is it simply more trade and production across several countries – buying Russian beer in US supermarkets and telemarketers in India calling hopeful clients in Britain? Or does it mean something more fundamental? Most economists and economic sociologists talk of trade, investment, and labor (e.g. Stiglitz 2003), while others talk of technological changes and high-speed communications that bring social actors into closer contact and lead to blending or even convergence of cultures (Castells 2000). (When I talk of "globalization" and a "global economy," I mean trends towards global economic *practices and structures*.) The second weakness is that analysts and commentators often look at *outcomes* – manufacturing spread out across many countries, with its negative impact on labor or the environment – but do not always focus on *processes* or *mechanisms* of change and structural reproduction. The third intellectual muddle is confusing "market" and "capitalism." Recall from Chapters 1 and 2 that economists tend to talk of "markets" as a natural state of human affairs – relatively free production and exchange, with an equilibrium of exchange and pricing. Sociologists talk of "markets" or "capitalism" as a system of institutions, structures, and practices – social forces underneath exchange, production, and pricing. Yet many analysts take "global market" at face value as expanded exchange – but where are world-level *structures* or *institutions* in which the global economy, like domestic economies (or any social structures), are structured and embedded? Much analysis of "globalization" ignores the social fabric – a "market" is not the same thing as a "market *economy*." Even sociologist Manuel Castells falls into this trap. His definition of "global economy" – "an economy whose core components have the institutional, organizational, and technological capacity to work as a unit in real time, or in chosen time, on a planetary scale" (Castells 2000: 102) – looks merely at tools of exchange. Institutional and technological tools are primarily the rights of capital mobility and rapid communications that allow for immediate coordination. Just as Durkheim saw improving communication and transportation increasing social density and leading to fundamental changes in social solidarity, Castells sees modern communications technology, especially the internet, behind a new global economy. But this is not so different from and no more useful than the economists' conception of an economy as exchange.

One distinction may be useful: much "globalization" may be "internationalization," different degrees of interaction between firms and clients outside their home country – not an increasingly powerful set of global *structures* or *actors*, but instead firms simply looking further afield. For example, English football (soccer) clubs began recruiting players from overseas because it became legal to do so – and so why not expand the pool of potential talent? Yet clubs looked for recruits primarily in countries with similar language, culture, and climate to that in England (e.g. Australia and Northern Europe). The market for English football remained primarily domestic; there was no global force making it shift hiring practices (McGovern 2002).[4] This may sound like picking nits, but it is not: "internationalization" means expanding access to resources and sales, while "globalization" implies a fundamental trans- formation of economic structures and institutions beyond national societies. Put another way, the unit of analysis for internationalization remains firmly embedded in national economies; for globalization, the unit of analysis is a global system (Hirst and Thompson 1996). Increases in global movement of capital, goods, and people are important – but what are their real foundations? Is Castells right – we live in a global economy – or is McGovern right – we look further for goods and services, but foundations remain sub-global? World-systems theorists argued for thirty years that capitalism is a global system; dependency and other theorists, however, demanded to see specific world-level institutions. Here is the fulcrum of the debate: global elites versus global institutions. But what *is* going on?

Forces for and against globalization

The "global economy" may be more myth than reality, and I return to this later. However, something is behind increased global exchange which must be encour- aged by relatively structured social forces – but what forces? I suggest we look at *interests*, *ideologies*, and *institutions* that allow people to impose or resist global- ization. We cannot reduce one to the others: ideologies and interests may be linked but are not necessarily equal, and we cannot assume that interests lead directly to ideologies. Ronald Reagan and Margaret Thatcher were key to post-1980 globaliza- tion, but they deregulated their respective economies because of their ideologies – and they found like-minded people in business and politics (e.g. various economists, such organizations as the World Bank and International Monetary Fund, international business groups). Mexico opened up its economy to foreign investors because elite technocrats making economic policy shared the neoliberal ideology – but the United States and IMF demanded austerity programs and economic liberalization in return for aid packages.

Promoting globalization

First, we look at *interests*: Whose interests are served by globalization? This seems simple: business! An integrated global market of free trade offers businesses cheap labor and raw materials and new markets. Yet the issue is more subtle and complex. Whose interests are served by *what form* of globalization? Free global markets are not equally helpful to all businesses. Fledgling businesses might be better served by protection rather than immediate global competition. One secret to the success of South Korea and Japan is that the state provided aid and protection from foreign competition until their industries had developed and could compete in the global market – what Peter Evans (1995) called a "greenhouse" developmental state. Larger firms, with capital and know-how, are better able to compete globally, and they may be more interested in open markets. When NAFTA opened up the Mexican market, American agribusiness beat some domestic producers on the Mexican market (especially in corn, subsidized by the US government), although other Mexican exports hurt American farmers (McMichael 2004: 175). The same is true for labor: American workers might be threatened by cheaper skilled labor in China, but they also have comparative advantages *vis-à-vis* laborers in Europe, where labor law is more generous to workers but at the same time less favorable to labor costs and business efficiency.

Globalization can also serve state interests. According to Obstfeld and Taylor (1998), state elites face a "trilemma." States cannot have fixed exchange rates, capital mobility, and an active monetary policy (e.g. economic intervention) *at the same time*. Something has to give. If a state has capital mobility and active monetary policy, holders of capital will move their wealth around in response to policies. After World War II developed states tried to implement fixed exchange through the Bretton Woods institutions and activist monetary policies to avoid a repeat of the Great Depression; capital mobility was still suffering the shocks of the 1930s and World War II. When financial capital finally recovered by the 1960s, economic strains emerged among developed economies: for example, high interest rates and low growth in the United States or loss of control over the economy in Europe (Obstfeld 1998). Leaders in developed countries were loath to give up monetary policy; economic theory stressed the importance of markets for capital and currencies. Fixed exchange rates were jettisoned and capital mobility encouraged. The trilemma, then, was an incentive for state elites to relax controls over capital – the beginning of current globalization.

Interests alone are not enough, for people or groups may have vague interests that are focused or clarified by *ideologies*. Businessmen want profit, but do they see profit coming from a low-tax, low-welfare economy or a high-tax, high-welfare economy that guarantees everyone will have some pocket-money and good health? Recall how Keynesianism's activist, regulatory policy style came under attack from neoliberal economists who saw it as the source of stagnation in the 1970s and who claimed that free markets and democracy go hand-in-hand. Popular business publications (*Business Week*, *The Economist*, *Wall Street Journal*) echoed this ideology, taking it for granted as timeless wisdom: market intervention was unnatural and harmful, even for society's underprivileged. Neoliberal ideology seemed to have support from history: the end of communism after 1989 seemed to herald free markets and neoliberal ideology as victors at the "end of history." The survival of Soviet communism in a capitalist world provided hope and legitimacy for leftist ideologies. However, economic decay, environmental degradation, political dictator-ships, and ultimate collapse of real socialism besmirched left-wing ideologies: look where they led in the Soviet Union! Following the end of communism, East European countries looked West, to the European Union: inclusion into democratic, capitalist, developed "Europe" and freedom from past Russian domination. As a minister from a Baltic country once remarked, they would do whatever the Europeans wanted, in the hopes of inclusion into the broader European market and polity.[5]

Finally, interests and ideologists without collective representation and power are inter-esting only as a passing fancy. With power – that is, when linked to *institutions* – they become real forces to contend with. Globalization is not just an ideological posi-tion or some elemental force of nature – it is a project of a new modernity enforced by a set of organizations through various institutions. Some central institutions can be crucial to this process: for example, the piecemeal deregulation of capital markets in the United States, or the October 27, 1987 "Big Bang" liberalization of London financial markets to investment from any source, to any destination. Along with capital mobility came the need for expertise, and a few major firms (Moody's, Standard and Poor) began applying their metrics of normality to judge the credit-worthiness of foreign firms or countries.[6] If these encouraged greater mobility, it was not neces-sarily a direct force imposing (or attempting to impose) global integration and econ-omic commonality. For this, the most important forces are transnational institutions that promote global markets – the International Monetary Fund (IMF) and World Bank, the World Trade Organization (WTO) – and leading states with political and economic power, principally the United States, European countries often working through the European Union, and Japan. The IMF and World Bank distribute billions of dollars for development and stabilization projects: the IMF gives loans to help stabilize curren-cies and balances of payments, while the World Bank funds projects that address deeper structural problems, such as weak infrastructure, education, inequality, or welfare reform. The WTO offers the possibility of entering a larger group of coun-tries trading with each other with few tariffs and more open markets – good for exporters. These organizations do not offer their advantages freely. They want members' economies to follow their model of normality: minimal states supporting basic infrastructure and public goods; low taxes and state expenditures (thus lower budget deficits); currencies eventually strong enough to be traded freely; open markets for investment and repatriating profits (taking profits out of the country); stable property rights; and liberal labor markets. Latin American, African, and East European countries had to promise to implement such reforms in return for aid – although reforms were not always implemented as promised or did little good.[7]

Resisting globalization

One of Polanyi's (1944) insights into market societies and economies is that soci-eties can bite back. If a global market is truly emerging, we should expect at least some segments of "global society" (disparate and disorganized as it may be) to resist. Globalizing forces themselves can create resistance through two means. First, global capitalism generates exploitation and resentment that can explode into open, mobilized discontent. Firms may relocate production to Latin America or Africa because wages are lower and leaders there welcome the employment – already creating a potential backlash in developed countries. If profits do not stay in the new host economy, and employees gain little support from their states or unions, expect further fuel for the fire. Central American farmers harvest coffee at cheap rates and learn that foreign firms are making enormous profits – why not share the wealth? What is important at this stage is whether the exploited can mobilize. This requires leadership, material resources, and meanings and symbols to legitimate protest and provide a rallying cause. This leads to the second means by which globalization creates its own resistance: the very terms "globalization" and "global economy" create a symbolic enemy. Imagine popular protest against the WTO in Seattle (1999) or against global capitalism in London (2003) without "globalization" – against what would people protest?[8]

Resistance, however, has not been on a global scale. Naturally, organizing non-elites across the world is a tremendously difficult task (as organizing is generally). Organizing requires resources that the poor and less well-off do not have. In his revision of Marxism, Vladimir Lenin noted that workers had little time or learning to understand the dialectical and exploitative nature of capitalism. They did not truly understand their class position and power or the need for revolution to change the system entirely. Rather, they suffered from "trade union consciousness": the desire to improve their immediate situation with better wages, fewer hours, and more benefits – all the while leaving capitalism alone. The communist revolution needed help from dedicated, learned revolutionaries. Freed from toils of everyday labor and with access to money, these revolutionaries would educate workers by printing pamphlets and organizing workers' study sessions on Marxism's wisdom, sparking class consciousness and activism. We may have our doubts about communism and Lenin's leadership, but he made a powerful point: resistance does not arise on its own but requires organization, especially leadership and resources (whether money or people). This is a tall order in deprived areas hardest hit by liberalized trade. Further, not everyone is exploited. MNC managers benefit, but so do the middle classes in France, Germany, and Russia: cheap clothing made in China gives them more cash left over to spend on other consumer goods.

Resistance leaders must not only be good at raising money and organizing people; they must also be able to use symbolic resources successfully. In other words, they must be good at marketing: successfully gaining access to and appearing sympathetic before a wider global audience (Bob 2005). Whom do they pitch their claims and cause to – New York corporate lawyers or sympathetic NGOs who have access to the media or decision-making? How do they get access to them – waiting for NGO representatives to arrive in Mexico, or using e-mail and faxes to transmit their claims and their spin on events? Not only must resistance leaders market themselves to the world; they must also market themselves to their followers. The rebels in Chiapas, Mexico (1994) intentionally called themselves "Zapatistas": Emilano Zapata was a popular peasant leader in the 1910 Mexican Revolution, known for his sense of justice and ability to understand and articulate the claims of Mexican peasants (Womack 1968). With this label the resistance leaders drew on symbols of the Revolution that the *Mexican government* used to legitimate power and that common people still revered. Fundamental Islamic movements linked to al-Qaeda include a moral regeneration and anti-capitalist rhetoric, ironically couched within their own alternative globalist vision (global Islam). Economists claim that a global economy will provide gains for all if firms, countries, and people are willing to *restructure* and meet the challenges – but this nonchalantly undervalues the pain and hides the complexities and costs of change in the simple word "restructuring." Small wonder that Rodrik (1998) complains that few understand or appreciate the economics of global trade when it is marketed in this offhand fashion, and resistance is more dynamic and creative – and realist.

New phenomenon – or return to the norm?

A few perceptive pundits (e.g. McRae 2006) have asked whether globalization is so novel. Commentators, anti-globalism activists, business elites, and politicians speak of "globalization" as a new and unclear (and frightening) wave engulfing us in uncertainty – but maybe we have been there before. Nation-states as we know them are relatively new (Tilly 1990), and before their advent people in adjacent and distant territories traded in goods and capital. In fact, in his discussion of the emergence of capitalism, Max Weber rejected the thesis that modern European capitalism emerged from increased trade, because it had been around for centuries (Weber 1987 [1923]). The elite had land holdings in different parts of Europe, and even in new empires abroad. If we look at the most developed countries in the nineteenth century, we see interdependence. British capital helped the expansion of American railroads and mining (Gaventa 1980; Roy 1997), and the British Empire was partly an economic zone of investment, for example, in tea in India. French investment drove the expansion of Russian railroads in the early twentieth century (for military reasons), and Russian industry depended on foreign capital and know-how: German industrialists ran some of Russia's most important firms (Blackwell 1968; Rieber 1982).

If we examine capital flows and exchange of goods over the past 100 years, a striking pattern emerges: exchange in capital and goods peaked in mid-1914 and then declined. Only in the 1990s did global trade and investment come close to those levels seen before the outbreak of hostilities in August 1914 (Feenstra 1998: 33, 35; Obstfeld 1998: 12–13). Before the war, national economies were well connected through cross-national ownership and trade. Money and goods flowed fairly freely, and investors could read about local economic conditions in far-flung parts of the world. Because of the severity of hostilities among the leading industrial countries, World War I severely disrupted this global integration. Global trade began to recover in the 1920s, but 1929 provided another devastating shock. As we saw in Chapter 4, Western political leaders responded to the Great Depression with a combination of welfare and attempts at autarky. The Great Depression spread between countries because of trade interdependence and currency values linked through the gold standard. When one economy crashed, others lost markets and capital, spreading the problem. Part of the Keynesian response was an activist state that used two important tools: protectionism and deficit spending. Further, states

BOX 8.1 A BRIEF HISTORY OF MEXICAN DEVELOPMENT AND THE REVOLT IN CHIAPAS

When import substitution industrialization and increasing debt to the developed world became too much to bear, the Mexican government turned to the United States and her economic allies for aid. In return for debt relief, the Mexican government was forced to privatize state-owned enterprises, reduce state expenditures, open up the market to investment and ownership from abroad, and open up its market to global exchange. This the Mexican leadership did, in the process squeezing the Mexican people and opening up the economy to competition from more efficient producers from abroad. In the late 1980s, Mexican leaders negotiated member-ship in NAFTA, which would further open up Mexico's market. Mexican president Carlos Salinas hoped this would bring in American investment and aid Mexican exports to the United States. However, this dream was unfulfilled; instead, there was economic and political disruption. First, to encourage investment, the Mexican state kept the peso artificially high, borrowing and spending foreign currency to help keep the peso rate high on the world currency market. The hope was that as investment and economic performance improved, the state could eventually make enough in taxes to pay its debts and to allow the currency to float on its own. Unfortunately, the debt proved too much, and in late 1993 the peso collapsed, as foreign investors sold pesos and other assets. In addition, Mexican agribusiness was losing to cheaper food imports from the United States before NAFTA – and entry into the new trade bloc with the United States promised little good for most Mexicans.

In the face of economic shocks and the neoliberal logic of global markets and the domi-nance of capital over labor – especially foreign capital over local labor – the revolt in Chiapas exploded on January 1, 1994. After years of neoliberal reform, local farmers and artisans were increasingly impoverished. They also believed in local markets, local ownership, and local entrepreneurship; exploitation by MNCs and foreign investors in the name of "market efficiency" struck them as illegitimate and unfair. Following the opening up of the economy, foreign firms were buying local land and sending in their own employees and technology to harvest coffee or take timber – depriving the local population of their earlier livelihood and potential employ-ment. Using the language of democracy and rights for all (including women), the Zapatistas struck out in armed rebellion against the Mexican state. They issued communiqués to broader international audiences, criticizing government leaders and the international business com-munity for exploitation and intrusion into local life. Chiapas did not bring confidence to international investors already worried about Mexican debt and the peso's sorry state. It took an appeal to president Bill Clinton – and Clinton's appeal to Congress and the international community to bail out Mexico – to help stem the financial crisis and provide some stability to the peso and the Mexican economy. However, the Chiapas revolt was not broken; negoti-ations continued for many years, and relations between the local population and the Mexican state remain as strained as ever – and Chiapas remains a stark symbol of a moral economy on the comeback, values of local rights and community over the broader, impersonal, exploita-tive global "market." Chiapas is not the first example of such a revolt, nor is it the last. The question is whether trends in international investment and business will generate sufficient momentum to sustain the global market against future Chiapases – or whether diverse local communities will be able to organize enough to strike back.

Sources: Centeno (1996); McMichael (2004).

increased controls over their economies and trade as part of mobilization in World War II, effectively honing the political authority over markets developed in the 1930s. Protectionism – privileging home industries *vis-à-vis* imports through taxation of imports or subsidizing domestic firms – is not new: American economic growth in the nineteenth century was due in part to protectionism, and the British mercantile economy closed off the empire from trade with the outside world to guard British capital and interests – a system that finally ended when the British state and economy were crippled by World War II. The other tool, state deficit spending, would keep economies operational. This provided a cushion against interdependency and its effects. What happened was that in the 1930s and 1940s state control increased *qualitatively* (in form) as well as *quantitatively* (in degree).

This means that 1914 to 1980, especially 1930 to 1980, was an *aberration* from the historical norm. Global financial markets and capital availability were hit hard by the Depression and world wars; only by the 1970s had they recovered. The modern wave of global interdependency and exchange is a *return to the norm* – and even so, we have not yet returned to the same level of integration as before World War I. Economies have always been interdependent to some extent. Ask any historian of Latin America how dependent those countries were on Western capital and markets. Modern MNCs have more capital now than forty years ago, giving them more leverage, but no Latin American would claim globalization is new. If anything, globalization seems new to Western populations because other countries are developing: China and South Korea have more educated workers than before, and firms there can produce goods that were once restricted to the US or Europe. We feel the heat of competition. But this is little different from competition within counties – globalization becomes an expansion of the normal state of affairs, with more competition but also more markets and more growth opportunities. We may also be more attuned to a return to the norm because there has, in fact, been a fundamental shift since 1914: states are more active in the economy. Keynesianism and welfare, organized working-class movements, and an appreciation of the state's balance *vis-à-vis* economies are well developed now. As we return to a global *economic* norm, the political picture has shifted. States and their citizens had more freedom in the "deviant" period, and now it is more constrained, which might account for some of the attention and worry.

Globalization versus regionalization

One important issue is to what extent the new economy is more regional than global. Neil Fligstein (2001a: ch. 9) claims that international trade has increased – but that trade is between developed countries, and tends to be regional. The United States and Canada are each other's largest trading partners; East Asian countries trade primarily with each other. European countries also trade primarily with each other, enhanced by the creation of the European Union and adoption of uniform standards (e.g. weights and measures, labor and trade laws) for member countries and the introduction of a common currency for some members.[9] Despite trying to prove the existence of a global economy, Castells (2000: 110–16) has to admit the importance of regional trading. His counter-argument is that trade beyond regional blocs is expanding – but there is more to an "economy" or "market" than trade. One interesting support for regionalization is homogenization of corporate structures. In a truly global market, competitive efficiency pressures firms around the world to adopt "best" corporate governance (Williamson 1996). Yet despite supposed global competition or World Bank and OECD attempts to promote common rules and standards, Khanna *et al.* (2006) show that *regional*, not global, diffusion of practices is the norm. Countries near each other, who engage in constant trade, adopt similar corporate governance laws. Beyond this, globalization's impact is limited. While businesses worldwide have begun to adopt some similar policies (driven by foreign direct investment and capital markets), these are not always implemented, i.e. they are decoupled (cf. Chapter 5). National and regional practices remain robust.

This suggests that significant economic integration may be *regional*. While the popular image is Japan, China, and Korea exporting to the United States and Europe, the reality is that these countries trade with and invest more in each other, creating an informal regional trading and investment bloc (Fligstein 2001a: 196–203). Alongside this, formal regional zones have been developing. Two important regional zones are the European Union and NAFTA (North American Free Trade Agreement); weaker variants include the Asian Pacific Economic Community (currently centered on Japan, although with China gaining strength one wonders what the real center will be), and the Commonwealth of Independent Nations (some countries of the former USSR), centered around Russia. The EU organizes most European countries into a single economic zone, with its own rules and, for some members, a common currency (the euro).[10] Rather than being a wider cross-country legislation, NAFTA is a set of beneficial trade agreements (e.g. lower restrictions and tariffs on trade and investment across borders), although within NAFTA the dollar is the informal currency. Thus, the question is whether the real face of the future is a global economy run by the WTO and "homeless" multinationals with industry and trade concentrated unequally across regions – much as the American economy is unified but has unequal concentration of capital and trade (e.g. the "rust belt" versus the West and South) – or a world economy balkanized into regional associations of differing strengths. This latter version would not be so different from the more recent global economy, except that, instead of various national economies, there would be strong blocs of super-national economies.

Regional groups can provide important barriers to globalization if member countries have sufficient resources and leverage *vis-à-vis* others. The European Union is not simply a trading bloc like NAFTA. It is more integrated, with formal rules and policies for all member countries: for example, all members must use the metric system, and human rights are increasingly applied to the workplace – although some countries such as Great Britain retain "opt-out" rights that allow them to ignore particular rules at their discretion. The EU can also provide barriers against outside forces: European countries have enough capital, industry, and market size that other countries cannot simply ignore the EU or force them to dismantle policies. (The EU challenged Microsoft on anti-competitive practices and has challenged the United States over claims of unfair trade practices.)

On the other hand, the internal politics of the EU suggest limits to super-national economic (and political) organization. The EU began as an "elite social movement": a project conceived by state elites (especially in France and Germany) who set out to cajole other countries to accept their vision of a new economic order (Fligstein and Mara-Drita 1996). The rationale for integration was to improve economies and well-being, avoid another world war, and provide a counterweight to the USSR and the United States. But the EU project also included harmonizing European economic and political cultures: social democratic principles were enshrined in laws defending labor, welfare, and the environment against the potentially destructive market. Yet British economic culture was less social democratic, with greater appreciation for individual initiative and more distrust of the state. Negotiations over expanding and institutionalizing the EU's powers in the European Constitution brought these different economic cultures into confrontation. In fact, both the British and French publics saw the constitution as leaning too much in the other direction. The British public saw the EU and its constitution as an unaccountable bureaucratic juggernaut. (It did not help that the EU constitution was over 250 pages of legalese, while the British constitution remained traditional and unwritten.) But the British did not have a chance to defeat the EU constitution in a referendum: the French beat them to it. The majority of French voters found the new constitution too Anglo-American: too many freedoms to business and too few provisions for social protection. The constitution ended up further dividing, not bridging, economic cultures. While the EU and euro survive, the project without a constitution faces further obstacles to integration, including subsidies and the limits of EU authority.

The disconnect: global economies and national institutions

At present it is difficult to predict what the immediate future will be – a global economy or regional economies – but I would bet (were I a betting person) on the latter. There have been historical movements of global integration, but regional forces (especially national states and societies) persist. Many economic changes or effects remain the result of *domestic* forces or of local decisions in a global context. Japanese competitors hurt the American steel industry in no small part because American steel leaders chose less efficient technology when they modernized. Auto workers in Detroit and other industrial workers in the Northeast "Rust Belt" lost their jobs not only to foreign competitors but also to cheaper labor in the South. As Ford and General Motors cut auto-making jobs in Michigan, Saturn and Honda opened factories in Tennessee and Ohio. As Pittsburgh and eastern Ohio deindustrialized, Charlotte and Seattle have been growing. Changes in America's economy are due to movement of capital *within* the country. Further, despite increasing trade between countries, investors prefer to invest in their home countries: American, Japanese, and French investors put more than 90 percent of their assets in American, Japanese, and French equities (Obstfeld 1998: 22–3). Information costs are part of this – an American will spend time and effort trying to fathom out the French market (different laws and language) – but this does not explain the extreme degree of investment at home, and the incredibly low rate of diversified investment across different countries, which one would expect from rational actors in a global market. This remains a daunting puzzle for economists, and it suggests that the global economy is not a state to which we return naturally.

I suggest there is an easier answer: transaction costs linked to the absence of a global state underpinning global trade. Here we come to the disconnect between a *global* economy and *national* institutions. One of the most powerful lessons of economic sociology is the importance of structures of *power* that can enforce and reproduce the structures, rules, and meanings that hold an economy together and give actors stability and constraints. Economies are grounded in institutions of property ownership, value and currency, and exchange (including defense of contract). Where are the world-level institutions to make a global economy operate? Integrated national economies have national institutions of property and exchange: stock markets, rules and fields of corporate governance, courts or other systems for recourse during disputes. Currently, there are no such institutions at the global level (cf. Fligstein 2001a: 209–11). The New York Stock Exchange is important to the global market – but it follows *American* laws and is embedded in *American* structures and politics. Authority within the World Trade Organization comes from agreements between *individual* countries. When one state violates WTO rules, the punishment is supposed to be sanctions from member states – not from some central body that has sovereignty over its members and an independent police force to enforce rules and decisions.

History shows that a capitalist market economy (or any integrated economy) requires a capitalist *state* to create and enforce it (Polanyi 1944; Weber 1987 [1923]; Evans 1995). Economists often assume that the movement of capital (e.g. capital flight) will force integration – economies that don't play by the rules don't get investment. Yet economies continue to show variation. The threat of capital flight may encourage *marginal* policy changes, except in dire cases (e.g. post-socialist countries). The reality, as we saw in Chapter 3, is that states created capitalist economies by developing capitalist societies and by eradicating barriers to integration. States and different elites factions engaged in competition and conflict over boundaries of exchange – protected local producers' markets versus expanded markets led by national elites and the state (Lie 1992). That is, integration of *national* markets did not evolve out of mystical imperatives to utility maximization or competitive efficiency; they emerged out of conflict over the *control* of trade and production. Further, nation-states enforced national currencies as the primary means of exchange or store of value – not only to expand trade but also to aid tax collection and build political authority (Bensel 1990; Sellers 1991). This created a border around a national economy: money was economic power, and the state controlled the national currency. Just as states monopolized the legitimate use of violence, they also monopolized the legitimate printing and circulation of that totem of economic power: money.[11] In post-socialist Russia this led to games of resistance; in the early years of the independent American republic, its absence led to Shay's Rebellion.[12]

This is the rub: the global economy does not have a global state to create or enforce it. The WTO and United Nations are not a global state. Without a global state to enforce a global market – a global state with an independent army and police force and sense of sovereignty above that of its members – that global market is on weak legs. As the experience of the League of Nations and the United Nations shows, individual countries' leaders and populations are loath to give up political sovereignty to a greater body, even in the name of economic gains. This problem with globalization also affects regionalization. Regional economic zones also need a regional power to enforce rules – but regional hegemony (e.g. the United States) or a few countries negotiating integration (e.g. the EU) are easier to organize.[13] Only the European Union comes close – rules made in Brussels by bureaucrats and Members of the European Parliament (MEPs) are supposed to be binding to member nations, and the euro further integrates participating economies. But even for the EU, those rules and adherence to the euro (including rules about limits to budget deficits, which France and Germany quickly violated) are enforced not by the power and potential violence of the EU, but by the power of individual member states (some of whom can "opt out"). This has led to two Achilles' heels for the EU. First, it resembles the United States under the failed Articles of Confederation – a loose alliance of sovereign entities, not a unified state. Second, the attempt to add teeth to EU power has bred the accusation that the EU is a "United States of Europe," not a bloc of sovereign states – something that still troubles many Europeans.

Nationalism and national identities remain a counterweight to globalization. As national economic integration once threatened local interests, global integration threatens national interests. Local communities resisted integration into national markets, but failed: Why won't national resistance to inclusion in the global economy fail just the same? The answer is simple, yet most analysts miss this point entirely: the global economy is not backed by a global state to break that resistance, and nation-states are better armed than local regions once were. When economists talk of globalization as increased trade and capital mobility that forces countries to open up their markets, they ignore power and institutions once again. Nation-states emerged from war (Tilly 1990); the kind of global war necessary to create a global state will likely destroy us all. Countries go along with globalization because their elites gain (and maybe their populations do sometimes). But free market capitalism was discredited in the 1930s for a time; who is to say that economic nationalism will not return? While countries may become more dependent on each other, what might happen in global economic recession or even depression, as in the 1930s? When this happened in the past, nationalism was a powerful clarion rallying elites and shocked populations. Economies and political elites have not managed to devise an economy that does not have its crashes – and attacks on the welfare state have taken away the very social safety net that has helped societies survive recessions and economic shocks. What will happen when the next major shocks occur – say, as the world's stocks of oil begin to dry up? Countries with relatively vibrant economies and militaries will be in good positions, although their elites will be sorely tempted to use varieties of nationalism to rally their suffering populations.

And the moral is ... ?

Hegel once claimed that the owl of Minerva takes flight at dusk: we gain wisdom and insight too late, only when an historical epoch or event has run its course.

Globalization may be an inevitable trend, with a global state (or a powerful business cartel) not far away. It may also be an historical oscillation that will change again. If I read today's newspaper I see proof of globalization *and* of its weakness. It is too early to tell which way the world will go, but it is not too early to discern how we should address this issue. Organized interests and ideologies push for greater freedom of trade between countries, but they (so far) cannot create the necessary institutions of enforcement. Today's world is complex and confusing (as economies have always been); reducing and simplifying it to "globalization" only adds to the confusion. In addition to increased trade and labor competition are regional blocs, competition within countries, global organizations such as the WTO and IMF, and a resurgence in nationalism and (maybe) in left-leaning ideologies critical of market predominance. Trade unions and democratic politics gave non-elites some means for justice and protection; if they could pressure the state, they could force changes in the economy. In a global economy without a global state – even if that global economy is little more than greater mobility of goods and capital – average people in Argentina and America have lost that means to justice and protection. There is a lot going on out there; we need to make sense of *what* is happening and *how*, especially the structures of power that are arising or declining.

One final point: information technology *has* made the world smaller. Between the internet and CNN I see breaking news as it happens, minute-by-minute: the war in Iraq, political or judicial decisions, news of corporate mergers or scandals. I am bombarded by information wherever news agencies can set up satellite dishes or someone has access to the internet and the motivation to write a blog. This makes me *feel* linked to the rest of the world. But is this real globalization – interdependence and connectivity beyond my locality – or is it the *illusion* of connectivity? There are structural links across countries. American and European corporations once exploited non-European populations, and still do; but now those populations offer cheaper labor and new markets. The periphery is getting its revenge, and thanks to information technology I know this. But is this *qualitatively* new? I know more, I can send e-mails to the farthest reaches of the globe, I have the impression of being part of something wider (and feeling even more powerless as a result) – but how much of that is real and how much is virtual, an illusion borne of information overload?

The challenge of economic sociology *vis-à-vis* globalization is twofold, then. First, we must be more precise about what "globalization" is, how new and different it is, and how it really operates – the social forces and structures at work. This demands that we be careful and rigorous with our analyses and arguments: being aware of assumptions, considering important variables (such as institutions and power) and how they operate globally, and *then* sifting through the data and engaging in debate. It also requires us to take stock of the insights economic sociology provides about past and present economies – so that when we study globalization, we have clear ideas of what and how to study it. Second, we must become more active in public discourse, so that discussion of globalization's causes and effects can be rid of illusions and more firmly grounded in reality. Both of these require that economic sociologists take steps to take stock of and organize their insights – providing an intellectual and normative agenda. This is the goal of the Conclusion.

Conclusion
Remaining challenges of economic sociology in the new millennium

We have come to the end of *our* journey – but the journey of economic sociology continues. In these final pages I want to recap the important lessons and suggest possible further steps forward – and I hope the reader will add his or her two cents. While economic sociology may have *scholarly* insights that rival those of economics, there remains work to do. First, there are still gaps in empirical knowledge and theory. Second, as Fligstein (2001a) rightly points out, economic sociology will not have the same status as economics until it translates its scholarship into a broader agenda. While economics and economic sociology have a *descriptive and explanatory* side – where economic sociology has scored important goals against its rival – economics has a relatively uniform and overt *normative* agenda that economic sociology lacks. Even if economic sociology describes the world better, economists can provide a *goal* along with a roadmap. Economics has a single dominant paradigm – microeconomics, with rational choice and efficiency at its heart – which, driven by seemingly objective mathematical formulae, seems to provide iron-clad claims. Even if they are far from true, they have influence in the public sphere, because it is easy to translate the complex math into straightforward, seemingly common-sense arguments: competition, open markets, and minimal politics are good for everyone (economies are apolitical), and the economic tide of growth will rise and lift all boats. Even when there is dissent among economists (as there once was between neoliberals and neo-Keynesianists), there is still a sense of unity over a few basic theoretical and normative claims.

In this Conclusion I lay out an agenda for economic sociology that includes theoretical and social-political issues: what we should address in our empirical work and teaching, and what we should fight for in the political realm. I make no claims to the perfect agenda, and I am sure I am slighting some people's favorite items. But it is a start. I begin with the intellectual–theoretical agenda – what the scholars need to work on more – and turn to the public or social agenda – what we should say to public audiences.

The lessons

I simply highlight key lessons and insights on which we can build in academic studies and in broader discussions and discourse. The key is embeddedness. We are embedded in structural relations: we know people personally or are linked to them through official rules (employee and owner, politician and voter); we are linked to resources (owning or not owning property, having access to political power). We are embedded in cultural meanings and symbols that provide "tool kits" (Swidler 1986) for making sense of the world and acting within it.

Structure and actors

Actors structure and shape each other. This does not simplify the picture, but there is no magic bullet: I would be lying if I said that we need only look for structure to fully understand economic history and practice. Recall inequality: structures shape classes and mobility. Industrialization – a structural change – helped create a working class and drew young men and women from the farm. Yet classes also shape economies, as the stories of the American corporations and American doctors showed. This is because structures are not solid, immovable objects like cinderblock walls. Rather, they exist through people's everyday practices (Giddens 1984). Strong and weak ties, networks and structural holes, class relations to property, relations between firms and employees and states – these persist and have importance because we give them meaning in everyday life. We do not question property relations because we take them for granted – and if we do not, there are plenty of elites, fellow employees, and police officers who do. Their practices reproduce structures. But if we understand structures, we can ride them as a surfer rides a wave: the surfer has to take the waves the ocean gives him or her, but he or she can use these to his or her advantage.

Economies, then, are not just free competition, utility, and efficiency alone. Whether efficiency is all-important depends on structures. The best employees may not make it because of class, race/ethnicity, or gender in class-biased, racialized, and gendered economies. To claim that existing structures of firms or inequality somehow must serve efficiency is to *assume* efficiency, not to demonstrate it. This provides an added lesson: economies are political. Structures inherently shape individuals' or groups' interests and ability to articulate and act on them (or not). Inefficient workers may be lazy or incompetent – but they may also be playing games of resistance (Burawoy 1979), working enough for themselves but not as hard as they can (unless managers can unite employees' interests with those of the firm).

Economies and power culture

If structures are reproduced by everyday practices, then we must dig deeper into those practices, and this leads to another important lesson: the importance of power and culture. Culture provides meanings and understandings of what is normal; it is our knowledge of what we *can* and *should* do. Economic strategies and structures are not always based on economic rationality, but rather on the logic of legitimacy. Power is the means to act and impose. Without power, we cannot overcome resistance. But these two do not act in isolation: they work together, what scholars in the tradition of the late French historian Michel Foucault call "power-culture." Cultural categories shape legitimate, available action: are we supposed to maximize or satisfice, and what – profit, employees, sales, share value? Yet culture by itself might be unimportant: why should I accept the categories and logics of economic structure and action around me? Here power enters: the ability of elites or collectives (e.g. fellow employees) to impose behavior upon me. This gives us a new twist on economic structures: they are really practices of power-culture. Economists of globalization talk about investors moving their capital and production around to get the best deal, but this is over-simplified – it sounds like eighteenth-century business, with firms or investment run by a few people, rather than by the complex firms that we have today. Now, different levels of managers, consultants, and brokers study, advise, deliberate, and invest. And they do so in a context of state and global politics that they may try to influence. In other words, simply to say that capital goes where it has the best deal hides more than it explains. *Who* decides what the "best deal" is – owners of capital, managers of capital, investment analysts? What are their models of "good economic practice"? What are their interests, and who are their masters – what are the relations of power-culture of the organizations and professions in which they are embedded? Does my broker really examine the stock market objectively when he invests my money, or is he using my money to play games with his co-workers and bosses, to achieve status with short-term gains that will lead to long-term loss? The twenty-first century is not an era of one owner deciding where his capital should go; it is a game of many players, with competing ideas of normal economic practice, embedded in complex and sometimes confusing relations of authority, accountability, and status.

These lessons, from discussions throughout this book, suggest key issues and questions we should always ask about policies, structures, behavior, and change. Power, culture, structure, and institutions are key – not just as abstract concepts, but as concrete social "facts." Economic structures and practices do not simply reflect competition or resource endowments alone, as economists have assumed since the days of David Ricardo. Economies are complicated beasts, and the following sets of questions and issues are starting points to help us make sense of those beasts.

- *Who* socially constructs reality, creating our categories, institutions, structures? Economies are not just competition, supply-and-demand, and objective market prices and efficiency. Value, business strategies and goals, and measures of success (such as profit or efficiency) are socially constructed meanings, as the story of post-socialist Russia clearly shows. Economic reality does not socially construct itself – actors do this. Which actors are important depends on who has access to the resources of power-culture. In countries with centralized states and political culture that privileges state authority (e.g. France or Japan), state officials are important actors. In countries where states are less privileged (e.g. the United States, Canada), business elites are more prominent.

- What resources do successful actors have – organizational authority, access to institutions of law or media, property and wealth, connections to people with institutional resources? The more money, networks, or manpower one has, the greater the possibility of socially constructing economies. This may be through direct force or dependence: making others do what they otherwise would not do by threatening to withdraw support (e.g. firms leaving countries or trading partners, employees going on strike) or to "attack"(e.g. through industrial sabotage, undercutting competitors in price wars, or donating money to agreeable political parties or candidates).

- What strategies lead to successful reconstruction of power-culture in organizations, fields, and economies? Simply having resources alone does not guarantee success, and in fact the strongest do not always win (Dobbin 1994). Jeffrey Pfeffer (1992) and Neil Fligstein (2001b) claim that economies are political, and so to successfully change an organization, field, or economy, actors (owners, managers, or others) must mobilize money, people, and legitimacy. This means creating or using networks to build alliances; manipulating the meanings and symbols of laws, events, and social myths that legitimate their claims and solutions and rally others to their cause; and cleverly using institutions and laws to back up or impose claims and actions.

- For economic change, what are the differences or "distance" between existing meanings, power relations, and practices and those of our "target," the kind of economy we want? The greater the difference, the harder change will be. Radical change threatens people: they feel their interests will be hurt, or they feel frightened by the uncertainty of new, unfamiliar economic practices and relations. Post-socialist change has been difficult exactly for this reason: Russians, Ukrainians, Poles, and others went from a system of welfare, production-based business strategies, and collective or state ownership to a system of reduced welfare and profit, sales-based business strategies, and private property. Workers felt threatened by a new world where unemployment and a wealthy capitalist elite – what they had long been taught were the face of evil – were a reality. In the United States, socialized medicine implied "socialism," which is illegitimate in American political and economic culture. This means that designing successful change demands not only manipulating networks, meanings, and power. It also means mapping out existing economic power-culture, what new power-culture might look like, and how to change cultural categories and power relations without creating too much confusion and resistance.

- What are the fields of economic structure and action, and what meanings dominate those fields? An economy is not unstructured; changing it means understanding its structure, and here fields are crucial. By studying fields, we can discern the important actors – who can foster or resist change, with what power – and what the existing economic meanings are that we must change. In Europe and East Asia, states are more important in fields; one can lobby the state for fundamental change in economic action. In North America, states are less important; fields are dominated by firms and the stock market. This makes change more difficult: it requires many actors and meanings to challenge and change.

These questions and issues can help us further develop theoretical and empirical material. There remain many unanswered questions. For example, sometimes we do act like rational actors, but at other times we follow routines or act on emotion. What determines when we are rational, routine, or emotional? In addition, fields structure economies, but how do field structures and boundaries emerge? How do fields emerge in different countries, and do they look differently? There is much research on American fields, but less on fields elsewhere. We understand the role of the state in the economy, but we know less about the actual everyday practices of state–economy interaction: in other words, we have much *macro*-level data, but little *micro*-level data. Still, we have learned quite a bit, and this can help us develop a social-political, or normative, agenda for the public and political spheres.

The intellectual–theoretical agenda

Ideas are important: they are the categories and cause–effect relations that we apply to problems and solutions in the world around us. To provide a powerful and accurate normative agenda, we need an orderly intellectual agenda: not only cataloging knowledge, but also noting improvements and exploration that are further needed.

Breaking out of the shadow of economics

Economic sociologists have spent too much time in the shadow of economists. While one can understand why – economics has a longer history and stronger pedigree at present – fixating on economic theory does not necessarily help advance the field any longer. Too much economic sociology spends too much time being preoccupied with economic theory: either developing theory that addresses economic theory point for point, or taking economic theory and simply adding a few structural variables (Zelizer 1988). In fact, much of Mark Granovetter's (1974, 1985) pioneering work does not provide a fundamental challenge to economic theory: rather than providing an alternative, Granovetter adds networks to general economic theory. Addressing economic theory point by point, and admitting insights and overlap, is useful at the start – but not for developing an alternative paradigm potentially richer in theoretical and empirical detail. We already have the foundations for that paradigm in the founding work of Marx, Weber, and Durkheim, and in the caches of data from the past twenty years.

Further, economic sociologists need to expand their field of vision and sources of ideas. Political sociology and political science have benefited from cross-fertilization: not only with each other, but with history and anthropology, and even with economics. Political scientists have gained paradigms (modernization or institutional theory), and political sociologists have gained powerful empirical data insights (e.g. from comparative politics) that helped shape state-centered theory. Political sociologists have even used neoinstitutionalism to study change (e.g. the rise of states and social movements). Economic sociologists may take inspiration from economists, but there are plenty of ideas from political sociology that can be incorporated.

For example, political sociologists have generated data and insights on power and culture in political structures and action; these are now part of the usual canon of tools and ideas. In economic sociology, however, such a power-culture approach remains underdeveloped, despite the insights it can provide (e.g. Fligstein 1996). Ideas from the study of social movements are particularly enticing (cf. Hass 1999, 2005): the importance of "framing" meanings and legitimacy, or of using structure to generate opportunity.

A more unified theory

Economic sociologists lack a unifying paradigm and a normative argument. As we saw in Chapters 1 and 3, there are different fundamental approaches, from the Marxist and Weberian frameworks to Durkheimian modernization theory and neo-Durkheimian neoinstitutionalism. There is no single voice: from one side comes talk about the power of structures *or* organizations, from the other the centrality of values *or* of fields and isomorphism. Whether these different theories can eventually be melded into a single paradigm remains to be seen. However, we recognize that economic sociology has also been helped by having multiple theories in competition. Marxists and Weberians in battle with each other (and with economists) are forced to correct and perfect their arguments. The result is better Marxist and Weberian theory, and perhaps an eventual merger of the two into an overall better "grand unified theory."

Competition helps us hone our arguments, but it should also contain elements of agreement over key terms and units of analyses; otherwise the competition can degenerate into intra-disciplinary squabbles and politics. At some point Marxists, Weberians, and Durkheimians (and others) will have to step back and look objectively at the facts and theories and move towards a greater synthesis. This may mean chucking out some cherished claims – class conflict for Marxists, functional rituals for some Durkheimians – but it may also mean retaining some key ideas and developing them further (for example, a concept of class and class interests closely linked to organizational dynamics). We economic sociologists must bring together disparate strands of research and theorizing, so that structure and culture, power and process, micro and macro come together fruitfully. Network-based studies will need to include power and cultural elements: the meaning which people in different societies and historical moments give to "friend" or "contact," for example. Is a "friend" supposed to reciprocate – do I have the right to demand favors – or is "friendship" more instrumental? How do networks help facilitate mobilization of fields or resistance – or how do culture and social skills help or hinder the use of networks to mobilize resources (cf. Fligstein 2001b)? Analyses privileging structures and institutions need to make sense of the micro-level and everyday economic practice. How do networks help reproduce macro-level structures and institutions beyond the elite level (which scholars have studied fairly well)? Perhaps one starting point is to rethink "institutions," "structures" and "networks," and "power" as components of *practices* – in a sense, bring in insights of microsociology and symbolic interaction too long neglected in economic sociology (but developed in studies of social movements).

Perhaps one way to make sense of all the insights in this field is to begin with methodological individualism – from the individual, as economists do – but instead of assuming rational choice, we look at when people are calculating, ritualistic, and emotional. From here we explore how people adopt or apply meanings to their networks in different contexts. This means taking stock of how networks and local communities inform our beliefs and tool kits of meanings (micro-level structure and power); and how cognitive systems of thought (see Chapter 1) shape the application of meanings. From there we can map out the direct and indirect networks that link people together: who knows who and authority in those relations; and relations between people through institutions, e.g. property (owner or manager versus employee). This is similar to Randall Collins' (1981) idea of "interactive ritual chains," extended chains of networks that people reproduce ritually and that create the structure through which power and institutions operate, and that help maintain continuity (e.g. class relations to property) or help spread change or resistance. Yet we cannot stop with networks. When I think of what influences my actions, structural relations are not enough. I look out into the world – at the media (news or MTV), at what my colleagues or students are doing or saying, at advertisements and the assortments of goods and services available – and from this I reckon the dominant categories and logics of legitimate behavior that I should adopt. That is, in the logic of *game theory*, I look beyond networks and community to make sense of my broader context. Here, I think, is an important missing piece to economic sociology: applying game theory to networks, culture, cognition, and power. This adds a collective dimension that can help us further make sense of change and continuity, and the mechanisms by which economic institutions and practices operate. The market, supposedly, is buyer and seller interacting; we have already explored the nature of that interaction, but there remains more to do.

The normative (social-political) agenda

The public agenda are normative claims, based on the intellectual foundations, that we should try to make to politicians, journalists, and especially fellow citizens. In the midst of the debates and cacophony there lurks an interesting, important, and unusual normative agenda focusing on power, structure, and culture. We should not throw out economists' concerns with growth and efficiency – but we should not assume that the two automatically generate justice or equal opportunity.

Social justice

Most sociologists are left of center. Analyses usually invoke the role of the state in investing in and protecting markets and societies. Where economists often see welfare as a drag on the economy (although there are a growing number who admit its importance as well), sociologists are usually quick to defend welfare and state intervention, no doubt because inequality and poverty are historically important topics of study in sociology. Yet the welfare state no longer enjoys the political legitimacy it once had (e.g. in the 1960s era of the "Great Society"). Sociologists have been on the defensive and sometimes slow to understand that there are indeed negative sides to welfare provision or state interference in the economy. What *should* policy-makers do? Lower taxes? Regulate firms – but how, without making the state too powerful? Create balance between firms, states, and civil society? But this required historical accidents to work in Sweden. Encourage a workers' revolution, even though Soviet socialism was a nightmare? Weberians are skeptical.

The state is an important part of the solution, but it is not the entire solution. Ironically for left-of-center sociologists, part of the solution may lie in what Republican president George Bush called "a thousand points of light": civil society. While Bush provided no plan for enhancing civil society – and Republican support for big business contradicts the empowerment of civil society *vis-à-vis* powerful corporations – that does not mean we cannot push the rhetoric to a logical conclusion. The communitarian tradition, usually linked to Amitai Etzioni, sees future progress through local organization and civil society, not necessarily through states or larger organizations. Smaller local organizations are more likely to be responsive to individuals: there is more communication, face-to-face contact, and accountability. Creating this, however, is problematic. Organizational elites are not likely to give up their power, and even smaller organizations may fall prey to the Iron Law of Oligarchy. And can we afford to lose large organizations that can accumulate resources and achieve the economies of scale that help improve our lives?

Structures and balance

One lesson from studies of democracy is the importance of *balance* (e.g. Moore 1966). If one group of actors – the state, bourgeoisie, nobility – becomes too strong, political rights for other groups are in jeopardy. Much is the same for economics: if one sector is too strong, the entire economy (and polity) can suffer: that dominant sector can siphon resources or demand protection and rents, at a cost to other sectors. Sweden works because of a balance between the state, business elites, and organized labor. America's economic "golden years" coincided not only with global hegemony (no small contributor) but also with greater balance between business and labor. With balance, different actors have to negotiate with and listen to each other. As we saw with East Asia, communication can facilitate innovation. Further, balance can aid the creation or survival of *trust*. If different groups cannot do each other in, then they may be more likely to engage each other without the need for defensive posturing. Distrust only breeds costs: the need for longer contracts and negotiations, for more lawyers and surveillance.

But how can we create balance and trust? This is often an accident of history. England had a relatively weak state and a merger of the nobility and bourgeoisie. The United States lacked a feudal aristocracy and had fragmented state power (Moore 1966). The Founding Fathers created some balance when they proposed a divided government, but they lived before the era of corporations. *Creating* balance, instead of stumbling into it, requires that actors with power give up some of that power: from business to unions, for example. Yet actors, from state officials and business elites to union leaders, do not like to give up power easily. One solution may be what Charles Sabel (1993) calls "studied trust." Collective structures and rituals bring rivals together and force them to recognize common interests and identities with each other and with the broader community in which they are embedded – promoting cooperation and innovation. Such organizations as the United Nations are supposed to foster studied trust, although the structure of power – with the Security Council the important decision-maker (and permanent members having veto power) – hurts this potential. It may be that creating practices of studied trust requires a massive and all-encompassing crisis that convinces the vast majority of people – employees and managers, citizens and elites, rich and poor – that they are in the same boat, that they must work together, and that they must create the conditions to *keep on* working together. The Great Depression did this to an extent, but the lessons of that era were not fully learned; the Keynesianist solution broke down because it was not fully implemented (let alone understood) (Piore and Sabel 1984).

This is structural balance. We also balance priorities, in particular the thorny "choice" of freedom versus order (or security). This has been particularly important for developing nations or those undergoing reforms. Democratic reforms in 1990s Russia coincided with economic and political *dis*order; Vladimir Putin's democratic credentials are not stellar, but he is popular because he has brought *order* that has corresponded with economic improvement. While "First World" countries did not face this issue directly, "security" is one buzzword in the post-9/11 world, and with increased competition from labor in developing countries, one wonders how long it will be before American or British voters are told that their wishes must be restricted in the name of being globally competitive: capital will have to win out over popular choice lest it flee elsewhere. Yet it is uncertain that such "discipline" of discourse and popular politics is so crucial to investment. Firms invest in different areas for a variety of reasons: not only cheap labor or few taxes and restrictions on activity (e.g. labor laws), but also to make inroads to a local economy, to take advantage of some other local advantage (skilled labor), or to be near to other complementary businesses. Business leaders may believe that employees and non-elites should follow rather than participate (cf. Domhoff 1998: 282–3), but sometimes non-elites have good ideas – something German and Japanese managers realized when they institutionalized closer contact and exchange of ideas between managers and line workers. As well, there is no guarantee that order will provide growth; democracy can also be correlated with growth, as in post-socialist Eastern Europe. Giving non-elites a voice and participation in decision-making may reduce elite power and profits, but it may also alert us to issues we must address to maintain growth. "Freedom versus order" may be a false dichotomy – the key, again, is balance.

Deliberation at heart

My final normative recommendation follows this last point (balance of priorities) and the lack of a single paradigm. Economists may have a general, uniform intellectual and normative agenda – but maybe we should be careful to offer a unified platform.

This smacks of the elitism (elites know best) that led to tragedy: whether the mess of Soviet communism, where an elite party assumed to know what was best for its society; or of the messes created by neoliberal policies in the United States, Great Britain, or Mexico, promoted and implemented by technocrats with Ph.D.s in economics who thought they understood social Truth but were no more correct than their Bolshevik brethren. But if we should avoid a united front, what should we advocate if we are not to be silent? We should encourage *deliberation*. Gutmann and Thompson (1996, 2004) claim that the real heart of democracy is deliberation: we discuss issues and policies as a society, and from rational, well-articulated arguments decide what we as a group think is best. Every person and claim gets a chance to be heard; from there we talk and decide. Since Marx, sociologists have been concerned about power and average people; rather than partake in power by claiming we know best, we should encourage the empowerment of people everywhere. We should encourage democratization of economies as well as of polities. Let business elites, blue-collar employees, and white-collar personnel vent their worries, hopes, and claims – and proceed to discuss how to address them. At this point, sociologists can step in to suggest *how* to implement what empowered people decide.

In fact, deliberation may be absolutely necessary when competing policies or logics cannot be reconciled and when it is unclear that one is inherently superior to the other. Academics and policy wonks debate the merits of Policy X versus Policy Y, but ultimately claims to superiority have less to do with comparable worth measured through a common metric than appeals to power, emotion, or ethics. Here deliberation beyond politicians and professors is necessary to explore nuances of policies and why one should be chosen over the other. Too much welfare can hurt productivity; but too great a stress on productivity has human costs. Overly strong unions are not the answer to productivity and justice, but neither are temp workers without stability or benefits. We cannot sacrifice the environment for economic growth, but neither can we sacrifice growth for the environment. Finding policies in the perfect middle may be impossible, but the various costs and benefits – economic but also moral, personal, and symbolic – must be deliberated and weighed up.

For a concrete example, consider American versus British university education. The American system is a market system. Professors, like American professionals generally, have better pay and more resources available. They have more autonomy in research and teaching. Tenure is a nightmare to obtain but is a powerful reward. The British system has permanent positions that do not include tenure, leaving lecturers in a sometimes precarious position. Pay and resources for teaching and research are less than in the United States. British universities are micro-managed and suffer near-feudal hierarchy, problematic accountability, increasing bureaucratic demands and workloads, and evaluation according to metrics that have little to do with real quality of teaching and research. To be blunt, British education more and more resembles the Soviet ministerial system, as Baroness Blatch noted in the House of Lords.[1] (see also Amann 2003) However, the American system is costly, with tuition rising faster than inflation; despite loans and scholarships for athletes, needy students, and bright students, many blue-collar and even white-collar children face the prospect of enormous student loans. If American education provides better teaching and research than its British counterpart, it also produces more inequality. And so – which system is better? If Vladimir Putin wanted to reform Russian higher education, should he choose the American or the British model? Rather than a clear "best practice," there is a trade-off. One could take examples from employment – more support (or coddling) for European employees, but also less productivity and higher unemployment than in the United States. Which is "better" (and who defines "better")? Here deliberation becomes crucial: what are we willing to trade? Sociologists can contribute not only many voices, but also a respect for nuances and dimensions to every policy and an appreciation for empowerment that comes from inviting people from all roads of life into the arena of debate.

This may sound utopian – but neoliberal economic policy, like Marxism, is utopian as well. I doubt an economy as large as that in China or America can have an enormous town hall meeting over economic policy, even if every family had a computer and access to the internet. However, republican democracy was designed to cope with this issue of large numbers of people, and we do have representative institutions for deliberation: Congress, Parliament, and so on. Why not expand the debate to economies? To an extent we do this already: debates over taxation, workers' rights, welfare, and the like occur in Congress or Parliament or the Duma. However, many issues are off limits: for example, profit margins and corporate investment are the territory of shareholders. The challenge is expanding the scope of debate, beyond overarching policies to the nitty-gritty of everyday economic practice and the major questions of what a "Good Economy" looks like. Part of that challenge is making the debate communal. Rather than have managers and shareholders on one side and union leaders (elected by employees) on the other, we have all people involved in production and exchange vote for representatives who will deliberate economic policy.

To overcome this challenge we have to confront a pressing issue: the public versus the private. Democracy is public: all members of the polity (citizens) participate. Capitalism is private: the only participants in decision-making are those who own property (shareholders) and their agents (managers). Economists believe this is an efficient system: private property encourages responsible use of resources.[2] Yet employees also have a stake in their business, and there is no reason to believe that they are less responsible than managers and owners. (Workers may steal paperclips, but managers use the company plane or other perks.) And private property is no guarantee of accountability: there are always moral hazards, and property can breed opportunism.[3] Finally, if investors provide capital, employees provide labor. Neoliberals privilege investors and Marxists privilege workers, but each side needs the other. To create deliberation, we must find a way to retain advantages of private property while empowering non-owners. Eradicating private property is not the answer; *transcending* existing limitations of creative thought and the narrow interests of those who benefit are necessary.

In fact, deliberation might find support in economists' own logic. They believe that competition creates efficiency and progress. Deliberation and deliberative democracy are competition and a marketplace of ideas. They can allow pressing issues to be heard and addressed that might be ignored because they threaten elite interests or because people fail to see them. Sociologists are adept at identifying relations of power that economic theory misses or hides; and sociology is not hampered by a single dominant paradigm and pressures to adhere to it. We are well prepared to facilitate discussion of ideas and how to implement them. However, until existing institutions open up debate, and until economic sociologists get across their ideas to a broader public, economists will continue to dominate discourse.

Sociologists stress embeddedness in social structures and forces, and it sometimes seems that people have no agency – no capacity to act. This is the *pathos* of sociology: good at telling us how powerless we are (unless we are elites), bad at telling us what we *can* or even *should* do. To make the subject more attractive, economic sociologists must develop concepts of agency and structure to show us where the limits of action are – but also to show us *how* we can create opportunity or at least maneuver and survive within the limits of individual agency. This will make economic sociology useful for average people: rather than say how powerless we are, economic sociologists will tell us what we *can* do and give us some hope in the process. This can help us liberate economic sociology from its narrow academic confines and the classroom. I hope that I have added both to classroom discourse and provided a few steps towards that liberation. This subject is too interesting, and too important, to leave to politicians, elites, and economists.

Concept guide and glossary

Below I give some basic concepts, events, people, and firms that are mentioned in passing but whose history and significance are not fully explained in the text. I also list some important terms and concepts for reference.

Austerity program Programs for reforming and improving a country's economic performance that involve drastically reducing state expenditures (e.g. on welfare or subsidies for firms). Such programs are carried out to reduce a state's debt and taxes and to encourage competition by taking the state out of the economy; firms and people will be forced to produce more and work better for less, becoming leaner and meaner and, in theory, engines of growth.

Autarky A situation of being independent and shielded from the effects of the global economy. Attempted in the Soviet Union and, to a lesser extent, in Latin America after the 1930s Great Depression.

Bubble A speculative boom fueled by large amounts of money. (See **speculation**.) In a bubble, the value of some good – shares, land, or in the eighteenth century Dutch tulips – goes up as more and more people buy the good in the hope that the price will go up and they can sell it for a profit. Hence, the value of the good inflates like a bubble. These goods become overvalued, and at some point people no longer buy the good – usually after some convincing signal of their overvalued status – and the price quickly drops as those holding the good sell to get at least some money. This is the bursting of a bubble.

Culture The "symbolic-expressive aspect of social behavior" (Wuthnow 1987: 4) through which we create meaning and embed it in physical entities and rituals. Different forms of culture include values, symbols, rituals, scripts, and schemas.

Dot-com Nickname given to small firms that opened in the second half of the 1990s to provide certain internet services, in particular sales services. Dot-coms required little overhead and initial investment, and so the initial share prices were low. However, given the newness of the internet and general intoxication with its perceived endless opportunities, demand for dot-com shares skyrocketed, driving up their prices and creating a bubble. The bubble began to deflate in the United States around 1999, but picked up speed and burst after the election of George W. Bush at the end of 2000.

Embeddedness A situation of being linked to one's social context. To say that firms are embedded in society or politics means that the firm's people and procedures are linked through networks, laws, culture, and dependency to their surrounding society, rather than being totally independent of it.

Export-oriented industrialization (EOI) Economic policy in which a country orients the production of goods and services for export, usually to developed countries or neighbors. This is usually associated with successful East Asian economies in the 1970s and 1980s.

Fields Communities of organizations whose leaders assume have affinity and similarity. Because fields are communities, field members watch each other to determine what normal and legitimate strategies they should adopt.

Game theory A branch of economics that looks at how rationally acting individuals interact with imperfect information about each other. Game theory essentially embeds individual choice in other individuals' choices, making interaction important. Interaction is like a game (e.g. poker, chess): we try to figure out what other people will do, and then consider how their actions shape the costs and benefits of our own choices.

Glass ceiling and glass cliff Informal organizational forces that hinder women's upward career mobility or success. While glass ceilings may be based on discrimination, they may also be based on cultural and structural forces: women unable to walk the fine line between acting male and female enough to satisfy male superiors; women lacking role models or allies (especially women allies) among superiors. Glass cliffs are a result of legitimacy: firms in trouble hire women to signal their willingness to undertake radical changes that would probably not help the firm survive anyway.

Institutions Collective rules (formal and informal) and procedures that create roles, relations, and meanings. Organizations, states, private property, and constitutions are institutions because they are rules that create collective meanings, procedures, and roles. Institutions are difficult to change because they are collective – meanings must be changed for a large number of people. The greater the change, the more power is needed to impose new meanings.

Import-substitution industrialization (ISI) Economic policy in which a country produces goods it once imported, with the goal of keeping profits within the country. In Latin American ISI, states were important owners and investors in new industries.

Isomorphism The process of matching one pattern to another. Organizational isomorphism is a process in which one organization's structure and strategies match another's. There are four forms of organizational isomorphism (DiMaggiio and Powell 1983): coercive, normative, mimetic, and competitive.

Multinational corporation (MNC) Corporations that operate in many different countries (hence "multinational"). While an MNC will have its corporate headquarters in one country – usually a developed country in which it was born, to be near capital markets and recruiting grounds for top managers – it does not necessarily owe loyalty to that country, and it will shift production around the globe to maximize access to sales and markets and minimize the costs of labor and other inputs for production.

Neoinstitutionalism A branch of organizational sociology that examines why organizations have particular strategies and structures. Neoinstitutionalists focus less on how rules shape costs and benefits and efficiency (as NIE does), and instead they study how institutions shape legitimacy. Further, neoinstitutionalists claim that organizations are embedded in *fields*.

New institutional economics (NIE) A branch of economics that focuses on the role of institutions. Institutions are rules that dictate the costs and benefits of action, thus shaping what we do. Formal law is very important in this approach because it shapes costs by making something legal or illegal. For this reason, NIE is sometimes called "law and economics."

P/E ratio Ratio of price to earnings. The higher the ratio, the better the return on investment – the better the productivity or performance of the investment.

Power The capacity to make others do what they might not otherwise do. Power takes many forms, from control of media and discourse to control of resources one needs (e.g. wages, life). Power may be direct – me forcing someone else to do something by threatening to shoot them or fire them – or it may be indirect – as when firms shape students' education choices by giving hiring preferences to, say, sociologists rather than economists. (Roy 1997)

Pyramid (sometimes referred to as Ponzi scheme) A *pyramid* is a scheme for attracting money from one source to pay off another. If interest is involved, then each successive sum borrowed increases, until the borrowing cannot cover previous debts, and the pyramid collapses.

Rational choice A theoretical view of human nature that sees people as having fairly stable preferences, sufficient knowledge about their economic or social world, and the drive to obtain enough goods to maximize their utility (satisfaction from use value of goods). Rational choice assumes that we weigh the costs and benefits of different choices, and we take the choice that provides the most gain for the least cost.

Satisfice Reaching a level of "good enough," rather than maximizing. For example, managers who satisfice profit do not reach maximum possible profit; they reach a level that is sufficient to meet current needs (paying debts and wages and demonstrating competence to shareholders). People may satisfice because maximizing utility or profit is too difficult: there are too many variables or factors to control, demanding too much time and energy.

Speculation Obtaining profit by manipulating price and availability. For example, if I buy shares or land and sell them when the price is higher, without adding any value (e.g. carrying out repairs on a home or developing the land), then I am making a profit simply by waiting for the price to go up. This is *speculation*. Crudely put, it is buying low and selling high – but the price goes up *not* because I added value, but because demand drove the price up. Sometimes speculation can be constructed when one group buys a good – land, stocks in certain types of companies – and then creates a positive image for that good, so that others will want to buy it at a higher price.

State That bureaucratic organization that claims a monopoly over the use of violence for a given territory. The "state" should not be confused with "government." "State" refers to the entire bureaucracy. "Government" refers to those who lead the state – in a democracy, elected officials of all branches (or, in the case of some court judgeships, appointed and approved by elected officials). "Regime" means the top leadership of the government.

Structure Patterned, fairly stable relations between multiple entities (people, states, organizations, classes). Structure can take different forms. Networks are relations between people based on knowledge. Organizational structure is formal relations of authority or work interaction (vertical or horizontal relations). Class structure is relations of different classes to relations of production, and from this relations to each other.

Sunk costs Investments that cannot be recouped after they are made. For example, raw materials (iron and steel, rubber, glass) may be used to make a machine, which costs, say, $1 million. The machine can be sold for scrap at, say, $100,000, but the remaining $900,000 cannot be recouped. This is the sunk cost – a cost sunk into a venture, literally. (If the machine is resold, its value will be lower due to age and wear – creating the same result.)

Notes

Chapter 1

1 This is partly because economics graduates work in directly applicable jobs (e.g. accountants or financial advisers). Sociologist graduates traditionally work in social control (social workers, police, criminologists, teachers).

2 In Marxism, humans are *homo faber*, "man the maker." Humans realize themselves through producing. Depriving people of control over production deprives them of identity and meaning, creating alienation. One way to understand this is to think of surrogate motherhood: a woman is hired to bear a child, and after birth she gives the child to the paying parents for her wage. Yet the biological mother has developed a "mother" identity and emotional link.

3 I consider here *American* economic sociology. British sociology languished until the 1960s (Collins 1994: 43), and its own economic sociology remains underdeveloped.

4 Economists see path dependence as "sunk costs," a narrow understanding of history. Economists assume people's choices are as free as possible and do not consider culture, power, structure, and institutions. Rare economists (e.g. Nobel prize-winner Douglass North) take history seriously, but their work is marginal to economics (but not economic sociology).

5 This corrected an "oversocialized" view in sociology (Granovetter 1985). In functionalism (dominant until the 1970s), structure and culture program people, leaving no room for agency. If economists saw people as too free, sociologists saw them as programmed.

6 This suggests that weak ties are more beneficial than strong ties, because people who are close to you know what you know already. However, before we replace all our friends with weak ties (a lonely existence), we should consider the use of strong ties. These people are close to us (colleagues or friends) who provide strategic advice and support (letters of recommendation, psychological help), for example, for promotions (Podolny and Baron 1997).

7 For an example of categories and meanings, take pre-university education. In the United States there are two types of schools, "public" and "private": public schools are funded by local governments, and private schools are financed by individual tuition payments. In the United Kingdom, "public schools" are non-state organizations (subject to state regulations) and funded through tuition, and "state" schools are state-run and funded. Note the difference in the meaning of "public." In the US, state-run schools are "public" because they are run by a state embedded in the public – the central idea of American democracy is that a state exists because the public wants it, and the state is run by the

people and is *part of* society. A school outside governmental control would be private, like private property. In the UK, "public" means non-state – an *opposition* between state and society. This reflects Britain's feudal past – which was absent in the United States. This seemingly minor detail reflects a larger understanding of political culture and relations between states and societies.

8   Consider choosing a job. Income is quantifiable, yet meaning and satisfaction are trickier. Economists discuss "psychic costs" – the distress or other emotional impact of changing a job (or making any decision) – but there is no reliable method to operationalize or measure this.

Chapter 2

1   An equivalent is assuming a frictionless surface in introductory physics. We add real-world complications (e.g. friction) later. Economists often exclude social friction (culture, politics).

2   Suppose I earn $100 per month, and the following month my salary increases by 5 percent ($105). If inflation is 10 percent per month, I need *$110* to buy the same goods – my new wage has not kept up. This is "real wages" controlled for inflation, a measure of real purchasing power. Most people think not in terms of real wages but in terms of nominal (face) value.

3   "Transitive" means order that is not violated: If A>B and B>C, then A>C. If I like ice-cream more than sex, and sex more than movies, I must like ice-cream more than movies. The assumption is necessary for the mathematics of economics models.

4   One could argue that buying products made in one's own country is *collectively* rational. If I buy imports, I hurt domestic producers, who shut down, creating unemployment and hurting my economy. Most mainstream economists do not address collective rationality, assuming that the gains from free markets eventually help everyone (in the perfect world).

5   Another theoretical result is that markets "clear": by the end of the day all goods should be sold at "market" price. This implies that imperfections should wash out: cheaters should be chased from the market because information of their cheating spreads and people avoid them.

6   I observed this first hand when giving a talk about economic sociology to Russian students and American economists in St. Petersburg, Russia. To empirical and theoretical claims that corporate change follows power, meaning, and policy, the American economists repeatedly objected that changes follow efficiency. When I provided empirical disproof of their claims, including empirical data that survival of Russian firms depends more on networks than sales, they still protested that efficiency *had to be* central. This was classic cognitive dissonance and the power of cultural idioms (or blinders).

7   Great Britain switched partially to metrics, with further switches scheduled for 2010. Under European Union legislation, economic exchange must be metric. Market sellers can be fined for selling only in pounds (without kilograms). The British measure distance in miles (speed limits are miles per hour) and drink

beer in pints. One sees cases where market sellers refuse to sell in metric (using pounds for weight) because it is not "British."

8 The film does show basic game theory in early segments, and Nash's biographer Silvia Nassar goes into detail about Nash's work on game theory. Nash's own work is mathematically complex but not immune to criticism – like economics, it has a consistent internal logic that does not always correspond to how human beings really think and act.

Chapter 3

1 Serfs were peasants in feudal societies tied to the land and owing allegiance to the landlord. They were not slaves, but their rights were restricted. The landlord was obliged to make sure they survived to work his land, and they owed him rent or part of their produce.

2 English and German textile owners used different means to evaluate productivity and payment: the English used the amount of yarn weaved (market output), while the Germans used the number of times workers moved their shuttlecocks (labor) (Biernacki 1995).

3 Interestingly, Spain was flush with gold and silver from their empire in Latin America – yet Spain did not develop the same vibrant industrial economy as Britain and France.

4 This does not mean that "capitalism" need be "industrial." Western capitalism is increasingly driven by services and intellectual output. Further, an alternative model of industrialization was Soviet state-centered socialism, which I address in Chapter 7.

5 France has been the ideal-type case for Marxist theory, but debate has raged since the 1960s over the accuracy of the Marxist description of French class structure and the Revolution. Some historians and sociologists find a more complex class structure, and Moore (1966) even suggested that in England the nobility and bourgeoisie melded into a single ruling class.

6 The question of "when" capitalism "emerged" is thorny. Some might claim that capitalism, as a system of production and exchange based on money and private property, already existed by the fifteenth century (Braudel 1982).

7 They might work their employees hard to keep them in God's good graces as well. Generally, the link between godliness or moral purity and work was one link between Protestantism and capitalism, as other scholars have shown (e.g. Foucault 1980).

8 As Orson Wells put it so well in the movie *The Third Man*, Italy was ravaged by centuries of war, and what emerged? The Renaissance. Switzerland had centuries of peace, and what did they produce? The cuckoo clock!

9 This is the general logic of policies, especially American policy, towards China: helping China's economy might increase their military capacity, but it will also encourage the growth of a middle class, along with middle-class values for capitalism and democracy. Compare this to American policy towards Cuba: containment.

10 Increasingly, multinational corporations with headquarters in core countries use the World Trade Organization and bilateral trade agreements to claim intellectual property rights over drugs and biotechnology. Peripheral countries must then import drugs from corporations in the core and prosecute attempts in their own countries to produce cheap analogous drugs.

11 The British and French empires emerged not only for economic reasons (raw materials and new markets) but also for military reasons: to keep resources away from competing states. Britain's expansion in the subcontinent was partly to guard the routes between Britain and India.

12 When OPEC countries raised the price of oil drastically in the early 1970s, they deposited their new-found profit in American banks. To make profit on these deposits, the banks needed to lend that money out. Latin American countries such as Mexico, Brazil, and Argentina, took out vast loans (at low interest in the 1970s) to finance their programs.

13 Also important is the history of *populism* in Latin America: mobilization of the non-elite (e.g. unionized workers, peasants) against the state and elites (cf. Collier and Collier 1991).

14 One Japanese practice has been to offer a lump sum on retirement, rather than generous pension packages for the remainder of a retired person's life. This forced Japanese employees to save for retirement, giving the Japanese a higher savings rate than in the West.

Chapter 4

1 In the 1980s there was talk of "privatizing" garbage collection, road repair, and education. In the UK the state-owned railroad monopoly was privatized, but after accidents and mismanagement, many politicians and pundits demanded renationalization.

2 This contributed to the American Civil War. Northern industrialists wanted tariffs against European imports. Southern cotton growers were afraid that European countries would in turn raise tariffs on American cotton.

3 This is "instrumentalist" because individuals use institutions like *instruments* (tools) for their own interests. In contrast, "structural" Marxism sees structures shaping strategies.

4 One might argue that the American model is superior because it has allowed *constant* growth. Japanese, German, and French models sparked rapid growth only for short periods, followed by stagnation. In the end this might be true; *however*, we have to determine to what extent American growth was due to other factors such as economic and political dominance. Were the United States not a superpower, its policies may have been less successful.

5 This contrasts with the stereotype of individualistic American politics. Historically, local communities were as important as individuals – in contrast to British political culture, which locates sovereignty in elite individuals. Alexis de Tocqueville (1966) noted how important local communities were and the maxim "politics is local" reflects American political logic.

6 Not all mergers were judged to violate this law: the Supreme Court approved the merger that created U.S. Steel as in the interests of efficiency, not price-setting.

7 Consider British education and the introduction of state-funded "comprehensives" to attack private (non-state) schools. Comprehensives were to provide free schooling and bring together children of different classes, to promote meritocracy and eliminate strongly ingrained class barriers. By the 1980s, elite and middle-class parents scrambled to get their children away from working-class comprehensives into private and church-run schools.

8 This may seem contradictory: how could the *state* create market behavior? Officials feared that professionals would resist market reforms; increased control would overcome resistance. Also, professionals were among Thatcher's critics. State control would shut them up.

9 In the United States or Great Britain, the "nation" is conceived of as a collection of rational, autonomous individuals with inherent civil rights. In France, the "nation" is a single organism. Individuals (citizens) are individual parts of this larger organism, and ultimately the collective is more important than the individual. French leaders historically could make decisions in the name of the collective good that might violate minority rights. The most recent example is a decision to ban headscarves and other religious symbols in state schools – which would evoke outrage in individualist Britain and America.

10 German national identity (Greenfeld 1992: ch. 4) envisioned a *volk* (a people) unified through blood and expressed through the state – legitimating corporatist relations.

11 German economic problems in the 1990s stemmed from post-communist reunification. The East German economy was weaker than that of capitalist West Germany. Reunification required support and investment to the east (absorbing and supporting workers let go when inefficient socialist-era enterprises shut down).

12 Another aspect of Japanese economic logic is maintaining informal networks. These allow actors to negotiate and save face, to work out problems that in public might cause scandal or raise costs (e.g. spurious lawsuits). According to Kester (1996), the use of networks to coordinate business helps reduce "transaction costs" – costs of groups dealing together. Dense personal networks facilitate trust and make it possible to punish cheating through reputation and patronage rather than costly, time-consuming courtroom processes.

13 "Economic nationalism" – growth as a political means to mobilize resources and discipline – remains understudied (but see Greenfeld 2003).

14 Partly for this reason, Japanese elites and policy-makers have not rejected their state-centered policy model, despite such continuing problems as weak transparency in financial institutions, due to which bad loans and debt perpetuate recessionary trends.

15 Another example of shared ideology is *mercantilism* pursued before the nineteenth century. States granted monopolies for a fee rather than allow competition. Mercantilism also involved empires and political control of markets rather than competition.

16 Economists argued that currency values should be set in a market. However, when investors judge a country's currency, they not only look at its economy – they also judge its politics. Currency speculators may fear that Leftist policies will weaken the American (or British) economy and the dollar (or pound), and promptly sell them. Like a self-fulfilling prophesy, their fire sales weaken the dollar (or pound). Creating a world currency market created *instability*: politics and ideologies now shaped judgments of currency values.

17 Under monetarism, central banks have been wary, even obsessed, with inflation, and monetarists look for a level of "natural unemployment." When unemployment dips below this level, wage competition leads to inflation, and central banks raise interest rates to maintain some unemployment. Economists are uncertain about the natural level of unemployment.

18 Katznelson (1985) also argues that, for this reason, American political parties are less ideological and more ethnic or neighborhood-oriented than European parties. State bureaucracies handed out money for public works (e.g. repairs, construction) and welfare; parties could only compete by selling ideologies. American parties controlled the purse strings, and party leaders could hand out money to favored neighborhoods in return for votes.

19 In the first case, the shadow economy cannot easily be eradicated by reducing regulation, because that regulation has a non-economic base. Take drugs: if the majority of a population thinks it is immoral, then their democratically elected leaders will likely continue to fight against drug use (unless the costs threaten to bankrupt the country). Arguments to legalize drugs on grounds of cost follow an economic logic or are ambivalent to the moral dimension.

Chapter 5

1 Down-sized professionals and managers did not always find equivalent jobs afterward; many found getting a white-collar job difficult. "Career coaches" and networks were of little use (Ehrenreich 2005).

2 Emergent properties are traits of a collective that cannot be reduced to individuals. Organizations have collective identities and practices that are not just those of individuals. A large number of people act as one, with common cause and identity that transcends individual beliefs or actions. This does not mean that there is a larger entity with the same real existence as its individuals – simply that collective actions are greater than the sum of their parts.

3 This does not always solve the problem of performance. A manager paid in shares has the incentive to maximize share value, but he or she can still manipulate data and carry out quick operations (e.g. laying off workers and selling property) that temporarily increase a firm's value. She can then sell the shares when they are high and make good money.

4 In one passage in his opus, *The Principles of Scientific Management*, Taylor discussed a conversation with a skilled worker whom he portrayed as not particularly able or intelligent – yet the worker had engaged in complicated jobs for himself as well as for the firm.

5 An example from politics is how American presidents promote laws or pursue policies that gain political support (e.g. George W. Bush's use of 9/11 imagery and patriotic rhetoric during the war in Iraq. Democratic presidents do much the same). In business, one example is the "poison pill" which managers devised to save themselves from corporate raiders (Davis 1991). In the 1980s, as corporate raiders went after firms, managers feared for their careers and had boards of directors rewrite their contracts, such that if they were fired they would receive immense rewards. A successful corporate raider would have to pay out a large amount of money to fire old managers of his new acquisition – hence the phrase "poison pill."

6 The following is drawn from the history behind the collapse of Rover in 2004: "Life After Rover: The Chequered History of Rover," broadcast on BBC Radio 4, March 27, 2006.

7 Certification is a symbolic resource. Medical doctors need an MD, complete internships, and medical board examinations. While these may provide a baseline to judge competence, certification also gives doctors symbolic capital to signal that they are "normal" doctors.

8 Not all sectors have stable fields. Take restaurants. Start-up costs are smaller than for an automobile factory, and there is a less desperate need to avoid uncertainty. There are also many more restaurants than automobile firms, hindering coordination.

9 DiMaggio and Powell do not discuss "competitive isomorphism" in detail. If an organizational strategy provides powerful advantages in the marketplace, competitors will have to adopt it or face difficulties. However, this is all things being equal.

10 This creates a moral hazard: lecturers fulfill bureaucratic demands and produce the required four publications regardless of the real scholarly quality. Anecdotal evidence on this aspect of British higher education abounds; rigorous studies of this are few, for political reasons.

11 The author worked for six years at an English university and experienced first hand these bureaucratic demands and colleagues' exasperation with the system (see also Amann 2003).

12 One might argue that this is competition: Ford had to adapt to new market conditions. However, Ford and GM had been in competition already and followed different strategies to avoid direct competition (Fligstein's "conceptions of control," below). In adition, were competition really the heart of the matter, we would not see the overall patterns of isomorphism – adaptations when they are not necessarily rational or provide added market value.

13 These isomorphisms need not act in isolation; for example, state policies (coercive isomorphism) might lead to an initial shift in conceptions of control, with the result that managers with a particular background (e.g. finance, or marketing) are recruited to lead firms in the new environment. At this point normative isomorphism kicks in as well.

14 New institutional economics (cf. Williamson 1985) posits a similar logic: vertical integration was a means to avoid opportunism in costly production such as steel or cars.

15 Some readers may think neoinstitutionalism ignores corporate power, but it really does not. So long as there have been corporations, there have been corporate elites and organizational power. However, *by itself* "corporate power" cannot explain variation in strategies and structures that Fligstein documents – it is necessary but not sufficient. Neoinstitutionalists add a cultural dimension to power. Where Prechel sees the MLSF emerging from corporate power and interests, Fligstein sees a new conception of control. The two explanations are not contradictory but are two sides to the same phenomenon.

16 We see this in everyday life: pretending to conform without really conforming in practice. To use Goffman's terms, our "front stage" goes along with demands others make, while our "back stage" and how we really do our work does not change.

17 This does not mean that Japanese and South Korean economies are *totally* in *keiretsu* and *chaebol*. Many small firms service these conglomerates or operate independently.

18 This is an interesting irony: the hierarchical, bureaucratic corporation emerged in an historical epoch when the project of modernity was to *control* the environment, not *react* to it. The corporation was partly an attempt to control all aspects of production: obtaining materials, transforming them (labor and technology), and distributing them (Piore and Sabel 1984). The more "reactive" logic of smaller firms reflects the *geist* of disillusionment with the modernity project: confidence in mankind's ultimate ability to control the world resulted in tragedies such as the *Titanic*, world wars I and II, and the confusion of 1970s stagflation.

19 This is one potential argument for a national health care system in the United States: it frees companies from costs of medical care, while providing that care to the population at large and maintaining labor productivity (which falls if employees' health declines).

20 This resembles the Japanese "just-in-time" supply system. A manufacturer (or store) reduces overhead costs, especially storage, by receiving only materials or goods it needs at that moment – thus "just in time". (This requires a reliable system of inventory and predicting need.) Temp workers are a "just-in-time" equivalent for labor.

21 There is some difference in temp work across countries. In Europe, labor laws make simple hiring and firing difficult, support part-time work, and provide better unemployment benefits. This makes unemployment higher: people receive benefits while waiting for a good part-time job. In Great Britain, even female part-time employees (salaried, not temporary) who work for a firm for six months qualify for maternity leave. However, temp work is growing in the UK, and in France nearly 70 percent of new jobs are temporary (see Box 6.2).

Chapter 6

1 This led to a thorny legal issue in the pre-Civil War American South: is somebody legally "black" if (s)he looks white but has a black grandparent or great-grandparent ("blood")?

2 Erik Olin Wright (1978) claims that such groups occupy "contradictory class locations." While *structurally* they resemble the proletariat – all they own is labor (mental labor) that they sell on the market – their social status and rewards put them closer to the bourgeoisie.

3 These studies of intergenerational mobility compared fathers to sons – mothers and daughters were left out. This is partly due to the gendered nature of research and work – but to be fair, data covered the 1940s to the 1970s, when women were not as emancipated as later.

4 Recall that countries have different policies and state–economy relations. Still, these countries have private property, bureaucratic organization, factories and so on: similarity *and* variation.

5 They discovered this by adding socialist countries to their data set (e.g. Poland, Hungary). Mobility under socialism did deviate from that in North America and West Europe – but education and state-driven industrialization also differed under socialism.

6 This is not to say that white-collar children are inherently smarter or better behaved. They can be just as "deviant" as blue-collar children. They are less likely to get caught (they may have cars and travel to other communities to misbehave), or authorities are less likely to punish them and harm their futures (Chambliss 1973).

7 If my lawyer friends can be believed, when they recruit, partners of elite law firms take prospective hires to good restaurants several times – not only to eat well at the firm's expense, but also to see how prospective colleagues act in a setting where they will later meet important clients. Knowing about wine and forks becomes more than silly chat and table manners.

8 Wilson (1997) notes much of the same in his study of inner-city poverty and African-Americans in Chicago. Employers – white *and* black – were hesitant to hire black males from the inner city for fear they would be bad employees, would engage in unlawful behavior (e.g. theft), or would bring spurious lawsuits (e.g. about discrimination).

9 It does not follow that lay doctors were less competent or more dangerous. Given the undeveloped state of medical research and knowledge, they could have been *less* dangerous than doctors trained in European universities.

10 Doctors did much the same against HMOs and Bill Clinton's proposals for national health care reform – although given health care costs, doctors have been less successful against HMOs, and it is uncertain how long they can avoid socialized medicine when an increasing number of *employed* blue-collar and white-collar workers cannot afford medical insurance.

11 Randall Collins (1975) shows that engineers, in contrast to doctors and lawyers, could not mobilize; their fates remained linked to companies. This suggests an alternative history: the hospital as factory and doctors (like engineers) its employees.

12 There is a dispute over the difference between race and ethnicity: some authors see the two as essentially variations of the same thing, while others see ethnicity as more fluid (people move between them more easily) and race as more fixed

(assumed to be a permanent feature of the individual) (cf. the exchange between Bonilla-Silva 1997, 1999, and Loveman 1999).

13   This was not the only case of anti-Semitism in Europe. The first ethnic cleansing was in England: Edward I forced Jews to wear yellow tablets and later expelled them. In pre-1917 Russia, Jews had to live in the Pale of Settlement, an area on the fringes of the Empire including Poland, Belarus, and Ukraine. Only a few Jews could leave the Pale each year.

14   British National Party members were aghast to learn that their leaders asked a Greek descendant to stand as a BNP candidate in a local election. While of European blood, the candidate appeared to have darker skin, and some rank-and-file members complained that party leaders had betrayed them by putting him forward in a party "for whites" (*Guardian*, April 8, 2006, p. 1).

15   For example, two major data analyses (European Commission 2003, 2005) make no mention of race or ethnicity in analyses of joblessness, income, poverty, or housing situations. Instead, gender, age, and "class" (vaguely understood) are the axes of analysis. This may be because European sociologists were more concerned with *class* – although ethnic and racial *politics* occupied a place in European history, which may have hindered public discussion of ethnic inequality. In addition, Marxism was powerful in European sociology, privileging class over race and ethnicity until the emergence in the 1980s of a new discourse on "social exclusion."

16   In October 2005, the United Nations' Global Commission on International Migration recommended liberalizing the movement of labor across borders – to widen *gastarbeiter* policy.

17   Becker claims that husbands and wives rationally decide that this maximizes overall utility (e.g. income, time, and effort). Hochschild (1989) tested Becker's claims and found them wanting.

18   Here culture and rational action may work together. Women may feel that male-dominated subjects are too risky (low chance of success) and turn to female-dominated professions. As well, with few role models, women may not feel comfortable or learn survival skills in male-dominated professions; available role models make them comfortable elsewhere.

19   This may seem innocuous, but think again. Two male colleagues in a bar after hours seems innocent. A man and a woman going out together after work risk the rumor mill of an affair.

20   Coercive isomorphism can sometimes help women. Beckman and Phillips (2005) found that law firms were more likely to promote women to partner status if clients had women in key leadership positions. Hiring women increased their legitimacy *vis-à-vis* these clients.

21   Western women were not the first to experience the second shift: Soviet women knew this only too well. Soviet policy supported equal rights for women (although there were curbs in the 1930s, e.g. against abortions). However, men traditionally had little to do with household chores. Women had to do their jobs and then seek out hard-to-obtain household goods (e.g. food, toilet paper), which usually involved waiting in long lines – a job in itself.

Chapter 7

1   I was in St. Petersburg in March 2006. The amount of recent construction was impressive; the surface impression was of a country on the move. After a week of observations, interactions, and discussions, I saw that corruption, rent-seeking, and anti-entrepreneurial practices are alive and well. Oil money had spread to firms, the state, and some people's pockets. I am unconvinced that foundations for sustainable non-oil growth are firmly in place.

2   The inefficient state sector would maintain employment until the private sector had developed sufficiently to employ enough people to prevent a political back-lash. Gradualists claimed that China supported their position, and one could say that even Poland turned to gradualism when it slowed privatization.

3   Consumers did sometimes complain and got solutions. There were also attempts to remedy low-quality output in the 1960s, but bureaucratic politics got in the way (Arnot 1988).

4   Certain firms specialized in legal services for quickly closing firms and reopening them as entirely different legal businesses – a "corporate veil" that helps owners avoid paying debts. In the US, parties can "pierce the corporate veil" to pursue debtors. In China, a 2005 law on corporate governance aims to do the same (World Bank 2006a).

5   While one person or group controlled many firms in a single sector (monopoly or oligopoly), the legal fiction was that many small firms created an illusion of widespread ownership.

6   In January 1992, when liberalization was introduced, prices jumped by nearly 40 percent; in October 1994, the ruble value *vis-à-vis* the dollar dropped by 40 percent in *one day*.

7   In a fit of nationalism, Russia's "Public Chamber" proposed fining firms for publishing prices in *u.e.* – the ruble is the national currency, after all.

8   This comes from my summary of media accounts and discussions with Russian sociologists.

9   One interesting difference between corporate governance in China and Russia is that Chinese law allows for punishing managers for bad performance. This remains problematic in Russia – in part because Soviet-era managers were able to gain shares in their enterprises and avoid being sacked for their performance (Djankov and Murrell 2002).

10 Yeltsin's tactics were somewhat similar, except enterprise managers were more concerned with security than with profit. Given legacies of Stalin and Brezhnev – insecurity from one, conservatism from the other – managers were accustomed to a bureaucratized economy and securing their positions. Entrepreneurship entailed risks which were anathema in the Soviet system, and so they used new freedom to secure income, rather than augment it by developing new goods or efficiency. Russian managers were also more fearful of foreign investment and competition.

11 After Stalin's death, the Soviet regime gave collective and state farm laborers the right to work on their own private plots and sell the produce at farmers' markets.

12 Unfortunately, I have not come across a rigorous study of this aspect of foreign attitudes and investment *vis-à-vis* Russia and China. I propose this based on disparate studies of Western foreign policy. For the sake of space I cannot go into greater empirical detail here.

13 Here the Chinese post-socialist economy resembles Russia's: a strong reliance on informal networks. In Russia's case, networks underpin the shadow and virtual economies; in China, they facilitate the organization of production and exchange, and also corruption.

14 Yang (2004) suggests that Chinese entrepreneurs use networks to play on "institutional holes," gaps between actors in different institutional contexts. This can help generate value and corruption, or both simultaneously.

15 Gaddy and Ickes (2002) hold to basic premises of neoclassical theory (efficiency and rational choice), but they can explain the virtual economy only by referring to *social values*. Most Russians support welfare and strong national defense. Inefficient firms must survive if they produce either. Yet reconciling rational action and values, tastes, and the like remains the Achilles' heel of rational choice and economic theory. Some economists (e.g. Shiller *et al.* 1992) even claim that values were unimportant to post-socialism.

Chapter 8

1 This is even more apparent in post-socialist Russia, where English words flooded the business world: *biznes* (business), *marketing* (marketing), *menedzhment* (management), *nou-khau* (know-how), *po faksu* (by fax). In many of these cases a Russian word could suffice (e.g. *delovoi* rather than *biznes*, *upravlenie* rather than *menedzhment*).

2 Readers who want such data may examine books that focus on these data (e.g. Castells 2000 or McMichael 2004).

3 "The Nationalist Resurgence," *The Economist*, March 4, 2006. Online via Business Source Premier. Available HTTP: <http://www.economist.co.uk>.

4 It is true that English football is linked to the world football (soccer) association FIFA, but FIFA is not a global market; it is more a confederation of national and regional football associations, and its main power is control over the World Cup.

5 My thanks to John Markoff for relaying this discussion from his own experiences.

6 When either firm changes Russia's rating, the news generally makes major headlines in the Russian business media.

7 After the failure of neoliberal reforms to inspire confidence or growth in Russia (even hurting much of the population) and the example of different paths to growth in China and Asia, criticism of the IMF and World Bank grew stronger from non-academic circles. After 2000, both organizations began to take a longer look at their neoliberal advice.

8 Alternative left-leaning rhetoric gained new life in Latin America after 2001. As George W. Bush's foreign policy appeared more about bluster and less about democracy and security, populist Venezuelan president Hugo Chavez challenged American hegemony and promoted welfare-style policies, including providing

cheap oil to Cuba. Pro-welfare, anti-globalization rhetoric began to spread to other countries and elections in the southern cone.

9 The euro is the currency for France, Germany, Luxemburg, Belgium, the Netherlands, Austria, Spain, Portugal, Italy, Greece, Ireland, and Finland. After a tumultuous debate, Britain stayed out of the euro for economic reasons (the Labour government was not convinced of benefits) and from nationalist reaction against losing a national symbol (pound sterling).

10 EU members are Austria, Belgium, Cyprus, Czech Republic, Denmark, Estonia, Finland, France, Germany, Greece, Hungary, Ireland, Italy, Latvia, Lithuania, Luxemburg, Malta, Netherlands, Poland, Portugal, Slovakia, Slovenia, Spain, Sweden, and Great Britain.

11 Thus Woodruff (1999) sees barter and the problem of monetization as symbolic of political fragmentation in post-socialist Russia.

12 In Shay's Rebellion, Massachusetts farmers refused to pay their debts in a particular "specie" (particular money, not general currency like the euro or dollar). Obtaining this specie was difficult, and so the farmers demanded that they be allowed to pay their debts in kind (barter) or through a more general currency that was easier to obtain. While the rebellion failed, some segments of the elite (especially those around Alexander Hamilton) used this event to support their demand for a national bank actively supporting a unifying national currency.

13 An interesting issue is what will happen in East Asia. Will countries there negotiate a common regional structure, or will a local hegemon emerge? At present, China is the hot economy, but it is not yet strong enough to impose its will on its neighbors. On the other hand, historical memories prevent closer integration (e.g. the behavior of Japanese soldiers towards Chinese and Koreans during World War II still hinders relations).

Conclusion

1 United Kingdom Parliament, House of Lords, March 21, 2001: Column 1486. Online. HTTP <http://www.publications.parliament.uk/pa/ld200001/ldhansrd/vo010321/text/10321-08.htm>.

2 Some scholars believe this is essential to civil society and democracy. There must be a private sphere beyond state control and for a balance between the individual and collective. However, an entirely "privatized" world kills civil society as well: some individuals or groups will have more resources than others and disproportionate leverage in deliberation. Further, an individualized world risks the drawbacks of free riding and the prisoners' dilemma (see Chapter 2).

3 Consider super-profits of the late 1990s dot-com bubble. A friend who worked on Wall Street at the time told me how dot-com shares were inflated *legally*. Brokerage firms would examine different formulas for evaluating a firm's worth. They tweak the formula providing the highest value, give it a new name, and leak it to the business press as a justification for dot-com wealth. In the end several investors made a killing while others lost investments.

Bibliography

Acker, Joan. 1990. "Hierarchies, Jobs, Bodies: A Theory of Gendered Organizations." *Gender and Society* 4: 139–58.

Afanas'ev, M., P. Kuznetsov, and A. Fominykh. 1997. "Korporativnoe upravlenie glazami direktorata (po materialam obsledovanii 1994–1996 gg)." *Voprosy ekonomiki* 5: 84–101.

Alchian, Armen, and Harold Demsetz,. 1972. "Production, Information Costs, and Economic Organization." *American Economic Review* 62: 777–95.

Aldrich, Howard E., and Roger Waldinger. 1990. "Ethnicity and Entrepreneurship." *Annual Review of Sociology* 16: 111–35.

Alford, Robert, and Roger Friedland. 1985. *Powers of Theory: Capitalism, the State and Democracy.* New York: Cambridge University Press.

Almond, Gabriel, and James A. Coleman. 1960. *The Politics of Developing Areas.* Princeton, NJ: Princeton University Press.

Alt, James E., and Kenneth A. Shepsle. 1990. *Perspectives on Positive Political Economy.* New York: Cambridge University Press.

Amann, Ron. 2003. "A Sovietological view of Modern Britain". *Political Quarterly* 74: 468–80.

Amsden, Alice. 1989. *Asia's Next Giant.* New York: Oxford University Press.

Anderson, Perry. 1979. *Lineages of the Absolutist State.* London: Verso.

Andes, Nancy. 1992. "Social Class and Gender: An Empirical Evaluation of Occupational Stratification." *Gender and Society* 6: 231–51.

Arnot, Bob. 1988. *Controlling Soviet Labor: Experimental Change from Brezhnev to Gorbachev.* Armonk, NY: M.E. Sharpe.

Aron, Raymond. 1965. *Main Currents in Sociological Thought, Vol. 2.* New York: Basic Books.

Arthur, W. Brian. 1989. "Competing Technologies, Increasing Returns, and Lock-In by Historical Events." *Economic Journal* 99: 116–31.

Åslund, Anders. 1995. *How Russia Became a Market Economy.* Washington, DC: Brookings Institution.

Bates, Robert (ed.). 1988. *Toward a Political Economy of Development.* Berkeley: University of California Press.

Baxter, Janeen, and Erik Olin Wright. 2000. "The Glass Ceiling Hypothesis. A Comparative Study of the United States, Sweden, and Australia." *Gender and Society* 14: 275–94.

Becker, Gary. 1957. *The Economics of Discrimination.* Chicago, IL: University of Chicago Press.

—— 1976. *An Economic Approach to Human Behavior.* Chicago, IL: University of Chicago Press.

—— 1981. *A Treatise on the Family.* Cambridge, MA: Harvard University Press.

—— 1985. "Human Capital, Effort, and the Sexual Division of Labor." *Journal of Labor Economics* 3 (Supplement): S33–S58.

Becker, Kristina Flodman. 2004. *The Informal Economy*. Stockholm: SIDA [Swedish International Development Cooperation Agency].

Beckman, Christine M., and Damon J. Phillips. 2005. "Interorganizational Determinants of Promotion: Client Leadership and the Attainment of Women Attorneys." *American Sociological Review* 70: 678–701.

Beissinger, Mark. 2002. *Nationalist Mobilization and the Collapse of the Soviet State*. New York: Cambridge University Press.

Bem, Sandra Lipsitz. 1993. *The Lenses of Gender*. New Haven, CT: Yale University Press.

Bendix, Reinhard. 1974. *Work and Authority in Industry*. Berkeley: University of California Press.

Bensel, Richard. 1990. *Yankee Leviathan: The Origins of Central State Authority in America, 1859–1877*. New York: Cambridge University Press.

Berger, Peter L. 1991. *The Capitalist Revolution. Fifty Propositions About Prosperity, Equality, and Liberty*. New York: Basic Books.

Berger, Peter L., and Thomas Luckmann. 1967. *The Social Construction of Reality*. Garden City, NY: Anchor Books.

Berliner, Joseph. 1957. *Factory and Manager in the USSR*. Cambridge, MA: Harvard University Press.

Bernstein, Basil. 1975. *Class, Codes and Control*. London: Routledge & Kegan Paul.

Bian, Yanjie. 1997. "Bringing Strong Ties Back In: Indirect Ties, Network Bridges, and Job Searches in China." *American Sociological Review* 62: 366–85.

Bielby, Denise D., and William T. Bielby. 1988. "She Works Hard for the Money: Household Responsibilities and the Allocation of Work Effort." *American Journal of Sociology* 93: 1031–59.

Bielby, William T., and James N. Baron. 1986. "Men and Women at Work: Sex Segregation and Statistical Discrimination." *American Journal of Sociology* 91: 759–99.

Biernacki, Richard. 1995. *The Fabrication of Labor: Germany and Britain, 1640–1914*. Berkeley: University of California Press.

Bihagen, Erik, and Marita Ohls. 2006. "The Glass Ceiling – Where Is It? Women's and Men's Career Prospects in the Private vs. the Public Sector in Sweden 1979–2000." *The Sociological Review* 54: 20–47.

Black, Cyril. 1966. Dynamics of Modernization. A Study in Comparative History. New York: Harper & Row.

Black, Cyril *et al*. 1975. *The Modernization of Japan and Russia: a Comparative Study*. New York: The Free Press.

Blackbourn, David. 1984. "The Discreet Charm of the Bourgeoisie: Reappraising German History in the Nineteenth Century," in David Blackbourn and Geoff Eley (eds), *The Peculiarities of German History* (pp. 159–290). New York: Oxford University Press.

Blackwell, William L. 1968. *The Beginnings of Russian Industrialization. 1800–1860*. Princeton, NJ: Princeton University Press.

Blasi, Joseph, Maya Kroumova, and Douglas Kruse. 1997. *Kremlin Capitalism. Privatizing the Russian Economy*. Ithaca, NY: Cornell University Press.

Blau, Peter M., and Otis Dudley Duncan. 1967. *The American Occupational Structure.* New York: Wiley.

Blinder, Alan, Elie R.D. Canetti, David E. Lebow, and Jeremy B. Rudd. 1998. *Asking About Prices: A New Approach to Understanding Price Stickiness.* New York: Russell Sage.

Block, Fred. 1977a. *The Origins of International Economic Disorder.* Berkeley: University of California Press.

—— 1977b. "The Ruling Class Does Not Rule: Notes on the Marxist Theory of the State." *Socialist Review* 33: 6–28.

Bob, Clifford. 2005. *The Marketing of Rebellion: Insurgents, Media, and International Activism.* New York: Cambridge University Press.

Bonilla-Silva, Eduardo. 1997. "Rethinking Racism: Toward a Structural Interpretation." *American Sociological Review* 62: 465–80.

—— 1999. "The Essential Fact of Race." *American Sociological Review* 64: 899–906.

Bourdeau, Pierre. 1984. *Distinction: A Social Critique of a Judgment of Taste.* Cambridge, MA: Harvard University Press.

—— 1990. *The Logic of Practice*, translated by Richard Nice. Stanford, CA: Stanford University Press.

—— 1996. *The State Nobility*, translated by Lauretta C. Clough. Stanford, CA: Stanford University Press.

Bowles, Samuel, and Herbert Gintis. 1976. *Schooling in Capitalist America.* New York: Basic Books.

—— 1986. *Democracy and Capitalism.* New York: Basic Books.

Braudel, Fernand. 1982. *Capitalism and Civilization. 15th–18th centuries, Vol. II: The Wheels of Commerce.* New York: Harper & Row.

Braverman, Harry. 1974. *Labor and Monopoly Capital: The Degradation of Work in the Twentieth Century.* New York: Monthly Review Press.

Burawoy, Michael. 1979. *Manufacturing Consent.* Chicago, IL: University of Chicago Press.

—— 1985. *The Politics of Production: Factory Regimes Under Capitalism and Socialism.* London: Verso.

Burawoy, Michael, and Pavel Krotov. 1992. "The Soviet Transition from Socialism to Capitalism: Worker Control and Economic Bargaining in the Wood Industry." *American Sociological Review* 57: 16–38.

Burt, Ronald. 1992. *Structural Holes.* Cambridge, MA: Harvard University Press.

Cancio, A. Silvia, T. David Evans, and David J. Maume Jr. 1996. "Reconsidering the Declining Significance of Race: Racial Differences in Early Career Wages." *American Sociological Review* 61: 541–56.

Cardoso, Fernando, and Enzo Faletto. 1979. *Dependency and Development in Latin America.* Berkeley: University of California Press.

Castells, Manuel. 2000. *The Information Age: Economy, Society, and Culture Vol. 1: The Rise of the Network Society* (2nd ed). Oxford: Blackwell.

Centeno, Miguel A. 1994. "Between Rocky Democracies and Hard Markets: Dilemmas of the Great Transformation." *Annual Review of Sociology*, 20: 125–47.

—— 1996. *Democracy Within Reason* (revised edn). University Park: Penn State Press.

Centeno, Miguel A. 1997. "Blood and Debt: War and Taxation in Nineteenth-century Latin America." *American Journal of Sociology* 102: 1565–605.

Centeno, Miguel A., and Patricio Silva (eds). 1998. *The Politics of Expertise in Latin America*. New York: St. Martin's Press.

Central Intelligence Agency (CIA). 2006. *The World Factbook. Russia*. Online. Available HTTP: <http://www.odci.gov/cia/publications/factbook/print/rs.html> (accessed April 17, 2006).

Chambliss, William. 1973. "The Saints and the Roughnecks," in J.M. Henslin (ed.), *Down to Earth Sociology* (pp. 180–94). New York: Macmillan.

Chandler, Alfred D. 1962. *Strategy and Structure*. Cambridge, MA: MIT Press.

—— 1977. *The Visible Hand*. Cambridge, MA: Harvard University Press.

—— 1990. *Scale and Scope*. Cambridge, MA: Harvard University Press.

Chase-Dunn, Christopher, Yukio Kawano, and Benjamin D. Brewer. 2000. "Trade Globalization Since 1795: Waves of Integration in the World System." *American Sociological Review* 65: 77–95.

Coase, Ronald. 1937. "The Nature of the Firm." *Econometric N. S.* 4: 386–405.

Cohn, Samuel, and Mark Fossett. 1995. "Why Racial Employment Inequality is Greater in Northern Labor Markets: Regional Differences in White–Black Employment Differentials." *Social Forces* 74: 511–42.

Coleman, James. 1998. *The Foundations of Social Theory*. Cambridge, MA: Harvard University Press.

Colignon, Richard. 1997. *Power Plays*. Stony Brook: SUNY Press.

Colignon, Richard, and Chikako Usui. 2003. *Amakudari: The Hidden Fabric of Japan's Economy*. Ithaca, NY: Cornell University Press.

Collier, David, and Ruth Collier. 1991. *Shaping the Political Arena : Critical Junctures, the Labour Movement, and Regime Dynamics in Latin America*. Princeton, NJ: Princeton University Press.

Collins, Randall. 1975. *The Credential Society*. New York: Academic Press.

—— 1980. "Weber's Last Theory of Capitalism." *American Sociological Review* 45: 925–42.

—— 1981. "On the Microfoundations of Macrosociology." *American Journal of Sociology* 86: 984–1014.

—— 1994. *Four Sociological Traditions* (revised edn). New York: Oxford University Press.

Commission for Racial Equality (UK). 2006. "Statistics: Labour Market." Online. Available HTTP: <http://www.cre.gov.uk/research/statistics_labour.html.pr> (accessed April 10, 2006).

Commons, John. 1934. *Institutional Economics*. Madison: University of Wisconsin Press.

Crouch, Collin. 1999. *Social Change in Western Europe*. Oxford: Oxford University Press.

Curtin, Polly. 2006. "Father Figures." *Guardian*, April 8, Work Section, p. 3.

Cyert, R.M., and James G. March. 1963. *A Behavioral Theory of the Firm*. Englewood Cliffs, NJ: Prentice-Hall.

Dahl, Robert. 1957. "The Concept of Power." *Behavioral Science* 2: 201–5.

Dalton, Melville. 1959. *Men Who Manage*. New York: Wiley.

Davies-Netzley, Sally Ann. 1998. "Women Above the Glass Ceiling: Perceptions on Corporate Mobility and Strategies for Success." *Gender and Society* 12: 339–55.

Davis, Gerald. 1991. "Agents Without Principles? The Spread of the Poison Pill Takeover Defense through the Intercorporate Network." *Administrative Science Quarterly* 36: 583–613.

Davis, Kingsley, and Wilbur Moore. 1945. "Some Principles of Stratification." *American Sociological Review* 10: 242–9.

DiMaggio, Paul J. 1982. "Cultural Capital and School Success: The Impact of Status Culture Participation on the Grades of U.S. High School Students." *American Sociological Review* 47: 189–201.

—— 1988. Interest and Agency in Institutional Theory," in Lynne Zucker (ed.), *Institutional Patterns and Organization* (pp. 3–21). Cambridge, MA: Ballinger.

—— 1990. "Cultural Aspects of Economic Action and Organization," in Roger Friedland and A.F. Robertson (eds), *Beyond the Marketplace. Rethinking Economy and Society* (pp. 113–36). New York: Aldine de Gruyter.

—— 1991. "Constructing an Organizational Field as a Professional Project: U.S. Art Museums, 1920–1940," in Walter Powell and Paul J. DiMaggio (eds), *The New Institutionalism in Organizational Analysis* (pp. 267–92). Chicago, IL: Chicago University Press.

DiMaggio, Paul J., and John Mohr. 1985. "Cultural Capital, Educational Attainment, and Marital Selection." *American Journal of Sociology* 90: 1231–61.

DiMaggio, Paul J., and Walter Powell. 1983. "The Iron Cage Revisited: Institutional Isomorphism and Collective Rationality." *American Sociological Review* 48: 147–60.

—— 1991. "Introduction," in Walter Powell and Paul J. DiMaggio (eds), *The New Institutionalism in Organizational Analysis* (pp. 1–38). Chicago, IL: Chicago University Press.

Djankov, Simeon, and Peter Murrell. 2002. "Enterprise Restructuring in Transition: A Quantitative Survey." *Journal of Economic Literature* 40: 739–92.

Dobbin, Frank. 1994. *Forging Industrial Policy*. Cambridge: Cambridge University Press.

—— 1993. "The Social Construction of the Great Depression: Industrial Policing During the 1930s in the United States, Britain, and France." *Theory and Society* 22: 1–56.

Dobbin, Frank, and John R. Sutton. 1998. "The Strength of a Weak State: The Rights Revolution and the Rise of Human Resources Management Divisions." *American Journal of Sociology* 104: 441–76.

Domhoff, G. William. 1998. *Who Rules America? Power and Politics in the Year 2000*. Mountain View, CA: Mayfield.

Dore, Ronald. 1973. *British Factory, Japanese Factory*. Berkeley: University of California Press.

Durkheim, Emile. 1947. *The Division of Labor in Society*. Glencoe, IL: The Free Press.

—— 1965. *The Elementary Forms of Religious Life*, translated by Joseph Swain. New York: The Free Press.

Dye, Thomas R. 1990. *Who's Running America? The Bush Era*. Englewood Cliffs, NJ: Prentice-Hall.

Edwards, Richard. 1979. *Contested Terrain*. New York: Basic Books.

Ehrenreich, Barbara. 2005. *Bait and Switch: The (Futile) Pursuit of the Corporate Dream*. New York: Metropolitan Books.

Emirbayer, Mustafa. 1996. "Useful Durkheim." *Sociological Theory* 14: 109–30.

—— 1997. "Manifesto for a Relational Sociology." *American Journal of Sociology* 103: 281–317.

Epstein, Richard. 1992. *Forbidden Grounds: The Case Against Employment Discrimination*. Cambridge, MA: Harvard University Press.

Erikson, Robert, and John H. Goldthorpe. 1987. "Commonality and Variation in Social Fluidity in Industrial Nations. Part II: The Model of Core Social Fluidity Applied." *European Sociological Review* 3: 145–66.

Erikson, Robert, John H. Goldthorpe, and Lucienne Portocarero. 1979. "Intergenerational Class Mobility in Three Western Societies: England, France and Sweden." *British Journal of Sociology* 30: 415–41.

—— 1982. "Social Fluidity in Industrial Nations: England, France and Sweden." *British Journal of Sociology* 33: 1–34.

—— 1983. "Intergenerational Class Mobility and the Convergence Thesis: England, France and Sweden." *British Journal of Sociology* 34: 303–43.

European Commission. 2003. *The Social Situation in the European Union 2003*. Online. Available HTTP: <epp.eurostat.cec.eu.int>

—— 2005. *Europe in Figures. Eurostat Yearbook 2005*. Online. Available HTTP: <epp.eurostat.cec.eu.int>

Evans, Peter. 1979. *Dependent Development*. Princeton, NJ: Princeton University Press.

—— 1995. *Embedded Autonomy*. Princeton, NJ: Princeton University Press.

Evans, Peter, Dietrich Rueschemeyer, and Theda Skocpol. 1985. *Bringing the State Back In*. New York: Cambridge University Press.

Eyal, Gil, Evan Szelenyi, Eleanor Townsley, and Ivan Szelenyi. 2001. *Making Capitalism Without Capitalists: The New Ruling Elites in Eastern Europe*. London: Verso.

Fajnzylber, Fernando. 1990. "The United States and Japan as Models of Industrialization," in Gary Gereffi and Donald Wyman (eds), *Manufacturing Miracles* (pp. 323–52). Princeton, NJ: Princeton University Press.

Featherman, David L., F. Lancaster Jones, and Robert M. Hauser. 1975. "Assumptions of Mobility Research in the United States: The Case of Occupational Status." *Social Science Research* 4: 329–60.

Feenstra, Robert C. 1998. "Integration of Trade and Disintegration of Production in the Global Economy." *Journal of Economic Perspectives* 12: 31–50.

Fligstein, Neil. 1990. *The Transformation of Corporate Control*. Cambridge, MA: Harvard University Press.

—— 1996. "Markets as Politics: A Political-cultural Approach to Market Institutions." *American Sociological Review* 61: 656–73.

—— 2001a. *The Architecture of Markets*. Princeton, NJ: Princeton University Press.

—— 2001b. "Social Skill and the Theory of Fields." *Sociological Theory* 19 (2): 105–125.

Fligstein, Neil, and Iona Mara-Drita. 1996. "How to Make a Market: Reflections on the Attempt to Create a Single Market in the European Union." *American Journal of Sociology* 102: 1–33.

Fossett, Mark A., Omer R. Galle, and William R. Kelley. 1986. "Racial Occupational Inequality, 1940–1980: National and Regional Trends." *American Sociological Review* 51: 421–9.

Foucault, Michel. 1977. *Discipline and Punish: The Birth of the Prison.* Translated by Alan Sheridan. New York: Pantheon Books.

—— 1980. *Power/Knowledge: Selected Interviews and Other Writings, 1972–1977,* edited by Colin Gordon. New York: Pantheon Books.

Frank, Andre Gunder. 1967. *Capitalism and Underdevelopment in Latin America. Historical Studies of Chile and Brazil.* New York: Monthly Review Press.

Frank, Robert H. 1990. "Rethinking Rational Choice," in Roger Friedland and A. F. Robertson (eds), *Beyond the Marketplace: Rethinking Economy and Society* (pp. 53–88). New York: Aldine de Gruyter.

Friedland, Roger, and Robert Alford. 1991. "Bringing Society Back In: Symbols, Practices, and Institutional Contradictions," in Walter Powell and Paul DiMaggio (eds), *The New Institutionalism in Organizational Analysis* (pp. 232–63). Chicago, IL: University of Chicago Press.

Friedman, Milton. 1953. *Essays in Positive Economics.* Chicago, IL: University of Chicago Press.

Friedman, Milton, and Rose Friedman. 1980. *Free to Choose.* New York: Harcourt Brace Jovanovich.

Gaddy, Clifford, and Barry W. Ickes. 2002. *Russia's Virtual Economy.* Washington, DC: Brookings.

Gambetta, Diego. 1993. *The Sicilian Mafia. The Business of Protection.* Cambridge, MA: Harvard University Press.

Gaventa, John. 1980. *Power and Powerlessness.* Urbana: University of Illinois Press.

Gerber, Theodore, and Michael Hout. 1998. "More Shock than Therapy: Market Transition, Employment, and Income in Russia, 1991–1995." *American Journal of Sociology* 104: 1–50.

Gereffi, Gary. 1990. "Paths of Industrialization: An Overview," in Gary Gereffi and Donald Wyman (eds), *Manufacturing Miracles* (pp. 3–31). Princeton, NJ: Princeton University Press.

—— 1994. "The International Economy and Economic Development," in Neil Smelser and Richard Swedberg (eds), *The Handbook of Economic Sociology* (pp. 206–33). Princeton, NJ: Princeton University Press.

Gereffi, Gary, and Donald Wyman (eds). 1990. *Manufacturing Miracles.* Princeton, NJ: Princeton University Press.

Gerschenkron, Alexander. 1962. *Economic Backwardness in Historical Perspective.* Cambridge, MA: Belknap Press.

Giddens, Anthony. 1984. *The Constitution of Society.* New York: Cambridge University Press.

—— 1990. *The Consequences of Modernity.* Cambridge: Polity Press.

—— 2002. *Runaway World: How Globalization is Reshaping Our Lives.* New York: Routledge.

Glasner, Angela. 1998. "Gender and Europe: Cultural and Structural Impediments to Change," in Joe Bailey (ed.), *Social Europe* (pp. 77–120). London: Longman.

Goldhagen, Daniel. 1996. *Hitler's Willing Executioners.* New York: Random House.

Goldstone, Jack A. 1987. "Cultural Orthodoxy, Risk, and Innovation: The Divergence of East and West in the Early Modern World." *Sociological Theory* 5:129–35.

—— 2000. "The Rise of the West – Or Not? A Revision to Socio-Economic History." *Sociological Theory* 18: 175–94.

Gorman, Elizabeth. 2005. "Gender Stereotypes, Same-gender Preference, and Organizational Variation in the Hiring of Women: Evidence from Law Firms." *American Sociological Review* 70: 702–28.

Granovetter, Mark. 1973. "The Strength of Weak Ties." *American Journal of Sociology*, vol. 78: 1360–80.

—— 1974. *Getting a Job*. Cambridge, MA: Harvard University Press.

—— 1985. "Economic Action and Social Structure: The Problem of Embeddedness." *American Journal of Sociology* 91: 481–510.

Gray, John. 1998. *False Dawn: The Delusions of Global Capitalism*. New York: The New Press.

Greenfeld, Liah. 1992. *Nationalism: Five Roads to Modernity*. Cambridge, MA: Harvard University Press.

—— 2003. The Spirit of Capitalism. Nationalism and Economic Growth. Cambridge, MA: Harvard University Press.

Grossman, Gregory. 1977. "The 'Second Economy' of the USSR." *Problems of Communism* 26: 25–40.

Grusky, David B. 1983. "Industrialization and the Status Attainment Process: The Thesis of Industrialism Reconsidered." *American Sociological Review* 48: 494–506.

Grusky, David B., and Robert M. Hauser. 1984. "Comparative Social Mobility Revisited: Models of Convergence and Divergence in 16 Countries." *American Sociological Review* 49: 19–38.

Gustafson, Thane. 1999. *Capitalism Russian-style*. New York: Cambridge University Press.

Gutmann, Amy, and Dennis Thompson. 1996. *Democracy and Disagreement*. Cambridge, MA: Harvard University Press.

—— 2004. *Why Deliberative Democracy?* Princeton, NJ: Princeton University Press.

Haggard, Stephan. 1990. *Pathways from the Periphery*. Ithaca, NY: Cornell University Press.

Haggard, Stephan, and Robert Kaufman (eds). 1992. *The Politics of Adjustment*. Princeton, NJ: Princeton University Press.

Hall, Peter. 1986. *Governing the Economy*. New York: Oxford University Press.

—— 1989. *The Political Power of Economic Ideas: Keynesianism Across Nations*. Princeton, NJ: Princeton University Press.

—— 1992. "The Movement from Keynesianism to Monetarism: Institutional Analysis and British Economic Policy in the 1970s," in Svein Steinmo, Kathleen Thelen, and Frank Longstreth (eds), *Historical Institutionalism in Comparative Politics: State, Society, and Economy* (pp. 90–113). New York: Cambridge University Press.

Hamilton, Gary, and Nicole Woolsey Biggart. 1988. "Market, Culture, and Authority: A Comparative Analysis of Management and Organization in the Far East." *American Journal of Sociology* 94 (Supplement): S52–S94.

Hamilton, Nora. 1982. *The Limits of State Autonomy*. Princeton, NJ: Princeton University Press.

Handelman, Stephen, 1997. *Comrade Criminal*. New Haven: Yale University Press.

Hannan, Michael T., and John H. Freeman. 1989. *Organizational Ecology*. Cambridge, MA: Harvard University Press.

Harrison, Stephen, and Waqar I. U. Ahmad. 2000. "Medical Autonomy and the UK State 1975 to 2025." *Sociology* 34: 129–46.

Hart, Keith. 1990. "The Idea of Economy: Six Modern Dissenters," in Roger Friedland and A. F. Robertson (eds), *Beyond the Marketplace. Rethinking Economy and Society* (pp. 137–60). New York: Aldine de Gruyter.

Hass, Jeffrey K. 1997. "Making Markets: Rationality, Institutions, Culture, and Economic Change in Russia." *Problems of Post-Communism* 44: 44–51.

—— 1998. "To the Undiscovered Country: Institutions, Authority, Culture and Russia's Transition to the Market, 1988–1997." Ph.D. dissertation, Department of Sociology, Princeton University.

—— 1999. "The Great Transition: The Dynamics of Market Transitions and the Case of Russia, 1991–1995." *Theory and Society* 28: 383–424.

—— Forthcoming. *To the Undiscovered Country: Power, Culture, Economic Change, and Russia's Market Experiment, 1988–2000*.

—— 2005. "Trials and Tribulations of Learning the Market. Culture and Economic Practice in Russia's Market Transition," *The Carl Beck Papers in Russian and East European Studies*. Pittsburgh, PA: Center for Russian and East European Studies, University of Pittsburgh.

Hauser, Robert M., and David B. Grusky. 1988. "Cross-national Variation in Occupational Distributions, Relative Mobility Chances, and Intergenerational Shifts in Occupational Distributions." *American Sociological Review* 53: 723–41.

Heckathorn, Douglas. 1990. "Collective Sanctions and Compliance Norms." *American Sociological Review* 55: 366–84.

Hendley, Kathryn, Peter Murrell, and Randi Ryterman. 1999. "A Regional Analysis of Transactional Strategies of Russian Enterprises." *McGill Law Journal* 44: 433–72.

—— 2000. "Law, Relationships, and Private Enforcement: Transactional Strategies of Russian Enterprises." *Europe-Asia Studies* 52: 627–56.

Hensel, Richard. 1990. *Yankee Leviathan: The Origins of Central State Authority in America, 1859–1877*. New York: Cambridge University Press.

Hirsch, Paul. 1986. "From Ambushes to Golden Parachutes: Corporate Takeovers as an Instance of Cultural Framing and Institutional Integration." *American Journal of Sociology* 91: 800–37.

Hirsch, Paul, Stuart Michaels, and Ray Friedman. 1990. "Clean Models vs. Dirty Hands: Why Economics Is Different From Sociology," in Sharon Zukin and Paul DiMaggio (eds), *Structures of Capital. The Social Organization of the Economy* (pp. 39–56). New York: Cambridge University Press.

Hirschman, Albert O. 1977. *The Passions and the Interests*. Princeton, NJ: Princeton University Press.

Hirst, Paul, and Grahame Thompson. 1996. *Globalization in Question*. Cambridge: Polity Press.

Hobsbawm, Eric. 1975. *The Age of Capital*. New York: Random House.

Hochschild, Arlie. 1989. *The Second Shift: Working Parents and the Revolution at Home*. New York: Viking.

Hoffman, David. 2002. *The Oligarchs. Wealth and Power in the New Russia*. New York: PublicAffairs.

Humphrey, Caroline. 2002. *The Unmaking of Soviet Life. Everyday Economies After Socialism*. Ithaca, NY: Cornell University Press.

Huntington, Samuel. 1968. *Political Order in Changing Societies*. New Haven, CT: Yale University Press.

Iganski, Paul, and Geoff Payne. 1999. "Socio-economic Re-structuring and Employment: The Case of Minority Ethnic Groups." *British Journal of Sociology* 50: 195–215.

Jacoby, Sanford. 1985. *Employing Bureaucracy: Managers, Unions, and the Transformation of Work in American Industry*. New York: Columbia University Press.

Jensen, Michael C., and Meckling, William H. 1976. "Theory of the Firm: Managerial Behavior, Agency Costs, and Capital Structure." *Journal of Financial Economics* 3: 371–94.

Johnson, Chalmers. 1982. *MITI and the Japanese Miracle*. Stanford, CA: Stanford University Press.

Julius, Deanne. 1997. "Globalization and Stakeholder Conflicts: A Corporate Perspective." *International Affairs (Royal Institute of International Affairs 1944–)* 73: 453–68.

Kanter, Rosabeth Moss. 1989. *When Giants Learn To Dance*. New York: Simon & Schuster.

Katznelson, Ira. 1985. "Working-class Formation and the State: Nineteenth-century England in American Perspective," in Peter Evans, Dietrich Rueschemeyer, and Theda Skocpol (eds), *Bringing the State Back In* (pp. 57–84). New York: Cambridge University Press.

Kellner, Douglas. 2002. "Theorizing Globalization." *Sociological Theory* 20: 285–305.

Kennedy, Paul. 1987. *The Rise and Fall of the Great Powers*. New Haven, CT: Yale University Press.

Kester, W. Carl. 1996. "American and Japanese Corporate Convergence: Convergence to Best Practice?," in Suzanne Berger and Ronald Dore (eds), *National Diversity and Global Capitalism* (pp. 107–37). Ithaca, NY: Cornell University Press.

Keynes, John Maynard. 1936. *The General Theory of Employment, Interest, and Money*. London: Macmillan.

Khanna, Tarun, Joe Kogan, and Krishna Palepu. 2006. "Globalization and Similarities in Corporate Governance: A Cross-country Analysis." *The Review of Economics and Statistics* 88: 69–90.

Kim, Ssangmoon, and Eui-Hang Shin. 2002. "A Longitudinal Analysis of Globalization and Regionalization in International Trade: A Social Network Approach." *Social Forces* 81: 445–71.

King, Lawrence. 2003. "Shock Privatization: The Effects of Rapid Large-scale Privatization on Enterprise Restructuring." *Politics and Society* 31: 3–30.

Kornai, Janos. 1992. *The Socialist System*. Princeton, NJ: Princeton University Press.

Kotkin, Stephen. 1995. *Magnetic Mountain. Stalinism as a Civilization*. Berkeley: University of California Press.

—— 2001. *Armageddon Averted*. New York: Oxford University Press.

—— 2004. "Heir, Apparently. Why Russia Wants Putin." *Financial Times Magazine* 45 (March 6), pp. 16–22.

Lachmann, Richard. 1989. "Origins of Capitalism in Western Europe: Economic and Political Aspects." *Annual Review of Sociology* 15: 47–72.

—— 1990. "Class Formation Without Class Struggle: An Elite Conflict Theory of the Transition to Capitalism." *American Sociological Review* 55: 398–414.

Levy, Marion J. 1966. *Modernization and the Structure of Societies*. Princeton, NJ: Princeton University Press.

Lie, John. 1992. "The Concept of Mode of Exchange." *American Sociological Review* 57: 508–23.

—— 1997. "Sociology of Markets." *Annual Review of Sociology* 23: 341–60.

Light, Ivan, and Stavros Karageorgis. 1994. "The Ethnic Economy," in Neil J. Smelser and Richard Swedberg (eds), *The Handbook of Economic Sociology* (pp. 647–71). Princeton, NJ: Princeton University Press.

Lindblom, Charles. 1977. *Politics and Markets*. New York: Basic Books.

Lipset, Seymour M., and Hans L. Zetterberg. 1959. "Social Mobility in Industrial Societies," in Seymour M. Lipset and Reinhard Bendix (eds), *Social Mobility in Industrial Society* (pp. 11–75). Berkeley: University of California Press.

Lipton, David, and Jeffrey Sachs. 1990. "Privatization in Eastern Europe: The Case of Poland." *Brookings Papers on Economic Activity* 2: 293–341.

Lipton, David, Jeffrey Sachs, Stanley Fisher, and Janos Kornai. 1990. "Creating a Market Economy in Eastern Europe: The Case of Poland." *Brookings Papers on Economic Activity* 1: 75–133.

Logan, John R., Wenquan Zhang, and Richard D. Alba. 2002. "Immigrant Enclaves and Ethnic Communities in New York and Los Angeles." *American Sociological Review* 67: 299–322.

Loveman, Mara. 1999. "Is 'Race' Essential?" *American Sociological Review* 64: 891–8.

Macaulay, Stewart. 1963. "Non-contractual Relations in Business: A Preliminary Study." *American Sociological Review* 28: 55–67.

MacLeod, Jay. 1995. *Ain't No Makin It* (revised edn). Boulder, CO: Westview.

March, James G., and Johan Olsen. 1984. "The New Institutionalism: Organizational Factors in Political Life." *American Political Science Review* 78: 734–49.

March, James G., and Herbert Simon. 1958. *Organizations*. New York: Wiley.

Markoff, John. 1997. *The Abolition of Feudalism*. University Park: Penn State Press.

Marshall, Gordon. 1980. *Presbyters and Profits: Calvinism and the Development of Capitalism in Scotland, 1560–1707*. Oxford: Oxford University Press.

McCall, Leslie. 2001. "Sources of Racial Wage Inequality in Metropolitan Labor Markets: Racial, Ethnic, and Gender Differences." *American Sociological Review* 66: 520–41.

McCloskey, Donald. 2003. "The Rhetoric of Economics." *Journal of Economic Literature* 21: 481–517.

McGovern, Patrick. 2002. "Globalization or Internationalization? Foreign Footballers in the English League, 1946–95." *Sociology* 36: 23–42.

McGuire, Gail. 2002. "Gender, Race, and the Shadow Structure: A Study of Informal Networks and Inequality in a Work Organization." *Gender and Society* 6: 303–22.

McMichael, Philip. 2004. *Development and Social Change. A Global Perspective*. Thousand Oaks, CA: Pine Forge Press.

McRae, Hamish. 2006. "Is the Bank of England Right to be Nervous?" *Independent*, January 18, p. 29.

Meyer, John W., and Brian Rowan. 1977. "Institutionalized Organizations: Formal Structure as Myth and Ceremony." *American Journal of Sociology* 83: 340–63.

Michels, Robert. 1959. *Political Parties*. New York: Dover Publications.

Miliband, Ralph. 1969. *The State in Capitalist Society*. New York: Basic Books.

Mills, C. Wright. 1959. *Power Elite*. London: Oxford University Press.

Mintz, Beth, and Michael Schwartz. 1990. "Capital Flows and the Process of Financial Hegemony," in Sharon Zukin and Paul DiMaggio (eds), *The Structures of Capital* (pp. 203–26). New York: Cambridge University Press.

Mizruchi, Mark S. 1996. "What Do Interlocks Do? An Analysis, Critique, and Assessment of Research on Interlocking Directorates." *Annual Review of Sociology* 22: 271–98.

Montgomery, James D. 1998. "Toward a Role-theoretic Conception of Embeddedness." *American Journal of Sociology* 104: 92–125.

Moore, Barrington Jr. 1966. *The Social Origins of Dictatorship and Democracy*. Boston, MA: Beacon Press.

Morris, Aldon, and Carol McClurg Mueller (eds). 1992. *Frontiers in Social Movement Theory*. New Haven: Yale University Press.

Murrell, Peter. 1991. "Can Neoclassical Economics Underpin the Reform of Centrally Planned Economies?" *Journal of Economic Perspectives* 5: 59–76.

—— 1992. "Evolution in Economics and in the Economic Reform of the Centrally Planned Economies." in Christopher Clague and Gordon C. Rausser (eds), *The Emergence of Market Economies in Eastern Europe* (pp. 35–53). Cambridge: Blackwell.

—— 1993. "What Is Shock Therapy? What Did it Do in Poland and Russia?" *Post-Soviet Affairs* 9: 111–40.

Nassaar, Sylvia. 1998. *A Beautiful Mind*. New York: Simon & Schuster.

Nee, Victor. 1989. "A Theory of Market Transition." *American Sociological Review* 54: 663–81.

—— 1996. "The Emergence of a Market Society: Changing Mechanisms of Stratification in China." *American Journal of Sociology* 101: 968–92.

Nee, Victor, and David Stark (eds). 1989. *Transforming the Economic Institutions of Socialism*. Stanford, CA: Stanford University Press.

Nelson, Joan (ed.). 1990. *Economic Crises and Policy Choice*. Princeton, NJ: Princeton University Press.

Nelson, Richard, and Sidney Winter. 1982. *An Evolutionary Theory of Economic Change*. Cambridge, MA: Harvard University Press.

North, Douglass C. 1981. *Structure and Change in Economic History*. New York: W.W. Norton.

—— 1990. Institutions, Institutional Change and Economic Performance. New York: Cambridge University Press.

—— 1991. "Institutions." *Journal of Economic Perspectives* 5: 97–112.

North, Douglass C., and Robert Paul Thomas. 1973. *The Rise of the Western World*. New York: Cambridge University Press.

Nove, Alec. 1972. *An Economic History of the USSR*. New York: Penguin.

—— 1977. *The Soviet Economic System*. Boston, MA: George Allen & Unwin.

Obstfeld, Maurice. 1998. "The Global Capital Market: Benefactor or Menace?" *Journal of Economic Perspectives* 12: 9–30.

Obstfeld, Maurice, and Alan Taylor. 1998. "The Great Depression as a Watershed: International Capital Mobility over the Long Run," in Michael Bordo, Claudia Goldion, and Eugene White (eds). *The Defining Moment: The Great Depression and the American Economy in the Twentieth Century* (pp. 353–402). Chicago, IL: University of Chicago Press.

O'Donnell, Guillermo. 1973. *Modernization and Bureaucratic-authoritarianism*. Berkeley: University of California Press.

Offe, Claus. 1984. *Contradictions of the Welfare State*. Cambridge: MIT Press.

Olson, Mancur. 1965. *The Logic of Collective Action*. Cambridge, MA: Harvard University Press.

—— 1982. *The Rise and Decline of Nations*. New Haven, CT: Yale University Press.

Organization for Economic Cooperation and Development (OECD). 2002. *OECD Economic Surveys 2001–2002. Russian Federation*, Vol. 2002/5. Paris: OECD Publications.

Pager, Devah, and Lincoln Quillian. 2005. "Walking the Talk? What Employers Say Versus What They Do." *American Sociological Review* 70: 355–80.

Parker, Robert. 1994. *Flesh Peddlers and Warm Bodies: the Temporary Help Industry*. New Brunswick, NJ: Rutgers University Press.

Parkin, Frank. 1979. *Marxist Class Theory: A Bourgeois Critique*. New York: Columbia University Press.

Parsons, Talcott. 1951. *The Social System*. Glencoe, IL: The Free Press.

Parsons, Talcott, and Neil J. Smelser. 1965. *Economy and Society: A Study in the Integration of Economic and Social Theory*. New York: The Free Press.

Parsons, Talcott, Robert F. Bales, and Edward A. Shils. 1953. *Working Papers in the Theory of Action*. New York, Free Press.

Paterson, Thomas. 1979. *On Every Front. The Making of the Cold War*. New York: W.W. Norton.

Perrow, Charles. 1986. *Complex Organizations*. New York: Random House.

—— 1993. "Small Firm Networks," in Richard Swedberg (ed.), *Explorations in Economic Sociology* (pp. 377–402). New York: Russell Sage Foundation.

Pfeffer, Jeffrey. 1981. *Power in Organizations*. Marshfield, MA: Pittman.

—— 1992. Managing with Power: Politics and Influence in Organizations. Boston, MA: Harvard Business School Press.

Piore, Michael, and Charles Sabel. 1984. *The Second Industrial Divide*. New York: Basic Books.

Pipes, Richard. 1990. *The Russian Revolution*. New York: Knopf.

Piven, Frances Fox, and Richard A. Cloward. 1979. *Poor People's Movements*. New York: Vintage Press.

Podolny, Joel, and James N. Baron. 1997. "Resources and Relationships: Social Networks and Mobility in the Workplace." *American Sociological Review* 62: 673–93.

Polanyi, Karl. 1944. *The Great Transformation*. Boston, MA: Beacon Hill.

Polyani, Karl. 1957. "The Economy as an Instituted Process," in Karl Polanyi, Conrad M. Arensberg, and Harry W. Pearson (eds), *Trade and Market in the Early Empires* (pp. 243–70). New York: The Free Press.

Porter, Michael. 1990. *The Competitive Advantage of Nations*. New York: The Free Press.

Portes, Alejandro. 1994. "The Informal Economy and its Paradoxes," in Neil J. Smelser and Richard Swedberg (eds), *The Handbook of Economic Sociology* (pp. 426–49). Princeton, NJ: Princeton University Press.

Poulantzas, Nicos. 1978. *Political Power and Social Classes*. London: Verso.

Powell, Walter. 1985. *Getting into Print*. Chicago, IL: University of Chicago Press.

—— 1990. "Neither Market nor Hierarchy: Network Forms of Organization," in E.E. Cummings and B. Staw (eds), *Research in Organizational Behavior* (pp. 295–336). Vol. 12 Greenwich, CT: JAI Press.

Powell, Walter, and Laurel Smith-Doerr. 1994. "Networks and Economic Life," in Neil J. Smelser and Richard Swedberg (eds), *The Handbook of Economic Sociology* (pp. 368–402). Princeton, NJ: Princeton University Press.

Powell, Walter, Kenneth W. Koput, and Laurel Smith-Doerr. 1996. "Interorganizational Collaboration and the Locus of Innovation: Networks of Learning in Biotechnology." *Administrative Science Quarterly* 41: 116–45.

Prechel, Harland. 1990. "Steel and the State: Industry Politics and Business Policy Formation, 1940–1989." *American Sociological Review* 55: 648–68.

—— 1997. "Corporate Transformation to the Multilayered Subsidiary Form: Changing Economic Conditions and State Business Policy." *Sociological Forum* 12: 405–39.

Putnam, Robert. 1993. *Making Democracy Work*. Princeton, NJ: Princeton University Press.

Quadagno, Jill. 1988. "From Old-age Assistance to Supplementary Security Income: The Political Economy of Relief in the South, 1935–1972," in Margaret Weir, Ann Shola Orloff, and Theda Skocpol (eds), *The Politics of Social Policy in the United States* (pp. 235–64). Princeton, NJ: Princeton University Press.

Reddy, William. 1984. *The Rise of Market Culture: The Textile Trade and French Society, 1750–1900*. Cambridge: Cambridge University Press.

Reskin, Barbara, and Patricia Roos. 1990. *Job Queues, Gender Queues: Explaining Women's Inroads into Male Occupations*. Philadelphia, PA: Temple University Press.

Rex, John. 1998. "Race and Ethnicity in Europe," in Joe Bailey (ed.), *Social Europe* (pp. 121–36). London: Longman.

Riain, Sean. 2000. "States and Markets in an Era of Globalization." *Annual Review of Sociology* 26: 187–213.

Rieber, Alfred J. 1982. *Merchants and Entrepreneurs in Imperial Russia*. Chapel Hill: University of North Carolina Press.

Rieder, Jonathan. 1985. *Canarsie. The Jews and Italians of Brooklyn against Liberalism*. Cambridge, MA: Harvard University Press.

Ritzer, George. 1993. *The McDonaldization of Society*. Thousand Oaks, CA: Pine Forge Press.

Rodrik, Dani. 1998. "Symposium on Globalization in Perspective: An Introduction." *Journal of Economic Perspectives* 12: 3–8.

Rogers III, William M. 2004. "The African-American Experience in the Recent Recession and Job Loss Recovery." Online. Available HTTP: <http://www.americanprogress.org/> (accessed April 12, 2006).

Rostow, W.W. 1965. *The Economics of Take-Off into Sustained Growth*. New York: St. Martin's Press.

Roy, William. 1997. *Socializing Capital*. Princeton, NJ: Princeton University Press.

Rozman, Gilbert. 1981. *Modernization of China*. New York: Free Press.

—— (ed.). 1991. *The East Asian Region. Confucian Heritage and its Modern Adaptation*. Princeton, NJ: Princeton University Press.

Ryan, Michelle K., and S. Alexander Haslam. 2005. "The Glass Cliff: Evidence that Women are Over-represented in Precarious Leadership Positions." *British Journal of Management* 16: 81–90.

Ryvkina, Rozalina. 1999. "Ot tenevoi ekonomiki k tenevomu obshchestvo." *Pro et Contra* 4: 25–39.

Sabel, Charles. 1982. *Work and Politics: The Division of Labor in Industry*. New York: Cambridge University Press.

—— 1993. "Studied Trust: Building New Forms of Cooperation in a Volatile Economy," in Richard Swedberg (ed.), *Explorations in Economic Sociology* (pp. 105–144). New York: Russell Sage Foundation.

Saxonian, Anna Lee. 1996. "Inside-out: Regional Networks and Industrial Adaptation in Silicon Valley and Route 128." *Cityscape: a Journal of Policy Development and Research* 2: 41–60.

Schumpeter, Joseph. 1976. *Capitalism, Socialism, and Democracy*. New York: Harper & Row.

Scott, James C. 1976. *The Moral Economy of the Peasant*. New Haven: Yale University Press.

—— 1985. *Weapons of the Weak*. New Haven: Yale University Press.

—— 1990. *Domination and the Arts of Resistance*. New Haven: Yale University Press.

Scott, Joan. 1986. "Gender: A Useful Category of Historical Analysis." *American Historical Review* 91: 1053–75.

Sellers, Charles. 1991. *The Market Revolution*. New York: Oxford University Press.

Shiller, Robert J., Maxim Boycko, and Vladimir Korobov. 1992. "Hunting for *Homo Sovieticus*: Situational Versus Attitudinal Factors in Economic Behavior." *Brookings Papers on Economic Activity* 1: 127–81.

Shirk, Susan. 1993. *The Political Logic of Economic Reform in China*. Berkeley: University of California Press.

Shonfield, Alfred. 1965. *Modern Capitalism*. London: Oxford University Press.

Simmel, Georg. 1990 (1907). *The Philosophy of Money*. London: Routledge.

Simon, Herbert. 1945. *Administrative Behavior*. New York: Wiley.

Skocpol, Theda. 1976. "Review of *The Modernization of Japan and Russia*". *Contempoary Sociology* 5: 756–8.

—— 1979. *States and Social Revolutions*. New York: Cambridge University Press.

—— 1980. "Political Response to Capitalist Crisis: Neo-Marxist Theories of the State and the Case of the New Deal." *Politics and Society* 10: 155–201.

Skocpol, Theda. 1992. *Defending Soldiers and Mothers*. Cambridge, MA: Harvard University Press.

Slomczynski, Kazimierz M., and Tadeusz K. Krauze. 1987. "Cross-national Similarity in Social Mobility Patterns: A Direct Test of the Featherman–Jones–Hauser Hypothesis." *American Sociological Review* 52: 598–611.

Smith, Adam. 1981 (1776). *An Inquiry Into the Nature and Causes of the Wealth of Nations*. Indianapolis, IN: Liberty Press.

—— 1982 (1759). *The Theory of Moral Sentiments*. Indianapolis, IN: Liberty Press.

Snow, David A., and Robert D. Benford. 1992. "Master Frames and Cycles of Protest," in Aldon D. Morris and Carol McClurg Mueller (eds), *Frontiers in Social Movement Theory* (pp. 133–55). New Haven, CT: Yale University Press.

Snow, David, E. Burke Rochford Jr., Steven K. Worden, and Robert D. Benford. 1986. "Frame Alignment Process, Micromobilization, and Movement Participation." *American Sociological Review* 51: 464–81.

Solnick, Steven. 1998. *Stealing the State*. Cambridge, MA: Harvard University Press.

Soto, Hernando de. 1989. *The Other Path*. New York: Harper & Row.

Spenner, Kenneth I., Olga O. Suhomlinova, Sten A. Thore, Kenneth C. Land, and Derek Jones. 1998. "Strong Legacies and Weak Markets: Bulgarian State-owned Enterprises During Early Transition." *American Sociological Review* 63: 599–618.

Stark, David. 1996. "Recombinant Property in East European Capitalism." *American Journal of Sociology* 101: 993–1027.

Stark, David, and László Bruszt. 1998. *Postsocialist Pathways*. New York: Cambridge University Press.

Starr, Paul. 1982. *The Social Transformation of American Medicine*. New York: Basic Books.

Stiglitz, Joseph. 2003. *Globalization and its Discontents*. New York: W.W. Norton.

Strauss, George. 1992 (1955). "Group Dynamics and Intergroup Relations," in Mark Granovetter and Richard Swedberg (eds), *The Sociology of Economic Life* (1st edn) (pp. 307–12). Boulder: Westview Press.

Sutton, John R., and Frank Dobbin. 1996. "The Two Faces of Governance: Responses to Legal Uncertainty in U.S. Firms, 1955 to 1985." *American Sociological Review* 61: 794–811.

Swartz, David. 1997. *Culture and Power. The Sociology of Pierre Bourdieu*. Chicago, IL: University of Chicago Press.

Swidler, Ann. 1986. "Culture in Action: Symbols and Strategies." *American Sociological Review* 51: 273–86.

Tarrow, Sidney. 1998. *Power in Movement. Social Movements and Contentious Politics* (2nd edn). New York: Cambridge University Press.

Taylor, F.W. 1911. *The Principles of Scientific Management*. New York: Harper.

Thompson, E.P. 1963. *The Making of the English Working Class*. New York: Vintage Books.

—— 1971. "The Moral Economy of the English Crowd in the Eighteenth Century." *Past and Present* 50: 76–136.

Tilly, Charles. 1986. *The Contentious French*. Cambridge, MA: Harvard University Press.

—— 1990. *Coercion, Capital, and European States*. Cambridge: Blackwell.

—— 1998. *Durable Inequality*. Berkeley: University of California Press.

Tilly, Louise, and Joan W. Scott. 1978. *Women, Work, and Family*. New York: Holt, Rinehart & Winston.

Titmus, Richard. 1971. *The Gift Relationship: From Human Blood to Social Policy*. New York: Pantheon.

Tocqueville, Alexis de. 1955. *The Old Regime and the French Revolution*, translated by Stuart Gilbert. New York: Doubleday.

—— 1966. *Democracy in America*, translated by George Lawrence. New York: Harper & Row.

Tversky, Amos, and Daniel Kahneman. 1974. "Judgment Under Uncertainty: Heuristics and Biases." *Science* 185: 1124–31.

—— 1981. "The Framing of Decisions and the Psychology of Choice." *Science* 21: 453–8.

Underwood, Simeon. 2000. "Assessing the Quality of Quality Assessment: The Inspection of Teaching and Learning in British Universities." *Journal of Education for Teaching* 26: 73–91.

United Nations. 2005. *Human Development Report 2005*. New York: United Nations Development Program.

Uzzi, Brian. 1997. "Social Structure and Competition in Interfirm Networks: The Paradox of Embeddedness." *Administrative Science Quarterly* 61: 35–67.

Valenzuela, J. Samuel, and Arturo Valenzuela. 1978. "Modernization and Dependency." *Comparative Politics* 10: 535–57.

Verdery, Katherine. 1995. "What Was Socialism, and Why Did It Fall?," in Daniel Orlovsky (ed.), *Beyond Soviet Studies* (pp. 27–46). Washington, DC: The Woodrow Wilson Center Press.

Volkov, Vadim. 2002. *Violent Entrepreneurs: The Use of Force in the Making of Russian Capitalism*. Ithaca, NY: Cornell University Press.

Wade, Robert. 1990. *Governing the Market*. Princeton, NJ: Princeton University Press.

Wallerstein, Immanuel. 1974. *The Modern World-System*. New York: Academic Press.

Warren, John Robert, and Robert M. Hauser. 1997. "Social Stratification Across Three Generations: New Evidence from the Wisconsin Longitudinal Study." *American Sociological Review* 62: 561–72.

Waters, Mary C., and Karl Eschbach. 1995. "Immigration and Ethnic and Racial Inequality in the United States." *Annual Review of Sociology* 21: 419–46.

Weber, Max. 1930. *The Protestant Ethic and the Spirit of Capitalism*, translated by Talcott Parsons. New York: Charles Scribners' Sons.

—— 1978 (1922). *Economy and Society*, translated by Guenther Roth and Claus Wittich. Berkeley: University of California Press.

—— 1987 (1923). *General Economic History*, translated by Frank H. Knight. New Brunswick, NJ: Transaction Books.

Weede, Erich. 2002. "The Transition to Capitalism in China and Russia." *Comparative Sociology* 1: 151–67.

Weir, Margaret, and Theda Skocpol. 1985. "State Sructures and the Possibilities for 'Keynesian' Responses to the Great Depression in Sweden, Britain, and the United

States," in Peter B. Evans, Dietrich Rueschemeyer, and Theda Skocpol (eds), *Bringing the State Back In* (pp. 107–68). New York: Cambridge University Press.

Westney, D. Eleanor. 1987. *Imitation and Innovation.* Cambridge, MA: Harvard University Press.

Wharton, Carol, 1994. "Finding Time for the 'Second Shift': The Impact of Flexible Work Schedules on Women's Double Days." *Gender and Society* 8: 189–205.

White, Harrison. 1981. "Where Do Markets Come From?" *American Journal of Sociology* 7: 517–47.

Wight, Jonathan. 2005. "The Treatment of Smith's Invisible Hand." Mimeo, University of Richmond, Department of Economics.

Williamson, Jeffrey. 1996. "Globalization, Convergence, and History." *Journal of Economic History* 56: 277–306.

Williamson, Oliver. 1975. *Markets and Hierarchies.* New York: Free Press.

—— 1985. *The Economic Institutions of Capitalism.* New York: Free Press.

—— 1994. "Transaction Cost Economics and Organization Theory," in Neil Smelser (ed.), *The Handbook of Economic Sociology* (pp. 77–107). Princeton, NJ: Princeton University Press and the Russell Sage Foundation.

Willis, Paul. 1977. *Learning to Labor.* Aldershot: Gower.

Willmott, Hugh. 1995. "Managing the Academics: Commodification and Control in the Development of University Education in the U.K." *Human Relations* 48: 993–1027.

Wilson, James Q. 1989. *Bureaucracy. What Government Organizations Do and Why They Do It.* Cambridge, MA: Harvard University Press.

Wilson, William Julius. 1997. *When Work Disappears. The World of the New Urban Poor.* New York: Vintage Press.

Womack, John, Jr. 1968. *Zapata and the Mexican Revolution.* New York: Vintage Press.

Women and Work Commission. 2006. *Shaping a Fairer Future.* London: Department of Trade and Industry.

Woodruff, David. 1999. *Money Unmade. Barter and the Fate of Russian Capitalism.* Ithaca, NY: Cornell University Press.

World Bank. 2005. "China at a Glance." Online. Available HTTP: <http:www.worldbank.org> (accessed February 10, 2006).

—— 2006a. "China Quarterly Update – February 2006." Online. Available HTTP: <http:www.worldbank.org> (accessed February 10, 2006).

—— 2006b. "China Quick Facts." Online. Available HTTP: <http:www.worldbank.org> (accessed February 10, 2006).

Wright, Erik Olin. 1978. *Class, Crisis, and the State.* London: New Left Books.

Wright, Erik Olin, Janeen Baxter, and Gunn Elisabeth Birkelund. 1995. "The Gender Gap in Workplace Authority: A Cross-National Study." *American Sociological Review* 60: 407–35.

Wuthnow, Robert. 1987. *Meaning and Moral Order*, Berkeley: University of California Press.

—— 1996. *Poor Richard's Principle.* Princeton, NJ: Princeton University Press.

Yakovlev, Andrei. 1999. "Ekonomika 'chernogo nala' v Rossii: mekhanizmy, prichiny, posledstviia," in Teodor Shanin (ed.), *Neformal'naia ekonomika. Rossiia i mir* (pp. 270–91). Moscow: Logos.

Yamagata, Hisashi, Kuang S. Yeh, Shelby Stewman, and Hiroko Dodge. 1997. "Sex Segretation and Glass Ceilings: A Comparative Statics Model of Women's Career Opportunities in the Federal Government Over a Quarter Century." *American Journal of Sociology* 103: 566–632.

Yang, Keming. 2004. "Institutional Holes and Entrepreneurship in China." *Sociological Review* 52: 371–89.

Zeitlin, Maurice. 1974. "Corporate Ownership and Control: The Large Corporation and the Capitalist Class." *American Journal of Sociology* 79: 1073–119.

Zelizer, Viviana. 1985. *Pricing the Priceless Child.* New York: Basic Books.

—— 1988. "Beyond the Polemics on the Market: Establishing a Theoretical and Empirical Agenda." *Sociological Forum* 3: 614–34.

—— 1997. *The Social Meaning of Money: Pin Money, Paychecks, Poor Relief, and Other Currencies.* Princeton, NJ: Princeton University Press.

—— 2002. "Enter Culture," in Mauro F. Guillen, Randall Collins, Paula England, and Marshall Meyer (eds), *The New Economic Sociology: Developments in an Emerging Field* (pp. 101–25). New York: Russell Sage

Zucker, Lynne G. 1986. "Production of Trust: Institutional Sources of Economic Structure. 1840–1920." *Research in Organizational Behavior* 8: 53–111.

—— 1987. "Institutional Theories of Organization." *Annual Review of Sociology* 13: 443–64.

—— 1988. "Where Do Institutional Patterns Come From? Organizations as Actors in Social Systems," in Lynne Zucker (ed.), *Institutional Patterns and Organization* (pp. 23–52). Cambridge: Ballinger.

Zukin, Sharon, and Paul DiMaggio. 1990. "Introduction," in Sharon Zukin and Paul DiMaggio (eds), *Structures of Capital. The Social Organization of the Economy* (pp. 1–36). New York: Cambridge University Press.

Zysman, John. 1983. *Governments, Markets, and Growth.* Ithaca, NY: Cornell University Press.

Index